Africa Alone
Odyssey of an American Traveler

Also by Sandy McMath

SOUTHERN PASSAGE

COLUMBUS AND COMPANY *publishes original personal accounts of discovery, travel, innovation and ordeal by observers whose primary occupations may be other than writing but who, for a variety of reasons, have found themselves involved with the unusual and written about it. Expedition narratives, natural history research papers, Peace Corps journals, war letters, flight and cruising logs, product-invention histories, archeological field notes and survival diaries are examples. Send* descriptions only of *available manuscripts unless otherwise requested. A finders fee for exceptional material is available, contingent upon publication. Suitable ventures underwritten.*

Cover photo: Driving at noon through a harmattan sandstorm in Cameroon's Sahel, near Lake Chad.

Back photo: On the road to Bangassou, Central African Empire.

Dedicatory photos: Lewis Wallace: alone (r), and with the author, then aged 12, following their rescue on January 9, 1954 by Governor Sid McMath (leading horse). George Douthit, Arkansas Democrat.

Africa Alone
Odyssey of an American Traveler

Sandy McMath

COLUMBUS AND COMPANY,
SAN FRANCISCO
Discoverers' Press

93 08632

Copyright 1983 by Sandy McMath
Published 1983 by August House

Second edition published 1988 by COLUMBUS AND COMPANY, SAN
FRANCISCO, *Discoverers' Press*, Post Office Box 1492, 300 Valley Street,
Suite 201, Sausalito, California 94966 (415-332-5545).

ISBN 0-935304-52-5 **Hardback Edition**
ISBN 0-935304-53-3 **Quality Paperback**

Library of Congress Catalog Card Number 83-070535
    McMath, Sandy
    Africa Alone: Odyssey of an American Traveler
    Little Rock: August House
        1983

COLUMBUS AND COMPANY, SAN FRANCISCO, *Discoverers' Press,*
1988

Cover design by Madeline Collins
Book design by Ira Hocut
Maps by Carron Bain Hocut

All Columbus and Company Books are produced on acid-free paper which
exceeds the minimum standards set by the National Historical Publica-
tions and Records Commission.

COLUMBUS AND COMPANY

SAN FRANCISCO

DISCOVERERS' PRESS

McMath journeyed through Africa, often at great risk, for 18 months. He dug for fossils with Mary Leakey, was held at the point of a machine gun, and roamed widely in his Land Rover under a general air of unease. This is a satisfying travel book, written in the fine tradition of 19th-century adventurers.

—Washington Post Book World

McMath, a lanky, good-natured, former Marine took a two-year leave of absence in 1976 from his Arkansas law firm to follow a dream: to drive from Paris to the southern tip of Africa. Along the way, he won the confidence of Mary Leakey at the famed fossil site in Tanzania . . . In Rhodesia, he narrowly missed becoming the victim of a terrorist raid on a nunnery.

The author's ingratiating style and eye to detail make this a special book.

—The Virginia Pilot

Africa Alone captures the essence of Africa as surely as the drums beat out a tribute to the day.

—Southwest Times Record

A true-adventure classic of our time!

—Perrin Jones

Africa Alone is at once a spellbinding account of a grand adventure and a stirring documentary of modern times in lands that, for most of us, exist only as puzzle pieces on a map. McMath's vivid narrative brings the continent to life, without stripping it of its mystery. The reader learns and enjoys in equal measure.

—Janet Fullwood,
Dallas Times Herald

Africa Alone succeeds primarily because of the straightforward nature of its narrative style. The language is direct and bare of literary flourishes, and McMath's intentions seemed to have been to allow the presented material to create its own emotional impact . . . *Africa Alone* reads quickly, and each chapter serves as a catalyst to the imagination.

— Arkansas Democrat

Africa Alone is the kind of book with which generations of armchair travelers have idled away long evenings.

— The Houston Post

From Morocco — where beggar children literally stoned him — through the Sahara with its endless sandstorms to the big game country of Kenya . . . the quality of his storytelling wins over the reader.

— United Press International

The miles of travel described by Sandy McMath create even greater wonder when one traces the route across expanses of desert, marshlands, forests and mountains . . . [His] style is personal and easily read and even poetic . . . The story of Africa is one of pain and struggle . . . He may not have all the answers, but he has the right questions.

— Arkansas Gazette

Foreword

Sandy McMath's lively account of his lone safari through Africa is an entertaining and stimulating read.

It was my pleasure to have Sandy's help at Olduvai Gorge when I broke my ankle at the time I was endeavoring to set up a new camp at the 3.5 million year old site of Laetoli, thirty miles away.

Sandy was invaluable. He had a natural rapport with my African staff, although he and they understandably had some language problems.

Nevertheless, Sandy had a road built and the camp organized for me whilst I was incapacitated – a true friend in need.

Moreover, he was sensitive to the atmosphere of my camp: the wild animals, the birds and the dogs, above all to the ambiance of the Serengetti.

Reading chapters of his book relating to other parts of Africa, I get the impression that wherever he went he was able to assimilate the background and spirit of each place he visited.

This is a rare quality in travelers and makes his book thought-provoking and important for people interested in the changing face of present-day Africa.

– Mary D. Leakey
National Museum of Kenya
Nairobi

Acknowledgments

I owe hundreds of men and women a debt of gratitude. Many of them were companions of the road, whose observations, adventures or mere passings are reflected in this account – some by name, others anonymously.

But to the following a special acknowledgment is due, for without them the story would perhaps never have found its way to the reader: Virginia Brooks, my determinative junior high school English teacher; Charley Cook, Ancil O'Neal and Rick Wright, for their invaluable mechanical and logistical help; Jenny Byers, Polly Prewitt, John and Betsy Harris, Phil and Bruce McMath, Mart Vehik and Leland Leatherman, for their steadfast support; Pamela Curry, who loyally devoted herself to typing the manuscript; and to my parents, Anne and Sid McMath, who provided special encouragement throughout.

I am particularly indebted to Dr. Mary D. Leakey of Olduvai Gorge, my friend and teacher, who patiently shared with me many of the secrets of Africa's archaeology – and twice acceded to my requests to present extensive summaries of her work at the University of Arkansas.

– SSM
Summer 1988

To

LEWIS WALLACE

My Old Companion From
The Grant County Days

FRANCE

SPAIN

Baleanc
Islands

Mediterranean Sea

TUNISIA

MOROCCO

ALGERIA

LIBYA

EGYPT

MAURITANIA

MALI

NIGER

CHAD

SENEGAL

GUINEA-
BISSAU

GUINEA

UPPER
VOLTA

GHANA

NIGERIA

SUDAN

DJIBOUTI

SIERRA
LEONE

IVORY
COAST

CENTRAL
AFRICAN
EMPIRE

ETHIOPIA

LIBERIA

TOGO

BENIN

CAMEROON

CONGO REP.

SOMALIA

EQUATORIAL GUINEA

ZAIRE

UGANDA

KENYA

GABON

RWANDA

BURUNDI

TANZANIA

AFRICA

ANGOLA

ZAMBIA

MALAWI

MADAGASCAR

ZIMBABWE
(RHODESIA)

MOZAMBIQUE

SOUTH
WEST
AFRICA

BOTSWANA

(NAMIBIA)

SWAZILAND

Atlantic Ocean

SOUTH
AFRICA

LESOTHO

TRANSKEI

Indian
Ocean

PROLOGUE

During the mid-1950s I spent a great portion of my waning childhood with Lewis Wallace, the family's black handyman, hunting in the International Paper Company's hardwood forest that bordered our farm near the Grant County community of Cane Creek.

No sooner would the dust settle behind the big yellow "No. 10" school bus than I'd grab my .22 long rifle, and Lewis and I would head for the woods—provided, that is, that "Miss Anne," as Lewis called my mom, didn't see us before we got beyond the garden fence. Otherwise, we'd have to face our respective drudgeries of chores and homework.

But on Friday nights, Lewis's chores were easier, and I'd have no homework to do. After supper we'd load Ol' Red into the pickup, a persevering white '52 Chevy, drive to the back gate and disappear for hours, doing what we both loved best—coon hunting. One January night we didn't return, and half the county was mustered out to search. We were found eighteen hours later—tired, wet and hungry, but otherwise intact. "We wasn't lost," said Lewis. "We was just confused."

Wallace was a jack-of-all-trades—carpenter, farmer, undertaker and part-time preacher. He was also a genealogist of sorts, having, he said, traced his ancestors back to Alabama before the Civil War. Beyond that, Wallace knew only that they had come in bondage to the New World. Consulting our battered Rand McNally Atlas (opened to the western regions of the Dark Continent), he speculated, I remember more than once on the Wallaces' African genesis.

Talk of Africa wafted with the smoke of many a campfire, while from some distant hollar, Ol' Red's resonant bays drowned the yelps of lesser hounds. (The dog had been a gift to my dad from the Northwest Arkansas Coon Hunters' Association, the members of which still considered him "Governor Sid," although he had by then left office, after two terms as the state's then-youngest chief executive.)

Africa even became for a time an obsession, stirring me to wander with Stanley in search of Livingstone and with Conrad into the heart of darkness, rather than tarry with Mrs. Thornton in the doldrums of long division at Sheridan Consolidated Junior High.

Through adolescence, college and war, Africa abided within me, and there sprouted a yearning to venture one day myself into the lands from which Wallace's people had come, and perhaps beyond them into the great emptiness of the Sahara itself.

Looking back now, I am certain that this reverie was made resolute by the reports in 1959 of the discovery in what was then Tanganyika of the fossil skull of *Zinjanthropus* (East Africa Man) by Mary Leakey, and subsequent news of the work of the Leakeys that seemed to establish Africa as the cradle and crucible of man. I devotedly followed these events through the *National Geographic* and the Leakey television documentaries of the period.

Finally, in 1969, while stationed with the Marine Corps in San Diego, following my return from Vietnam, I attended a lecture by Dr. Louis B. Leakey. Shaking hands with me afterward, he extended me a hearty invitation to "pay us a call" should I ever get to East Africa. Perhaps he was only being polite, but I knew that one day I would accept his offer.

Allons! after the great Companions, and to belong to them!
They too are on the road—they are the swift and majestic
men—they are the greatest women . . .

Walt Whitman

CHAPTER I

On July 11, 1976, I left Paris alone for the Cape of Good Hope in a 1974 Toyota Land Cruiser—the same one I had driven for three years while practicing law in Little Rock.

I had shipped it from Port Elizabeth, New Jersey, to Southampton, England, for a fraction of the cost of finding and fitting out a good used Land Rover. Besides, I figured—correctly, it turned out—that the little vehicle would make the trip as well as anything more elaborate.

Having studied the several historic routes across the Sahara, I had chosen the least traveled: across the Moroccan and Spanish (or western) Sahara to Senegal. Not having previously driven over such terrain, I decided to test myself and my jeep at Cabo Beberias, on the Spanish island of Formentera. Any gremlins would, I hoped, be discovered there.

Formentera I knew from previous visits to the home of an old friend, Antonio Tur Gabrielet. Seeing Tony was reason enough for choosing Formentera—plus the fact that the Balearic chain of islands, of which Formentera is the smallest, was not far out of the way, easily accessible by car ferry from Barcelona.

Tony's spacious but crumbling *finca* was on La Mola, the small elevation on the tip of the island. The only visible sign of civilization from the place was the bleached white tip of El Faro al Fin del Mundo ("the lighthouse at the end of the world").

Tony was something of a Balearic folk hero, an artist and poet who had forsaken the Paris café life of a Franco exile in the '50s and returned to his native Ibiza, the nearest island, to paint and sculpt local scenes. Harried by the commercial bustle of Ibiza's burgeoning tourist trade, he soon decamped to Formentera. His clients for many years were mostly English tourists, but recently some wealthy Spaniards had begun purchasing his work. But he was perhaps more renowned for his culinary art, particularly his paella, served only after hours of tedious preparation to maddeningly starved guests buoyed with generous droughts of *tinto*, the ubiquitous and tasty table wine of Catalonia.

On virtually any given evening, Can ("house of") Gabrielet would play host to an eclectic coterie of islanders and tourists who would walk or motorbike the two miles from La Mola's solitary hamlet, Nuestra Señora del Pilar. Among them would be, invariably, an entourage of rowdy but good-natured

14

young Spanish bohemians who would sing and dance and chant the *anti-facista* poetry of Garcia Lorca and Miguel Hernandez until the wee hours.

Formentera is a magical island, with legends of ghosts and spirits of the full moon. There are caves in La Mola which have never been fully explored and which some say contain the bones of Roman and Moorish slaves. The island's *salinas* (salt flats) were worked by both. Formentera was a place of exile for "witches" during the Spanish Inquisition.

For several weeks I stayed at Can Gabrielet and made regular runs across the fine, powdery sands at Midjhorn Beach and the punishing rocks at Beberias, a desolate Sahara-like wasteland on the southern end of the island. There were no mechanical problems, but I learned to deflate the tires from 23 to 11 pounds per square inch for better sand driving.

By ferry from Ibiza, I sailed to Alicante, from which I drove first to Granada (paying a ritual visit to the Alhambra) and then to Málaga, following the coast to Gibraltar and on to the port of Algeciras.

I made a few odds-and-ends purchases in Algeciras, including four twenty-liter yellow plastic water jugs. I would keep them half filled, which made for better weight distribution. I carried one on each corner of a tough, steel toprack I'd purchased in Paris. Across the front of the rack I lashed eight jerry cans, each containing five gallons of premium gasoline. With the fifteen gallons in my regular tank, plus the spare tank's 23, I had a cruising range of over 1,000 miles calculated at thirteen miles per gallon. (Actually, at the low speeds of desert travel I frequently averaged fifteen.)

I entered Africa by ferry from Algeciras to the Spanish coastal enclave of Ceuta, the last European colonial possession on the continent. The ferry was late leaving and as an orange sun settled into the Atlantic through the Straits of Gibraltar, I felt the poetry in the Spanish *a tardecer,* which is the "coming of the late afternoon." To the south, the purple mountains of Moroccan Africa loomed in the mist above Ceuta. I paused at the enclave only long enough to top off with gas, then drove straight to the border some five miles south of town.

The Spanish customs process was perfunctory, but the Moroccans were detailed and thorough, operating from a formidable blockhouse, which was surrounded by several score of loitering peasants and hustlers who surged around me as I stopped my jeep and got out. The abrupt, almost hostile guard waved me to one side for inspection. Locking the doors, I became so harried by the hustlers that I left the key in the ignition. The only thing to do was to try to work the vent with a screwdriver, during which I broke the glass and cut my hand. Fortunately, the hitchhiker whom the guard ordered me to carry to Tétouan was a carpenter. He invited me to his home, made a wood filler for the window in his shop, and fed me generous portions of Ramadan soup and skewered goat. The fee: eight dirhams. Devout Muslims never drink, and even the less devout attempt to forego alcohol during Ramadan. Nonetheless, his son fetched me a cold Spanish beer from a neighboring shanty. A dozen neighbors huddled about the hood of the jeep while I spread out the Michelin map and showed them Africa. None of them had seen a map before and they could not grasp the concept of terrain being represented on paper. I was to encounter this phenomenon on many

15

subsequent occasions.

At Tétouan, for the first time, I watched small boys playing at the ubiquitous African game of stick-wheel (or roll-a-wheel), a solitary game in which one runs along with a stick shuttling a small wheel, usually about six inches in diameter. I would later see children in Swaziland 5,000 miles away playing the same game.

In the town's center I found a cheap hotel with access to a garage with the help of a gaunt, hollow-eyed young Moroccan who boasted that he had studied English in a Peace Corps class. He offered to buy me a beer. I had not enjoyed the first one and had a Coca-Cola with him instead. We sat at a sidewalk café in a plaza near the hotel.

"How much do you want?"

"How much? How much what?"

"Hash, man. Hash," he said.

His father and brothers had a farm in the mountains and I could buy as much from them as I wanted. He suggested five or ten kilos "for you own use" and maybe 100 (about 230 pounds) to "take back to Europe."* When I told him I was not interested, he was understanding—"smooth" would be the word. Why didn't I go to his place and try some? It wasn't the "bad stuff" people smoked in the States. I begged off, thanking him for the pop, and bade him good night. The hotel bouncer (clerk he was not) demanded that I fetch my passport or sleep in the streets: "Police arrest me if I no have your passport." This is a military as well as a tax-control measure, and strictly enforced.

Tired and queasy from the bad beer-Coke combination, I searched for the garage, got lost and wound up pursued by urchins for a handout. When at last I walked into the garage, the two "guards" were in the front seat of my jeep, in the process of removing the radio. I knew then why they had insisted that I leave it unlocked.

The following night I camped on the beach at Larache. The surf there recedes over a quarter of a mile at low tide. It was a strange sensation to seek it by sound in the night fog, which hid everything, even the campfire. With me were some Spanish silversmiths on their way north from Tan Tan, where they had purchased silver for a quarter of its price in Europe. As the beach fire crackled, they talked of the hamlet of La Union in the mountains of Colombia, where they intended to begin an agricultural commune. When I told them I knew the hamlet—having stayed there once when hitchhiking through South America—and that the surrounding countryside was very poor for farming, they said that they sought refuge as well as land, and that if the mountains did not work out they would move into the Amazon rain forests. They were an intense lot, except for the handsome Greek-Indian

---

*Through Spain, of course. A favorite trick of Moroccan dope dealers is to turn in their customers to the Spanish police, for the reward. As anyone knows who has traveled there, Spain jails anyone (even pregnant women) for an automatic six years who gets caught with any amount of marijuana or hashish. For hard drugs, the penalty is much worse. There is no time off for good behavior in Spain, and the jails are full of would-be millionaires who were going to get rich quick, as well as people who just didn't think.

wife of the eldest. Her name was Maria and she had grown up in Kenya. Her jet-black hair glistened in the firelight, and she walked majestically upon the sand. These people, whom I met walking on the beach at dusk, were gone before first light.

I tarried at Rabat, the capital, only long enough to be rebuffed by the police in my attempt to get a permit to cross the western Sahara. All of the *pistes* (routes through the sand), they said, had been mined by *polisario* guerillas.

South of Rabat I became accustomed to the sight of Moroccans astride puny burros which trotted smartly along the shoulder of the road. An open cut or sore frequently festered on the burro's rump, which the rider jabbed with a stick to goad it on. Trundling behind at a respectable distance would be two, perhaps three, plump veiled women laden with produce and infants. Along the highway, roadside vendors sold honeydew and watermelons. The honeydews were especially good. One had to be careful to leave nothing within reach on the seat; otherwise an "assistant" would grab it while the driver's attention was distracted by the vendor.

I checked into the class "C" Lincoln Hotel in Casablanca, to wait until Monday mail call at the American Express agency. When Monday came, I read my mail at the Cafe Des Negociants at the corner of Rue Colbert and Avenue Mohammed V, a seedy, high-ceilinged, '20s-style rendezvous where I was serenaded by passing motorists. Hornblowing is compulsive in Casa: as soon as a light changes, everyone honks. The lights along Avenue Mohammed V were not synchronized, and this resulted in a discordant fugue. I moved to the bus station's bar, where I found a long backbar with tar-splotched mirrors. On the wall hung a 1936 Air France travel poster, the figures of which could have walked out of Bogart's *Casablanca*. Speaking of the movie, Esperanza, the "Play it, Sam" piano bar, no longer exists—if indeed it ever did. There was a boarded-up Pension Esperanza which did not look the part.

Tourists do not tarry in Casa—there is little for them to do. The big leather and clothing markets are in Fès and Marrakech. Geared to light industry—shipping in particular—Casa's central medina reflects the local workers' needs (simple clothing, scrap lumber, tools, used tires, and appliances).

A restaurant in an old hotel in the medina attracted scores of Arabs at the breaking of the fast. I followed the crowd and entered a lobby with elaborately colored tile walls that rose into random archways. Here and there were secluded cubicles, in one of which two handsome black women in purple robes ate with a young Arab in a grey business suit. Most of the diners ate on small wooden tables, and everyone was served Ramadan soup, followed by kebab. The waiters seemed to know each client's taste for hors d'oeuvres and spices and seasoned his plate accordingly. The soup was thick and meaty, with lots of hot goat cheese. The kebab was tender, served with hot yellow beans garnished with olives, garlic, onions and tomatoes. For dessert, there was sweet watermelon and banana salad, followed by mint tea blossomed with herbs and cloves. The tab was six dirhams—about $1.50.

The only other residents at the Lincoln Hotel were black Mauritanian students. At the time there was a close link between the two countries, and Morocco's universities (here and in Rabat) had several score Mauritanians enrolled, primarily in agronomy. The Moroccan service academies also train Mauritanian lieutenants and ensigns, several of whom I met. These were young Negroes from the interior. To a man, they supported the *march verte* (green march), the Moroccan euphemism for King Hassan's attempted annexation of the old Spanish Sahara and its subsequent partition with Mauritania.*

A weak Spanish government decided to withdraw in 1975 rather than hold an orderly plebiscite in the colony under U.N. supervision. As the Spanish left, the Moroccans went in, only to find that they had bitten off more than they could chew: about 5,000 *Saharois,* Spanish Foreign Legion veterans, went into the desert and have been fighting the Moroccans ever since with aid from Algeria and Russia. They run circles around the Moroccans—killing and capturing hundreds. Morocco's King Hassan wants the desert because it has the world's largest deposit of phosphate. There is little mining now, though, because the *polisario* blow up the mining equipment and destroy the tracks on the narrow-gauge railroad that carries the ore to the sea.

Mauritania used to mine phosphate on its own territory, but even that can't be done profitably now, because the *polisario* attack these installations with impunity, disabling them and capturing both native workers and French technicians. The French, who supply both Moroccans and Mauritanians, have had to pay high ransom to free their countrymen.

The young Mauritanians are disdainful of their Moroccan peers, many of whom smoke hashish. The Mauritanians live a spartan existence—out of scrupulosity as well as necessity.

My second night in Casa, I wandered into a clothing store, where the attendants produced a gallon jar of what they said was export hashish. When I protested—as I had in Tétouan—that I never used, much less bought the stuff, they promptly sold some to two American boys, about nineteen, who had just arrived from Amsterdam. The price: about 500 dirhams (officially $250) worth each. The parties retired to the back of the store for the transaction. They said they were regular customers.

Just outside the shop, several legless beggars crawled by. According to the attendants, they are cared for by the people in the market and seem never to be stepped on. Occasionally, a passerby will hand one a coin or a crust of bread.

At the foot of the main market street I observed that the taxi drivers followed the expedient of pushing their cabs to the head of the line, each

---

*Morocco, which became independent in 1956, now has a kind of parliamentary democracy. Hassan is still boss, but most local opposition is permitted. Communist and monarchical abolitionists, however, are not. According to *Amnesty International Report,* 1977, there are several hundred political prisoners in the country. See *Report,* p. 83.

helping the next. Fuel was very expensive, the equivalent of $1.70 per gallon ($1.25 with tourist coupons).

Arriving just before noon the next day, I found that the Centre de Sante l'Arsa Moha (the French-staffed local health center) had neither gamma globulin, the anti-hepatitis shot, nor the shot for tetanus. I had wanted to renew both.

The hospital did have a collection of scorpions and spiders in tightly sealed jars of formaldehyde. One of the scorpions was as large as a small lobster. These are kept so that a victim, by identifying the one that most resembles the one that stung or bit her or her child, may have the appropriate antitoxin administered. A number of children die each year from such attacks.

In the outer office and in the shade of the portico, scores of patients waited for the doctors to return from their two-hour lunch break. Most were mothers with infants who had come for vaccinations against cholera.

Leaving Casa, I drove to Marrakech and found a cheap but clean pension away from the street. Terribly fatigued, but so hot and sticky that I couldn't sleep, I lay with a wet towel over my face. I had almost dozed off at 3:00, when I was awakened by a most incredible wailing. It was punctuated by hissing and clucking and long sopranic sighs that conjured images of a coven of witches. This, I soon learned, was the morning prayer of Ramadan from the central mosque received on the transistor radios of my fellow guests. As I listened, there came a rhythmic chant, supported by a chorus an octave higher of the assembled faithful. This continued for half an hour, then again there was silence. During the next few days I became accustomed to this morning interlude and in fact looked forward to it. Implicit in these ritual Islamic incantations, I reflected much later, was surely an acknowledgment of the awesome emptiness of the Sahara.

Toward 8:00 one morning, I was walking along a street adjacent to the market, when I came upon ten sacks of flour clearly labeled:

SOYA ENRICHED
Gift of the People of the United States
Not to be Sold or Exchanged

The message was repeated in a half-dozen languages. Beside the sacks was a gaggle of peasant women with bowls and plastic pails. Money was being paid to the vendor, who in turn would pour a measure of the flour into each woman's container. When he saw me, he dispersed his customers and refused to sell or even quote me a price. I had seen this sale of American-aid food in Vietnam and Peru and was to see it again in Chad and Rwanda.

I returned to the pension after a long walk and wrote up the journal of the past few days. Although I had set myself the task of making daily entries, I would eventually go as long as a week before bringing the log current. But here, toward the beginning of the trip, I considered three days a terribly long delay and was most anxious not to fall further behind.

Shortly after 3:00, I awoke from a short nap and decided to walk to the medina. As I passed the rows of open-air stalls and prepared to enter the labyrinthine passageway of the medina, I was surrounded by a host of begging urchins. These children, some barely ten years old, badgered tourists mercilessly with demands for gifts of money and offers to act as "guides."

Entering the canvas-covered passageway, I winced as I inhaled the nostril-piercing dust-air of stale urine, dung and incense. No other market was comparable to this, I thought. Not even in the great market of Istanbul are one's senses so assaulted by such pungent sounds and smells.

As I was about to pass into the souk of the rug merchants, a cockeyed boy I had seen the day before approached. He asked if I had found the leather for which I had been looking. He had seemed shy, hanging back when the others had hounded me into a jewelry shop. The merchant had thrown them out and I had not seen the boy since. "Would you like to visit the shop of my uncle, a leather merchant?" he asked. I was assured that the leather was of the highest quality. Against my better judgment, I accepted the invitation. Anyway, it was refreshing to be with a child who was not tugging and shouting at me. And as long as I was with him, I hoped, the others would leave me alone.

We turned down a side passage and came to an opening where six or eight smaller passageways converged. The boy led, quickly now, and soon we were walking among corpulent, white-robed Arabs. No *petit commercants* these, but prosperous merchants every one.

A burly tailor groaned past with a great ream of blue cloth on his back. He was followed by two assistants, one pulling, the other pushing, an oxcart-sized trolley on which were piled a dozen bolts of assorted colors. At length, the boy stopped and pointed to a doorway of a small leather shop. "My uncle," he said. A heavy, black-seched Arab with a white goatee smiled and motioned us inside.

"Assiez-vous, Monsieur, s'il vous plait."

He thanked the boy and contrived in Arabic an errand for him. When the lad had gone, the uncle asked where I had come from and where I was going. When I told him, he said that the western Sahara was most dangerous. He himself had never ventured there, but he had had friends who had done so. "It is no good alone," he said.

He brought the conversation around to leather bags and produced some, but they were too flimsy and the prices too exorbitant. We haggled perfunctorily for a time, but finally I stood to go. He shouted at the boy, who had returned and was eavesdropping, and when they had agreed in Arabic, the uncle said to me in French that the boy would show me to the medieval wall at the south gate of the city. I had heard that it dated from the first settlement here in the twelfth century and had asked directions to it.

The boy led me into a ghetto even more decrepit than the one next to the market. As we walked, he looked over his shoulder as if to make sure he had taken the right direction. Following his gaze, I saw a half-dozen children with dirty faces and clusters of flies at their eyes. These were not market tykes, but urchins of the shanty town beyond the souk, seldom entered by tourists.

As we came to the wall I saw that the gate did not open directly onto the city but into a chamber or vestibule which lay at a right angle to it. I poked around the wall for a few minutes, noticing all the while that my little entourage had grown to about twenty. Inspecting the fortification both from the vestibule and from the sand flats on the outside, I could tell that a determined defender could only be starved into submission. The works were similar to those of southern Europe during the Middle Ages, particularly the mutual cover of extended parapets and gates and the narrow wedge-shaped slots in the walls which enabled an archer to shoot well but not become a target himself.

I thanked the cockeyed boy for showing me the wall and asked to return to the market. I had walked just a few paces, when I turned and saw that the fly-eyed urchins had doubled in number. Singly at first, and then in unison, they began chanting the monotonous *"Donnez-moi cadeau, donnez-moi cadeau."* Not to be outdone, my former guide darted to the front, his cockeye wide with excitement: *"J'etais un bon guide,"* he repeated several times. "Give me ten dirhams."

I had started to tip him but discovered that I had only a ten-dirham note. Had I given him that I would have been beseiged for *cadeaux* by them all. I told him that I would give him something when we returned to the medina. But he was not stayed and resumed his whining, all the while jabbing his first three fingers into his mouth ("I am poor and hungry. Give me money to buy food"). I smiled and resumed walking, repeating that I would tip him in the market.

They came on, their feet raising a cloud of dust. They now numbered some 40, and at each new neighborhood, more children joined the procession. It was funny, I thought for a moment, and I mimed the pied piper and made a comical face. Ahead, a woman holding a small child glanced hurriedly at the mob and disappeared into a doorway. The door slammed shut and was followed by the muffled sound of a difficult bolt sliding home. Beyond were two more women, obviously brought to their doors by the noise. I shouted at them as politely as I could: "Where is the street to the market, to *centre ville?"* The first woman, who was suckling an infant, gave a confused grimace and soon another door was bolted. Her neighbor likewise vanished. Then, to my dismay, the passage narrowed through a two-foot neck and ended in a dead end. In a window overhead I caught the flash of a woman's brown hand drawing shutters and the report of their slamming echoed off the pale green mud walls.

I was about to turn when I felt a sharp blow in the small of my back, followed by another on the top of my head. Flakes of rock powdered into my face as a half-dozen stones struck the wall. As each youngster crammed into the cul-de-sac, he too began stoning.

"Hey!" I shouted, throwing up my arms to protect my face. No use. A flash of pain shot through my nose. I wiped away blood, looking frantically for a friendly, even a playful face, but there were none.

Just then, toward the mouth of the passage came an old man pushing a wheelbarrow full of what looked like cement. I waited until he was completely blocking the way, then ran and leaped—pushing him to the side and springing with one foot in the middle of the load. Momentarily startled, my pursuers dashed to the bottleneck, but the old man had recovered and was asserting his right-of-way.

I sprinted for what seemed like minutes, somehow picking my way back through the maze of passages until I reached the main thoroughfare. Squatting merchants were chatting, while a burro stood silently by and two infants played in the dirt. The merchants started at the strange red-bearded intruder who had so suddenly stumbled, out of breath, among them. The oldest, a kindly man with a full set of white teeth, smiled and directed me toward the medina, and in moments, I was again among the rugs, incense and leather. I did not return to the shop of the uncle.

Later, when the siren ended the fast, I thoughtfully ate but a single bowl of soup. And I cannot remember a more delicious tea than that which I drank that night in the stall of the cloth merchant Muhammed Ali Ben Hassan.

One of the letters I had received at Casablanca said that my sister, Patricia, was to be married the next Saturday, September 5th, in Little Rock. Everyone hoped I'd show, but I wasn't really expected. Nor was Joel Cooner, the best man. Strangely, he too was thought to be in northern Africa, although no one knew exactly where. Deciding to surprise Patricia, I placed a call to Little Rock from the Hotel Marrakech. She was just leaving for the church. After a long chat, she admonished, "If you see Joel, tell him that we are just as mad at him as we are at you for not being here."

Later I pined at her words as I walked through the medina, stopping at last at the stall of Muhammed Ali. He was pouring tea and motioned for me to sit and have a glass. He sent a boy for herbs and mint and began talking about the day's sales. Not very many tourists came in September, he said. Ramadan is bad for them because all but the most expensive restaurants obey the fast and it is hard to find food.

As we sat I began to amuse myself by calling out to the small knots of tourists who passed. Some thought it odd that an American was selling in the souk. I would shout something such as, "Hey, come and see Muhammed's Saturday night specials!" This continued for some time until, suddenly, a bearded fellow demanded, "Hey, aren't you Sandy McMath?" I moved aside the lantern, the better to see.

"I'm Joel Cooner—Patricia's friend. I'm supposed to be the best man at the wedding, but I don't think I'll make it!"

Joel was driving one of those red double-decker London buses that enterprising tour operators load with students for Morocco and India. When he was off, he lived in Marabella in Spain. We spent the night reminiscing as only Arkansans can.

The big red bus was a magnet to the gamins of Marrakech. Children clustered around, tapping at the windows and trying to climb aboard. The passengers drew the curtains, but the tapping continued. Some of the children threw rocks, and others spat through the open windows. Joel eventually had to park the bus in a residential area far from the market.

22

The first level of the bus was the lounge and kitchen. Upstairs was a sleeping area for twelve people. It was crowded, to say the least. The ten passengers, most of whom were well-nourished young American women, swapped chores and on the whole coped well, considering the cramped environment.

Joel's job was about finished. The passengers were going their separate ways and the owner back to London. I told Joel he was welcome to ride south with me, although we would probably go no further than Zagora because of the war. I recounted my failure to get a permit from the police in Rabat. A second attempt at Marrakech had been likewise unsuccessful. After a day or two he decided to come along.

The terrain on the other side of the Atlas Mountains waxes steadfastly into reddish-orange and ocher wasteland, the beginnings of the Sahara itself. Except for the beds of the *draas* (dead rivers), the landscape is utterly barren of life. A poignant example of the power of the desert is the long, fragile fingers of green palms extending along the length of the beds of these once-proud rivers. To either side of the *draa* there is nothing but rock and sand. Although the *draas* are usually dry, they sometimes have subsurface water at a depth of several feet. The water level falls as you go south until, at the Tagounite Oasis, it completely disappears. Of course, the *draas* do have flash floods during the rainy season and then, for a moment, dead rivers revive again with a fury.

From the ridge you can look out to the southeast toward the great western emptiness, one of the most extensive and desolate reaches of the planet. Except for the hard-surfaced road to Tindouf in Algeria, one would cross no sign of man for more than 1,000 miles. Joel and I, however, did not go beyond Zagora. We toured the irrigation projects there (horticultural experiments of the Ministry of Agriculture) and talked to some nomads who were not accustomed to foreigners. Their village, an oasis unmarked on the Michelin map, lay several miles from the larger village of Foum-Zguid.They came to town once a month on their camels. They were perhaps half-castes of Arab and Berber (the so-called "blue people") stock. Although we saw several of the Berber in Zagora, we did not come upon an encampment of them until Essaouira on the coast.

It became our custom to drive out from the nearest town in the late afternoon and choose a place to camp. Camping too close to a village invited begging children and thieves. Uncannily, however, no matter how seemingly abandoned the place we stopped, a Moroccan would invariably appear as if by magic.

Our fears of theft proved unfounded. The *draa* people were helpful and friendly. One night we returned very late to a campsite in a stand of palms in the riverbed north of Zagora. We inflated our air mattresses and lay down— Joel next to the vehicle, I not very far away under a large bush. Two youngsters walked by not twenty feet away. I could see their silhouettes in the starlight and could tell by their hesitation that they had seen us, although they kept on walking.

Shortly thereafter, as I turned over to get into a more comfortable position—*kapow!* The pillow section of my air mattress exploded. I jumped completely off the ground. With the flashlight I discovered thorns two inches long on the bush underneath. Not long after we ceased laughing at the incident, a dim yellow light approached us from across the valley. It came on for a long time swaying slowly back and forth, specterlike, until it reached the *draa,* and then I saw that there were three small children with a lantern. A little girl carried a plate of fresh dates. They had been sent by their mother. We gave them each a dirham, although they did not ask us for money. I thought it sad that we should assume that they must have been sent to sell rather than to share their fruit with us. Still, I was sure that their mother could use the three dirhams. After they had stood and stared and smiled at us for a long time, they walked back across the *draa,* and we watched their lantern until it disappeared.

Unable to continue southward from Zagora, we turned back and headed west toward the Atlantic, the unimproved earth road a wretched rock furrow that churned and jerked us no matter how slowly we drove. Although the *piste* finally became a pavement at Taliume, the initial 80 kilometers were the roughest I crossed in northern Africa.

About 30 kilometers from Agdz, we came to a small hilltop village which was unmarked on the map. It was isolated, austere, and primitive, with dirt-floored huts and communal open-air hearths. It was as if time had passed it by and left it in another dimension beyond our ken. Fly-covered naked children, their skin caked with the red earth, ran to meet us as I foolishly drove toward the village gate. No sooner had we dismounted than they surrounded us and began begging. They seemed so hard and their shouts so strident and menacing that we decided to beat a hasty retreat. Somehow, Joel managed to lure most of them aside into the central compound, while I walked, as casually as one could under the circumstances, back to the jeep on the pretext of retrieving something I'd left there. Remembering my similar encounter in Marrakech of the week before, I was more than a little nervous. There was no way out of the village except the way we'd come, which meant that the jeep would have to be turned around. This I just managed to do by scraping the front bumper down one wall and backing into the opposite, whereupon the children charged out of the enclosure. I yelled for Joel but he waved me on, calling that he would run behind. Thus we sped over 300 yards—I in the jeep at 40 miles an hour, and Joel sprinting before a screaming mob of rock-throwing waifs. Just as he climbed aboard, the lead demons caught up with us and jumped onto the rear, clinging to the spare tire and window latch. As we fled onto a sandflat below, they tumbled gleefully away, cavorting in exaggerated somersaults. Their comrades, now far behind, gave up the chase.

Joel and I traveled uneventfully to Agadir, then back up the Atlantic coast to Casablanca. We tarried several days in Essaouira, where I finally accepted that I would be unable to cross the western desert but would have to attempt a direct frontal assault on the central Sahara.

Late that month, I sailed to Marseille on the packet boat *Massalia*. There I stocked up on some additional spare parts and changed to Dunlop all-terrain sand tires, buying an extra spare for the roof rack.

Joel was to have met me in Algiers and accompanied me at least as far as Tamanrasset. Unfortunately, personal matters intervened, and I was unable to keep our rendezvous—much to my loss, for Joel was a seasoned traveler and loyal companion.

CHAPTER II

Ten weeks later I was in Algeria on the road to Tamanrasset, the oasis at the base of the austere and desolate peaks of the Hoggar Mountain range. In the second-class lounge of the ferry *Marseille* I had met five young Frenchmen who invited me to join them for coffee. They were crossing to Kenya in a converted Mercedes troop carrier, filming along the way a documentary for French television. Painted on one side of the carrier was the panda bear of the International Wildlife Fund.

The group was headed by Jean Michel, a freelance photographer and television producer. He and his wife, Marie Paule, and their friends, Renée and Patrick, were accompanied by a young friend, Christian, who had come aboard at the last minute when a third couple backed out. None of them had previously traveled the Sahara, but had read a great deal about it. We hit it off well enough and decided to convoy for a time together.

We camped the first night at Blida, in a crevice beneath a cliff above the town. Marie Paule and Renée cooked dinner while Patrick and Jean Michel pitched the sturdy two-man expedition tents—inflating their rubber floors with Peugeot bicycle pumps.

Driving into Blida, we sought the baker to replenish our dwindling supply of bread. Inside the sweltering adobe hut, the ovens were tended by apprentices who shoveled the hot dough with long polelike paddles. We had been unable to buy bread at the previous village because the Algerian army, in what was to become a common occurrence, had preempted us. Standing outside the bakery were armed soldiers facing a small crowd of sullen villagers while four of their comrades, in rapid bucket-brigade fashion, heaved box after box of loaves into a troop truck. At Blida, though, the army was nowhere to be seen and there was plenty for all.

As we continued southward into increasingly desolate terrain, I would occasionally drive ahead of the others and stop to enjoy the silence on an elevation from which I could view in a single sweep the dreamlike geology through which we were passing. Sometimes we would cross a plain of fine gravel, each pebble of a seemingly uniform size. Occasionally, there were patches of sand from which protruded wrinkled fingerlike slags extensively weathered by the wind. The sun cast ominous shadows from these monoliths, which seemed to have been sown at random by some mythological deity.

At one point, as far as one could see to the north and east, there was a flat uninterrupted plain of finely ground gravel, not a pebble of which was more than a quarter-inch in diameter.

One could not help but sense a purposeful order in all this, a feeling—more of anticipation than of dread—of being confronted by an essence whose language was the opaque geometry itself. Some have said that the essence of the Sahara is silence, and indeed there was frequently an absence of sound so absolute that, were it not for the rush of my breath or the deliberate crunch of my boots in the sand, I could as well have been deaf.

It had been an uneventful day. We had only seen one other vehicle—a double-suspensioned bus plying its way between Aïn-Salah and Tamanrasset. We had stopped to film, so we were able to hear the engine from its first faint groan far to the south as it pitched and yawed across the void. We were as a ship becalmed as another passed on the horizon oblivious to our presence.

When the bus had passed, we resumed the positions we had taken at dawn, Jean Michel and I in the Toyota and Patrick driving ahead in the Mercedes. Jean Michel wanted to film them as they descended to the mosque at Moulay Hassan. Moulay Hassan had been a kind Arab who protected the *source* (fresh-water well) which now bears his name. The well is a half-mile walk up into a nearby rock cluster or "mountain," which is the only major elevation around. There, Moulay had raised a few goats and grown some potatoes and onions. Being a good man, he constructed a small rest shack for travelers from which he dispensed cups of mint tea to desert wayfarers. When the old man died, this tradition of hospitality was carried on by his sons. Eventually, a mosque was constructed where he had been laid to rest.

The legend developed that a sojourner will have a safe crossing of the Sahara if he circles thrice around the mosque. The deep ruts circling the mosque attest to the seriousness with which the legend is accepted. The devout, of course, also dismount to pray.

From the road above the hamlet, Jean Michel and I waited for our companions to descend. We could see several giant desert lorries which had themselves just concluded the circling. One flatbed was still turning in a cloud of dust.

Then our friends reached the roundabout, and there sounded the clack and whirr of film until the ritual was concluded. We then followed in the jeep. I was relieved to have completed the third circle and indeed drove halfway around again to make sure.

Parked to one side was a Formula One Italian racing driver in full battle dress whose sponsors had flown him and his racer here as a promotional. Renée wondered aside to me whether Allah would be pleased at this use of his mosque.

Taking the free tea was by custom mandatory, but it was sweet and fresh. The boy behind the plank-on-barrels which formed the counter smiled as he granted my request for a refill. At this moment I mistakenly neglected to remind myself that my companions were in a hurry. When the boy told me how to climb the ravine to the *source*, I decided to explore. I shouted this to the others as they talked with the Italian.

Among those stopped for mid-morning tea was a grizzled Catholic missionary from Mali in a Peugeot van. Monkishly dressed in seche and robe, he was traveling north with two petrol trucks. He wanted me to take his photograph, which I did, and then the two of us started up the ravine. I was climbing much faster, however, and soon had left him. In about a quarter of an hour I came to the *source:* a narrow hole in the ground with no cover. Two rusty iron buckets were tied to a length of rope. If one were thirsty enough he could lower one of the buckets into the slimy, brackish water which lay at about fifteen feet. Luckily, I thought, I had filled my water jugs at Aïn-Salah. The mountain was bare of vegetation, even near the well. Perhaps I should not have been so squeamish, I thought. This water had probably meant the difference between life and death for many a desert traveler. At least old Moulay, or some thoughtful person, had provided buckets. I remembered tales with unhappy endings, such as the Italians who had died at a well in Mali only twenty feet from water because they had no bucket and rope. A gust of hot wind blasted my face, and I knew that I too would greedily gulp this water if I had no other. Suddenly I remembered my companions. Scampering down the ravine, I ran upon the monk, sitting on a rock and catching his breath.

"Say, weren't you with those French fellows?"

"Yes, that's right."

"Well, they have gone on. I think they blew for you two or three times."

I thanked him and hurried down to where I could see the mosque. Sure enough, only the petrol trucks, the priest's Peugeot and the Toyota were there: the Mercedes was gone. Not that there was any danger. Although you are officially prohibited from traveling alone, many do so anyway, usually waiting at the outskirts of town for others so that all can pass the police check in convoy, then drive on alone.

I knew that my recent companions would be going about 30 to 35 miles per hour and that I would eventually overtake them. The trail was fairly well defined with the tracks of the large trucks from Moulay Hassan. Sure enough, twenty minutes later I saw my companions. They had stopped in a field of gravel next to a *draa.* Their tool chest had been emptied onto a blanket and Patrick was on his back working on the trailer hitch. The trailer was heavily overloaded with everything from spare parts to food and tents, and it had jerked along like an oversized toy behind the troop carrier.

Although I made no secret of my annoyance, they were so good-natured that it was difficult to be put out with them for long. The women had gotten out the teapot and had a fire going. Renée carried some towels to a folding chair near the fire and spread them out to dry. She and Marie Paule then went around to watch Patrick fix the trailer hitch. Jean Michel was busily photographing the damage. I raised my hood and had begun removing and brushing my sparkplugs when someone shouted, *"Feu! Feu!"* Marie Paule ran to the van door, which was hanging slightly ajar, and began to beat the deck with a towel. Beyond her the flames had caught the curtains and were lapping toward the roof. The interior of the van was quickly filled with smoke. The men ran toward the door with handfuls of sand, which they uselessly heaved into the cabin. I remembered that they had stored several jerry cans of fuel in the back.

Quickly, I ran to the Toyota. The fire extinguisher was between the door and the seat on the driver's side, but the door was locked. Opening the passenger door, I scooted across and grabbed the canister, opening the driver's door as I did so with my free hand. I jerked off the safety frame and hurled myself toward the van. The foam quickly shot out and was soon smothering the fire. *"Ca suffit!"* screamed Jean Michel. "That's enough!" There was a half-inch of foam on his camera gear near the door.

"You mean you don't carry a fire extinguisher?" I asked.

"One can't think of everything," he shrugged.

Fortunately, the damage was mostly cosmetic—a couple of curtains and two or three towels. The rest of the gear was intact. I was never able to determine exactly what had caused the accident, although I suspected one of the towels had caught on from the tea fire and then set off the curtains.

My friends were indeed in a great hurry. Their impossible schedule and overloaded vehicle would have doomed them to mishap and frustration in a futile personal war against the desert had it not been for Renée's and Marie Paule's light-hearted dispositions and culinary talent.

It was another four days before we reached Tamanrasset. The Mercedes became stuck in the sand more often as we ventured deeper and deeper into the desert. These moments became routine "immediate action" drills, in which I would pull up close by and Jean Michel would jump down, remove my sand tracks from the overhead racks and place them ahead and under the front wheels of the troop carrier. It was necessary, of course, to place them exactly parallel so that they could take the rear wheels as well. Everyone would get out and push. Twice I gave them a tug with the chain.

It is easy to forget the most elemental necessities when one is planning a very complicated overland expedition—particularly with so many sponsors needed to defray expenses. Still, my ten days with the Strasbourg raid convinced me of the necessity of keeping things as simple as possible. Murphy's Law is no stranger to the Sahara: If anything can go wrong, it will.

Tamanrasset is one of the four chief terminals in the Sahara, the others being Marrakech, Timbuktu and Agadez. It has an abundant supply of fresh water. Except for a few goats, however, it is wholly dependent upon the outside world for food.

The French used the oasis as their southern base for exploration and their perennial campaign against the Tuareg, ancient masters of the Sahara whom they never totally subdued. The town serves today as the Algerian government's desert capital and military base.

The town is about a mile and a half in length with one hard-surfaced street which is the last stretch of a five-mile blacktopped highway that runs from the airstrip. The "tar" has wrinkled in the sun, and the potholes are worse than no road at all. There are perhaps a dozen short side streets, unpaved, which end in the desert.

Tamanrasset is the site of the annual Sahara trade fair sponsored by the

Algerian government for most of the nations of north and west Africa. The fair was underway when we arrived. Among the most colorful items for sale were bolts of cloth from the Ivory Coast in Nigeria and Tuareg silver from the Aïr Mountains in Niger. (Morocco, Algeria's arch enemy, is not invited, although a number of items featured originate there, such as leather bags, slave bracelets, silver necklaces and spurs.)

There were two places to stay in Tamanrasset. The first was the "camping" area, where you could park your rig next to a nearby thatched cabin divided into two rooms. There were about a dozen of these dirt-floor huts together with a tea room and kitchen of the same design, all surrounded by a ten-foot wooden wall patrolled by two sworded Tuaregs. It is impossible to get in after 10:00 p.m., even if you are a registered guest. The cost: ten dinars (two dollars) per night. The second hostelry is the Hotel Sahara, where single rooms start at twenty dollars a night.

Near the town center was the almost-completed University of Tamanrasset, with its beautiful, arched Muslim architecture of bright red brick. The university covered more than two acres and was an impressive indication of the regime's intention to rechannel oil revenues into education and agriculture. The school was to be a laboratory for irrigated farming and desert horticulture.

Tamanrasset looks most beautiful in the morning. Before dawn, I would rise and walk the periphery of the town. At its southern extremity there is, suddenly, nothing: the trees stop; the street stops; houses, shanties, power lines, and gas stations are not to be seen. The dirt road veers off into the desert, where its tracks disappear into a field of sand. Above is Mount Laperrine, named after the intrepid French pilot and explorer who, in 1924, died there of thirst beside his crashed plane before a rescue party could reach him.

The town is still a major stop for trans-Sahara travelers, most of whom are drivers of the giant desert trucks that run on the Algiers-to-Kano route; the rest are "overlanders," travelers like myself. Occasionally, one sees suited-and-tied foreign businessmen or Algerian government functionaries who fly in at the small airport, stay a day or two, then fly out again. Then, of course, there are the oldest and most professional desert travelers of all, the Tuaregs. Neither Caucasian nor Negroid (some say they are the descendants of the ancient Libyans whom the Romans pushed into the desert), they can be seen coming and going in small caravans of from fifteen to twenty camels. They camp in the desert well beyond the town. From behind their blue veils they keep a wary and disdainful eye on those whom they consider interlopers; they do not mingle with the European or the Arab. Tuaregs do, however, recognize a lower caste of their tribe among their Negro servants (the Bouzous) whose condition of servitude is one of the oldest forms of African slavery. I am reluctant to give it that name because it is more of a caste relationship than slavery in the Western sense of the word. A Tuareg slave, for example, is entitled to protection and sustenance, and he may leave his master if he feels mistreated.*

---

*Yet, the traditional form of bondage still exists in the Sahara. It is abetted by the

Although Islamic, the Tuareg do not adhere to the more rigid Muslim strictures, particularly with regard to women. Indeed, it is the *men,* not the women, who wear the veil—always a bright blue cloth beneath the seche. Women are not only not excluded from the tribal council but may predominate in the decisions.

Tamanrasset was no exception to the general rule that in any remote outpost of humanity there will appear certain eccentric local characters whose pleasure it is to welcome, entertain and panhandle visitors. Tamanrasset had two: Chi Chi and Jo Jo. Although some visitors, in hobnobbing with one or both of these gentlemen, parted with a great deal of cash, they also, I am convinced, got great pleasure and satisfaction in doing so.

Chi Chi was an expatriate Greek who had somehow found his way to Djanet in the eastern Algerian Sahara several years before. He had closed a small restaurant there and moved to Tamanrasset when the drought drove out the Tuareg and destroyed Djanet's fledgling government-sponsored tourist business.

His restaurant here was in an old mud dwelling, leased from the village, in which he had managed to set up a kitchen with three young helpers from Algiers, whom he drove mercilessly. From a block away one could hear Chi Chi shouting, "Mohammet!" at the young spindly-legged waiter who was constantly shattering the crockery.

Chi Chi's weakness was Scotch whiskey—or, really, anything potent he could hustle from overlanders in the camping. He was at the gate at sunup when it was opened by the guards. But whatever might have been his relationship to the bottle, he ran the best restaurant in town: ten dinars for thick, lumpy bean and goat soup, and a plate of tender goat or mutton with boiled potatoes, garlic, onions and salad. The clientele consisted of a half-dozen young French high-school teachers and their visiting wives, overlanders, police and army officers and local bureaucrats. Chi Chi was the source of local scuttlebutt on such things as when to buy bread. Tamanrasset was

---

Tuareg, as well as by the Toubou in Chad and by Arab traders in the Sudan. Until World War II, Arab chieftains throughout the Sahara engaged in outright kidnapping and detention in forced labor of other Arabs, blacks and half-castes—not to mention an occasional Englishman or American who was unlucky enough to fall into their hands. Such raids or *razzias* are mostly a thing of the past. However, Saudi and Persian Gulf merchants still provide a market for young black children— mostly girls—who are sold into bondage by their parents. Officially this traffic in human beings goes under the euphemism of "labor procurement" or "employment service" but it is nothing other than slavery. Twice in northern Niger I saw young black girls in Tuareg camps who were obviously in transit. According to an impeccable source in Agadez, such children are carried into the sand sea of Bilma where, relayed from caravan to caravan, they eventually reach Port Sudan on the Red Sea where they are shipped in *dhows* directly across to Saudi Arabia or to the Persian Gulf.

having chronic bread "shortages"—i.e., only enough for the army. As at Blida, a squad of riflemen kept off angry villagers while what bread there was was loaded up for the barracks. Chi Chi advised an early arrival at the bakery since the baker always secretly prepared an extra batch. The soldiers slept late and didn't know about it.

Arriving at the bakery the next morning, I saw that it was surrounded by coffee-colored old Arabs selling dried jaw-breaker dates and thimblefuls of salt. I was surprised at how tough and unchewable these dates were. We learned that the good dates are all exported. These were the rejects. Aside from being dry, they were covered with dirt and other unappetizing material. A Peace Corpsman, John Burns, whom I met at the camping, showed me how to clean and remoisten them by dipping them quickly into hot water and letting them sit for a few minutes.

Chi Chi always seemed to have fresh export dates, not to mention fresh bread and vegetables. He also had feed sacks of onions and garlic when none could be found elsewhere. No one knew where this booty came from, but he must have had a special deal with the regular truck drivers.

The other character in Tamanrasset was Jo Jo. Actually, Jo Jo "visited" Tamanrasset but lived at a place called Tahabort Source, which was a mud and thatched split-level dwelling eighteen miles into the desert and built over the small mountain spring for which the site is named. The spring seeps into a pool which is enclosed in a small "closet" just behind the entry room. A pipe runs from the pool to a faucet outside the lodge where visitors may draw drinking water, wash their clothes and bathe. The *source* is the only fresh water between Tamanrasset and Hirhafok, 140 miles to the north on the other side of Assekrem, the great peak of the Hoggar range.

The lodge contains four large rooms on the ground floor, including a tea room spread with soft tattered carpet remnants. At night, hitchhikers and caravan passengers are invited to throw down their sleeping bags there. Hot, sweet mint tea is brought by one of four handsome Tuareg servants on a magnificent silver service. One does not always pay for his tea nor for his supper: Jo Jo has a mercurial (and selectively forgetful) generosity. With a great flourish he will enter his *salon du thé* and hold court with his guests. He tells them of his travels, which are vast: Mexico, South America, Europe.

But even with this traveling abroad, Jo Jo is still a man of the Sahara. He has been to Timbuktu and Gao and across the sands of Bilma. There is a large poster board in the "reception" with Jo Jo's postcards, photographs, letters and newspaper clippings from many countries. Jo Jo keeps in touch with his friends up and down the Sahara by letters which he sends via overland travelers. I was pleased to carry one of these to the boss of the Sahara Hotel in Agadez.

Jo Jo has no vehicle but rides the eighteen kilometers to town and back with whomever among his guests might be going. In town, he appears suddenly, mysteriously, with a wide smile, his even wider girth draped with a billowing shirt and the baggy trousers of his Islamic sect. He demands: "A la source?" Of course, you are going and you invite him aboard. As you head out of town, he suddenly remembers an errand or three, and friends to see. One must make such calls before finally being permitted to enter the sand

"Welcome, my friend, to Tahobort Source," is Jo Jo's oft-repeated greeting. Foothills of the Hoggar range, Algeria. Photograph by Camille Alonzo.

fields toward Assekrem. Jo Jo invariably takes up the entire right side so that if anyone is riding in the passenger seat they are forced into the rear. There is a noticeable corrective swing to the chassis once he scrambles out. He is ever observant for the surprising amount of edible vegetation in the desert. Once he spied sprigs of mint growing under a bush. There was no way I or the others could have seen it. Jo Jo hopped out, ran 40 feet to the bush, and harvested several handfuls, holding them up in triumph like a small boy.

This garrulous, ambiguous, thriving and suspicious fellow is typical of the Arab merchants of the Sahara: he must be clever but kind in order to survive. He must remain flexible, amiable, but always watchful in even the most cursory dealings. Yet once he is committed to a bargain he will fulfill it. One's word is one's bond in the Sahara.

The reciprocal giving of *cadeaux* is a custom constantly observed. Jo Jo's gifts are his banquets, sometimes attended by high officials. (One of the displayed letters of thanks from former guests was from the American ambassador.) To these banquets he invites the district governor, police chief, and even the town's four traffic policemen. He hopes they will steer well-paying clients his way and see to it that his modest enterprise is not expropriated. Among his detractors are zealous young party officials who see in Tahabort Source a stubborn redoubt of capitalism. Yet even these critics enjoy an occasional skewer of Jo Jo's fatted goat.

I drove out to Tahabort one morning with Peter Sutton and Camille Alonzo, an intrepid English couple in their early 30s who were heading to Nigeria to seek jobs in the booming construction trade there. They drove a 1953 British Army ambulance, which Peter had converted into a camper. I met them outside the camping in Tamanrasset, where they had decided to park rather than pay the four-dollar nightly fee.

The Hoggar, beyond the *source*, is a graveyard of extinct volcanoes. A million years ago they presented a formidable presence, smoldering and grumbling and heaving slag over a tropical landscape. During subsequent centuries, wind and sand have sculpted them into such contorted shapes that they rather resemble a potter's discards. Some peaks are twisted and bent at convex angles that seem to defy gravity. One looks like the tufted pendule of a Victorian nightcap, another like a fishhook suspended at a 30-degree angle to the horizon, another like an arrowhead. Depending upon the season and time of day, the colors of the Hoggar change from pink-violet to reddish-orange to purple. A child with a jumbo box of crayons could draw the Hoggar correctly, in the course of a single day, using every color but green.

We had decided to take my jeep into the mountains, to Assekrem. The 140-mile trip would take us through extremely difficult terrain, and it was doubtful that the old Austin ambulance could make the steep grade. The afternoon before, we had gone to town to buy bread and food. Unable to find enough potatoes, onions or garlic for a week, we decided to try Chi Chi, who produced an entire feed sack full of vegetables. What we didn't need, he said, was to be delivered to the father at the hermitage.

Before leaving, we transferred most of my equipment to the ambulance, keeping only a jack and three jerry cans of gas. Camille provided bread and goat cheese, and I donated several tins of meat and fish. John Burns, who joined us, threw in a sack of dates. Olga, Camille's German shepherd, crouched eagerly in the back.

The *piste* from Chez ("the home of") Jo Jo rejoins the main tracks to Assekrem about three miles across the sand, beneath a particularly high and solitary cone which stands like a sentinel above the valley floor. From there the tracks meander northward through a *draa* into successive small fields of boulders and sand furrows. The only sign of life was a single adobe-like hut on a knoll above a 100-foot gorge cut through bedrock by eons of flash flooding. There was a depth gauge alongside the concrete piling built parallel to the cliff wall. At first glance it seemed ridiculous to have the measuring stick so high: it must have been 25 feet from the base of the stream. Then I noticed that caught near the top of the gauge was a patch of dried brush, an ominous reminder of the depth and fury of the water when it came.

There was no sign of life for over 40 miles through the boulder-strewn landscape until we passed a Tuareg in a small canyon who was grazing four camels on some tough sage that evidently had found enough moisture to grow there. He made no sign of greeting.

We arrived at the foot of Assekrem around 4:00. The road was steep and blocked by rock slides in several places. Without four-wheel drive, the ascent would have been impossible.

At the top of the pass we were directly opposite the "Three Sisters," enormous peaks rising together to the southwest. The road there reaches its highest point at about 9,000 feet. Alongside is a refuge for travelers. This is rather like a mountain lodge one might find in an American national park. There is a large central room with a fireplace, a sleeping room with two dozen one-man mattresses, and a kitchen, which was locked. It was quite late, so we stowed our gear as quickly as possible, setting up the camping stove in the central room and arranging our food and utensils for dinner. It would be dark when we returned from the summit.

The climb was steep and Peter groaned under the sack of vegetables. About halfway up, there suddenly burst down the trail a team of four burros smartly driven by a wiry bare-chested little man in black trousers who shouted for us to give our produce to "the bishop." He was the resident priest who was hauling up firewood from the shed next to the refuge.

The summit we found dominated by a small chapel, next to which was a concrete stylus placed by the Auto Touring Club of France in 1939, upon which was outlined in silhouette each peak on the horizon.

Olga, who had climbed with us, had run ahead and entered the chapel, growling. I managed to retrieve her just as there appeared a robed cleric. He motioned for us to be silent and to follow him. He led us through the chapel to a small library with volumes in both French and Tomachek, the language of the Tuareg, of which Father Foucould, founder of the mission, became a master. Foucould translated the Bible into Tomachek and various verses of Tuareg poetry and folklore into French. He alternated his mission between the Assekrem hermitage, which was completed in 1911, and that in Tamanrasset. He devoted himself not only to translations but also to the freeing and training of Bouzou slaves. He was killed in Tamanrasset on December 1, 1916, by rebelling Tuaregs.

Our guide introduced himself as the "Bishop of the Sahara." His circuit was the largest in the world: over 1,000,000 square miles.

"So you know Chi Chi?" he asked, looking at the sack.

We told him how we had been befriended by Chi Chi, and he nodded understandingly. He had known the Greek in Djanet, before the drought.

The sun was now well below the shoulders of the sisters and receding quickly. As it dropped into the earth, the shadows of the mountains fell backward upon each other—black iron shadows, undisturbed by clouds or atmosphere.

I followed the trail alone until it came to a precipice several hundred yards from the summit. There was a dead fall some 500 feet into a ravine, the bottom of which, completely shadowed now, was invisible. It was necessary to use the flashlight to climb back down to the ridge.

When I arrived, Camille was boiling rice, beef stew and peas. After a hard day's drive and the climb, we were famished. We shared our dinner with a nun from Strasbourg, France, who had come for three weeks of meditation. She slept alone in the woodshed, climbing each morning to the summit, where she meditated until dusk. She spoke only after dark. She said that she was on her own and not permitted to use the hermitage.

We had looked forward to a long night's sleep but the refuge was also hosting a family of rambunctious field mice who were determined to forage, gnaw and scamper throughout the night. Though we succeeded in clubbing several of them, they sent in two replacements for each casualty.

After feeding the dead mice to two starving dogs, we drove on toward Immalman, an abrupt and solitary mesa where several climbers have lost their lives over the years. Upon arriving, we saw two Land Rovers with "British Bilma Sands Expedition" stenciled on their doors. In a hot plastic tent alongside the vehicles were two young British women reading paperback novels. They were the expedition's nurse and "secretary." The men had left before sunup to attempt the summit.

Nearby huddled a young Tuareg, his arms clapsed around his knees as if meditating. "He's been like that for two days, since we picked him up at the village just east of here," the nurse said. "He wants to go to the fair at Tam." He had insisted upon waiting during the several days necessary for them to complete the climb. He had some dried meat and a gourd of water. "He hasn't asked us for a thing," the nurse said.

The expedition had driven north by compass and sextant from N'Guigmi in Niger on Lake Chad. They had come across the sand sea to the oasis of Bilma itself. From there they had headed north by northwest to Adrar Bous and, finally, Djanet, from which they had come to Immalman. They had had no major problems, although several times one or the other of the Land Rovers had become stuck in the sand. They did not have the long-range radio equipment customarily carried by European expeditions on such crossings. (I later encountered in Agadez a French expedition, a west-to-east [Mauritania to the Nile] crossing by a convoy of specially equipped desert trucks, which was monitored by satellite from Paris.)

Their mission was about finished. It had initially been to explore a certain improbable range of mountains (in southwestern Algeria) which had recently been revealed for the first time in detail on a satellite photograph. They had been surprised to find their approach blocked by a succession of deep gorges. It seemed that after they crossed each gorge, the mountains lay just as far away as before. They had marched ten days toward them without success. Having allotted only two weeks' provisions to this phase of their enterprise, they were unable to continue. They had gone on to Lake Chad, resolving to return another year.

Leaving the Bilma expedition we descended on a punishing trail. The road had been all but washed away, and again, it was necessary to navigate through substantial rock slides. Once we came very close to skidding out of control on the loose gravel and careening into a gorge. Upon reaching the plain, however, the *piste* turned into tracks again, in the soft but bouyant sand of the *draa*. We followed this soft tarmac for twenty miles until we came to the Tuareg village of which the English woman had spoken.

The village was "V"-shaped, approximately 300 yards on each leg—and we approached from the closed end of the "V." As I turned off the main tracks, I saw only a herd of goats and their shepherd, and an old woman squatting in the shade of a mud hut. A few fires smoldered further on. The goat boy blew on his whistle and in no time we were surrounded by children. Some of them produced little wooden cups and bowls to sell. Others chanted, *"Donnez-moi cadeau."* Fearing I might hit one, I turned to take the right fork. As I did, the children disappeared. They had known we would have to enter the village from the other tracks, so they had raced across the *draa* to the lower fork. Sure enough, two minutes later, there they were in the middle of the road. Every child in the village! There must have been 40 of them. Camille chanced a photo, and this set off a row of feigned disapproval coupled with intensified demands for *cadeaux*. A few old women stood in their doorways watching. There was not a single adult male to be seen.

The *piste* broadened into a flat wide course of tracks which frequently disappeared into the sand. We followed it by following the terrain—if you always stay on whatever particular contour or in whatever stream you find yourself, the tracks will usually reappear. Some ten miles further on, we came to two thick-limbed, stubby trees, each about fifteen feet high with radii of about fifteen feet. They appeared dead, and Peter took the axe to cut some firewood. Nothing doing. The wood was green and hard and oozed a thick green sap. It deflected the axe as if it were concrete.

A quarter-mile beyond the trees, we came to a wide gravel streambed where two Australians, Rex Monroe and Phil Tilley, sat on the hood of their Land Rover. They had parked near the bank and turned around to take a rest. The remnants of a picnic lunch lay on the ground. We exchanged information and they told us that we were only about an hour from the main tracks to town. They had wanted to drive to Djanet but had decided against it because they could not find an accompanying vehicle. We told them about Immalman and the road to Assekrem.

They indicated that they wanted to leave soon for Agadez and suggested that we might want to travel together. We arranged to rendezvous at Jo Jo's later that week.

The tracks again disappeared into a wide level plain of sand but the surface was much firmer and I was able to achieve a speed of 60 miles per hour for as long as fifteen minutes at a time. The sensation of such speed in such emptiness was one that I would soon take for granted, but which at that moment was one of the most exhilirating experiences I had ever had.

It was sundown when we reached town, and after buying bread, we headed out toward Tahabort Source. Just as we were about to drive into the desert Jo Jo made his customary surreptitious appearance from the shadow of a wall. With ease he navigated our return to the *source* over a different, trackless route.

The days at Chez Jo Jo's turned into a week during which we studied our charts and worked on our rigs. There was good water for washing and bathing, and we filled our tanks and jugs from the source. John and I threw our sleeping bags in Jo Jo's tea room alongside those of the Tuareg servants—each with his sword by his side. Jo Jo slept in his study, a small room above and behind the tea room from which his snore reverberated throughout the lodge.

There were, of course, no sanitary facilities, and whenever anyone needed them, he had to venture into the desert. There was an allotted place just north of the lodge, but it was in full view of the faucet and the clearing where the Tuaregs plucked chickens and peeled vegetables.

Pete was a jack-of-all-trades—carpenter, mechanic and tinkerer—who would eventually get any job done, puttering about in his own slow way. Camille was the interpreter (she spoke fluent French and knew quite a bit of Arabic) and a superb cook. (Pete bragged that he had taught her how to cook during their six years of living together.) They had dozens of recipes and a score of exotic spices to go with them in the small kitchen which was in the front end of the truck's lounge/bedroom. They had managed to put together a miniature kitchen which was the model of camping efficiency. They had one of each pot, skillet, and casserole dish that would be needed to produce their regular recipes. Their small stove burned camping gas.

Being very English, Peter and Camille had morning and afternoon and high tea, to which John and I and anyone else in the vicinity were invited. They had been on the road for about six months in southern Europe, Morocco and northern Algeria. Thus far, they had had no major difficulties with the old ambulance which, after its army years, had been a mail truck for the British Postal Service, from which Peter had bought it at auction in 1975 for $1,500.

Although Jo Jo's banquets were outstanding, the daily fare was less appealing. The food was overly vinegared with a kind of stale sauce, and the potatoes and macaroni were overcooked. Hence, John and I began to eat with Peter and Camille, each of us contributing a quantity of our own provisions and taking turns cooking and washing up.

The last day of the fair there was a ceremonial parade featuring the Tuareg and Bouzous. There were two groups of the latter, each consisting of about 30 men with short nineteenth-century muskets, into which they stuffed smelly black powder. Each group had a single rhythmic chant which was repeated over and over again as they danced and shimmied and shook their rifles in the air. They wore white robes festooned with tin and silver bangles.

In between the two sections of prancing Bouzous came the Bouzou women, who emitted, rolling their tongues, a shrill gutteral trill like the cries of some exotic fowl.

Behind the Bouzous came five rows of four camels each, mounted by Tuareg warriors resplendent in white and blue robes and blue veils, swords hanging at their sides. Between the rows of camels came the Tuareg women, who were surrounded by a circle of guards who, with hands on the hilts of their swords, looked menacingly at the crowd and waved back those who came too close. The Tuareg women wore no veils but only smiled, their teeth resplendent in their brown faces.

Although there was no band, the rattling trills of the Bouzou women and the cacophony of drums and chants of the riflemen provided a surprisingly easy, graceful marching rhythm. The procession gently wound its way from the prefecture of police to just past the post office, where it turned right and headed toward the fairgrounds. Suddenly, there appeared a contingent of gruff Arab policemen—some dozen of them with olive uniforms bristling with pistols and black leather belts. They began shouting at the marchers and pretended to direct them along the route that they were going—as if they had not been proceeding properly.

The police were directed by a suave young Arab in a dark suit who darted officiously back and forth between the marchers and the reviewing stand, which was set in a kind of corral just inside the fairgrounds. There he conversed with his superior, a striped-suited functionary in dark glasses who sat among some dozen civilian and military officials, also in dark glasses. These had been chauffeured around the parade in Mercedes sedans, bathing the marchers with dust. The Tuaregs were made to wait at the gate while the Bouzous were hustled inside. Children scampered about under the legs of the camels as the Tuaregs gazed with evident disdain at the spectators. The graceful Tuareg women looked about regally from within their circle of warriors. Meanwhile, the contingents of Bouzous, each in its turn, shimmied to the center of the ring and on signal pointed their rifles down inside the circle and fired. The report startled the crowd as well as the camels, and it was several moments before the smoke and wadding from the muskets had cleared the air. The salute was repeated by the second contingent, and this was followed by a kind of passing-in-review of the Tuaregs on their camels. The parade then disbanded.

It should be noted that the parade is the highlight of the year for the Bouzous, who had been practicing their ceremony on the local playing field every night for the previous week.

In the next few days we cleaned and checked out our vehicles and reviewed the maps of the road ahead with the Australians. They too had come to Jo Jo's and were now ready to head south. We decided to leave in convoy early the following Saturday.

Before we left, I dropped John Burns off at the north end of town, where he hoped to catch a ride to Algiers. Later he wrote that it had been a week before he had been able to get out.

John had arrived in Niger, the country immediately to the south, in the fall of 1974 and had been assigned to dune control at the village of Keita in the Sahel. There he had been able to see firsthand how the Sahara expands into lands ravaged by indiscriminate strip burning, wood gathering, and overgrazing of goats. (Interestingly, most of what is now the Sahara was, within the last 1,000 years, habitable plains and forest.)

John's efforts at Keita had attempted to educate the local people as to the best way to prevent the spread of the sand, through the planting of seedlings of tamarisk trees, parkinsonia and prosopis around the edges of advancing dunes.

Many of the seedlings, of course, had perished in the dry soil; others had been eaten by goats as soon as they sprouted. "We only got something like five out of one hundred seedlings that lived to become saplings," he said. And many of the saplings that escaped the goats had been felled by villagers gathering fire wood.

Eventually, John had been able to muster the support of the village chief, who persuaded his constituents to assist in gathering millet stalks and other compost. John seemed to have had more success than most Peace Corpsmen I met who were involved in similar projects.

When his time was up in the fall, he had hitchhiked north to Agadez and on into the Aïr Mountains. There he had bought a camel and struck out alone across the Bagzine range to the oasis of Timia, the last rendezvous of the Tuareg caravans to Bilma. After several weeks there—during which he had been befriended by a local chief—he had caught a ride in a petrol lorry to Tamanrasset via the French uranium mine at Arlit.

CHAPTER III

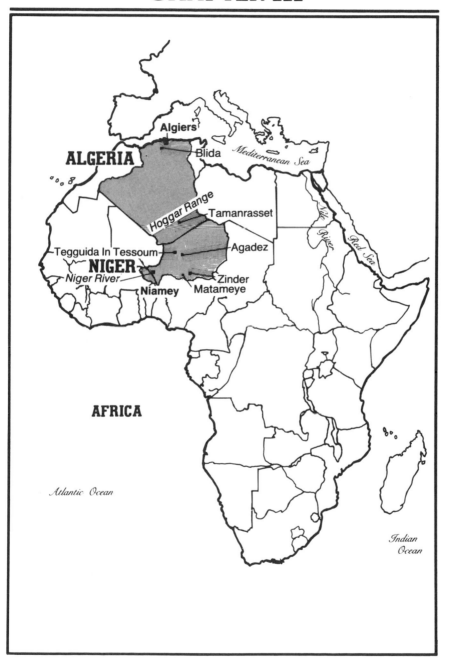

Before driving south into the desert from Tamanrasset, one is required to obtain a permit from the local police. This involves filling out a form which says you are aware of the dangers involved in such a crossing and are prepared to risk them. As mentioned earlier, no one is permitted to leave except in convoy with at least one other vehicle.

At dinner the night before leaving Chez Jo Jo, we agreed upon an order of travel and signals to be given in case of emergency. Because sound travels poorly in the desert, visual signals were essential. Thus it was decided that if a vehicle broke down or one of us otherwise had to make a long stop, he would turn on his headlights and leave them on. To inquire whether a halted vehicle was in trouble, the one ahead would flash his lights twice; the reply for "all is well" was the same signal. Failure to respond would be treated as a breakdown.

Because they were the slowest, it was decided that Pete and Camille would drive ahead in the ambulance. I would follow, and the Australians would bring up the rear. Each of us had experienced the nuisance and uncertainty of uncooperative partners who sped off on their own, so it was encouraging to be once again with reliable companions.

Among the tales of the desert woe is that of the traveler gone to the next oasis for help and returning to find his stranded vehicle looted and stripped. As on the high seas, an abandoned unit is considered fair "salvage" for anyone who comes along. On the Sahara, almost every truck driver carries a tool kit with which he can salvage a complete engine in half a day.

A good many breakdowns result from an overestimation of the desert-worthiness of one's vehicle and one's own mechanical ability. Some even attempt the crossing in light Combis or similar vans that easily bog down in the deep sand, lose oil and overheat. Even with a sturdy vehicle, failure to bring along basic spare parts (for example: alternator, water pump) can spell disaster. Surprisingly, such fundamentals as an adequate supply of fuel and a good compass are frequently overlooked. One fellow, a Frenchman, allowed as how he didn't need a compass: "Me, I just follow the tracks . . ." But not long ago two of his countrymen had perished doing just that: the tracks they had followed had abruptly ended in the middle of nowhere. The travelers had apparently left the *piste* to view some distant ruins. On the way back they'd picked up what looked like a fresh trail and followed it. A Free

French veteran in the rescue party recognized the tracks as those of an Allied convoy, circa 1942. The convoy had passed early in the morning in dew-damp sand. After drying in the sun, the tracks would remain, perhaps for centuries—the wind covering, then uncovering them with successive gusts of sand.

The results of navigational or mechanical errors could be seen occasionally looming in the distance, sometimes called to our attention by the reflection of sunlight from a shattered windshield. These abandoned wrecks lay like the bleached bones of a great fish on an uncharted beach. We would approach such ruins reverently, for some of them were doubtless the remains of machines which had carried intruders such as ourselves into the emptiness.

By 3:00 the first afternoon out of Tamanrasset, we had traveled about 40 miles over alternate sand and corrugations when, toward the top of a long depression, the road forked and it appeared that the more recent and frequent tracks led to the east. I followed these for a good while, until I reached a ridge where I scanned the horizon with the binoculars. Far in the distance two plumes of dust were disappearing over a rise. Little did I suspect that this was Pete and Camille, from whom I had become separated.

In a quarter of an hour, when they had still not arrived, I backtracked to the fork, whereupon I encountered a battered semi loaded with Nigerians returning from the fair. They took the western fork without hesitation, leading me to realize immediately my error. Cresting a hill, I found my friends lounging at afternoon tea in the shadow of a dune. A snakelike cornice of rock extended several yards from the dune to provide protection from the wind and concealment from any unlikely passersby. There we camped for the night.

During our after-dinner coffee, there arose to the south the unmistakable hum of a heavy engine. Soon there appeared two trucks making their way slowly toward Tamanrasset. It took them half an hour to disappear, and when they had, it was dark. An hour later, a giant petrol tanker passed about a mile out into the *piste*, a searchlight towering above its cab like some monstrous eye. After that, there was silence.

The Aussies had a portable shortwave radio on which we listened to the news from the BBC World Service. For two weeks this was our only contact with the outside world. Much of the news concerned Africa, particularly the wars in Zaire and Rhodesia. During the weather the commentator mentioned winds in the Sahara. The reception was unexpectedly clear.

When the others had gone to bed I took a flashlight and walked out a ways from camp toward the belt of Orion, which lay in the southeast at about 35 degrees. After about ten minutes, I could barely discern the outline of our three vehicles beneath the rock. The only sign of life was the wavering amber eye of the fire's last coals. Above, the stars of the Milky Way shone, uninterrupted by clouds or pollution. I sat for a long moment on the sand and let the laminated needle of the compass find north. I shot an azimuth back toward the shadow of the rock. I noticed that I had begun heading down a gentle slope into a plain of boulders. A lift of dunes began to my right and extended in an ever-widening "V" as it settled into the horizon.

Overhead two shooting stars arced, one behind the other in rapid succession. A satellite coursed along the handle of the Big Dipper and disappeared.

As I paused to button my field jacket, a light caught my eye: it was not celestial. It was a fire. I looked away for a moment to make sure I was not seeing things, then looked again. Sure enough, against the backdrop of a distant ridge was a campfire. My curiosity aroused, I crept toward it, taking care lest I stumble. My progress was slow, and in a ravine, I lost the fire altogether. But when I emerged I found myself on a crest less than 100 feet above it.

All about on blankets and sacks were sprawled a dozen Arabs. One sat on a folding chair, and as he talked he leaned back on the rear legs. Beyond were two canvas-covered five-ton trucks parked facing each other. As I watched, one of the men carried an armload of wood from one of the trucks and threw it on the fire. He then sat down and picked up a small transistor radio, which began crackling with sharp, undulating Arab music.

Beneath the truck on the right was another, smaller fire. Around it were huddled other forms. I could tell from their voices that they were Africans, probably Nigerian tradesmen or helpers returning from the fair in Tamanrasset. Their destination would be Zinder or Kano. Occasionally, one of them would walk over to the Arabs' fire to get something from a small sack.

I let my mind wander. I knew that not long ago this would have been a camel caravan—that instead of the trucks, there would have been 100 camels placidly resting from the long day's march. After an interlude, I decided that it would be best not to disturb them and carefully made my way back to our camp.

The next morning, I took Olga for a long walk and returned to the ridge. On reaching the top I could see no trace of the caravan except the dead coals of the fire and the tracks of the trucks which led down toward the *piste.*

Before leaving Tamanrasset we had filled our gasoline tanks, jerry cans, and water jugs. My toprack was creaking and swaying under the weight of twelve such containers, a sixth spare tire, and a trunk of camping gear. Traveling in shallow sand at 40 miles an hour, I struck a sudden depression. The entire right side of the rack ripped away, and it took two hours to refasten it. It was necessary to place the jerry cans and water jugs in the back of the jeep. I was wary of driving with the gasoline there, but there was no other choice.

Around noon we came upon a Nigerian truck with a broken axle. The twenty-odd passengers were huddled resignedly in the shade of the truck. When some of the Africans presented bottles and jugs for water we obliged. In no time Camille had dispensed a salt tablet to everyone. Seeing that there was nothing further we could do, we started to push on, but Peter could not get the ambulance to start. For two hours he and Rex were under the hood testing first the fuel pump, then the filter, and finally the fuel lines, where, it became apparent, the problem lay. Many of the Africans clustered around. This was most annoying, since a lot of tools and equipment were lying about. When they refused to move, we had to lock everything up in the cab except what was actually being used at the moment. When one young man reached

46

for a wrench that was lying on the fender, Olga lunged at him and had to be restrained. Fortunately, he was not bitten. After that, we had no more trouble from these people.

Finally, Pete closed the hood and stepped down, his long face bearing the look of a guardedly optimistic surgeon—an expession to which we were to become accustomed during the next two weeks.

The engine started on the first try and we were off. For the next two hours we made fairly good time, and when we came to a long smooth plain of hard sand we maintained an exhilarating 50 to 60 miles an hour for untold minutes. There was not the slightest interruption in contour. Phil and Rex would pull even with me at a distance of, say, 100 yards, then slowly, we would veer apart—each following his own independent trajectory until we were separated by miles of emptiness. When we caught up with Pete and Camille, whom we had given a half-hour's lead, we would halt and tarry, then race again over the sand.

The surface remained hard, brittle as a fine winter frost on short grass: you could hear it whirr and crackle as the tires virtually hydroplaned over it. Occasionally, I had the sensation of flying. When a dune or other elevation would separate us, I had the illusion of vertigo. Once when we had broken formation and run ahead of them, it appeared that we had lost Pete and Camille. We searched with our field glasses for several minutes but to no avail. Just when we had given up and were about to retrace, we saw the ambulance emerge from behind a large dune-rock ahead of us.

Remembering the phantom caravan, I kept a close lookout lest they appear again off in the distance, huddled perhaps around their parabolic iron kettles having tea. I thought of several questions I would like to ask them. They must have made many voyages through the Sahara. Once, I saw what I thought were some trucks near the base of a dune. I drove toward them for an indeterminate time, leaving my partners veering to the southwest behind me. But upon reaching the place, I found only an abandoned Volkswagen van and an old Peugeot station wagon. Each had been turned on its side and stripped, apparently long before, and their paint was peeled away.

That night we built our fire in a small box canyon eroded out of a red-ocher slag much like that in the Hoggar. The slag was over half a mile from the *piste,* and behind it rose a giant castlelike mesa which we resolved to climb the next morning.

Everyone was still abed when I crawled out of my tent well before dawn and headed toward the base of the mesa. The sand was deep and loose, and walking was most difficult.

The eastern slope of the rock was solid, but as I proceeded to the southeast it became increasingly brittle and flaky until, finally, it was pure sand. As I rounded the face I found myself at the base of an enormous dune. Far above where the rock was still intact there was what appeared to be a gate. The sand was so steep that in order to climb without slipping I had to zigzag at wide angles.

At last I stepped into a level "walkway" of solid rock and was able to continue upright around what could have been the ramparts of a medieval fortress. A hundred feet further on were natural steps which led into another passageway, which led in turn to another, and so on, until eventually I reached the summit. There I found a remarkable view. Rising far to the southeast was a sea of dunes beyond which dawn was just breaking. Between the dunes and my perch were a half-dozen similiar mesas, each beginning to undergo the rapid morning color change from red to pink. Then, gazing below, I saw our camp. The others were up now and moving about, although I could not identify them individually. For a moment it appeared as if there were eight of them instead of four, so darkly were their shadows cast. Indeed, when Olga ran after a stick she looked like two dogs racing neck-and-neck across the sand.

When we broke camp we proceeded downhill due south instead of returning directly to the *piste*. Pete's truck had had difficulty making the long climb up the slope to the rock and it was feared that it might founder on the return. Thus we decided to rejoin the *piste* by intersecting it further on. Unknown to us, the trace veered some 30 degrees to the east. After an hour and a half, we decided that we should head due east, in order to be certain of crossing it. The further we drove, however, the deeper the sand became and the more difficult for Pete's heavy rig to traverse. Twice again, he was plagued with a clogged fuel line which took over an hour each time he repaired it. I was about to suggest that we backtrack—no easy task (even though we could follow our tracks) since we would be following much of the terrain uphill in deep sand and Pete was having enough trouble going downhill. Suddenly, Rex shouted that he had seen a *piste* marker, a stack of rocks which, though infrequent and unpredictable, was usually reliable. I looked with the binoculars, and sure enough, I could not only make out the marker but some tracks as well. Pete was at the time fixing his fuel line, so the Aussies and I drove over and reached the *piste*, about a mile and a half away. Half an hour later, we camped just off the trail, about 24 kilometers north of In Guezzim, the last post before the Niger border.

In Guezzim was, except for its sister border station of Assamaka in Niger 30 kilometers to the south, the only outpost for hundreds of miles. We had been warned that it was both inhospitable and bare—of food, fuel and water. The border guards were said to harass overlanders, and we were told that we should camp far enough above it so that we would not be seen by its restless garrison, many of whom were incorrigibles who had been sent there as punishment. We hoped, therefore, to complete all the necessary formalities and move on into Niger by the afternoon without having to camp nearby a second night.

Actually, we did not know for a fact that we would be able to pass into Niger, about which we had heard, while in Tamanrasset, reports of a *coup d'état* and a subsequent closing of the frontier. It was also rumored that Europeans would henceforth have to have visas. Because Americans had always had to have them, I had obtained one before leaving Paris. The

Australians had one, but from the French consul in London—a service performed by French embassies for former French colonies which do not have embassies of their own. Peter and Camille had not bothered. We decided, however, to proceed straight to the border and do what we could to persuade the officials there to let us all in. Since I had the only valid visa I would act as spokesman and, if any problems arose, would explain that when we had set out our papers were in order. Some Swedes in a Land Rover going north the first day had told us they had turned back when they met a van of French travelers in In Guezzim who had been denied entry. This heightened our own fear.

In Guezzim was a squatty, wind-blown bidonville—a shanty town of mud huts covered with a layer of sand and dust inches deep. Tied down on a makeshift landing strip was a red and white Piper cub said to belong to some tourists who had made an emergency landing. They had not had proper papers for Algeria, and the aircraft had been impounded. It blew up and down, straining at its moorings in the wind. This was the first really heavy wind we had had, and it seemed as if it were blowing for the sole purpose of giving In Guezzim a hard time.

It was suddenly a busy afternoon for the immigration officer. No sooner had Rex and I shouted him awake from his cot in the rear of the customs hut than two Combis bearing eight Swiss arrived from the south. The Swiss looked beat. One of the vans had been constantly breaking down since Agadez. It had taken them two weeks just to get this far. When we had shaken him awake, the customs officer ordered us in a thick whiskeyed voice back out into the sand-wind to stand at the tiny window from which business was conducted.

As we braced against the wind he staggered about in the hut and in so doing knocked over his work table with all of his official stamps and papers. He came to the window and shouted for the Swiss to collect their passports: he would attend to all of us at once. I smiled at Phil, who shrugged his shoulders, and we walked over to the Land Rover and stood with Pete, Camille and Rex, who had gathered there talking to one of the Swiss girls. The leader of the other group collected their passports and passed them through the window.

It was then that we noticed the van, about 100 feet away—a Volkswagen with French tags, its hood hard up against the wall of the first mud dwelling to protect the engine from the sand. There were yellow curtains tightly drawn over the windows. The Swiss were talking about their troubles and the condition of the road to the south when the door of the van opened and a skimpily bearded, pale-skinned youth in a white T-shirt descended rather hesitantly and walked toward the hut. The Swiss leader stepped away from the window and the officer called me over to verify our nationalities. While I was there, the T-shirted young man entered from the rear door. I could see them talking but it was impossible in the wind to tell what was being said. The young man was obviously subservient to the official, who was most abrupt. The official paused and leaned into the window, "Do you have medicine? Medicine? Give it to the boy." I replied that we had some medicine; though I did not really know what kind of medicine he needed, certainly we had between us about anything he might require.

As I relayed the request to Phil and Rex, the boy came around the corner of the hut. He had a high squeaky voice and a slight stutter. I asked in French exactly what medication he needed.

"Stomach. For pain for the stomach," he replied in English.

I asked how long he had been sick, whereupon he stated that the medicine was not for him but for his friend.

"How long has he been sick?" I asked.

"Oh, it's a girl," he said. "She has been sick, uh . . . since last night."

"How long have you been here?" Rex asked.

"Now for . . . five days," he hesitated.

"Five days? What's wrong, engine trouble?" Rex asked.

"No, no . . . visas. We are French and were turned back at Assamaka by the Nigerians. They said the new rules require visas for all Europeans, even French."

"But why are you here?"

"We're waiting—Michel—that's Renée's husband, she's the girl who is sick—has gone back to Algiers to get them. He took all of our papers. He left yesterday on a tanker truck north. It should take about ten days."

"At least," Phil said.

"How many of you are there?" I asked.

"Just the two of us now," he said. "We were three but the New Zealand girl left this morning on a water truck to Agadez."

"New Zealand girl?" I gave a description and asked him if it were she.

"Yes," he said.

So she had finally gotten a ride. I had met this girl in Tamanrasset about ten days before. She was trying then to hitchhike to Agadez. In the Sahara I did not take hitchhikers. I felt I was already overloaded and did not wish to risk breaking a spring. She hadn't had too much gear, although she was a large girl. She was hearty, self-reliant. She carried a light pack and slept under the stars. She didn't say much but wrote a great deal in her diary.

Rex came up with a handful of stomach pills.

"Thank you. *Merci*," he said, and he glanced over at the hut. I followed his gaze and saw that the officer was watching us. Nobody else said anything, and the boy thanked us again and walked back to the van.

I asked the Australians if they felt like something funny was going on. No one did, except that Rex thought the boy was not very healthy.

"Why didn't he just come right over here and ask us for the medicine?" I asked.

"Yeah," Phil said. "He didn't even say 'hello' when he walked over to the hut the first time."

"I think I'll go have a look," I said, and walked over to the van and knocked on the passenger door. The Frenchman opened the curtain a bit, recognized me, and opened the door. In the back of the van was a very lovely but disheveled girl with long black hair, which she was combing.

"Hi," she said. She looked hollow-eyed, pale.

"Hi, I hear you've been sick. I hope you are feeling better."

"Are you going to stay here tonight?" she asked. Before I could answer, she continued, "If you do, could you please pull up over here close to us?"

"Why?" I asked.

She told me that, having been refused entry to Niger, they had returned here and tried to send a message to the French consul in Algiers. But the immigration officer refused to send it, so her husband decided to hitch to Algiers on a truck which passed the third day. Just after dark, two soldiers came to fetch the women to the hut, saying they had to fill out some forms. The soldiers had been drinking. Denis, the boy, went with them. When they got to the customs house, the official was there with some other soldiers. They made the New Zealand girl stay in the front and took her into the back room, where she was ordered to undress. She refused, and for a long time they sat there looking at her and talking in Arabic between themselves. When Denis suspected what was going on and walked into the room, the soldiers grabbed him and pistol-whipped him. (He parted his hair and showed me a considerable gash just behind his left ear.) The officer then pulled out his revolver and, without pointing it directly at her, told her she must obey. She did as she was told, and each of them raped her. Afterward, they returned her to the front room and brought back the New Zealand girl. The New Zealand girl was there for only a short time before she became very sick; whereupon, the soldiers shoved her back into the outside room and took the French girl back and attacked her again. The boy was ordered back to the van and told that if he returned to the hut he would be shot.

I returned to my partners, who by that time had our passports and had pulled up alongside the "empty" gas station. We discussed what we should do. At first someone said that if they were in all that danger it seemed strange that they had not gone back to Tamanrasset. We had seen at least three vehicles going north the past three days, not counting the trucks. They could easily have gotten a ride with one of them if they wanted to. Then someone else pointed out that they did not have passports and that leaving would entail abandoning their van, in which they probably had a lot invested. The best thing to do would be to take them both with us to Assamaka, from where they could radio the French consul in Niamey. Surely, when the authorities in Niger were told what had happened they would let them proceed to Agadez.

I walked back to the van and told them what we had decided. They looked at each other, and the girl said, no, thanks a lot, but they would stay. Remembering the Swiss, I said that they could go back to Tamanrasset with them if they did not want to go to Assamaka with us.

"No, we'll just stay. Oh, there's one thing . . ."

"What's that?" I asked.

"Could you spare a pack of cigarettes?"

I didn't smoke, but Camille donated a pack of her Galouises.

We tried to purchase our fuel from the soldier in charge of the gas station. There were tanks with both diesel and super gasoline. "Finish. Complete," he said. However, as Pete fixed his fuel line we saw a government Land Rover and an army truck fill up. In Guezzim was not a friendly place.

The *piste* from In Guezzim to Assamaka was marked at irregular intervals with kilometer posts of 50-gallon drums. The drums, set at varying depths into the sand, were like buoys on great ocean swells, shouldering us gently between two atolls. The calm at midpoint was striking: the sky was a soft azure, and the sand-wind that had vexed In Guezzim had abated.

Assamaka is a dilapidated, mud-walled garrison whose existence is due solely to the presence of an ancient Tuareg wellspring. Water from the well drips constantly into a long wooden trough where the Tuareg water their camels and slake their own thirst, in that order. A note in an old guidebook said that the water was sulfurous and not potable, but we found it sweet and drank our fill. Just northeast of the trough is a solitary stand of bent tamarisk trees, sand-caked from the wind.

Assamaka was our first encounter with "Black Africa." The soldiers, customs officers—everyone was black. The inspection given to the vehicles here was the most thorough so far. Every box, trunk, hubcap was searched. I thought that they might be looking for dope, but they were searching for weapons. The government in Niger was more gun-shy at that time than most. Happily, there was no visa problem. The immigration officer returned with all our passports in about half an hour. We were told we were free to go on or to camp there for the night. Several Land Rovers and a Combi van of Swiss and French people had just received the word that they too were free to continue. Some of them had waited there for a week. According to the Swiss, the problem had resulted from a misreading of the regulations by a new bureaucrat in Niamey.

The calm into which we had come had been illusory, a momentary lull in a violent sandstorm, the mere fringes of which we had seen at In Guezzim. Just at dusk, when the haze had begun to thicken, three separate groups of Tuaregs with six camels each went into the desert several hundred yards. They left at about five-minute intervals, after watering their camels at the trough. The first group halted and waited for the others. For half an hour I observed them through the field glasses. They seemed to be haggling over a camel, for occasionally two of the men would walk over to one of the animals held by another and examine it, lifting its hooves as one might those of a horse. The business evidently concluded, they returned to the oasis single file, leading their camels back to the trough.

We had an early dinner and went to bed. The haze had become so thick that visibility was barely ten feet. Within an hour, the first unmistakable patter of sand began on the tent. I hurried out to the jeep, raised the hood and tucked a blanket securely around the block. The others did the same.

The wind increased until, at about 6:00 a.m., it suddenly subsided. The sun peeked through, and visibility returned to about a half-mile. We discussed whether it would be wise to head south so soon but decided finally to risk it. Pete and Camille took their customary lead, followed by the Aussies. As we rode out of camp, a small waist-high, hand-lettered sign read:

DON BE A FULE. FOLLOW THE STEAKS.

Only a fool would have disobeyed. The sand was the softest and most treacherous since Aïn-Salah. The truck had been overheating quite a bit, and

Pete slowed frequently, as if to stop. We feared a continuation of the chronic fuel-line problem, but somehow he kept rolling, and we made eight, ten, fifteen miles. The ever-present curtain of dust receded further, and at one point, it seemed as if it had stopped altogether. We could not have been more deceived. As we crested a small rise, the storm was upon us.

The gentle sand-spray which had been pelting us now became a broadside. Twisting corkscrewlike rivulets, about knee-high, were blown with a velocity that far exceeded the earlier wind and it became almost impossible for us to keep one another in sight, although we each turned on our lights. To make matters worse, many of the kilometer barrel-markers had been blown down, and some had completely disappeared.

Strangely enough, the sun occasionally found a funnel through which to peek, and through it we could glimpse patches of clear blue sky. At such times it was possible to follow the *piste* since not all of the tracks had yet been obliterated. However, they were going quickly, and it became obvious that unless we could find some markers soon to guide us on, we would have to stop. And it would have been foolhardy to continue to drive our engines into the oncoming sand.

Suddenly, the sun-hole closed and there was nothing but sand— everywhere now. It came in two channels, twisting spirals at about knee- to waist-high and a solid sheet above that level. Even with the windows rolled up tight, the granules cut through the glass, and within half an hour I must have wiped half an inch of it from the dashboard. With the windows up, the heat became intense and the air suffocating.

It was apparent that we had to stop and follow the correct sandstorm procedure of facing downwind and covering the engines. Rex and Phil, who were just in front of me, stopped when I flashed my lights. We agreed immediately and the two of us overtook Pete about a quarter-mile ahead. With the Land Rover on one side of Pete's ambulance and me on the other, the three of us faced downwind and stopped. It was 8:45 a.m., January 26. I wrote in my notebook:

> Storm now become vicious. We pulled off, finally, stopping with backs to wind. One rig on either side of truck . . . Sun, though clouded, is very bright. Then hidden. Sea of sand rushing past . . . All is swirling, twisting, snaking rivulets, torrents, all headed southwest. Can still see (faintly) blue sky in occasional holes. We were not wise to have left Assamaka . . . We are now twenty-one miles southeast of oasis . . . Fortunately we have plenty of water. Food no problem. Storm could last several days but can't tell just now.

We each kept a close eye on our oil pressure and temperature gauges. It would be necessary to clean air filters as soon as the storm had subsided. Although some travelers insist that the oil filter is better, I found my felt filter caught as much as the oil filter in the Aussies' Land Rover and was much easier to clean. Although a good cooling system needs no additional water, not many radiators are subjected to desert conditions like these. I was not surprised, therefore, to find that I had burned off a gallon of water since Tamanrasset. The temperature gauge was consistently registering more than halfway above normal.

As soon as we had covered the engines, Camille had hot spiced tea on the kitchen table. We were fortunate to have that big Austin. It made the long hours of waiting out the storm quite enjoyable—although Olga let us know in no uncertain growls from her perch in the cab that she did not enjoy it at all.

After tea, someone suggested a game of hearts. Perhaps inevitably, hearts soon became poker, using as chips the pegs of assorted colors from Camille's Mastermind game. The Aussies had not spent years in the Outback for nothing: Rex and Phil picked us all clean. I lost $40.

Occasionally the wind would seem to die. One of us would go out and walk around, only to find it blowing just as hard but from a slightly different direction. In the strange light our eyes had been fooled. Once I was certain that it really had stopped. I walked out several hundred feet and felt nothing. Far to the south I could even see the next marker. Then, on glancing skyward, I realized what was happening: the storm had risen perhaps 100 feet into the air. Its velocity was ferocious. Just as I returned to the truck, the storm fell to earth again, and my face and arms were riddled by the sand. After another couple of hours, the storm let up significantly, so we removed the blankets from our engines (dusting over a quarter-inch of sand from the blocks) and drove on some twenty miles. We had not followed the correct procedure of moving the vehicles every 25 or 30 minutes to prevent them from becoming covered with sand. Fortunately, due to the pitched angle of the incline where we stopped, there was only a modest buildup behind each vehicle and not the inundation frequently experienced in such storms.

It was during this last twenty miles that we finally realized that the incessant haze in the distance was the harmattan, the seasonal wind of the Sahel. While the sandstorm may have had an independent origin, it was certainly exacerbated by the harmattan so that the two appeared indistinguishable. Even when there is no wind, the haze of dust remains in the air, keeping visibility down to several hundred feet for four to six months of the year.

It was almost dark when I spotted through my field glasses a thin line of scrubby trees, the first we had seen except at the oasis. They were about three miles away and seemed at first to be a mirage. When we finally arrived, they were hardly larger than tall weeds and afforded no protection at all. But they were tamarisk trees, and it was good to camp near them.

We had no sooner set up camp than Olga crouched and began snarling. Seeing nothing, we were nonplussed. Then from a hidden depression came an old Tuareg on his camel. He seemed to think that we were lost and repeatedly pointed in the direction of the *piste*. When he finally realized that we were camping, he dismounted and sat on the back of Pete's truck and began a long monologue in Tomachek. He pointed to himself and rocked his arms (babies) and held up six fingers. He made stairstep-height signs (the oldest was as tall as he). He then pointed to the northeast, evidently the direction of his camp.

He had chocolate-leather skin and the weathered face of an American Indian. His eyes were coal-black. His hair was fine and dark with some trace of grey. Concluding his monologue, he was silent for a time, smiling and staring into the distance. Then he walked over to the nearest tree and pulled off one of its yellow fruit which was studded with needlelike thorns. While he was talking I noticed that the camel had been browsing among them, thorns and all. Our visitor pulled off the flowers, squeezed the fruit from the thorns and ate it. Olga was by then safely shut up in the front seat of the jeep from which her occasional growls and whining could be heard through a crack in the window.

The old man smiled approvingly at Pete, who followed his example with a grimace. I gave the fruit a try but found it terribly bitter and spat it out. The Tuareg just smiled and made a short inspection tour around the vehicles, mounted his camel and began riding away. When Camille came back with some hot tea for him, he was gone—high on his camel, disappearing into the haze.

We had discovered for comfort the seche, a strip of white or black cotton cloth some six feet long and two feet wide which is wrapped around the head, leaving a loose strip of maybe eighteen inches which is brought back, veil-like, across the nose and lower face. At first the garment feels constrictive, but breathing is much easier with it than without it. The cotton cools the hot air while filtering out sand and dust.

The next morning we were again enveloped by the haze—this time in a long desolate flat or plain that continued with no distinguishable relief for hours. The markers along this stretch were so few and far between that it was impossible to depend upon them. It finally became necessary for us to leap-frog, one vehicle ahead of the next, which in turn went ahead of the third, which remained stationary at the last marker. When the first driver had found a marker (frequently four or five miles away) he would have to back-track until his headlights became visible to the second, who in turn signaled the third, until all three vehicles had rendezvoused. Frequently the wind would pick up and obliterate our tracks completely. These were precarious moments. Fortunately, we maintained our compass readings so that we were reasonably certain of our direction and position.

The stakes had been placed long ago (in the early 1950s) by the French. They had not been regularly maintained. At the sometimes-inhabited village of In-Abangarit these markers continued out into the desert at 90 degrees from the present road. They marked an old *piste* that once lead to Tahoua, a village in southcentral Niger, across 300 miles of nothing. Evidently, the survey crew ran out of markers halfway out and never came back with more.

The first regularly inhabited village we reached in Niger was Tegguidda In Tessoum. It exists because of rich fields of salt found nearby. The southern ridge of town is the pit or mine where the salt is processed.

The pit is a ten-acre cloverleaf-shaped gravel pit marked with tiny craters a foot deep and three across. Next to each of these is a smaller hole about six inches deep and eighteen inches across.

Through the pit runs a muddy spring from which the women draw water to pour onto heaps of the red, salt-rich earth which is brought there by the men in the morning. They bring it from nearby flats in gourdlike pots and baskets which they carry, one on each end of a shoulder pole. Some carry only one potful without a pole. Their work is finished by 8:00 a.m. The midday stirring and mixing and churning is then performed by the women. The women mix the water into the earth until it becomes a thick brine. For several days the brine is stirred until the dirt settles. After evaporation, the resultant brine is poured into the smaller adjacent hole where the process is repeated. The water finally evaporates, leaving the salt, which is then traded for millet and sundries with the Tuareg and with the inhabitants of In Gall some 30 miles to the south.

Tegguida In Tessoum was the first village I entered in which the population was African.* They were the Hadad. There were no Tuaregs, no Arabs, no Europeans. There were two stores in Tegguida In Tessoum. They sold dates and matches and little else; there were no cigarettes, no flour, no green vegetables. There were a few tins of mackerel and sardines, but these were priced out of the reach of the people who lived there (500 CFA—two dollars—for a tin of mackerel). There was a half-full sack of millet, the top rolled down.

The village was plagued with flies. Even in Morocco, the children's eyes were not as weighted with the sucking insects as they were here.

One lad attempted to persuade me to carry his brother to In Gall. When I explained that I was already overloaded, he argued, persuasively, that his brother was light. When that didn't work, he argued that his brother was ill and must see a doctor and was, in any event, an excellent guide. I soon learned that this insistence on a favor was not unique to this village. An African will ask for a ride simply because he sees someone going in that direction. Perhaps it is just to be asking for something, or perhaps it is simply relief from boredom.

Before leaving Tegguida In Tessoum I went down into the pits and walked among the craters. At one an old woman plunged her hands into the brine, stirring it patiently as the idle young men who had followed me bantered playfully among themselves.

Altogether, Tegguida In Tessoum was bleak and depressing, and for a long time, I gave it no further thought. But five months later in Bed IV of Olduvai Gorge, I saw the hardened remains of an almost identical salt works dated at 400,000 years. Perhaps Tegguida In Tessoum had been in operation for a very long time.

And so, from the Sahara I slowly descended into the Sahel. In the past

---

*It should be noted here that the word "African" is used to refer only to persons of Negro descent. The words "Negro" and "Black" are seldom used in Africa. "Afrikaner" refers to those persons from southern Africa of Dutch descent. "European" is the word most used to describe whites who live in Africa, whether they be colonials or recent arrivals. My own personal preference is "Westerner"— although that too is confusing, since there are now a good many Eastern European and Cuban Communists on the continent.

This piste in the deep Sahara between Arlit and Tegguidda In Tessoum, Niger brings to mind a verse by Shelley: "The lone and level sands stretch far away. . . ." Photograph by John Burns.

seven years this band of semi-desert had become infamous for its dying and dispossessed people. Hundreds of thousands of square miles of its grazing land and water holes had dried away to join the Sahara itself.

Some have talked of the theft by the Sahara of the Sahel, but the country was not stolen; it was given outright. The present inhabitants are but the rear guard of those who have chosen over the centuries to sacrifice their green fields and bustling woodlands to the sand. The manner in which this has occurred is uncannily identical from Niger to Kenya coast.

Whole great forests have been burned to clear land which sometimes, but not always, grows forests again. When there is a drought it will grow only grass and shrubs. Here an African's wealth is measured not in terms of money or any other thing except his cattle and goats. The more of these animals he possesses, the greater is his wealth.

Custom forbids the routine killing of animals for food. Rather, a staple diet of milk and blood drawn from live animals is eaten instead of meat. Meat is a delicacy and is eaten only on special occasions—for one diminishes his status with the killing of an animal. Cattle can and do overgraze and destroy land but the goat is the plague of the Sahel. After the forest has been burned, and the drought has parched the land so that it is infertile to all but the most hearty grass and scrub brush, the goat will then eat these—down to and including the roots. With this, the land is finished. The sand will come and settle into silence, where a stream only decades before ran through green fields. What drought and goat don't destroy, man himself does with indiscriminate cutting for firewood of anything that grows.

This incessant southern march of the Sahara as the result of such gross negligence appeared to me as a sinister ballet in which man and his goats danced obliviously before the advancing sand. Nor is the tragedy played out only in the Sahel: four-fifths of Kenya, it is now estimated, is desert. One need only drive between Nairobi and the port of Mombasa to see how quickly the desert is claiming that country. (The technical name for the East African desert is "Ougaden," but it is really a southeastern extension of the Sahara.)

The road to In Gall was better than expected, and we arrived by 4:00 in the afternoon. We went immediately to the market to replenish our supply of vegetables and meat. The market was deluged by a heavy harmattan and everything was dusted with sand. While to us this was but another inconvenience, to the market people it was a plague.

Our leaving In Gall was delayed for over an hour when I just happened to stop at the local police station to ask directions to Agadez. One learns quickly in Africa never to ask a policeman or official for anything since he will immediately demand that you present your papers for inspection. Even in those instances—such as at the frontier—where such inspections are inevitable, one's passport, for example, should never be presented until it is specifically asked for, and then it should be handed to the officer opened to the visa of his country. These officers are usually barely literate and can only recognize their own visa and that of the country next door. Some, of course, have been trained to recognize those of South Africa and Israel.

We drove about ten miles southeast of In Gall where we camped a half-hour before sundown. By chance, we set up in a petrified forest. All about us were strewn fragments of fossilized limbs—some of them over three feet long.

We broke camp early the next morning and hoped to make Agadez by noon. That was not to be. Pete, while driving on an apparently safe stretch of lightly corrugated road, hit a dip and broke both his rear springs clean through. It was a miracle that his chassis did not slip forward off of the axle. Several efforts to shore up the springs came to naught, but it was decided that we would attempt to proceed as slowly as possible. I scouted the way, flashing my caution lights upon encountering rough terrain.

CHAPTER IV

It was almost 9:30 p.m. when we crawled into Agadez. The camping was five miles to the north, so we had to enter the town, find the road out again and slowly make our way over a very rough and deep sand *piste*. The camping was run by a German-speaking Frenchman named Joyce, from Strasbourg, who had settled in Agadez following World War II. He was particularly fond of German guests, who gather here in large overland groups with their giant machines and superbly equipped Land Rovers. There are several clubs who make the pilgrimage every year. The camp is quiet when they are away, but when they return the peace is broken with the cracks and snaps of Prussian voices.

Agadez is the southern hub of the Sahara. For centuries it was the destination of caravans from Tamanrasset, Timbuktu, and beyond. It is the northernmost outpost of the ancient Sultan of Zinder, who reigned over the central Sahara during the eighteenth and nineteenth centuries before—and for a good time after—the coming of the French. I was told, in fact, that he still lives there, holding court from time to time—although his power now is only ceremonial. At one time, his ancestors ruled from Bilma to Kano to Lake Chad.

The town has an impressive conical mosque that rises from the bidonville beyond the market and which is the destination of pilgrims from the surrounding area. The market is the largest between Algiers and Kano. Animals are butchered in the same stalls from which meat is sold. Young blacks and Tuaregs lounge about in their own groups, staring at each other and at the occasional European who drives through.

Near the clothing market a dozen young blacks sat eating ravenously from a small mountain of locusts—giant grasshoppers of the Sahel which had been dried to a crusty brown and which they ate as Westerners would potato chips or peanuts. These insects are a primary source of protein for Africans of the Sahel.

Joyce's camping consists of an area of about an acre surrounded with baobab and tamarisk trees. To one end of the compound is a large metal tank and well. The water is fresh and clean, and guests are invited to take all they need. The lodge has a small restaurant where Tuareg cooks prepare tasty European and African food. A half-dozen Tuareg guards and helpers assist guests in procuring vegetables from farmers who manage small truck gardens along the *draa* which runs behind the camping.

We parked our vehicles and hurried to the restaurant. Although he had just closed, Joyce reopened the galley and served up superb T-bone steaks, fries and a fine salad of local greens.

Joyce, while hospitable, was wary and collected the rent (two dollars) from each guest the first thing each morning. He made the rounds in the company of his largest Tuareg guard, a tall dark-skinned warrior who stared at us coldly from behind his blue veil.

The next morning we set about cleaning our engines. The sand had worked itself into the most remote crevices, and it was impossible to remove it completely.

Since it was required that we check in with the police station in Agadez, we proceeded, in spite of a heavy harmattan wind, to do so. The station was just across the street from the large single-story mud-walled houses of Peace Corps volunteers Lee and Barbara Morgan and the World Church Service agents, Ralph and Flossie Royer, who invited us in for tea.

The Royers had come to Agadez from Nigeria, where they had been in missionary work for 25 years. Ralph's territory was the entire Agadez area plus the Aïr and Bagzine Mountains. His efforts had been directed toward improving crop yields through irrigation and improved planting techniques. For example, he had taught the natives to construct wells so that they could hoist water using a bucket and rope pulled by an ox or camel. The bucket rises to a turning bar which tilts it into a trough that runs out into the patch. The simplicity of this system enables the farmer himself to maintain it. Hardy varieties of potatoes, cabbages and other vegetables have been introduced.

One of their worst enemies, according to Ralph, is the theory of foreign aid officials that anything can be solved, provided that the right technology is "thrown at it." The problem is that, in order to use technical equipment effectively, one must maintain it once it has been installed. These people have no way of repairing, for example, a diesel pump. Even if they had the spare parts—which are frequently unavailable—they do not have the training necessary to install them. The result is that the equipment is used until it breaks; then it sits idle, rusting. The well, on the other hand, not only serves the same purpose as the pump but can easily be repaired.

Ralph also bemoaned the overgrazing of goats and indiscriminate cutting of firewood: "The overall problem, of course, is that of cultural inertia—the people are simply part of a culture that has never heard of conservation. They live from day to day, taking from the land what they need to survive today, with no thought given to preservation for tomorrow."

Ralph took us outside and showed us some of their Irish potato seedlings and the frames used for making concrete walls for the wells. The concrete is usually mixed on the site itself, using frames supplied by the mission. The mission has a jeep, a truck or two, and a few laborers, including one qualified driver.

"The idea," Ralph said, "is to select projects which are simple and which the people can maintain themselves, using traditional tools and methods. If a project is helpful but not really necessary, the farmers will abandon it right away; and even if it *is* necessary—such as a water pump—they will abandon it if it is beyond their means to maintain. With the loss of one spare part, in other words, an entire crop will dry up while a new pump sits there idle."

Noting his success with small patches of truck, I asked him why he had not attempted to expand farmland into the desert. The answer was that the subsurface support level is so low that the water would run off. In addition, it was all he could do to keep the farmers busy on their own small plots. They would never be able to care for such a large project. In spite of all their drought problems, local farmers now supply 80 percent of the Agadez vegetable market. They ship potatoes, tomatoes, onions, and even wheat regularly to Arlit and Niamey.

Next door to the Royers, Lee and Barbara Morgan had been teaching English to local grade-school and high-school children for two years. They had become something of experts on the Tuareg, whose culture and migrations they had studied and from whose silver and leather handiwork they had compiled an impressive collection. They had decided to return to the States in the fall.

Barbara was an excellent cook and invited me over for lunch the afternoon I left. We shared many stories—they had traveled extensively in Niger and western Africa—and I invited them to visit me the next time they came to Arkansas.

Delivering the message to the proprietor of the Hotel Sahara for my friend Jo Jo in Tamanrasset, I told him that Jo Jo had assured me that I would receive a beer as my courier's fee. Whereupon, I was presented with my first Flag, the famous local brew which is the favorite of Peace Corps volunteers.

Back inside the market, I stopped at an egg and cheese merchant's. The camel cheese came in heavy thick dry bricks, yellowish-brown in color with a pleasant goat-cheese flavor. An attempt to haggle down with a child the price (250 CFA) of a dozen eggs was successful until the agreement was annulled by the child's father, who suddenly appeared in the doorway of the stall next door, wagging his finger and reasserting the higher price.

Young Tuaregs approached me to peddle their swords and silver bracelets. A bracelet could be had for 500 CFA; a sword cost 5,000.

We pooled our food budgets at the camping, and though we continued to take turns in the kitchen, I must admit that I was not called upon to do much other than wash up and set the table. It was the bearded, garrulous Rex who finally emerged as our master chef: his list of recipes was as inexhaustible as his good humor in preparing them under such adverse conditions and for such unappreciative diners as we.

It was at the Joyce camping that I met one of the most unforgettable characters of the Sahara. Mike Foster had been a scout, game hunter and tourist agent in Nairobi for years before finally coming here to work with a firm of adverturesome tour operators known as "Quest Four." A small operation out of London, their business is carrying tourists and scientists to remote sites in the desert. They are equipped for almost any expeditionary requirement, from mountain climbing and surveying to fossil hunting.

Mike was their chief scout and mechanic, keeping the fleet of three Land Rovers in top condition. When I met him, he had just returned from Adrar Bous, a seventh-century lakeshore living site in the northern sand sea of Bilma. He had become an expert on the Tuareg—the hard way. Having observed their caravans for many months in the winter of '74, he had finally met and won the confidence of their leader, who had soon invited Mike to join them.

He had had to purchase four camels—one to ride, and three to serve as spares and to carry provisions of firewood, millet and water. The millet was mixed with water or camel's milk to make gruel, the caravan's staple diet. But it was also used for trading with the Africans of the oasis for salt and dates. The camels might serve as a source of meat in an emergency, but it was hoped that they would survive to carry back the precious cargo.

Bilma is roughly 400 miles from Agadez, in about the center of the Grand Erg of Bilma, a sand sea the northeastern dunes of which rise to heights of 1,000 feet against the Aïr Mountains. Bilma would be a contender for the dubious distinction of being the most desolate place on earth. It is inhabited by the Hadad, Africans descended from slaves brought there long ago by the Tuareg to work the mines. They are now perhaps 500 in number. Other than the Hadad, there is only a military outpost with a small garrison of fifteen to twenty soldiers. Nearby are the remains of a French Foreign Legion fort. In the late '60s and early '70s, there was a Peace Corps volunteer stationed here but the post was abandoned in 1974. Bilma's only regular contact with the outside world is the fortnightly army mail flight from Niamey.

The Tuareg caravans are the only economical means of transporting Bilma salt and dates to the villages in the Sahel, where, although no longer necessities, they are in great demand—the dates as the choicest delicacies and the salt as feed for the cattle. An occasional truck does make the journey, but only in transit to or from Libya, carrying freight and workers for the Libyan oil fields.

A Bilma caravan today will be comprised of from 150 to 500 camels. People to whom I've told this say, "My, what a caravan—500 camels." I always pause for a few moments before telling them that as late as the 1890s, it would not have been uncommon for such a caravan to contain 20,000 camels!*

During Foster's journey, several of the wealthier drovers also carried a goat kid or lamb. And Foster, in addition to his measure of millet, packed along a few tins of corned beef and sardines—"Just to be on the safe side." After almost a week's monotonous waiting in the marketplace, the signal to depart was given (a series of slow, steady drumbeats), and the caravan headed out into the desert.

Not all of the drovers owned their animals. Some had only the animals of relatives and friends who had entrusted them to their care. Many of these

---

*See Thurston Clarke, The Last Caravan (New York: G.P. Putnam's Sons, 1978) for a colorful account. For the most exquisite commentary as well as photographs of this region of the Sahara the author has seen, see Renee Gardi, SAHARA (London: George Harrap, 1972).

drovers were younger men making the voyage for the first time.

At Telouess, the last oasis before the desolate Tenere Desert in the west of the Grand Erg, the Agadez group was joined by another caravan coming down from the Aïr Mountains. Together numbering some 300 camels, they set out into the Tenere, a vast sand and gravel wasteland in which the wind quickly destroys all tracks. Yet the Tuareg could navigate using the sun and even the wind itself—and, at night, the stars. Uncannily, they also followed the "lie of the dunes," which to the European means nothing, but which to the Tuareg is a sure clue to wind direction and, hence, direction itself, since he knows the point of the compass from which the gusts will come, depending upon the season and the time of day. A certain rock, a small craggy peak, a nameless *draa*—all meaningless to the intruder—are, to the Tuareg, signs, verily, of life itself.

The progress of the march (for the camels are not mounted until the very height of the afternoon) is slow and tedious. Each driver walks in front of his lead camel, the others following, tethered, behind. Mounting, usually at 2:00 in the afternoon, the men ride on until dark, sometimes even far beyond, into the night. Camp is made as simply as possible, the voyagers huddling around several small fires of a pooled supply of scarce wood. The signal to mount is given at first light, and woe be unto him who is not ready at the drum: the caravan will not wait. He must fend for himself; there will be no tarrying. If his animals have strayed or gone lame, or whatever the reason, he must catch a ride with another drover or remain by himself and make do as best he can.

Thus plodding its way, Foster's caravan reached Fachi, a small oasis of dateless palms and saline water, on the tenth day. Fachi is roughly two-thirds of the way to Bilma. There they rested for a day and replenished their water supply. The following morning they continued into the desert and, in the afternoon of the sixteenth day from Agadez, arrived at Bilma.

Although he had considered himself in top physical condition and well acclimated to the desert, Foster was quite fatigued. He was able to wash up and rest for several days while the Tuareg proceeded with their trading. Every camel had to be fully loaded with salt and dates, each quantity of which was received in trade for a traditional measure of millet. Although an elaborate bargaining ritual precedes the trading, the measure is almost always two cups of millet for one tablet or block of salt and one cup of millet for one cup of dates. The salt blocks are distinctively cut and can be seen in village markets throughout the Sahel. The design has held for hundreds of years.

After several days of trading and resting, the caravan set out on its return voyage. The second day out, disaster struck: Foster came down with hepatitis—although at the time he did not know the nature of his illness. His body ached and it was all he could do to stay astride his camel, which he rode even in the morning. The Tuaregs were understanding and tried to comfort him, but they had no medicine and there was not much they could do. In the heat of the midafternoon of the third day his headache reached the limits of endurance. He felt sure he would die.

By coincidence a German anthropologist and his wife had arrived at

Fachi. When the caravan reached the oasis on the sixth day, someone fetched the Germans and they nursed Foster at their hut for several days. By a second coincidence a party of British overlanders, whom he had known from a previous expedition, came through and they carried him back to Bilma, hoping he could catch the mail plane. By a third incredible coincidence, the plane came on its biweekly run the following morning and that night he was back in Agadez, Chez Joyce! It took him two months to recover. Still it was an experience for which he would take nothing.

The sun shone only one full day while I was in Agadez. I was told by Ralph Royer that that was something of an occasion. Normally the harmattan would hang in the distance until about 10:30 or 11:00 in the morning, when it would advance in full force. The air would remain smothered in sand, dust, and heat until an hour or so before dark, when the haze would retreat to the same monotonous middle-distance on the horizon. Sometimes at night there would be a clear sky so that from the stars one would receive the false promise of a clear dawn. But next morning the haze would still linger. The one good thing about the harmattan was that it blew flies before it. Indeed, I had the choice between the wind and the flies—at least for a time, since my eyes and skin could take only so much sand before I was forced to return to the flies.

The morning of our fifth day we decided to head our separate ways. Rex and Phil drove north into the Aïr Mountains. It was difficult not to go with them, but it was only three weeks until the International Academy of Trial Lawyers meeting in Abidjan where I was to rendezvous with my parents. I might have had time for a short jaunt but not for any side trips or prolonged breakdowns.

Mike Foster warned us strongly against going into the Erg of Bilma without a guide. Rex and Phil thought that they would be able to get one in the Aïr. Later I heard that they made Adrar Bous without a guide, then returned to Agadez and followed my trace to Zinder. By that time I was in Abidjan.

Peter and Camille wanted to repair the ambulance before heading south to Kano. We said goodbye, and I was later to hear from them that they had made it safely, Peter getting a job there with an Italian construction firm.

The road to Zinder was graded for ten miles, and I momentarily discounted the bad description given of it by the Morgans. After all, it had been three months since they had driven it. However, their report was, if anything, optimistic. The road became a roller coaster of deep corrugations interspersed with wind-blown sand fields. I passed only one vehicle, a slow-moving petrol truck, and as I emerged from its wake of dust, the road suddenly ended in a trench of deep sand. For the first time since In Gall it was necessary to go into four-wheel drive. I plowed along for an hour through what I knew must be the *piste*—yet there was not a single track. It was only by carefully checking in depressions away from the wind that I was able to find the remnants of tracks to verify that I had not strayed from the route. Once I looked for half an hour until I found what appeared to be a vehicle track. Yet my own was so clear beside it that I decided it was old and backtracked to double-check. Halfway up the hill I spied two large truck tracks perpendicular to my own. Following them, I found the road. This afterthought-and-backtrack routine recurred several times. About 10:00 p.m. I came to the village of Aberdissinat. When a crowd gathered around the jeep, I asked an important-looking older man if I could camp near the village. He did not understand and sent for the chief. The chief was much younger than the others and spoke very good French. He said there would be a good place to camp three kilometers further south. I thanked him and drove on through the village. The wind was up and the huts were partially obscured by the haze. A single electric light swung from a cord on the porch of the gendarmerie. From nearby came the putt-putt of a diesel generator.

Leaving Aberdissinat, I returned into the desert and drove until I came to a stand of scrub trees where I stopped and turned off the lights. All I could hear were crickets. Just as I had decided to dismount and set up the tent, I saw a flicker of light approaching through the haze. Whoever it was was taking his time. Presently, a tall man in a white robe walked into the clearing. I turned on the lights. He walked up to the window, smiled and said "Hausa." He was probably only curious, but I did not want to camp near a settlement, so I thanked him and drove on. Twenty minutes later I found another stretch of scrub brush which extended to a *draa* to the left of the road. The place was full of driftwood and small bushes wrapped with debris from a recent flash flood. The wind had died, revealing a full moon with a ring around it. I pitched the tent and ate some corned beef and peas, which I washed down with coffee and powdered milk. There was about me a great silence not broken even by the chirp of crickets, and after exploring the riverbed for a quarter-mile in each direction, I returned and fell asleep.

At first light I made coffee and took another long walk before heading south. Ten miles of sand later I crested a hill to find a semi backed into a corral of longhorn cattle. The Peulh, a tribe of region nomads, were selling some of their stock to a trader from Zinder. Just below the corral was a well, next to which four foot-high limb forks had been planted. In the neck of each fork was a wooden pulley. Each herdsman lowered his pail by hand into the water. When the bucket had reached the water, the herdsman would jostle it so that it filled and sank. He would then attach the free end of the rope to one of his animals—a burro or camel—and drive the animal along the path in front of the fork. One could tell the depth of the well by the length of the path. I walked one in 60 paces.

About 30 children, most of them young girls, gathered around the jeep. Their heads were shaved except for a small half-inch strip of hair in the center—an Islamic custom whereby the child's guardian angel has something to hold onto to jerk it out of harm's way.

Twenty kilometers further on, I came to an improved earth road. The road had not been maintained, and the corrugations were wretched. I managed to lessen their impact by keeping my speed above 40 mph, a difficult task in what became a blinding sandstorm. The heat inside the jeep was insufferable. Stopping at the village of Takoukant, I was given a mat by an old man at a fruit stand. We sat together against the side of his stall and weathered the storm for an hour and a half. His son brought tea while the old man lamented that he had nothing else to offer. Finally, somewhat rested, I thanked him and resumed my way to Tanout.

CHAPTER V

NIGER

Mediterranean Sea

Tegguida In Tessoum

Agadez

Zinder
Matameye

Niamey

Niger River

AFRICA

Atlantic Ocean

Indian Ocean

I decided to wait out the storm in Tanout. According to the Morgans, a friendly fellow from New Jersey named Alan Davis was the Peace Corps volunteer there. At first I was unable to find anyone who had heard of him, but a lame boy from the market showed me to the clinic of Marie Noel, a French Volunteer for Progress who lived near Alan. They were both so glad to have a visitor that that night there was a special fête at Noel's.

Their houses were similar, although Noel's was somewhat larger. Both were equipped with a concrete-floor "bath," a tiny closet to the rear of the house where a suspended shower bucket or bag was at the disposal of the bather. The water ran out a small drainpipe in the floor. There was no toilet—one simply went to a designated area in the back of the yard. The hot, dry climate quickly disposed of all waste.

Alan introduced me to Ibrahim Mainisara Yacouba, the 30-year-old son of the aging *chef de canton* (district chief). It was the burly, good-natured Ibrahim, really, who ran the canton, settling petty disputes and some serious ones, collecting taxes and generally showing the flag.

One of his jobs was an inspection tour on each market day of the surrounding villages. Sometimes he would take Alan on these, especially the more colorful ones of the Peulh at Aberdissinat and Takoukant. Frequently, local peasants would present him with produce or even a goat or two. He would share these gifts with Alan.

From time to time Alan would host Ibrahim in his home. Alan's place was a solid, breezy, high-ceilinged mud and plaster house, built in the 1930s. It had probably served at one time as a colonial officer's or teacher's house. It was surrounded by a large wall, although the gate was usually open to anyone who wanted to come for a visit, and many villagers did. There was a big kitchen with a camping gas stove which Alan used to boil water for his coffee. He boarded, though, Chez Marie Noel.

Alan's house belonged to a village hadji, a title taken by men who have made the pilgrimage to Mecca—although, recently, it has come to mean that a man has enough money to purchase some property and not necessarily that the bearer of the title has made the pilgrimage.

It was here in Tanout that I first woke up in the morning to the sound of women pounding grain into flour. The thud-thud-thud from the scores of huts reverberated through the dawn. I soon found the rhythm of African life to be ordered by pestle upon mortar in the morning and drum at night. There was never a village, no matter how small, that did not at night echo with the beat of drums. I found this to be true no matter where I journeyed. And there was no greater mystery then where these drums were: I would follow their cadence until it seemed certain that they were only just down the next row of huts or over the next wall. But just as I approached, the sound would disappear, only to reappear moments later behind me at twice the distance. I knew there must be many drums, but how they could so evade my finding them always remained a mystery.

On alternate nights, Ibrahim would host Alan. Ibrahim's house, like Alan's, was surrounded by a prestigious wall. Inside, however, the courtyard differed little from those of his less prosperous "subjects." His children ran naked in the dirt, and his wife and her family were immediately shy and withdrawn whenever strangers appeared. But in a house separate from that of the women Ibrahim had constructed a comfortable study which was furnished with a great double-mattress bed and a deep armchair. On the wall was a photograph of John F. Kennedy smoking a cigar.

Alan and Ibrahim could haggle like pawnbrokers. Ibrahim had bought a new radio and wanted to sell his old one to Alan. We took it to the repair shop, a hut behind the house of a nearby villager, for an independent estimate. Scattered among nets of spiders' webs were vintage French receivers, wires and plugs. A sizable crowd had followed us, and everyone began at once to give his opinion at the top of his voice. The price, to begin with, was too high, said Alan. Also, the set was dirty: it would have to be thoroughly cleaned and rewired. These defects were mitigated, however, when the nimble repairman adjusted a disc and the instrument blared forth.

In addition to cooking his meals, Noel gave Alan lessons in French each evening after dinner. Alan reciprocated with lessons in English although with considerably less regularity. Both had had house servants when they first arrived—holdovers from previous volunteers. However, after a few months, Alan let his go because there was "nothing at all for him to do around here." The lad now came every other day to deliver fresh water (25 CFA per bucket) and once a week to do the laundry (usually 150 CFA).

Over the years Alan's predecessors had left at the house over 200 paperback volumes. He had added to them another 100 or so, classics and detective fiction, mailed from friends in the States and swapped with other volunteers during occasional trips to Niamey. Night reading was done by lantern or candlelight.

Alan taught at the CEG ("sara j," as the French pronounced it), the local secondary school, from 8:00 until 11:00 in the morning and from 2:00 to 5:00 in the afternoon. He was enthusiastic but harbored no illusions about his students learning English.

"What's really important," he said, "is that they have some sustained contact with someone from the outside world. It makes little difference whether they are officially being taught English or mathematics." This sentiment, echoed by other Peace Corps volunteers, seems to have replaced the early elusive goal of achieving academic excellence in the bush.

My friend was, for all practical purposes, the deputy mayor of Tanout.

Friday, market day, he took me on a tour through the marketplace, where almost every vendor recognized him and shook his hand. The goodwill he had engendered during his eighteen-month tenure was everywhere evident.

The people of Tanout were mostly Hausa, a sedentary tribe that has lived throughout the Nigerian Sahel for centuries. Tuareg were rarely seen here, but three years earlier, at the height of the drought, thousands of them had straggled into the village looking for water for their dying flocks and for themselves. Some remained, camped in the desert several kilometers from town. Scores were in the market, selling leather, silver and blocks of Bilma salt.

At the north end of the market were some two dozen uncovered wells or shafts of wells, some over 50 feet deep. Children played about them, although some had fallen into the holes and perished.

On Saturday Alan had visitors from Matameye, a town twenty miles north of the Nigerian border. These were Keys and Dorothea Mantiveld. Keys was a Dutch veterinarian and agronomist. They had been in Niger two years. With them were Jackie Tierney, the town Peace Corps volunteer, and a young French agriculturalist named Ivan. Ivan lived at Kanche, thirteen kilometers north of Matameye. The four of them constituted the Western community in the 80 miles of southcentral Niger between Zinder and Kano.

That afternoon we drove out to the orchard of Oumar, a prosperous Arab farmer. The orchard was a green "island" roughly 200 yards square in the desert, about eight kilometers from Tanout. We were met by a Tuareg watchman who lived there. Dozens of orange and mangrove trees were covered with half an inch of dust from the harmattan. The watchman explained that many of the trees had died and the orchard had shrunk to half its original size. He had been watering the trees from a small well. The well was over 150 feet deep, judging from the length of the pull rope. Two years ago the well had gone dry and water had had to be carried from Tanout. Some water had returned, although it was muddy and brackish.

Most resistant to the drought were some tall date palms, about a dozen of them. Three had remained out in the desert about 500 yards away. We could see the still green fruit nestled high up under the leaves.

Next Oumar conducted us three kilometers to another oasis, where we were met by a robust hadji, Midrim, whose tract this was and who had gone on an hour before us to prepare for our visit. He had had his workers pick for us several honeydew melons, which, though pulpy and tasteless, were welcome thirst-quenchers. Midrim's surprise was a watermelon, which we broke open, Arkansas style, on the ground. The big sweet hunks were might tasty. He loaded us up with a second melon, dozens of bright red tomatoes, green peppers, onions and Irish potatoes.

This garden and several others nearby were tended by young Hausa from the village who took for payment enough for their families. Ibrahim said there was no stealing because the men guarded the plot carefully. One of them was at the oasis at all times. Once they had suspected that one of their number was taking more than his share, but the culprit turned out to be a goat that had worked its way through the thornbush fence.

That night Noel treated us to a feast of roast goat. Toward the end of the meal, I went to fetch some coffee at Alan's house. As I returned through the kitchen, a Tuareg was peeping at the guests through the service hole in the wall. He was at least six-foot-four, and his face had a deep bronze color, like an American Plains Indian. When he saw me, he hastened into an adjoining room and closed the door. A devout Moslem, Noel's closet friend had refused even to meet, much less dine with, infidels.

The next afternoon our visitors departed for Matameye, extending as they left a warm invitation for me to visit them on my way into Nigeria.

I stayed on with Alan for several days but knew I must move on if I were to meet my parents in Abidjan. Only two weeks remained. So, on the following Monday I drove south, to Zinder. Zinder has recently been replaced as a commercial center by Maradi, 120 miles to the west. But it is still the largest population center before Agadez to the north and Nguigmi on Lake Chad.

I wired my family from Zinder that I had arrived there safely and asked that they bring an extra air filter to Abidjan. While looking for the post office I ran into Ivan, who directed me to the Restaurant Moderne. There I ate a lumberjack meal for $1.50 (hot steamed beans, *frites* [fries], a huge green salad with tomatoes, and several side dishes of local vegetables). The chef said that according to the radio some English travelers had been lost in the Erg of Bilma for a week. A search party had been sent but hadn't found a trace of them. I hoped that Rex and Phil were safe.

It was well after dark when I turned off at Kanchee at what I thought was Ivan's house. I was immediately surrounded by a crowd of white-robed villagers who had just finished their evening prayers. What did I want? they demanded. I told them, whereupon a very stern elder shouted that Ivan was not there and he didn't know where he was and I had best move on. I tried the gate, but a ferocious dog lunged at it so I got back in and drove to Matameye. At the only electric light in town, a tailor was busily stitching and treadling on one of those prewar Singers found throughout western Africa. He led me to a house deep in the village. It was surrounded by a wall—next to the gate of which three beggars with belled canes stood chanting. The houseboy opened the gate just far enough to reach and hand them each a coin. When they had gone, he admitted me, but not the tailor. Jackie, Ivan and the Mantivelds were having dinner.

The Mantivelds' house was very tidy and European. There was running water from two 50-gallon drums on a ramp outside the kitchen window. The refrigerator was one of the thrifty, camping variety in which the beer is always cold.

After dinner, we adjourned to the garden where Keys made "Tuareg tea," which is heavy with mint and sugar and tastes like the Arab tea of the northern Sahara. Keys's tea-making was also done with great ceremony, beginning with the gathering of wood and the building of the small "teepee" fire.

Jackie invited me to stow all of my gear at her place and even gave me her

Nigerian tends goats in the market. Matameye, Niger.

big brass bed. The village chief had had the brass bed brought over and installed especially for her. She rarely used it, however, because it was "simply too big for me," and preferred the cot in the front room. Her house, too, had a large wall all around and a cozy sideyard. Her houseboy, Hammed, was expert at making peanut butter from ground nuts bought in the local market. After he had washed the dishes and done the laundry, he spent the day making peanut butter.

The agricultural disaster at Kanchee can be traced to the same causes as that in northern Niger: overgrazing by goats and strip-burning for wood.

Ivan had tried to concentrate on introducing sturdy breeds of cattle and other stock (for example, rabbits) to replace goats as a source of meat, while at the same time encouraging feeding from central feed lots with hay or grass gathered for the animals, rather than letting them graze about destroying vegetation and burning up energy. He explained to the farmers that their goats lose as much energy as they get from foraging. He told them that it is much more efficient to pen or tie stock and let them eat from a hayrack or trough, where several animals can feed simultaneously with no difficulty.

Ivan's hutches of experimental rabbits were in two rows of about 25 each. About every third hutch along the bottom row had been forced open by wild dogs and the occupants devoured.

Ivan developed several kinds of chicken feed in experiments with local

*McMath catches a few winks before heading into Nigeria. Taken in the
courtyard belonging to Keys and Dorothea Mantiveld, Matameye, Niger.*

grains. Concurrently, he had been searching for a better chicken. By crossing several well-known European and American breeds (Rhode Island Reds, for example) with the scrawny local variety, he hoped to find a stock which could peck out enough protein from the sparse semi-desert earth to survive. He had isolated one variety, but it was too slow for the dogs. Behind the hutches were two pens of healthy, feisty chickens. Each flock looked hearty enough, but one was freshly arrived breeding stock and the other was a second-generation cross, as yet untried against the dogs.

Ivan was one of the most clever and enthusiastic aid people I ever met. It was a shame that he had to leave without being able to train his replacement. (The replacement, a female Peace Corps volunteer, was being held up by bureaucratic bickering in Niamey.) Ivan soon returned to France to write and do consulting work.

Each of Jackie's male professors, several older students, and a Nigerian border official with other-than-scholarly intentions would come at least once a week to visit her. Ostensibly these visits were official, or at least in a spirit of friendship. In spite of having put in a long day of teaching, she would stop whatever she was doing and graciously receive them. Frequently, they would come by just as she had set dinner on the table. The guest would of course be invited to stay and eat (which he invariably did). One night, the persistent border official sent a messenger to order that she prepare dinner for himself and a colleague. When they arrived they found dinner long finished and an English class in progress. The Nigerian harbored no illusions after that.

The schoolhouse was just off the highway about a quarter of a mile toward Zinder, so early one morning Jackie and I walked together—she to teach and I to hitchhike to Abidjan. All of her pupils were on the road at the same time, giggling and chattering, as well as the merchants of the marketplace and young mothers with babies. I saw a hadji in an orange and purple robe close the rear door of his Peugeot van.

"Takeita?" I asked. That was, indeed, his destination. So I climbed in the back of the van, but not before giving Jackie a very friendly goodbye kiss which made her blush and raised a titter among the pupils.

The hadji mounted with a swirl of robes. As we drove away I waved to her, still smiling, her face blushed to a rosy pink. As the van accelerated, we left her surrounded by her army of pupils marching towards us like the hokey ending of a '40s movie.

I did not want to risk my vehicle in the theft-plagued cities along the coast. It was for the interior. So I accepted the Mantivelds' invitation to leave it in their compound. My clothing and tools I left at Jackie's.

Tuareg half-caste, sword at side, surveys market. Matameye, Niger.

CHAPTER VI

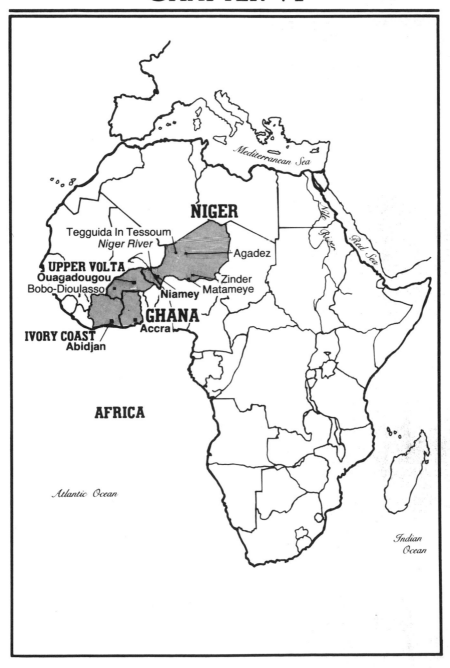

NIGER

Tegguida In Tessoum
Niger River

Agadez

UPPER VOLTA
Ouagadougou
Bobo-Dioulasso

Zinder
Matameye

Niamey

GHANA
Accra

IVORY COAST
Abidjan

AFRICA

Mediterranean Sea

Nile River

Red Sea

Atlantic Ocean

Indian Ocean

I hitched to Niamey in a succession of vans and trucks—some of which stopped for wood along the side of the road. Vendors sell it in packets weighing about 30 pounds each. It is gathered from trees previously burned and stacked.

I talked with the soldiers guarding the intersection at Takeita for almost three hours. But in a single moment my luck changed, when a five-ton fish-meal truck from Nguigmi on Lake Chad pulled in for inspection. The driver motioned me aboard.

Except for about 80 miles of dirt between Takeita and Maradi, the narrow road was blacktopped from Lake Chad to Niamey, a joint Italian-Canadian project finished in 1972, the only paved road in the Sahel. It was 27 hours to Niamey, but it would have been quicker had we not had to stop for scores of police *controles.*

All traffic must stop at these, and drivers dismount to present their papers. The procedure is for verifying vehicle ownership and load-limit compliance. But weapons and contraband are also targets. Firearms are prohibited to private citizens, and possessing one can be a capital offense. Searches are also made for radios and watches smuggled in from Nigeria. Possession of contraband, however, brings another penalty: dash.

Dash is exacted for two favors: allowing an overloaded vehicle to pass and ignoring contraband. How much dash must change hands, and how often, is always a matter of dispute. Pending the negotiations, the passengers sit sometimes for hours in 100-plus-degree heat.

Standard alibis are expensive repairs, a long period of bad business and already having had to dash heavily up the road. The latter excuse rarely works since there's a rigid pecking order among officials which limits the amount dashable by junior officers. The big dash is, of course, reserved for customs officers at the frontier. Niger was really not bad compared to Ghana and Nigeria, where bribery by even petty officials can be expensive.

My driver had little difficulty—perhaps because of his cargo of fish meal, a carefully protected foodstuff. But the passengers did have several cages of chickens, some blankets and straw mats, and an assortment of produce, including honeydew and watermelon, tomatoes, cabbages, several sacks of corn and some peanuts.

Among the passengers was an old Ghanian who had migrated eighteen years before to Senegal. He'd never been back to Ghana, having worked in Dakar and later in Mopti in Mali. He'd tried to go home once but was refused entry because his papers weren't in order. That was right after Nkrumah had died, and the government, fearing a *coup d'état,* refused reentry to expatriates without a special permit. So he had gone back to Mali for a few more years as a laborer with a French construction company, then to Nguigmi where he'd worked with the Canadians on the trans-Niger highway.

The truck did not stop except for police checks until we reached Maradi. There we parked beneath some baobab trees in a plaza near the market. The driver and his assistant went into a small restaurant. I sensed that this was the last chance to grub up, so I went in and ordered some almost-warm macaroni and chunks of cold mystery meat for 60 cents. Some scraggly goats ranged at the kitchen door; their shepherd was also the cook.

Afterward, I walked through the market and picked up some bananas and oranges. I was amazed at the variety of consumer goods, such as radios and cassette players. Maradi is the largest market, except for Kano, in the central Sahel.

When I returned to the truck the Ghanian said, "I like eat, too." I sensed the panhandle—had expected it ever since I had given him half of the dates, cookies, and grease balls (fried dough) I'd bought from a roadside vendor. I gave him 100 CFA. I thought he would go right in and eat—they had lots of plates in there for less than that—but he only pocketed the coin and smiled.

As we sat there we were surrounded by a bevy of Koran boys. Islamic code requires that they beg for their food, and they have better luck with the truck drivers and their passengers than with the market people they see every day. They made that mournful gesture of jabbing at the mouth with three fingers, head cocked submissively. As we drove away, they were chanting prayers under a tree with their marabout.

The streets of Maradi groaned and squeaked with mammy wagons and taxis, most belonging to El Hadji Such-and-Such, whose name (along with his el-hadjiness) was proudly painted on the driver's door.

We were there long enough to eat, gas up and recruit new passengers—a nursing mother with two small children, who settled somehow between the watermelons and chicken crates.

The police checks became rarer after Maradi, and we made good time. The countryside lapsed into bleak, scrubby desert with no villages between the main towns and with the only sign of life an occasional procession of Tuareg on their camels—too small an ensemble to be a caravan.

At 10:30 p.m. we drove into the central market of Birni Nkomni. It was Saturday night, and there was a celebration in progress. I lay back on my improvised armchair of chicken crates and straw mats and took in the scene. Small boys were selling what looked like hot chestnuts and peanuts. One lad had a kind of hot, stringy pink taffy which he sold in little dabs from his nut tray for five CFA (two cents). Also for sale, for ten CFA, was coke nut, the raw fruit from which is distilled cocaine.

A bar nearby disgorged one rowdy patron after another, each escorted off the premises by a bouncer whose musculature rippled through his "Woodstock" T-shirt. I saw that he had learned that manly American-teenager technique of rolling a pack of cigarettes up in his sleeve.

After half an hour I decided to mosey over and have a Flag. Most of the Peace Corps volunteers and other Westerners who know about that kind of thing say that Flag is by far the smoothest and lightest beer in Africa—both going down and the next morning. I certainly found it preferable to most others I tried.

Each country seems to have its own. Ostensibly national beers, these brews are really made under contract by one of the larger European breweries (such as Heineken or Lowenbrau) in plants which are pre-fabricated in Europe, shipped here and installed by Europeans. The barley, malt, yeast and other ingredients—all that—is shipped (sometimes flown) from, say, Amsterdam. There are also *true* local beers, made from distilled mangroves, bananas, pineapples, maize—you name it. In sampling these home brews I invariably got a case of firebreath not unlike that bestowed by white lightning.

No sooner had I stepped inside the bar than all eyes turned on me (not too many redbeards in Birni). They crowded in close, one beery question following another. They were particularly interested in the Sahara and Agadez, to which none of them had ever been. Several were young soldiers with bright red berets. Their sergeant was a friend of the bartender and did not pay for his beer.

On one stool was a peacock-plumed lady in a red mini. Although she was the sergeant's lady, they were not getting on too well. She finally settled down with an old man with a World War II French campaign cap who kept shouting from a table his disagreement with whatever was said at the bar. Whenever he became particularly annoyed, he would bang his cane on the floor. He was doubtless one of the vanishing Free French veterans who fought for France when most Frenchmen weren't fighting. These vintage warriors proudly wear their caps and medals and whatever is left of their uniforms. They enjoy high social standing and are often seen carrying decorative walking sticks bedangled with beads, strips of leather or feathers. In some villages, they live in honored seclusion, their houses fenced off and with a totem out front indicating their position. They receive a small pension from the French treasury which, unfortunately, is subject to local taxation. In order to collect the tax, the tax collector disburses the pensions. This makes it easier to take a larger share—both in taxes and in dash by petty officials who will hold up a veteran's money until he tips them to hasten the paperwork.

I guzzled a cold Flag and was being hustled for a round by the regulars when the horn sounded. Sprinting, I was barely able to scramble over the rickety sideboard before the truck sped off into the night.

The market had been hot and muggy, and I had removed my shirt. Now I found myself rummaging for a sweater and jacket, both of which proved inadequate in the 55-mile-an-hour draft. So I dragged my sleeping bag to the rear and struggled to arrange it among the watermelons. I had just dozed off when the truck ran off the road and down an embankment. As the dust cleared, we all crawled out to survey the damage. Everything appeared to be intact but the horn, which screamed plaintively into the night until it was disconnected. The driver called to me: "American, can you drive this?"

"*Oui,*" I said.

"*On y va!*"

Ten minutes later I was at the wheel of a five-ton Saviem hurtling through the dark night of the Sahel. There were no other vehicles. I drove for 100 flat miles before almost ramming a police blockade in the middle of nowhere. Two guards, one with a submachine gun at the ready, cautiously approached.

"*Bon soir, mon capitain,*" I said. The officer did a double take when his flashlight caught my face. He demanded my driver's license, whereupon I presented my expired 1976 Arkansas permit. He studied it carefully, then nodded and handed it back. The one with the submachine gun motioned for me to carry on. The glows of their cigarettes receded in the rear-view mirror as I resumed my improbable journey. A few miles further on, I made a rest stop and noticed that the driver had crawled into my sleeping bag and was sound asleep.

Next morning at sunup, a five-ton truckload of chickens, goats, watermelons, two nursing mothers, and a half dozen hadjis arrived in Niamey, Republic of Niger, driven by a red-bearded Arkansas hitchhiker.

The National Museum at Niamey was built near the city center with a commanding view of the Niger River. It is surrounded by trees and banks of grass on which "*Musee National*" is white-limed. There are a dozen separate pastel blue and orange complexes, each housing a separate display of Niger's diverse heritage, from native costumes and music to prehistoric artifacts. Dominating the latter exhibit is a magnificent fossilized skeleton of *Tyrannosaurus rex,* the carnivorous dinosaur which once roamed what is now the Tenere Desert. It is displayed just as it was found lying in the sand.

A Stone-Age building contains materials on the period of the last 6,000 years and emphasizes the Tuareg and the sedentary tribes of the oases, with particular attention given to cave or rock drawings of the last millennium. Among them is an exquisite sequence of animal paintings. Needless to say, the camel, which replaced the horse in the Sahara in about the twelfth century, is given the greatest attention.

One of the most informative exhibits is a Hausa village. Most of the population of Niger and northern Nigeria are Hausa. At one time they were the masters of westcentral Africa. As tradesmen, they have spread their language so that today Hausa is here what Swahili is to East Africa, the *lingua franca.* When the Tuareg of the Aïr haggle with the Hadad of Bilma over the price of salt and dates, they speak Hausa.

Although the Hausa are the most numerous tribe in Niger, the country has recently been run by the Djerma who live in the western region along the river. Djerma habits dominated the costume exhibit. I was an eavesdropper for half an hour to a spirited argument between two Djerma women over the authenticity of an apronlike garment on a model there. A young curator interpreted for me. Soon there were a dozen women participating. (The other men avoided the exhibit during the argument.)

To the museum's discredit, a number of small animals, including several monkeys and baboons, were kept in tiny box cages where they were tortured by children who poked them with sticks.

There is a work center for the disabled where one can purchase leather, wood and silver handicrafts. It is still actually possible in Niger to purchase a Tuareg sword or a Djerma pouch that has been made for use and not for tourists. Most of the customers of the work center are people from the countryside. On most market days peasants, as well as schoolchildren, can be seen crowding through its gates.

The museum not only is well planned and run but truly serves the Niger people. It was the single most efficient public-service institution I saw in Africa, with the possible exception of Richard Leakey's National Museum of Kenya, which is enabled by its American endowments to fulfill a prestigious international research role. The Nairobi museum, however, was not as much frequented by the African public as was the one in Niamey.

I stayed at the Hotel Domino, dead cheap at four dollars a night. The Domino had a decent European restaurant and a rowdy bar that geared up about 9:00 and exploded at 1:00. Two ferocious dogs patrolled the table of the two immense French ladies who ran the place. If you looked the wrong way, those dogs had you at bay and only the larger of the two ladies could pull them off. The dogs remained throughout the night. Their chief function (as in cheap hotels everywhere) was not to prevent breaking in but breaking out (i.e., leaving without paying the tab). As soon as anyone crossed the garden to enter the exit foyer in the morning, he would be bayed against the locked doors until the *gardien* came (a slow-walking old African with an ornate chief's cane). Before you could get out for morning coffee you had to bring your tab up to date. The old man did not read well, and the dogs became impatient as he fingered the ledger. Coffee was not served at the hotel in the morning, and one had to leave to buy it from nearby street vendors. The dogs started baying clients at about 7:00 a.m.

Niamey is a typical African town. Open sewers run alongside dirt streets where people huddle before fires at dawn to drink Nescafe with three to five tablespoons of sugar. One frequently gets not only coffee, but tea and coffee together, unless you very clearly specify that you want coffee only. The tea made earlier that day, or the day before, will simply be reheated and served with a dash of Nescafe. In Kano I saw well-dressed bureaucrats drink this brew at a street stall outside their building.

My most vivid memories of Niamey are the dawn mist of fog from the river and smoke from the street fires, and the people yet asleep under light blankets, and some without blankets, and the stirrings of those already awake to make their fires and wash themselves, and the thud of pestles behind walls.

Some effort is made by the ruling Djerma junta to recruit Hausa and Fulani functionaries, but there is much tribal rivalry, and to cooperate—even in the interest of national unity—might jeopardize one's tribal standing. The Islamic Hausa are extremely hostile to public schooling, one of the government's primary objectives, and very few are functionally literate. Many Hausa children do attend Koran schools, however, and one of the most common sights in any village is a class of Koran students clustered in the shade around a marabout. Their chanting—each a different prayer—continues until dark. In their hands they hold the slates on which they have copied in Arabic the prayers that they are singing.

At night these children walk about with empty bowls, begging for food. The boys generally come from another village and stay with friends of their family. But it is required that they obtain their own food. One will generally share with a fellow food he has begged, though on occasion I observed boys scuffling over prize morsels.

The Tuareg are excluded from the government in Niger as they are in the other Sahara states. This is because of their abhorrence of sedentary life and their absolute refusal to send their children to school. These former (and to some extent, present) masters of slaves find it demeaning to obey black officials. Although the Tuareg were able to resist citizenship with impunity while there was some water and grass left in the Sahel, the drought which destroyed their herds has forced them into the towns and villages, where they have gradually had to submit to authority. Oddly, the Tuareg reputation for honesty and reliability has made them sought after as *gardiens* of the homes of high officials as well as of Europeans. In Kano, for example, I stayed several days at a company rest house with some young Canadian surveyors. They were profuse in their praise for their Tuareg guards, whom they credited with having captured numerous thieves.

"It is best for the thief if one of us is here," one said. "They will always ask permission before they execute him and we can turn him over to the police. If we are away, they will hang him immediately."

They had recently returned from the bush to find an alleged culprit strung up on a tree in the backyard.

Not all displaced Tuareg are vagrants or guards or market peddlers. I talked to one in Tanout who was among some 40 workers coming home on vacation from the Libyan oil fields (on one of the rare trucks that cross the Erg of Bilma). He wore a blue veil, but as a bandana, and he boasted tight bellbottomed denims. I asked him how long he had been in Libya, and he said a year. He said there were many Americans there. He had visited Tripoli and Tunis and planned some day to go to Paris.

Later on I learned that the Libyan government surreptitiously recruits young Tuareg for service with the *polisario* of the western Sahara and the Toubou in northern Chad—fellow nomads who are fighting Western-backed governments.

The American Embassy's swimming pool was a three-minute walk from the Domino. There, on Saturday afternoons, Peace Corps volunteers ate hot dogs, drank Schlitz, and played volleyball.

At the time, there were about 80 Peace Corps people in Niger, most of them English teachers between 22 and 26. Individually, in their villages, the Peace Corps volunteers I met in Africa were open, friendly, hospitable—hungry for conversation. I was frequently the only non-P.C. visitor many had had, and I must have stayed briefly with over a dozen of them in Niger,

Chad and the Central African Empire.

In the capitals, such as Niamey, Peace Corps people become suddenly cliquish and condescending toward other Americans. Most are from upper-middle-class families and are recently graduated from so-called "prestige" schools. Their liberal training (and their view of "colonial exploitation," which they are here to assuage) makes them distrustful of other Americans whom they encounter, particularly career State Department bureaucrats, businessmen and good-old-boy construction workers with quite different views of Africans and their development potential.

Their ostensibly Spartan life and their self-image of being on the front line against poverty, ignorance and disease gives them an élan similar to that shared by elite soldiers who know that they are absolutely the best. And, indeed, many of these people are exceptionally talented.

The quickest way to Ouagadougou is by mammy wagon (so-called because most of the passengers on the small buses are mothers with tots), and I was told to be at the market at 7:00 a.m. sharp. Some of the buses were partially loaded with mats and chicken coops and net sacks of personal belongings. But the Ouagadougou bus was virtually empty, so I knew that the *patron* had been lying when he said it would leave at 9:00. A mammy wagon never leaves until it is dangerously overloaded. This one had a long way to go. Still, the *patron* demanded my fare of 3,000 CFA (about twelve dollars) in advance.

Once you pay, that's it. If it doesn't leave for two or three days (Peace Corps story), you get no refund. An old gent with a white goatee motioned for me to follow. He led me to where a well-loaded competitor was being gassed up and whispered, almost gleefully: "Ouagadougou" (pronounced "wah-gah-doo-goo," and often shortened to "waga"). I tipped him 50 CFA.

We crossed the Niger at 9:00. The foliage changed to thicker, stumpier baobab trees and leafier scrub brush. There remained the ever-present rusty sand, blown less severely in the Upper Volta than in Niger, but still generated by a seemingly pernicious harmattan wind.

I counted 32 police checks and three separate stops by motorcycle patrols, two *motards* (patrolmen) at each. I began to recognize a ritual: the *motards* were almost, but not quite, concealed under a shade tree. As soon as the bus driver would see them, he would pull over. In other words, it was not necessary for them to signal him to stop. He knew why they were there. Dismounting, the driver would approach and all but kowtow to the chief. The chief would not acknowledge him. Nor would either of them address the other *motard*, who, as soon as the chief began examining the papers of the driver, would spit and walk away. He would never be there when the chief took whatever it was he took from the driver.

I found more trees in Ouaga than in Niamey. There were several European bookstores and an ice cream parlor. The European community was mostly French (teachers, government advisors) with Americans (Peace Corps, UN) running a close second. As in Niamey, they tended to live in the European sector with their houses protected by a sworded guard who slept (and lived) at the gate. The *gardien* would keep there all of his belongings. Sometimes he might have with him a dog, thin and mangy, and frequently other male members of his family, all of whom participated in guarding the premises.

We arrived at 5:00 in the afternoon at the central market, and I found a room at the Pavillion Vert Hotel, two dollars per night. The mattress was too soft, so I threw it on the floor and put my sleeping bag on top. It was hot until 3:00 a.m.; then I needed a sheet. Having none, I used my poncho liner and slept through the night.

At the depot next morning there were twice as many people as there were seats in the second-class section of the Abidjan-Niger express. There were also goats, pigs (plenty of pigs now that we had left Islam) and chickens. One gent even carried a calf on board which he was forced by the conductor to shackle and ship as freight. (Goats, okay, but a cow?) I struggled in vain to breathe. Yet one learns from such experiences. The train stopped at virtually every station (there were fifty of them). The main stop was Bobodiùlaso, the only other city in Upper Volta and about halfway to Abidjan.

The name of the express was misleading, since the terminal at Ouaga was 300 miles from Niger. Completing it would increase the line's length by one-third and complete the railroad link to Lake Chad. This would be an ideal aid project of immediate humanitarian as well as commercial benefit. Niger, already Africa's second exporter of uranium, was soon to become a prime producer of coal. Enough had already been found to fuel the industry of the Ivory Coast, western Africa's fastest-developing country. Adequate transportation is essential.

With this export potential, not to mention its fish and cattle industry on Lake Chad, Niger should be able to honor reasonably scheduled repayments of a world bank or even a private loan for this purpose.

At each stop along the way, trilling children and young women advertised fresh water by shouting, "G'EE-BAY, G'EE-BAY." They held buckets of water into which, for five CFA, they would dip a cup and pass it to the passenger.

"BANAN, BANAN," they shouted, pushing bunches of green bananas toward the open windows. Chickens were for sale—most of them spitted to a sooty, crispy brown. Most were fresh, but you had to take care that the one you bought was thoroughly cooked. The vendor would let you peel back the skin to verify this. These *poulets* cost about 150 CFA (60¢) apiece.

There were scores of women with mangroves, some golden ripe but many green and terribly bitter. Bread was sold only sometimes. It came two feet long (thick and thin) and had nearly always been freshly baked that morning. While prices of fruit and meat were negotiable, that of bread wasn't: always 25 CFA for a small loaf and 50 CFA for a large one, no matter how many you bought at once.

Other vendors sold small, finely woven chairs and stools, hard-boiled eggs and cocaine nuts. Sometimes a seller would fail to collect before the train got underway and would run after it shouting and waving at the slow-paying customer. Invariably, the buyer would capitulate and toss the correct change alongside the tracks.

A passenger, from his window, could dine quite well and cheaply. A meal might consist of the following:

> Hors d'oeuvre: Hard-boiled eggs with peppers
> Entrée: Chicken, dried fish
> Dessert: Pineapple, banana, orange

Occasionally, there is coffee.

First-class passengers could sit in the dining car. Beer there cost 150 CFA (Flag) or 250 CFA (Heineken or Lowenbrau). The dinner—meat, vegetable, bread—was 500 CFA, without service, which was another fifteen percent. If you had a beer, the total was 650 or 750, and dessert was another 250. So for a complete dinner, with service, you paid 1,035 CFA—five times the price of the more interesting (and filling) track-peddler meal.

We came to real banana and peanut country the next morning, and the two together were delicious. Vendors also sold plantains, the big, pulpy bananas which are fried in palm oil or mixed with peanuts and baked. Peanuts (ground nuts) are made into a crunchy, sweet peanut butter which is better than any store-bought stateside brand.

The Ivory Coast is sometimes referred to as "the Kenya of Western Africa." One notices modern housing, highways, power lines and factories as soon as the train crosses the frontier from Upper Volta. Even the quality and variety of produce and poultry sold by trackside vendors improves: bananas are plumper and larger, pineapples juicier, eggs fresher, and fruit and vegetables are in an abundance not often seen on the continent.

This cornucopia remained in my mind for the rest of the trip, for I did not see such apparent African prosperity again until I got to Rhodesia. Even Kenya, with its rich west-country farms, did not exude such widespread abundance. The Ivory Coast is the world's third largest exporter of coffee and the fourth-largest exporter of cocoa (producing fourteen percent of it in 1975).

Abidjan, the capital, is certainly the most cosmopolitan city in Black Africa and probably, after Lagos, its largest port. One morning I counted 103 freighters of various sizes there loading or standing by. Of the ships in port or standing by, many were taking on timber and palm oil, which also feature among the country's top exports. Abidjan is the major base port for the world's fishing fleets which harvest the South and Central Atlantic. Its oil refineries process much of Nigeria's oil and natural gas.

(Later, when traveling through the forests of the south coast, I saw thousands of acres of palm oil plants—all carefully planted in seemingly endless symmetrical rows. The cool shade of those manmade forests was an inviting respite from the oppressive humidity. Once I tried to follow a row of palm to its very end, but after an hour it still stretched out before me as far as I could see.)

Abidjan's skyline is that of a modern industrial metropolis. It is the home of over 30,000 French workers and executives who run the country. It would not be accurate to say that they are only technical advisors, for they are the directors-in-fact (although not in name) of the departments of every bank, major hotel, and shipping company. There are efforts being made to train Ivoiriens to assume true management positions, but thus far they remain a distinct minority in these roles. One young bank clerk complained to me that there was little actual training of Africans and that the Europeans acted as if they were permanent in their positions. A law professor said that one major problem was getting educated young blacks to return to the country once they had received their degrees from European universities. Doctors, particularly, and even teachers and engineers, can always find better-paying posts in Europe and America.

Most European executives live out on the big hill above the harbor behind the giant Hotel Ivoire. There at dusk, down neatly paved streets, glow the bonfires of the *gardiens* at the gates of the rich, who also include many high Ivoirien officials. Each sentry carries a long Tuareg sword, probably brought from Niger by a young black migrant and sold in the market at Treichville, Abidjan's working-class district.

The price of a good street meal in Treichville is less than one-tenth that of the same meal at one of the European restaurants on the plateau, Abidjan's downtown, across the bay. This difference in price generally holds true for food, services and accommodations. There is an African price and a European price. To give an idea of the figures involved, it was possible to have fried plantain, a reasonably tender steak, fried or baked potato, pineapple and coffee on the street in Treichville for 175 CFA. Lunch at the African restaurant three blocks up the road from the National Museum of Art was still only 225 CFA—also for steak, French fries and bananas, but with rice and fresh green salad. The food at these places was clean and tasty, although the decor was rough.

On the other hand, at the Hotel Ivoire, virtually the same dinner, but garnished for the European palate, was 2,400 CFA. A hamburger was 1,200 CFA. The taxi ride from the hotel downtown was 600 CFA, and a single room (just for one night) cost 10,000 CFA, over $40. When it is considered that some African families buy only one or two loaves of bread a day, at 25 or 50 CFA, the contrast is startling.

The conspicuous coexistence of disparate lifestyles throughout not only Africa, but most of the third world, is one of the greatest ironies of our planet. But the disparity is more dramatic in Africa because it is the greatest. Even in most of the so-called "socialist" countries which have expelled all Westerners and abhor bourgeois consumerism, the party elite enjoy European privileges on a scale at least equal to that of top Ivoirien officials.

In addition to that of the exorbitant Hotel Ivoire, there were several less-expensive restaurants in Abidjan patronized by both Africans and Europeans. Among them was La Bossi Be, a Madagascan specialty house in Treichville where for 2,100 CFA, one could have a superb Indian Ocean meal with meat, salad, rice, soup and a number of vegetables, dessert, coffee and an after-dinner liqueur.

But such fare aside, Treichville is a world unto itself. Downtown on the plateau no one eats and sleeps in the streets. Over in Treichville, life *is* the street: people eat, sleep, socialize—spend the better part of their lives out in the street. Like those in Niamey and other African capitals—but even more so—the streets are filled with boiling pots and sizzling skillets, and the air is pungent with the aroma of smoking cocoa nuts and palm oil. Dowdy market women hawk eggs and plantain, and young boys tout stringfuls of shoal fish caught just that morning in the surf. The streets are lined with furniture, clothing, and jewelry shops.

Although these shops offer native clothing and crafts at prices below those of the central market, I saw not a single white shopper take advantage of them. The central Treichville market, however, is a different story. Vendors and hawkers of every description gossip and dicker with the relays of tourists bussed over hourly from the big hotels across the bay. Young street people walk about with transistor radios to their ears in the late style of American teenagers. Much of the music is Western pop, but there is a distinct African rock combining drums and castanets with guitars. It was a kind of "washboard" background with an almost-Latin rhythm. Most popular at the time were several groups from Cameroon whose albums were prominently displayed along with those of American rock stars.

Almost everyone in Abidjan rides the bus. (Europeans don't, but they really miss the best and cheapest—twelve cents—ride in town.) The buses are crowded and the air heavy with body odors, but I never rode one where I didn't meet a friendly Ivoirien eager to talk. The fare to Treichville was one-tenth the cost of a taxi to the Hotel Ivoire from downtown. (By apparent collusion between the municipal authorities and the taxi company, there was no public bus service *to* the hotel.)

I would take breakfast (cake and coffee) at a small pastry shop and coffee bar in Treichville. An adjacent bus-stop curb was about 30 yards long. For some reason, drivers never stopped at the queue but drove past, sometimes the full length of the curb, so that there was a great scramble as everyone ran to get on. The queue would form again, only to be overshot by the next bus.

Jack was an aerial spotter for the Spanish tuna fleet out of Abidjan. He had been there six months but had flown only six days.

"My job is to be here ready, willing and able to fly," he said. "If they don't order me up, that's their business."

Just his hotel bill averaged 170,000 CFA ($680) per month. It cost him, he said, at least $80 per day to live there.

At the bar with Jack was a French pilot named Francois. (He insisted on "Francis.") He flew African businessmen and government officials to Europe or wherever they wanted to go. "These people absolutely refuse to fly with an African pilot in the cockpit—even with a registered European pilot commanding," Francis said. Just the week before, he had flown an Ivoirien cabinet secretary to Paris. Before taking off, the secretary had ordered the African co-pilot to the passenger section. He told Francis he could "get his experience on the way back, when I'm not in the plane."

Jack was from Galveston and when he learned that I was a Razorback he invited me to join him and Francis and a gentleman named George from

Detroit, an executive with an American baby-powder company who said that he had fought with the British Eighth Army in northern Africa. He talked at length about the war and the role of gliders (he had been a glider pilot) in supplying and ferrying troops. Gradually the conversation came around to present-day Africa. George said he'd traveled the world over, setting up plants for his company, and that, of all the undeveloped places, Africa—because of its natural resources—had the greatest potential. Yet it was unlikely it would ever be realized because of graft and corruption that disrupted planning and commerce: "Sometimes we spend thirty, forty percent of our budget on a given project just greasing the palms of politicians. If one guy doesn't get his, he can foul up the whole program. . . ."

I allowed as how his company seemed, in spite of all that, to do a good business or they surely wouldn't be there. He admitted that that might be true, but, he said, "After the plant is set up and they are trying to run it on their own, it will break down from petty corruption and the inefficiency that goes with it."

One story of incompetence and corruption then followed another until I became weary and excused myself, thanking Jack for the dinner for which he had insisted on paying. It had been a good meal and they had been good company, but I was restless and needed a long walk. I entered the palm grove beyond the hotel and trudged up the beach. The surf was up near the high-tide mark, and the wind was at near-gale force. Some porters were retrieving awnings and beach chairs.

"Be careful of that surf," Jack had said when I mentioned it looked good for swimming. "A young African girl was snatched away last week by a big swell. Dragged her under right in front of her family. . . ." The girl had been carrying her baby. Miraculously, the child was washed ashore, alive, an hour later at almost the same place. There was no set pattern to the waves, he said. They would be normal, then a big one would wash up to the high-tide mark and take everything with it.

As I walked past the parking lot, I waved away the solicitous taxi driver who had already clamped on his meter. To them, all whites are rich turkeys. One driver had a meter that ran on two speeds, one being a special double speed for hotel fares. The meters normally began at 50 CFA, but I could see through the window that this one was already at 125.

I went on to the beach and walked for a good twenty minutes before I came to the road that led into Viridi. There I caught the last bus to Treichville.

The delegates from the United States to the International Academy of Trial Lawyers finally arrived on February 24. I was at the airport to meet them. The Arkansas contingent consisted of my father, incoming president of the Academy, my mother, and Jack and Doreen Deacon of Jonesboro. They were tired but in good spirits, and we had a cheerful reunion. Dad dutifully delivered the air filter I'd wired for—holding it out as he stepped down the gangway.

Following the usual hassle with misplaced luggage, we went to the Hotel Ivoire. The Academy was splitting its conference, four days in Abidjan and ten days in Nairobi. The theme of the conference was "World Peace

91

Through World Law." A number of African jurists were to be inducted as Fellows.

There were quite a few long speeches during the conference, not all of which were easy to follow. However, it was a rare opportunity to meet and visit with the politicians who ruled the farmers and nomads among whom I had been traveling. The view from the elegant towers of the palatial Hotel Ivoire was different indeed from that of the *piste.*

Among the entertainment at the hotel was a group of native dancers, some twenty of them, who performed twice daily in a red-carpeted warehouse-sized conference room hung with crystal chandeliers. So-called "exquisite, hand-carved" wood and ivory images sold for exquisite prices in the hotel souvenir shops. Occasionally, individual groups of drummers and musicians would perform for guests swimming in the labyrinthine concrete lagoon and garden which was the hotel's luxurious swimming pool.

There were a number of receptions and dinners at which I was able, courtesy of the Academy, to meet and visit with various African jurists, including the Chief Justice of the Supreme Court of Sierra Leone, the young mayor of Lagos, Nigeria, and His Excellency, President Houphouët-Boigny of the Ivory Coast.

President Houphouët-Boigny has been one of the few leaders in Black Africa to maintain public diplomatic contact (although informally) with South Africa. For this, he has been severely criticized in both African and Western circles. His reply has been that he serves as a reliable conduit for an exchange of views—and as an honest broker, himself an African, who can keep open the possibility of peaceful change through negotiations. He has cited as evidence of his success the recent ambiguous acquiescence of Pretoria to the principle of independence of South West Africa (Namibia), a development doubtlessly attributable to a variety of pressures but for which many give considerable credit to the Ivory Coast President. Indeed, so important does the South African government consider their link to Houphouët-Boigny that their foreign minister personally flew to see him on a moment's notice in September, 1977, when it was feared that it might be politically impossible for him to continue the relationship.

On the last evening of the convention in Abidjan, I had the opportunity to visit very briefly with the President. He expressed an interest in my journey and was curious to know how an overland traveler compared the Ivory Coast with other countries he had seen. I told him my general impressions, which were favorable. I also told him the Ivoirien people were certainly among the most hospitable that I had met. To this he replied, "Yes, we like foreigners very much and want more of them to come. And they can stay if they want to." Those few words seemed to summarize the country's economic policy: the attraction of as much foreign capital as possible by a wide-open economy that has virtually no restrictions on the repatriation of profits and capital.*

---

*Capital export takes two forms. First, salaries of European employees are frequently

This policy of the open door has been severely criticized as neocolonial. The fact remains, however, that there is less unemployment and higher per-capita productivity in the Ivory Coast than almost anywhere else in Black Africa.

One of the pleasures of traveling in out of the-way places is meeting other Americans. Except for my Peace Corps friends, I had visited with hardly any Americans before reaching Abidjan. The trial lawyers were a plucky, spirited lot with whom I shared hours of rich conversation. Some of them, such as Walter H. Beckham of Miami, had previously traveled in Africa. With his sons, he had spent several months hunting and photographing game in Kenya many years before.

The night before I separated from the lawyers, Jack Deacon suggested that he and Doreen and the McMaths have dinner together at one of the better Treichville restaurants. Somehow we decided on the Bossi Be. I would meet the others there since the restaurant was not far from my hotel. When they hadn't arrived an hour after the appointed time, I apologized to the maitre d' and headed uptown. Several miles away, as I was walking along the congested waterfront road, a taxi passed headed in the opposite direction. Looking out the rear window was Jack Deacon. We saw each other at the same time. Their driver had been wandering around Treichville for over an hour, unable to find the restaurant. I showed him the way and the Madagascan dinner we shared was by far the most succulent of any meal I enjoyed during my passage through western Africa.

The last day of their visit to Abidjan, the Academy members were driven south into the coastal palm forest around Grand Bassam Island. I missed their bus from the Hotel Ivoire but managed to hitch out with an off-duty taxi driver. We picked up a farmer who, luckily, knew the way. I jumped on the last barge just as it pushed off. On either side of us, boys in pirogues played chase. As we approached the center of the channel, there suddenly appeared three water skiers behind a sleek speedboat. This welcoming committee performed some ramp jumps and other daredevil acrobatics.

Grand Bassam is the sight of the local Club Mediteranée, the French resort syndicate which has lodges from the Alps to the South Pacific. I found its Grand Bassam camp especially exotic, bordering as it did the northern tip

---

fully payable in dollars or in their own national currency to their bank accounts back home. Thus, none of the wealth which they earn in the Ivory Coast is spent there. But this practice is one followed to a large extent throughout the underdeveloped world, and the Ivory Coast is no exception. Some countries, such as Tanzania and Zaire, do require that a small percentage of each employee's salary be paid in local currency and spent in the country. As a practical matter, however, this portion of an employee's salary is treated by his employer as expenses or "per diem," with the real salary still paid back home. The second form of capital export is the actual transfer of earnings and profits from the Ivory Coast to the corporations' European or American accounts. This is done both in payment for raw materials as well as in outright removal for investment elsewhere. Restrictions on this type of capital outflow are less stringent in the Ivory Coast than in any other major African country.

of twenty miles of virgin beach. Swimming, though, was prohibited due to a treacherous riptide. Mary Frances Allen, a friend from Virginia traveling with the group, waded out with me several hundred feet before we were frantically motioned ashore by two anxious lifeguards. We could not hear their shouts above the surf.

After a half-hour's rest our group was ushered into a thatched pavilion for a delectable picnic of roast pork and a variety of local vegetables and fruit. By 5:00, the last of my companions had shoved off for the mainland and I was alone again after five days of hearty comradeship. I waved at them until they disappeared down the lagoon. My mother and dad had especially enjoyed the island and were in particularly high spirits as they waved goodbye. I would not see them again for eighteen months. We had had a splendid reunion.

The maitre d' had kindly fixed me a box lunch and with it I set out south along the beach. Soon I was alone with the surf and, overhead, some friendly gulls. By nightfall I had made about five miles.

Walking with the heavy backpack in the sand was hard work, and I had to stop every 20 or 30 minutes to rest. I began looking for a place to camp with protection from the wind. Each time I would climb the bank there would be a hut just beyond the high-tide line. They were pumpkin-shaped, squatty little huts, and once in a while I thought I detected a form moving beside one or another of them. But there was little light and eventually these movements ceased—or at least I did not see them any longer.

The more tired I became, the more earnestly I searched for a campsite. Once I found a place behind a log on a hillock of sand and settled in, only to have a dog run up and stick his snout in my face. I then heard the sound of children in the trees. I did not wait for them to find me but gathered my gear and moved on. Finally I came upon a great tree washed ashore above the tide line. I scooped out a shallow depression in the sand alongside and again put down my sleeping bag, pulling up the poncho liner as a coverlet. Neither dogs nor children disturbed me this time, and I fell asleep gazing at the stars.

I awoke and, in the sea mist, saw what I thought were beachcombers. After a few moments I realized they were fishermen and that they were toting a pirogue toward the surf. There were six of them. In the fog they appeared to move in slow motion. Suddenly, the last one hurled into the pirogue what I knew was a net.

As they were about to launch their canoe, one of the men broke away and darted back into the treeline. Just as quickly he reappeared, carrying a long oar, which he handed to the others who were now aboard. Soon the craft could no longer be seen, although it was obvious where it was from the solitary figure standing on the beach looking after it. Then a dark form rolled under the curl of a swell and swiveled in its neck; it was they. The figure on the beach retreated into the treeline and disappeared.

I fastened the plastic girth which bound the pack to my hips, so that my shoulders merely balanced the frame but did not carry the weight. My feet sank into the cold wet sand. It felt good. My back was rested enough, and the chocolate bar and orange saved from the box lunch gave my legs energy to push on. It was easier to walk along the ripples of the tide on the just-wet sand and then to hurry inboard before the next wave came. The surf was every bit as unpredictable as old Jack, the fish pilot, had said. Once I was caught completely by surprise and found myself knee-high in a clutching surf, struggling to keep my balance against an insidious undertow. Occasionally, I would glance backward to see the distorted gashes of my footprints, methodically erased by the sweeping tide; another wave, and they were gone. I looked at my watch: it was 4:30 a.m. I had slept fewer than five hours. But I continued to walk as I had, my footprints disappearing behind me.

When the sun finally lifted the fog, I had come to the end of the island. Ahead was the mouth of the lagoon, which is joined by a river just as it empties into the sea. Just up the lagoon was a log shack, beside which was a beautiful pirogue almost finished yet still part of the tree from which it was being carved. .

On the sand a fiddler crab pranced back, forth and sideways and then walked completely around the building. Out on the lagoon two boys were fishing from a pirogue. Another was almost hidden in the trees next to the bank about 100 yards upstream. When he saw me he poled in my direction.

The fee to the mainland was 25 CFA, which I gladly paid, struggling to balance myself in the narrow bark. He made me squat down low—not sit—and hold on to my pack, which was balanced crosswise on the bow. When we reached the other side I scrambled up the bank and slowly worked my way along a trail to the village while dogs barked and mothers with small children came to their doors to stare. In the market I found a woman frying plantain, bought a plateful, devoured them and bought another. The lady volunteered to boil water for the Nescafe which I took from my pack.

The Ghanan border was about fifteen kilometers further on, across the river, and I haggled a boatman into reducing my fare to 150 CFA. I crouched low in the stern as the ferryman rowed mightily, hand over hand, with a double-bladed oar, his muscles rippling with his long, even strokes. Soon sparkling whitecaps leapt like schools of fish as the lagoon-river emptied into the sea not a quarter-mile away.

For 30 minutes he rowed. As we entered a long slough, the current became barely perceptible. After a while, we entered another branch, and still another, until finally we came to a landing on a bank pocked with recent footprints. A narrow trail led to a village and after filling my canteen from the well next to a small tin-roofed store, I walked on to the beach. The storekeeper had said there would be a truck for Assini but he did not know when, so I braced myself for a long walk to the border.

A couple of hundred yards further on I heard a sound like someone breaking open melons. In a clearing a small, wiry man was heaving fresh coconuts one by one onto the point of a stake. As he did, he twisted the husks and they flew off onto a pile. The nut itself the man tossed to his wife who dropped it into her basket. When he saw me, he heaved one of the nuts onto the stake and opened it, revealing the sweet white meat and milk inside. He handed it to me, and when she saw how much I enjoyed it, his wife handed him another to open for me. I devoured four of them in short order.

A bit further on I lay against a palm to rest and fell asleep. When I awoke the sun had moved two forks down in the tree just west of me. At that moment there came from the beach the chugging, coughing sound of a struggling engine. Hurrying to the treeline I saw approaching in the distance the most improbable beach buggy, a red mammy wagon that could have belonged to a misplaced entourage of circus clowns. The rig was running back and forth on the wet sand just ahead of the surf. It looked like a Model-A cab welded onto a Volkswagen van. The contraption was filled with villagers on their way to Assini to do their weekly shopping. I climbed aboard and nestled down between two young mothers and a toothless old man, and this is how I made my way into Ghana.

The Ivory Coast border check was easy. The officer in charge was asleep, and an assistant stamped my passport and waved me on. But I knew I was in trouble when, 200 yards down the beach, the Ghanan officer asked for my visa. I told him that I was in transit and had thought I could get a transit visa at the border.

"Impossible," he replied ... and so it began. It was immediately apparent that the driver of the Ghanan mammy wagon (a converted school bus) was in a big hurry. My pack was already on board, having been heaved up with the baggage transferred from the other vehicle. I tried to explain this, but my English was not his. Finally, he made it quite clear he was going to wait no longer. Somehow I prevailed on the immigration officer to let me talk to his chief at Assini. Maybe the chief could be persuaded to give me a special-entry permit so I could travel on to Accra and get a visa.

So into the new mammy wagon and another long ride. I could tell when we came to Assini by the ancient rusted freighter aground on the beach— straight on, as if it had tried to run right up into the town. Later I was to learn its strange story. There had been supernatural forces at work.

"You are in Ghana illegally. You have broken the law." This was George, the young immigration officer in Assini. He reared back in his chair. He was trying to stay cool, correct, although he was obviously nervous. It was late, well after closing time. Yet he was trying to set a professional example for the soldiers and customs officials who crowded into the small room to look at the weird American.

The conversation turned to how much money I had. As I started to answer, he barked orders to the others to inspect my pack at the customs shed. When they had gone, I asked him how much it would cost for a special permit.

"There is no such thing. You will have to return to Abidjan and get a proper visa."

I told him that I had heard that you could get a special transit visa to Togo (the next little country down the coast).

"Impossible," he said. "But it is too late now to discuss it. We close here at 5:00 and it is already 6:00. You have kept us an extra hour, my friend. Where will you sleep tonight?"

"There must be a small hotel."

"There is, but it is not a very good one. Besides I would like for you to be my guest. Come on."

We went to the customs shed to get my pack. A faint tingle of fear ran through me when I realized that I had not declared the twenty boxes of Kodak slide film or the Toyota air filter that Dad had delivered at Abidjan. The form had only asked for commercial items and I, of course, had none. The items had been set aside and a rather pompous customs officer insisted on conducting an inquiry—his first "violation" in three months' duty, according to my host.

I was made to empty my pockets and stand against the wall while they frisked me. Again, I had to dig out my passport and other documents. It was during this episode that I forgot to retrieve my shot card. (This became a nuisance later in Nairobi, where I had to get revaccinated against yellow fever, cholera, and smallpox to get a Zambian visa.) But, finally, he accepted my story and I was let go.

I arrived in time to observe a funeral for an elderly woman. The villagers had gathered to a child in the market square just behind the customs office. A score of masked and painted dancers swirled and shimmied, and my host was very proud of them. When we approached, the crowd of spectators gave way and the dancers nearest us smiled and strutted more stridently. A plump girl of about twenty, who was dancing but not costumed, ran up and took both of my hands and invited me to dance. I smiled but declined, nodding at my pack. She grinned and pranced back into the circle.

There were at least a dozen drums of all sizes and the beat was a rigid, frantic one. I saw that some of the young men wore bellbottomed trousers and some of the girls mini-dresses, brightly painted with flowers. Two young men ran alongside us and pounded a small drum decorated with feathers and beads. They followed us 40 paces or so, then snaked their way back to the arena. George spoke to an old woman who seemed to be in a hypnotic reverie. He said that she was the older sister of the deceased. Two younger sisters sat at her side.

We left the wake and walked through streets lined with pastel pinks and blues—colonial-era shanties, many with wide porches which were broken in places, with sections of the floor protruding. They reminded me of Carib houses I'd seen in Belize, Nicaragua and Panama.

In the center of the village near the asphalted highway there were quite a few mammy wagons, each with a biblical name or homily painted over the cab.

JESUS OF MARY
DO NOT BAD. HE SEE
HE KNOW
FORGIVE. BLESS
ZEBEDEE
JOSEPH
ISSAC

My friend's house was a mile from the customs office. Inside was a young teacher and her two small children. She hurried them into the kitchen when we arrived. They were living together, but the children were not his. She had been transferred here from another province, and it was convenient for them to share the house, one of the larger one-story dwellings in the town.

My host had gone to college in Accra and, after graduation, studied a year in London. He was hoping for a better assignment but had been here fourteen months and had had no reply to his several requests for a transfer. The young woman who was cooking our dinner stepped to the kitchen door to report that there was nothing to drink. He apologized, but I offered to buy him a beer later in the town.

"Professionally, I should not accept," he said. "I should not even have you here."

I told him I had thought I might go to Dix Cove. The Peace Corps people in Niger had said it was a superb beach and you could live there and eat fish—all you could hold—for three dollars a day. The problem was that in order to get a visa into Ghana one had to purchase $150 in *cedis,* the local currency, at the official rate. That rate was six to eight times the market value of the currency. The rule was enforced for tourists coming from Abidjan because they came in large numbers on organized tours. At the remote, rural border with Upper Volta, however, the rule was not enforced, and anyone who happened along could get in with no *cedis* at all. The Peace Corps people, long aware of this, always came in that way.

Supper consisted of two courses: a soup of fresh red fish and crab followed by chunks of beef in a spicy hot sauce. Each course was eaten with the fingers directly from a common bowl. The beef was accompanied by a thick starchy cornmeal paste with the texture of plaster which, custom demanded, be swallowed whole without chewing. We ate on the floor in the small bedroom which also served as a kind of den.

"The ship that is on the beach? How did it get there?"

"The English say that the storm blew her in, 1914, I think. The captain, he stay on board even after she hit the beach. When all the crew go, he shoot himself. They bury him in the middle of the main street which is called The Street of Captain Williamson. I will show you the grave."

"But how did such a big ship happen to just run aground? The ocean is pretty big. He must have had plenty of room to maneuver."

"The English say it was only the storm. They say he just couldn't keep it away from the beach or didn't see it."

"But what really happened?"

"The fetish. The spirit that lives in the lagoon. You see, there are two lagoons here. The fetish, he lived in one and he wanted to make love to the female fetish that lived in the other. But he had no way to do this—to travel down to the lagoon. So he drew in the ship with his power and rode it down there."

My host explained that the ship first beached at the point where the lagoon is nearest the surf, about 50 feet. Before morning it had slowly worked its way down to the present position just off the second lagoon. The crew jumped overboard and some were drowned in the surf. The captain was despondent and refused to come ashore. He shot himself the next night.

"You don't really believe all that about the fetish, do you?" I asked, before I could better compose the question.

"Yes, I do—You know, the people here, they celebrate this event every year on the anniversary of the coming of the ship. They say prayers and make gifts of food and jewelry to the fetish."

"How did the fetish get back up into his lagoon?" I asked.

"A fetish have many ways of doing what he want to do," he replied.

When we had finished eating we took a long walk and looked for a place to have a beer. My host was eager to point out that we might not be able to find one, but I had seen several bars in town and could not see a problem.

"Yes, but they only have enough beer to serve to their regular customers," he said.

I didn't understand, but after we had gone to three bars and been turned away I began to be a bit disappointed in my host's clout. Surely the local immigration officer rated a couple of beers. At the fourth place, after an initial rebuff, I explained that I was an American and would tip well for a beer. Whereupon the bartender looked around suspiciously, checked outside, then ushered us into a back room where we sat and drank two rounds of local brew. While my friend went to the restroom, the nephew of the barman came over to the table. I asked him why we had been turned down. He replied under his breath, "He very honest man. He no dash. They do not like him here."

Although I think my friend might have let me go on with a *laissez-passer* if I had insisted, I didn't. The next morning, after a sleepless, muggy night on his front porch, he found me a ride with the bus *ISSAC* the seven miles or so down to where a waterlogged old motor launch chugged people, pigs and chickens across the lagoon to the Ivory Coast. He explained my irregular status to the immigration officer there, who in turn passed me through to the launch.

After returning to Abidjan, I caught the next night's train to Bobo-Dioulasso. There for three days I tried to get a ride to Mopti, on the Niger River in Mali, in time to catch the last steamer of the season to Timbuktu. The border, however, was closed to all except specially licensed traffic, and none was leaving. When I got to Niamey, I learned that the steamer had been docked because of shallow water for over a month.

With greater luck than usual, I hitched in a series of mammy wagons, hadji buses and cattle trucks back to Takeita. There I got a ride with a carrion truck to Matameye. The trip took about a week. It was good to see Jackie and the Mantivelds after six weeks and to see that my jeep was still there. I replaced the air filter and gave it a test run. It was in good shape.

I stayed on in Matameye for about a week, resting, reading and talking to Jackie's students and fellow professors who came by, as usual, to borrow books and talk. Some of them had banking problems, but Jackie had long since mastered the technique of politely saying no. Amusingly, the Nigerian border official reappeared after an absence of several weeks: he had learned that I was back in town.

Mural on a missionary school, Bobo-Dioulasso, Upper Volta.

A funny thing happened when I went to check on the jeep at Keys's. The gate was locked and no one answered my calls, so, pitching my leather pouch onto the wall, I climbed over. But I forgot the pouch. After checking the jeep, I left through the door in the gate, which locked behind me. An hour later Mickery, Keys's handyman and servant, hailed me in the street. He wanted to know if I had just been over at the Mantivelds'. I said yes, how did he know?

"Did you lose something?" he asked. I had to think. "Oh, hell," I had started to say, when he said, *"Portefeuille.* You lost your billfold, man." He had come by just moments after I left and found it lying in the street. The wind must have blown it from the wall. Kids were playing everywhere. That could've been a disaster: over $100, my passport, 15,000 CFA (about $60), credit cards ... I tipped him well.

Jackie was a dedicated teacher. She would stay up until 2:00 or 3:00 in the

Hammed makes peanut butter in the courtyard of Jackie Tierney's Peace Corps house. Matameye, Niger.

morning, sometimes until dawn, correcting homework and writing encouraging notes to her pupils. She would then walk the mile to school and teach until 4:00, returning home to receive the first contingent of visitors.

Jackie's house had one window, which opened off of the front room eastward into the village. By 11:00 the harmattan would begin and Hammed would close the window to keep the house from becoming choked with dust.

Early that last morning—the morning I decided to split and left a note on the refrigerator to Jackie who had gone to Zinder with the Mantivelds—I stood back a few feet and looked into the village for the last time. The door was closed and there was very little light. Two old men and some small boys sat against the house beneath the window, and they were watching, too. We were watching together although they didn't know it. If they had, they would have stood and begged, and the window would have had to be closed.

Looking at the house from the road you would have seen the window as a single dark hole in the long, mud-brown wall of houses. Between the houses and the road was a 100-foot strip of deep sand in which groups of men were huddled, discussing the harmattan. A vendor was hawking among them hard-dried cakes of camel cheese while his three camels sat observing indifferently. A herd of goats straggled about, nibbling on morsels of discarded offal and mangroves and, seemingly, on the sand itself.

Four women stood chatting, their infants straddle-wrapped into the smalls of their backs. They stood apart from the seated councils of men, their visit momentarily interrupted by the intrusion of a bawling tyke, cuffed by a sister who was still defiantly clutching the *cause de guerre*, a plastic white-child doll. The sister pointed toward my window, her moist eyes swollen red with glaucoma, the badge of Sahara childhood. The flies which brought it to her and which would take it to her brother formed a black patch around each eye. From a distance she appeared to have two black eyes. She made a weak effort to wave them away and they moved just enough to dodge her hand and then lit again.

An infant boy crawled by on all fours, cackling, his mouth full of sand. He was attended by an older sister gleefully shouting encouragement. A cowed, emaciated dog, bearing the scars of Muslim outlawry, was wiser than to approach the children and slunk around the corner of the house and out of sight. Koran school boys, clustered beneath a tamarisk tree, began their dutiful incantations of Arab prayers under the watchful gaze of a marabout—their discordant voices a chorus unawares. A hadji bus, its roof stacked with dates and purple cloth and vegetables in rope sacks and goats and coops of chickens arrived from Zinder, drowning my reverie with its engine.

Tuareg camels rest in the market. Matameye, Niger.

CHAPTER VII

Mediterranean Sea

Nile River

Red Sea

CHAD
Lake Chad
Waza National Park
Kano

N'djamena
Fort Foureau
(Kousseri)

NIGERIA
Lagos

Lai
Mondou
Gore

CAMEROON
Yaounde

AFRICA

Atlantic Ocean

Indian Ocean

Baobab tree near Madugeri, Nigeria.

Twelve miles south of Matameye I crossed the border into Nigeria. My visa was to expire the next day, and it was only with the most vehement persuasion that I was able to obtain an entry stamp from the petulant immigration official. Duly admitted, I proceeded to Kano, a city both oppressed and oppressive. The harmattan dust was still a nuisance and provided an eerie backdrop to the din of shrieking horns and sirens, troops of crippled beggars and displaced immigrants from the drought-stricken Sahel.

At night the bedraggled and homeless slept on curbs and in the foyers of those buildings belonging to men who could not afford the robed and sworded Tuareg guards. Such a guard would build a fire on the street in front of the building he was protecting, mosquito netting and mattress just far enough out from the building so that he might catch whatever breeze might stir, yet leave no space for a thief. Windows and doors were locked and shuttered with metal grating.

I met some Canadian surveyors at the Grand Hotel who refused to abandon me to the thieves of the camping. If the thieves didn't get me, they said, the horses would: the camping is a Saturday racecourse. Recently several campers had been trampled during the first race. Racing and show riding are elite sports in Kano, where horsemen are attired in red English riding habits and black caps.

I was most grateful for the Canadians' hospitality and was tempted to linger in the air-conditioned comfort of their retreat, a model suburban home in a tree-lined district of such dwellings kept by Western firms as R-and-R houses for their engineers. My hosts' company was surveying rights-of-way for secondary roads in the Nigerian Sahel northeast of Kano.

Nigeria is in the waning years of its windfall oil boom. It has another twenty years according to some estimates—barely ten, according to others—before the oil runs out. The vast majority of the Nigerian people remain marginal participants in the prosperity, and no alternative economic plans have been made. (The federal budget gets 85 percent of its revenues from oil.)

But in spite of its enormous income relative to the rest of Africa, Nigeria runs one of the continent's largest trade deficits. Government checks so frequently bounce that foreign contractors refuse to pay their workers until the checks have cleared. Several firms have gone broke during months of interdepartmental wrangling over who was responsible for an overdraft. Other checks never arrive or come months late.

Graft and corruption are not only endemic; they are all but officially sanctioned. Every bureaucrat, from border-police chief to cabinet minister, demands his share of dash. Robbery, however, is frowned upon: each Saturday afternoon in the larger cities there are public executions of robbers by shooting. These are held in the local football stadium or on the beach, near Lagos.

If, as the result of a market hue and cry, a suspected thief is caught, his summary execution or mutilation by indignant villagers frequently follows. Revenge killings, by machete, of motorists who strike darting children or other pedestrians are also common. (Hence, the absolute rule: never stop if you hit someone. Proceed to the next town and report only to the federal police.)

During the February, 1977 International Black Cultural Fair in Lagos, suspected pickpockets were seized by the stadium crowd and passed up, row after row, to be thrown to their deaths on the concrete parking lot below. It was finally necessary to stop the program until police with rifles mounted the ramparts. An announcement was read over the public address system: "Please refrain from throwing human beings off the top of the stadium."

Although English is the country's official language, it was difficult, at least in northern Nigeria, to find anyone who could speak or understand English as it is spoken elsewhere. This is especially frustrating when it is seen that local papers and signs are printed in English. How can this be? The answer is that what the natives do speak and understand is "pigdin," which is an unrecognizable derivative of Victorian and colonial English and sounds very similar to (but is not the same as) Carib, the language spoken by Negroes in the Caribbean.

Although French-speaking Africans are sometimes difficult to understand, this is due largely to pronunciation and inflection and not to the fact that they are speaking a different language. Certainly pronunciation and inflection do play a small part in the inability of the average white to understand Nigerian English, but the regular use of run-together phrases and malapropisms has made it, for all practical purposes, another language. This anomaly is partially explained by the fact that British colonial policy did not, until very late, emphasize literacy, formal education being left largely to the missionaries. The French, on the other hand, educated large numbers of middle-level bureaucrats to fill leadership roles the British reserved for white and Indian civil servants. In addition, much of post-colonial French aid has consisted of secondary-school training with heavy emphasis on French language and culture.

Kano was historically, and is today, the southern terminus for the Saharan caravans from Tamanrasset, Agadez and Timbuktu. The giant oil tanker trucks that serve the Sahara south of Algeria ply from here. A growing share of European-Nigerian freight goes between Kano and Marseilles over the trans-Sahara lifeline. Merchants justify the additional cost of the overland route by pointing out that ships are often delayed for months (some over a year) unloading off Lagos. Ships are also easy prey for pirates who lurk in the unpoliced estuaries and marshes of the Nigerian coast disguised as fishermen. A Danish freighter was recently boarded and looted bone clean When her captain sought to intervene he was shot and dumped overboard.

Kano has dozens of filling stations but only one or two will have fuel at the same time and frequently none will have it. In this, the largest of African oil-producing countries, riots over fuel are so common that most go unreported in the local press. Although dealers hoard fuel to sell at quadruple the official price, the chief reasons for shortages at the pump are lack of planning and transportation failures. Tanker trucks are poorly maintained and the drivers are largely untrained as mechanics. Spare parts are often nonexistent, months being required to get a new starter or fuel pump for even a common late-model vehicle. Also, dash diverts shipments from one station to another with such frequency that planning is useless.

When a tanker is rumored to be arriving at a certain station, a line will form there. But there is no orderly advancement: drivers and passengers rush with empty jars and jerry cans to pumps where they fight over the nozzle. Police are assigned to patrol these events but seldom intervene. At Maiduguri, however, two military policemen with rifles effectively limited each customer to five gallons and enforced the rule against filling jerry cans.

A mile-long petrol line delayed my departure here for three days. Eventually, I was granted a visitor's letter from the local chief of police that advanced me to the head of the queue—along with a sergeant to enforce it. I was also exempted from the "no jerry can" rule.

Yet, on the whole, I found the Nigerians an expansive, friendly people. Even the beggars and urchins seemed to share in the national boom-town élan in spite of their not sharing the wealth. People on the street wanted to talk as soon as they heard I was an American. Unlike those in most other places, few wanted to emigrate to the States: a good sign, I thought—commensurate with the newly found pride of a raw, unsettled, rambunctious people on the move. The first question a Nigerian would invariably ask me was what I thought of his country. It was certainly an exciting place in which to live, I would tell him.

The scrub brush of the Nigerian Sahel yielded slowly to the marsh and woodlands of Cameroon's Waza National Park just south of Lake Chad. March's harmattan was in full gale, and it was literally "darkness at noon" when I came to the end of the paved highway near the Nigerian border.

Near Waza the landscape became cratered with small ponds, each with a single resident white heron. Although the ponds flooded over into the surrounding marsh in the summer rainy season, just then (March) they were quite low and fishable: the herons were feasting while families of peasants swept the bottoms with nets and seines. Although most of the fish were eaten locally, an occasional farmer was seen waiting alongside the road with a basket for market.

"Ici bon reparateur de pneu *(Here is a good tire mechanic)." Such mechanics are surprisingly efficient. Garage in Cameroon's Sahel.*

At the end of the blacktop there was a 50-yard-wide sand *piste* which traversed the Waza Park for 25 kilometers into Ford Foureau (now Kousseri) on the Shari River border with Chad. I reached the town just before dark and found the last ferry had already crossed to N'djamena, Chad's capital. It would be morning before another would sail.

Looking around I found the Hotel Logone and Shari, or Chez Magna. Inside was a bright red and yellow poster:

UNION NATIONALE
CAMEROUNAISE
UNION TRUTH DEMOCRACY

The poster showed a rising sun in six sequences, the last being fully risen. The poster was in English and French, since both are official languages. A third, German, is also widely used. Cameroon has the dubious distinction of having been under three colonial masters.

I asked for the least expensive single room and, I am sure, was given it. I drove the vehicle around back and locked it and tried to fall asleep in the windowless, steamy little cubicle. There was a crash. I jumped up, dazed. The empty bottle I had placed in the open doorway as a burglar alarm had rolled under the bed. I tossed away the poncho liner and leaned against the wall. As I did I shone the flashlight into the doorway and, behold: a scrawny rooster cackled, flapped his wings, and flew onto the roof. Arching his head, he let out a shrill crow, then looked down at me, his evil eyes reflected in the flashlight beam. It was 3:30 a.m. I lay back on the iron bed and thought about what a sweltering, humid, depressing night it had been. The room was a natural oven—soaking up heat during the day and holding it well into the night.

On the breeze wafted the sweet-sour stench of garbage and pigs. Unable to doze again, I lay there listening to the rooster scratch and flutter. He crowed again from the far side of the building and then was silent. They most frequently crow after another rooster has crowed nearby. I recalled lying awake on a flatcar at the River Sixaola on the border of Panama and Costa Rica and listening to the "doppler" crowing of the roosters. The crowing began so far away that it was barely audible. Then, as each rooster down the line responded to his neighbor, it became louder and louder, until the one just behind the banana siding crowed the loudest of all. His neighbor picked up the refrain, and his in turn, and so it went until the crowing became again inaudible—then it would come again. Here there was just the one rooster. Perhaps he intimidated the others or it was just too early for them. I dozed, to be finally awakened by sharp staccato voices quarrelling. I tried shutting the door but the heat was insufferable. The argument finally abated and was replaced by the soft chatter of children playing in the garbage. Sounds of morning.

I got up and washed in the pail of water I had been given, which had been drawn from the well adjacent to the garbage pit. A child trailing a crushed metal toy followed me to the toilet next to the well. The others stopped their playing when I emerged and gaped at me with wide, blank stares. Beyond them were several adults, gazing with the same child stares.

I had driven to the end of the road the night before in the red haze of the harmattan. It had ended in the water at the confluence of the Shari and Logone Rivers—abruptly, at the ferry landing. This morning I walked in a wide circle around the town. There were dozens of wide, empty dirt streets. Following one, I came to the town well, situated in a five-pointed intersection. Three men were busily filling five-liter tin pails which had formerly held kerosene. They were carrying these in the manner customary throughout the Sahel, one pail at each end of a shoulder pole.

In the estuary of the Logone there were scores of dugouts and flat-bottomed barges, some with small outboard motors. From several of the dugouts men were fishing with throw nets. Others were ferrying people the mile or so down to the juncture with the Shari, where they beached on the Cameroon side or crossed over to N'djamena. Below, women were washing clothes on a long, narrow slab of rock where a dry creek bed entered the river. The women were slapping their garments on the rock, and the rhythmic sound echoed up the ravine.

The Kousseri ferry was late. As it reached midstream I snapped a picture, provoking howls of protest. The ferryman tried to confiscate my camera, telling me that the ferry was a military installation and that taking pictures was forbidden. He said he would not permit me to board, but when he began motioning others around me I drove on anyway. This caused quite a ruckus, and when we docked on the other side he reported me to the police. I was made to follow the immigration officer to his chief, by whom, after half an hour's wait, I was interrogated.

"You must surrender your passport," he said. Reluctantly I did so, pointing out that my papers were in order and that I had a three-month visa.

"That's no good now," he said. "I will keep your passport here. You will receive a one-week visitor's pass. If you want to travel outside of N'djamena you must apply for a special permit. In the meantime, you will be arrested if you photograph any more military installations."

It took ten days to get the extended travel permit. Luckily I was granted permission to visit Lake Chad itself, which had been denied travelers for many months. I had met a Peace Corps mechanic and two well diggers who had agreed to let me convoy with them to Bol, the only village of any size on the lake. Unfortunately, the mechanic was able to fly out in a military aircraft, and the well diggers suspected me of being with the CIA and left without me.

Chad is another of those geographical abominations, the borders of which were drawn over cognac by European politicians whose other accomplishments included the Polish Corridor and German war reparations.

The borders have little ethnic or topographical relevance and instead reflect the exigencies of European colonial politics. These were usually dictated by the needs of plantation and mine owners and, where it existed, the railroad. Where none of these considerations was imperative, the lines were simply the whims of foreign secretaries or their nameless cartographers. African political reality was ignored.

In Chad, for example, the Toubou of the Tibesti have absolutely nothing in common with the sedentary Sara farmers of the south, from whom are drawn the French-favored officials who rule the country. The borders which dice the Tibesti and Bilma desert homeland of the Toubou in the north and west do not even follow a natural topographical contour.

Neither the Toubou nor the Sara (nor the Ouaddi of central Chad) has any cultural or political bond with the Hadad and Boudouma, who fish the lower Shari and Lake Chad itself. The latter two tribes, together with the Kotoko, have virtually no contact with the government except with tax collectors and functionaries who (in their minds) unjustly tax their fish and attempt to prevent them from trading with the Nigerians across the lake at higher prices. To these people it makes little difference who is in charge of the Department of Fisheries or who is President of the Republic.

The northern four-fifths of the country is Sahel or outright Sahara. Except for the Lake Chad tribes previously mentioned, the only people who live there are the Toubou—and an occasional tribe of Fulani just to the north of the lake.

The tough, no-nonsense, xenophobic Toubou were never conquered by the French. The most that can be said is that there was an occasional stand-off in the main oases and villages of Faya, Zouar and Bardai. Even at the height of French colonial power it took a special detachment of Legion-

Bearers of water near Fort Foureau, Cameroon.

Lepers near Bangor, Chad. Photograph by Sidney Jeffers.

naires operating out of Faya to assure this detente. There is nothing up there but spectacular desert landscape and a few hidden water holes known only to the Toubou. Occasionally an overly adventurous traveler would cross to Fort Lamy from Tripoli and report only friendly contact, but usually the roads were deathtraps, and many disappeared permanently along with their vehicles. This was almost the fate of Madame Francoise Claustre, the famous French anthropologist who was held captive there for three years. She had been released in February of 1977, just before I arrived. Her release was reportedly brought about with the aid of the megalomanic Colonel Qaddafi of Libya, whose "good offices" were used to channel a considerable ransom of French money and arms. The French had previously been unable to secure her release in spite of their having already paid a substantial amount. A detained French commander was executed by the Toubou when an earlier planeload of ransom arms accidentally landed and was seized in Niger. Qaddafi regularly recruits and trains guerillas for the Toubou from among the other nomadic tribes of the Sahara, particularly the Tuareg.

It was Chad's then-governor, Felix Eboue, who led France's African colonies to the Free French standard of de Gaulle in 1940. His heroism is

114

one of the high points of French colonial history. A Haitian, he was a district official at Bangassou in the Central African Empire, then French Equatorial Africa, before being appointed governor of that colony and later Chad. It was from N'djamena (then Fort Lamy) that Leclerc's division marched north to victory in the Libyan desert with the British Eighth Army in 1942. Chad has since held a special place in the hearts of Frenchmen and has been a favored recipient of French aid. Presently French troops maintain the Sara regime, at least in N'djamena, and France is Chad's largest trading partner.

The government's writ does not, however, run north of the road from N'djamena to Mongo-Abéché, and the road itself is subject to frequent ambush and mining by both Toubou and Ouaddi rebels. North of the road is the no man's land where the elusive Toubou move with impunity. In April, 1978, the Toubou had captured the government's last Saharan stronghold at Faya and ambushed a government relief column from Bokara, killing or capturing every one of its 500 soldiers.

Libya, meanwhile, has summarily helped itself to 25,000 square miles of uranium-rich Tibesti land contiguous to its borders on the pretext that the area was ceded to Libya by France in a 1936 treaty with Mussolini. There has been no report of the reaction of Libya's Toubou allies to this seizure.

I checked into N'djamena's Grand Hotel. It was relatively cheap—about $8.50 per night. There was even an air conditioner, although it only ventilated.

The main street, Avenue Charles de Gaulle, was lined with the decaying remnants of colonial-era storefronts. There were one or two bars and raggy boutiques. On one corner a loudspeaker blasted Chuck Berry and Fats Domino from a rock shop, skimpily stocked with T-shirts, blue jeans and denims. There were two general stores on the main street, one run by a young Indian and another by a Lebanese. Each of them sold "feed 'n' seed," cloth and sewing gear. A French-run hardware store sold a wide assortment of modern tools.

There were few people in the street during the day. Most of them were down at the market, a half-mile away, just across from the new Saudi Arabian central mosque. This impressive multi-minareted structure was being built at a cost of $4,500,000 by several hundred local laborers under the direction of Saudi engineers. When completed, it would house not only the mosque itself, but a modern library, classrooms and conference hall.

The market, which begins across the street from the mosque and extends to the river, is a cornucopia of fresh vegetables (many from garden plots or "polders" on Lake Chad). European women prefer its produce and meat to that found in the tidy air-conditioned French stores on the "strip" in the European quarter. Once again, in this market, I saw U.S.-aid grain being sold from its clearly marked sacks. No attempt was made to hide these transactions and there was a long line of buyers. Again, I was in no position to inquire as to the exact origin of the particular grain being dispensed. It did come from sacks stenciled with the shaking hands and the admonition that the grain was not to be sold or exchanged. Perhaps the original grain had

The Sahara Desert near Lake Chad. The only elevation for hundreds of miles, these mysterious monoliths are pocked with small caves.

already been distributed and the sacks refilled with commercial maize, but I doubt it.

Capitaine is the succulent, meaty, catfishlike *poisson* that abounds in the Shari-Logone and in Lake Chad itself. It tastes like the wild river catfish you used to get in Southern restaurants in the United States before they started serving those raised on fish farms with chicken feed.

The best *capitaine*—indeed the best meal in N'djamena—was at the Etoile du Tchad, a Lebanese restaurant that also served a delectable vegetable soup. The *capitaine* filet was cooked in a spice-herb sauce and served with green salad.

The Etoile was a good afternoon rendezvous and writing place. The Lebanese family who ran it and the African waiters were prompt and friendly. The clientele was evenly divided between local mechants and Europeans. Among the Europeans were a number of World Bank and U.S. officials. In poor countries like Chad, even minor officials of such organizations wield considerable power. They are consulted and flattered by government officials as well as other foreign bureaucrats.

The Peace Corps in Chad was reputed to be one of the most effective in Africa. The agency was run by Dick Walls, about 32, who had been there five years. He had an enormous library on the country and Lake Chad in particular, having begun as a volunteer before eventually becoming the salaried director. His budget director was Bob Smith, an amiable but tough black ex-paratrooper. The two made a good team. Well informed, efficient, and courteous, they were highly regarded by volunteers and embassy staff.

Lake Chad is the world's seventh-largest lake. It is surely the strangest, with an average depth of twelve feet and a maximum almost three times that. Sprinkled with tiny floating islands of vegetation, it is the child of the Shari and Logone River systems that drain northcentral Africa. With all that water constantly flowing into it, you'd think it would be full. It isn't, though, because the water is quickly absorbed by the desert or evaporates.

Water from the lake actually seeps through the Sahara for hundreds of miles, providing a northwardly extending water table under the sand sea of Bilma at depths of up to several hundred feet. The level of the water table varies, depending upon the terrain. It is not a gradually descending level, in other words. No one knows exactly how far the table extends since no hydrographic chart has been made.

Peace Corps well diggers, however, had a good idea how close the table ran to the lake. I visited at length one morning with two of them who were about to return to the field. The problem with modern wells, one told me, is that if they are too efficient they deplete the water table. Once the water is pumped out and the table has fallen, it will not naturally rise again. In addition, if the people don't maintain the wells, they eventually clog up, the pipes rust through, and they have to be replaced. They had not been able to train the natives to maintain and repair them, so the well diggers had to go out and do it themselves.* They follow a routine inspection-and-maintenance circuit and were just about to leave on one. They invited me to convoy with them as far as Bol, but when my travel permit came the next day, they had departed without me. I was told confidentially by another volunteer that they had suspected that I was with the CIA or one of the oil companies contending for drilling rights in the lake. A man alone is suspect.

Unable to find anyone going to Bol, and there being no military convoy, I decided to try taking a natron barge. A half dozen cross the lake weekly when the river is floatable. I walked up and down the bank but the farthest any of the barges there were going was to Mani near the mouth of the Shari.

It was very early and there was the faintest wisp of fog rising from the river. Morning life along the bank had begun, although a few late sleepers lay wrapped in blankets under upturned dugouts. Out on the river, boatmen poled early risers to the Cameroon side. In one pirogue a man was beating a goat which had loosened the rope with which it was bound. The animal was trying to jump into the river. The other passengers looked on passively. Upstream two muscular young men were fishing with throw nets deftly thrown overhead with wide, circular motions. A dozen naked adolescents had waded into the river among the barges to take their morning baths.

At the top of the bank the chants of Moslem prayers rose above the bustle

---

*There is a third problem: dependence upon a Peace Corps well often leads to neglect of a traditional well which is then useless when the new well breaks down.

of early commerce, as sacks of maize and vegetables were hauled down to the sausage-shaped, flat-bottomed river boats. When they can cross the lake, such barges ferry natron from Bol and Baga Sola, further to the north. Natron, or saltpeter, is used for consumption by both humans and animals. It is dug out of pits and fashioned into slabs like biblical tablets.

The mineral has a ready market in Nigeria and Cameroon, where it is transported by large semis and dozens of smaller trucks from the stockpile of slabs on the river bank. But when the boats stop running, so do most of the trucks. Some trucks belonging to SODELAC (Societe de Development du Lac), the government-sponsored co-op, ply the sand tracks between N'djamena and Bol, but the trip takes a week (both ways, including loading) and is not economical for commercial haulers.

I continued along the bank until I came to the barge *El Hadj Boo,* where a boy of twelve was heaving aboard sacks of grain. Alongside sat a dozen passengers with their bundles of personal belongings. One of them said that this very barge would go to Bol if the captain thought he could get through. It might leave that afternoon. The captain, however, was not there, and no one knew where he was. Encouraged, I walked on until I came to a fancy boat dock guarded by two sentries with sten guns. The hull of a speedboat moored there bore the seal of the United States Ambassador. In the cruiser next to it, an obese African in dark glasses sat in an olive canvas deck chair, casting with a rod and reel. His shirt read, "Bert's Dairy Queen, Highway 10 South." The guards did not appreciate my presence—nor that of the inevitable entourage of waifs in my train. Climbing the bank again, I spied a truck driver stretched out in his cab, apparently asleep.

"Bonjour."

His name was Pascal. He was from Yaoundé, in Cameroon. He knew the captain of the barge I had seen and would take me to see him. He locked his truck, and we walked for half an hour through streets I had not seen, although by then I thought I had explored the city thoroughly.

The morning came down one of those warm, cool, silken mornings where the spirit and the sunlight mingle, then burst together into a great wide smile. We walked down shaded passageways of gum arabic and red dirt streets dank with the sweet-sour stench of sewage and pigs behind walls. We saw people with dark leather skin and people with fair brown skin, spirits veiled in wind-danced cottons of red, white, purple and green, and naked elfin children playing at stick-wheel—the ubiquitous game of African childhood from the Niger to the Limpopo. The long dirt street stretched out beyond the eye's ken, the street itself a great wide smile, so that ahead you could see the spirits of the people walking, heads nodding toward you and away from you, and the children at stick-wheel. The pink-rust minarets of the mosque peeped through the harmattan, now blurring our eyes ever so slightly. Pungent musk and camel dung ambushed our nostrils—And through the arabesque, we heard the fleeting laughter of children and the coarse honest voices of the market.

We inquired at several mud houses before finally locating the captain. He was reserved but courteous, a light-skinned man with a short white beard. He was playing chess on a stump under a tamarisk tree with another barge captain. He said that no barges were able to make Bol because of the sand islands but that I could get to Baga Sola just north of Bol on the *Souay Bou*, which would leave from Mani the next day at noon. I was to tell the captain, one O-Maroe, that El Hadji Souay Bou had told me that I could ride *gratuit* (free).

This was, then, my best chance of seeing the lake. The problem was to get to Mani before noon the next day. I knew I could leave my rig with Phil Infilise, the Peace Corps ichthyologist, and his wife, Alice. They had been most hospitable and told me that if I was able to find a boat they would keep the jeep in their walled-in yard. I had not known how long I would be gone and certainly could not leave the vehicle unattended at Mani. A government convoy had been ambushed near there just a few days previously and there was a lot of guerilla activity in the area.

I thanked the captain and bade him farewell. Pascal then took me to the small market where the buses departed for Mani and other towns to the north. We breakfasted at the Etoile du Tchad where I treated Pascal (who never once asked for a gift) to *capitaine* and eggs.

Checking out of the hotel and leaving the jeep with Phil and Alice, I went to the terminal. Although a bus was rumored to be leaving at any moment, none appeared. Some soldiers came late in the afternoon and checked papers. The sergeant said that there had been another ambush and a holdup of a bus near Mani that morning and that a passenger had been kidnapped. About that time, I decided that discretion was the better part of valor and that Lake Chad would best be left for another day.

When I returned to the Infilises to get the jeep, Alice suggested that I might talk one of the pilots of the French flying club into taking me up. She and some of the other embassy wives had taken lessons there, and some of the pilots, she said, were quite good.

Jean Guy Gaynard had been a freight pilot for the Free French in northern Africa during the war. He now worked with the Red Cross and had been stationed here for the past six months. I didn't know it, but this was also his first flight over Lake Chad.

We headed down the Shari toward its mouth, soon sighting the Cameroon village of Goulfey and the hamlets of Dougia and Mani on the Chadian side. I counted eleven barges at Mani, one of them perhaps the *Souay Bou*, if it had not already sailed. Mani was not particularly large, maybe 300 people. There were other, smaller villages on to the north—each consisting of a few huts and a tin-roofed grain bin and police shack. The land in-between was barren except for an occasional stand of scrub brush.

Tugging at my sleeve, Jean Guy pointed to the northeast where, far on the horizon, loomed the four peaks of Hadjer el Hamis, the weird rock cluster which is the only elevation for hundreds of miles. Guiding ourselves by the monoliths, we flew above the river's mouth, which had by now diverged into tentacles of narrow channels snaking through thick marsh. Just to the east of the delta was the village of Karal, from which a dirt track wound toward the rocks of Hadjer, now some twelve miles in the distance. It

119

was hard to tell where the lake began and the marsh ended, except for black patches here and there which, upon closer inspection, were corrals of cattle.

Arriving at the elevations, we circled the rocks slowly at very low altitude. One had a gaping crevice, almost a cave. *What a splendid place to explore,* I thought. Finally turning toward Bol, our target, we headed on an azimuth of 340 degrees. The marsh now so completely carpeted the lake that we only knew it was there from the flickering reflection of the sun on the water beneath the vegetation.

After twenty minutes or so, we began seeing the first sand islands, extensions of the desert which oddly ran parallel to each other from northwest to southeast. There were hundreds of them, mostly deserted, although on the larger ones neat circular villages of the Boudouma appeared well above the water line. Invariably, attached to each settlement was a corral. Here and there between the islands drifted a solitary pirogue, some quite far from any village.

There now opened beneath us and to our front an almost uninterrupted horizon of blue, open water. Twice I saw what appeared to be large round-shelled turtles swimming on or near the surface. Once I saw a school of long, carplike fish. They were probably *capitaine.* It was revealing that the lake does, in fact, become an open body of water: I had heard from many that it was almost entirely marsh and the so-called "floating islands" of shrubs and other plants for which the lake is famous. You can go to sleep on one facing one direction and wake up facing another.

We flew at about 500 feet—although Jean Guy would dip in very low whenever something looked particularly interesting on one of the islands. As we approached Bol, the polders on the sand islands became more prominent. Polders are paddylike gardens in patches of rich subsoil between which are banked and diked sand dunes to keep the lake from flooding them when it rises. Every third year the water is permitted to enter the polders to replenish the soil. When the lake recedes, the dike is restored and the retained water slowly evaporates. The soil is very fertile and will produce two or three crops of corn or wheat a year. An increasing portion of the grain marketed in N'djamena comes from the polders of Bol and Baga Sola to the northwest.

As we came over the landing strip we saw that it was occupied by a herd of goats. Although we repeatedly dipped our wings, the strip officer—or whoever he was—made no attempt to disperse the animals but merely waved his arms up at us excitedly, I suppose to tell us that there were goats on the runway and we shouldn't land. While the goats were still contentedly grazing on the third pass, we circled the village once again and headed back toward N'djamena. We took an azimuth of 170 degrees until Hadjer el Hamis was once again in sight. From there we followed the river to the city. We had to hold for fifteen minutes for the takeoff of a Sudanese Boeing 747 and a Chadian Army DC-3.

The entire flight had lasted under four hours, but I had been able to see a wide area of one of nature's most unusual lakes. It is my hope someday to return and drive around the lake and northwards across the sand sea of Bilma. The region is one of the least explored on our planet and, with hostilities abated, future study will doubtlessly reveal much of geological and cultural import. While we were over the lake it occurred to me that there was something instrusive, presumptuous about our being there looking down upon these people. Most of them would never leave the lake; a good many would never see even the village of Bol.

One night at the Oasis Bar, the local watering hole for "good ol' boys," I met some American and British geologists working for a survey firm under contract to Conoco. They were looking for oil in Lake Chad. Rumor was they'd found it, but they weren't saying and I didn't ask.

They had a rest house in a building behind the bar, and one night they invited me up for dinner. When the conversation turned to the perils of the desert, one recounted how a drilling crew he was with once camped in a *draa* in the southern desert of Aden. As they were washing up they saw lightning in nearby mountains. Abruptly, the crew chief ordered them to break camp. They complained bitterly, but the chief replied that those who wanted to drown could stay behind. "Drown? You must be joking!"

Still, everybody packed up, and in fifteen minutes they had made it up the ridge. The sky was clear, showing stars, a full moon—not even a breeze. Suddenly, from the direction of the mountains came a phantom shadow down the *draa*, and in seconds, a wall of water ten feet high rushed through their abandoned campsite. The next morning, when they returned, the sand was as bleached and dry as when they'd left.

Before leaving N'djamena, I went by to say so long to my friend Basher, the garrulous little Syrian who ran the *souflaki* stand on the small unpaved side street between the hotel and the U.S. Embassy.

Basher was one of those free spirits who by happenstance had found his way to this forgotten corner of the planet and made a good living—and a good many friends—by selling tender, juicy mutton sandwiches dashed generously with fresh lettuce and onions and served, at the customer's choice, with one of two hot sauces, each of which was so hot you had to just barely touch the bread with the back of the spoon. I took mine emphatically *sans sauce.*

All the Peace Corps workers, embassy staff and Europeans in general knew Basher and ate at his sandwich stand. He served cold beer, which would be fetched quickly by his young Sara apprentice (who put too much hot sauce on the sandwiches he made). The beer was kept in an ancient French icebox in the tiny alcove where Basher lived in the house behind the stand.

Each night Basher would hold court on everything from deep-sea fishing to leggy Paris fashions (he disapproved), carefully, of course, avoiding local politics.

Basher had no patience with Arab politicians who he said spent too much time stirring up trouble against Israel in order to distract their people's attention from local economic problems. He was a favorite among the young Peace Corps volunteers and had collected many addresses toward that future day when his road would lead him to America.

121

Basher would not let me pay for my last two sandwiches, nor for the round of beers I ordered for my Peace Corps friends.

As I was leaving town, Peace Corpsman Steve Toy flagged me down. He was returning to his teaching post at Mondou and needed a ride.

The day was uneventful until, just the other side of the village of Mislippi on the road to Lai, we encountered an old woman with bottle-cap lips. Her lips had been stretched out over an inch so that they looked like two small saucers. Into each saucer had been affixed in some manner a Coke bottle cap. On her head she carried a five-gallon pail of smelly dried minnow-sized fish which she had been seining in a marsh nearby. Several other old women were still stooped and wading in the reeds.

Could I photograph her? I asked, to which she agreed. Then I motioned: a ride? Of course. Steve got out and helped her up, passing up her bundles and a little tin kettle of milk which she placed inside the pail of fish. She frowned as the engine started—wary. Then came a wide, toothless smile as she watched what it would have taken her an afternoon to walk whiz by in twenty minutes. It was twelve miles to her village and as we turned off the road onto the path she clapped with glee, knocking over her pail. The nauseating stench of raw fish and sour milk reeked through the jeep.

It was a poor village. The people who ran to meet us were drawn, hollow-eyed and emaciated. The children had protruding bellies.

The young men of the village, after some hesitation, came to take us away. We resisted politely but shook hands all around. The old woman's family bade us return to their area, which we did, sitting just outside her hut.

A young woman, surely her daughter, sat well away from the others, resignedly tending a puny, skeletal infant. How much longer this child could have lived I do not know, but it was obvious that he was dying. I asked the oldest boy if the mother had taken the child to the *medecin*. He only smiled.

Could we take him and his mother to Mondou? I pronounced it slowly, pointing first at the baby and then at the jeep. They all laughed politely, not understanding my gesture. Only the younger men still had teeth at all, and their front teeth were missing. I pointed at the child again and again at the jeep and said the word: "Mon-dou." Again, they just laughed, a sort of nervous, good-natured laugh, and shook their heads.

We sat on a mat which our recent passenger placed for us under a straw lean-to next to her hut. She disappeared inside and emerged with another, larger pot of milk than the one she'd spilled. It was creamed and she made a kind of doughy, plaster paste with some millet flour and poured it into bowls and offered it to us. We thanked her but declined, rubbing our stomachs to say we had already eaten. I was about done in from the fish-milk stench and doubted that I could have survived even a ceremonial tasting of her concoction. She smiled and withdrew the bowls, placing them carefully to one side. She continued to gesticulate her gratitude for the lift we had given her and for our being there with them.

These people were of the Massa tribe. Some members have even more greatly distended lips, which result in platter mouths several inches in diameter. The distortions are begun by their mothers or other village women when the daughters are still infants. The mutilation is designed to make them sexually appealing. I wondered whether lip ornaments were changed from time to time since pop-bottle caps had probably been unavailable in this woman's childhood. Still, appearances are deceptive and maybe she only *looked* 80 years old.

We cleaned out the jeep as best we could with some old newspapers in the floorboard. As we discarded the papers, they were seized by the young men. They would make good kindling for their fires.

The old woman was very happy with her fish and sour milk. She was proud of her family and her village and of her ability to repay our hospitality with her own.

We stopped at Lai to ask directions for the better road to Mondou. There were two roads and each had recently been flooded; we wanted the one least damaged.

Steve knew some Italian engineers who lived at Lai, and we stopped to visit. They lived in a well-equipped four-house complex with electric power provided by a portable generator. They were building a canal under contract with the World Bank. It was a pilot project designed to drain off flood waters from the Lagone River and irrigate local rice land. If the project was successful, other canals would be dug. Steve and I went out and inspected the project and it was formidable indeed, being some 50 yards wide and 20 feet deep and stretching 40 kilometers.

We were told that "the monk," a large gregarious priest, was the source of all road information. We found him at his monastery on the outskirts of Lai protected by a six-foot-high fence and a fierce German shepherd. He told us that we must cross the ferry at Lai and take the back road to Mondou. It was marked as difficult on the Michelin map, but the main road was, he said, impassable. The mission had lost two vehicles (broken springs) on it in the past month. We crossed the ferry and, although the road was bad, it was not as rough as we expected, and we made Mondou by nightfall. About halfway there, we were approached from the rear by a cloud of dust which, I surmised, was a police or military vehicle. I pulled over and as he passed we saw it was a new, chauffeur-driven, white Mercedes sedan: it was the Russian math teacher at Bangor on his way home!

We stayed that night on the porch of the Peace Corps house at Bangor— one of two graceful, dilapidated colonial homes on the banks of the Lagone. (Two Russian teachers share the other. They were invited to dinner but never came. They rarely did, Steve said.)

We made Mondou the next night at 8:00, and Steve and his roommate, Yves Robinson, a physics teacher and devout Quebecois, prepared an outstanding meal of rice and roast beef.

Before leaving the next morning, I went to the local brewery at the invitation of the amiable director, M. Georges Depachtere. The name of the brewery is Brasserie du Logone, the home of Gala Deluxe, an export beer. Mondou is the third-largest city in Chad, and Gala is its largest employer. The plant, a Heineken subsidiary, employs 250 local people, from the control laboratory staff (two young French-educated black chemists) to about 40 conveyor belt workers who bottle and cap the brew and cull rejects. As with most national brews, Gala enjoys a government monopoly, but I was unable to learn how much revenue it generated.

In the plant, I saw a forest of bright steel pipes and churning vats. Whirring dials and gauges showed the temperature, pressure and elapsed time of each batch. Here and there white-jacketed African attendants methodically inspected a gauge, adjusted a valve. One wrote intensely on a yellow clipboard. Another disconnected a great striated metal hose from one vat and secured it to another. Through a porthole you could see the frothing yellow liquid.

"This one now, 350 degrees," Georges said. "This batch should be about ready." The air was laden with the sweet dank odor of freshly spilled beer.

Back at the lab, I was left with one of the chemists. In excellent French he lectured me on the processes of zymurgy. Just then, he said, he was about the very important business of controlling the alcohol content of the batch I'd just seen. Gesturing to a test tube of beer, he added a blue solution. Sometimes, he said, it gets up to six, seven or even ten percent. "This is absolutely forbidden," he emphasized. "So we must make sure that it is no greater or less than 4.6 percent."

"Why 4.6 percent?" I asked.

Company doctors in Amsterdam, he replied, had determined that that was the medically allowable limit. Beyond that the average person becomes intoxicated before he has drunk his fill. In any event, it was now a government regulation. I did not pursue it further.

In August and September, when the river is high, the bottled beer is shipped by barge to N'djamena. At other times it is shipped by truck over the bad roads we had just traveled. Beer travels badly by any means, but especially by rocky road. Accordingly, the beer in N'djamena is flat and sour. The beer at the Brasserie was mellow, almost like Heineken itself. The director took me out behind the plant and showed me a damp and heavily shaded tin-roofed pen. Inside were five fat and smiling hogs. They were fed on the dregs and a little of the barley. "The French," Georges said, "must always have their pork."

Back at the office, Georges and I each had a small glass of his product. He then produced a dozen glasses boldly stenciled "Gala" in red and told me they would come in handy at the border. I filled my canteen with fresh water and Georges had a steward fill my bucket with ice. It was good to have cold water for the half-day it lasted.

I drove on south, reaching the border at Gore at 1:00 p.m. I did not see the barrier until I was right on top of it, whereupon I was arrested for speeding and disrespect. In another second I should have been shot, they told me.

Being the first overland traveler in some time, I provided relief from their boredom.

"Did you not see the sign?"

"Yes. And I stopped immediately."

They said I was going 80. I said I was going 30. And so it went. Finally, I produced the glasses, which they condescendingly accepted. Still, I was kept for an hour and permitted to go only on condition that I carry along a fur-loughed robber. He had just done three years of a six-year term in Mondou, he said, "for political offense." During our conversation he explained that he had looted the local party's kitty. He was going to Bassangoua in the Central African Empire to visit his family.

CHAPTER VIII

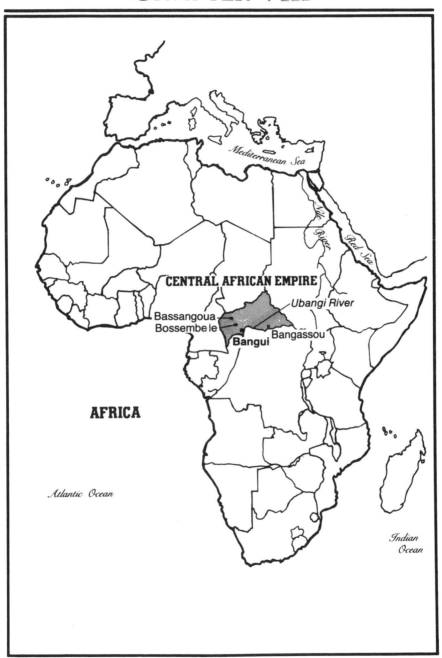

Mediterranean Sea

Nile River

Red Sea

CENTRAL AFRICAN EMPIRE

Ubangi River

Bassangoua
Bossembe le

Bangui

Bangassou

AFRICA

Atlantic Ocean

Indian
Ocean

Termite mound near Bossembele, Central African Empire.

The hitchhiker grinned. He was glad to be out of Chad. Where would he go now? He didn't really have a family in Bassangoua, he said. He was going to Bangui and try his luck there. It had begun to rain, and as the rain increased we fell silent. Tall, deep stands of timber appeared—beneath them knee-high red earth mounds: termite hills. An old woman sat on one of them, to her side a burden of wet straw and a net sack full of her belongings. She seemed to pay no attention to the rain. I thought of the old woman with the bottle-cap lips.

In Central Africa, if one arrives after noon at a border post he cannot pass until the police have finished their *dejeuner*—an annoyance taught by the French and suffered by every American who has visited Paris.

At the border post of Bemal the immigration officer, an obese captain in neatly pressed khakis, was eating his lunch under some nearby trees and lecturing loudly to some soldiers. After half an hour, I walked over, presented my passport and asked him if it would be possible for us to pass. At this he exploded with a lecture on how soldiers were not to be inter-rupted during their meal. When I asked how much longer that would be, he said, "When our business is finished here." When he finally did adjourn his dinner and re-open his post we were each made to produce our every item of equipment (including spare parts) for his personal inspection. It was 5:30 before we drove away.

As night approached the foliage became more dense and, although there were still wide stretches of sand and scrub brush, it was obvious that a major watershed had been crossed. It began again to rain and it must have continued without letup for two hours. When it finally lifted (as we crossed a rickety bridge and headed up the other side of a draw) a great swarm of moths suddenly descended upon us from the forest. Their bodies caked the windshield so that it was impossible to see. I managed to stop and, getting out, attempted to scrape them off, but to no avail. In a moment they had covered my body as well, down my back, in my eyes and mouth—I even swallowed one. Fighting to the front of the jeep, I saw that they had clogged the radiator grill. Rolling down his window, the hitchhiker called for me to turn off the headlamps. I did as he suggested and in no time they had risen above us. I scraped the windshield and we continued on for many minutes without lights, the eerie, humming sound of the moths quite audible above the sound of the engine. I had never seen anything like it. Suddenly, when we reached the top of the hill and started down the other side, they disappeared as quickly as they had come.

We had just left the moths behind us when there was a flash of fur and an ominous thud. My guest became agitated and called for me to stop. As I did, he jumped out and ran back into the night searching for whatever it was I'd hit. Moments later, he reappeared holding a dead rat by the tail. I could not believe it, and it took me several moments to realize that this fellow was going to put the thing in the jeep. When I protested he looked at me askance and replied: *"On mange bien ca* (This is really good eating)." I only relented when he began wrapping it in a shirt he pulled from his bundle. Even then I didn't fancy the idea of hauling around a dead rat, particularly one that size.

"What is it called?" I asked as we drove away.

"Cee bee cee (CBC),"* he replied. I later learned that in fact the people eat these regularly and that even some missionaries find them delectable.

Bossembele was about 150 miles south of the border. There was a steep hill just before the town, at the top of which burned a single electric light. A young man there directed us to the local Peace Corps house, to which I had been referred by Steve Toy in Mondou. Someone had run ahead to say a strange *blanc* was in town. I could see the improbable Americans in the light from their front room, standing like suspicious hill folk on the porch. A tall gent had his hands slung skeptically in his suspenders. Beside him was a woman in a long calico dress. Dave and Nancy, "urban planner," my guide said. Although he had taught English the first year, he had taken the new job when they changed the billet. She taught English at a town near Bangui. They were polite but guarded as they offered dinner. I accepted. I slept in the front room on the floor on my air mat. My hitchhiker found a place at an African house up the road. Did he want to leave his things in the jeep still? Yes. There was an orchestra of frogs and crickets, and I slept well.

I was up as usual at first light, retrieved several bananas from a cache in the back of the jeep and went for a walk. Nothing. Not even a dog. Crickets quiet. Silence. The bananas were the short fat kind, very sweet. I lay back on the air mattress and two hours later awoke with the sun in my face through the front door.

A visiting volunteer from Bangui needed a ride back to his post and I obliged. He had traveled the road several times before and knew, he said, some interesting side trails, including one that led to some remote but beautiful falls. The hitchhiker had, meanwhile, decided to stay over for a few days—perhaps to prepare his "CBC" while it was still fresh.

Dave and Nancy asked that we stay for lunch. The Russian teachers were coming, two shy, stout ladies about 26 (Eva) and 38 (Natasha): portraits of peasant earnestness. We spoke in French, which facilitated yet softened their evasive answers concerning their training in the Soviet Union and

---

*My phonetic spelling of the French pronunciation of the Latin "zibethica," or muskrat.

politics there. We didn't press, out of a kind of implicit honoring of detente—except that on one occasion I did briefly pursue the subject of freedom of immigration as an incidental follow-up to a question concerning Natasha's relatives. Natasha smiled and asked Nancy where she had bought the onions. For some reason onions were very hard to get in Bossembele.

They had been teaching Russian and mathematics here for a year and a half. The tour of duty is two years with no vacation. We talked at length about Dostoevski and other presumably innocuous nineteenth-century writers we had all read. They were interested in my trip, especially the Sahara. How had I managed to cross the desert alone? Was it dangerous? Wasn't I afraid? While they talked I wondered why Russians never visit foreigners alone. There are always at least two of them.

When saying goodbye, Natasha presented a gift for each of us from her handbag. Mine was a miniature wooden bear which I later cemented to the top of the dashboard. It stayed there until the Cape of Good Hope. No one would believe a Russian math teacher in the Central African Empire had given it to me. I reciprocated with two of the Tuareg bracelets I had brought along from Agadez. They seemed pleased with them.

The Bangui volunteer and I, and the lingering odor of "CBC," left right after the Russians, passing the rest of the day through more of the same savannah of red earth and termite mounds. Occasionally there were small stands of timber.

We made Bassangoua after nightfall and searched for an hour for the Catholic mission through hilly streets lined with white-waisted mangrove trees. Finally, we found it—a long wood-and-stone ranch-style building with an autocratic African maitre d'. The rooms were tidy and comfortable and outside were model gardens of greens and corn. The barnyard thrived with hogs and fowl. Among the latter were several score of white turkeys and a flock of guineas.

The generator stopped running at 10:00 p.m. and we lit the candles provided by the steward. We had just prepared for bed when two scruffy white cats appeared on the window ledge. They meowed incessantly and climbed through. I offered the remains of some canned sardines, but they were not hungry. When they absolutely refused to cease their monotonous whining, I doused them with the pail of water on the washstand. This had to be repeated twice before they finally got the message.

After a couple of cups of hot Nescafe on the hood of the jeep, we headed into the morning. We passed groups of hunters in taut loincloths, each carrying an identical four-foot shaft with a metal spear point at each end. The top point was about six inches long and jagged, the other about two inches and straight. Alongside each hunter was a lean, short-haired white dog with black spots. This was the first time I had seen men and dogs hunting. Islam was now far behind.

The next morning I walked from the center of Bangui toward the heights overlooking the town and the Ubangi River. There was a mist hanging low in the first rain forest since the Ivory Coast. The potholed Avenue Valéry Giscard d'Estaing led past the once ostentatious but now decrepit colonial administration building. Two guards with submachine guns loafed at the gate but stiffened as I approached. Above the fountain in the roundabout at the avenue's intersection with an unpaved street was a bronzed likeness of His Majesty, the Emperor Bokassa I, emperor of the Central African Empire.* The likeness was rusted and beginning to crack. The expression on the face was neither imperial nor menacing but decidedly indifferent. No water seemed ever to have run from the dirt-caked apertures of the fountain. One of those pink, rubbernecked vultures that are as common here as pigeons in other parts glided down as if to alight on the Emperor's shoulder, but thought better of it and flew away. A hundred yards further on, the street ended in a hill path through towering mahogany and iroko.

The higher I climbed, the greater the number and colors of butterflies I saw, offering the greatest concentration of them I had seen. They were gathered on every residue of moisture, especially fresh dung. You could tell where an animal had been by their clusters.

The trail was not well traveled, and I had to remove fallen boughs from it occasionally to pass. Once, like some fabled toadstool gremlin, I sat on a termite mound and watched droplets of dew sparkle like pearls in an enormous spider's web. In the shadows an occasional frog or cricket chirped away. Softly, the sun peeked through the holes in the second canopy of the forest, changing dark colors to hues of red and orange as it advanced. A red caterpillar crawled along the trunk of a tree where some butterflies hovered over fresh droppings.

I was awakened from my reverie by a spindly old African in khaki shorts with a butterfly net. He was walking up a trail, to the left, and did not see me. He stared transfixed at the congregation of butterflies; then in the flash of a frog's tongue he hooped them all in his net. Painstakingly, he cupped them in his hands and pressed them into pre-arranged triangular folds of note-book paper. Later, he would set them into various designs on cardboard and sell them in the Bangui market.

I was in Bangui about four days—just long enough to see some rust scraped off the undercarriage, a coat of tar and a lube job. About a block from the riverfront I found the Bangaise, a watering hole from the '50s famous for its backbar mural of an Arctic fishing scene: Eskimos, penguins, icebergs.

---

*Bokassa was officially "coronated" the following December in a comic-opera Napoleanic pageant of gilded thrones, golden coaches and ermine robes studded with mother-of-pearl. The cost: $30,000,000—more than the country's entire budget. (Annual per-capita income is $110.) Bokassa was one of the linchpins of French policy in Africa, due to the nation's vast potential mineral wealth (uranium, diamonds, copper) and strategic location. President Giscard d'Estaing frequently visited for hunting safaris and summit meetings with Francophone chiefs of state, particularly Mobutu of Zaire, a close relative and ally of Bokassa's. An ex-French army sergeant, Bokassa served in Vietnam and Algeria before returning to Bangui following independence in 1960. In 1966 he deposed his predecessor, who is now his successor.

The place is a hangout for upper-level bureaucrats. Younger Africans and Peace Corps volunteers patronize the New Palace Bar on the nearby roundabout.

The current of the Ubangi here was swift, and there were many whirlpools. Natives who plied the river did so close to the bank. There was a car ferry over to the direct road to Kisangani, but according to the American Embassy the road was far worse than the alternative route from Bangassou to Kisangani in the northeast.

I met a Hawaiian Peace Corps girl in a shop in Bangui where I had gone to try, unsuccessfully, to find some mailers. She was waiting outside: could she ride to Bangassou? Of course.

Before leaving town we made the required checkout through the central police station. Just that morning I had learned from some Australians that you had to have a special permit to circulate. There was a five-day wait and a fee of twenty dollars, if you were lucky. I decided to try without it. It worked. I was never asked for anything except my regular papers—and the Empire had police barricades and *controles* every twenty miles. These were red and white poles lowered across the road like railroad crossing barriers. They were always down. The official in charge would be far away in his hut. You had to stop, get out your papers and go find him. If you got there between 12:00 and 3:00 (or worse, after dark), you were usually out of luck. *Controles* also serve as rain barriers. After a rain, heavy vehicles are held up—perhaps for days—until the road hardens, although small vehicles with four-wheel drive are usually allowed to pass.

The first night we made Banbari, an old cotton- and peanut-barge port on the Ouaka River. The Ouaka is just wide enough to be navigable down to the Ubangi, 70 miles to the south—a two-day float. The town's several crumbling, colonial-era stores were virtually empty of provisions although there were a few cans of beans and bags of macaroni, some dried milk, and Mocaf beer. There was a bar, a half-acre terrace surrounded by six-foot-high plank fence. A hi-fi blared Cameroon rock to a houseful of young Africans in slacks and tight dresses.

A mile down a narrow track along the east bank of the river were the remnants of a peanut-oil mill built in the 1920s, its rusted wheels and gears long since fallen into disuse. It now served as a goat barn and a playground for the children of the grade-school principal who lived just above in the miller's house. A hundred yards back was another house shared by the town's Peace Corps volunteers, then on a visit downriver. As elsewhere, it was customary for volunteers to use each other's houses. My companion found the key and I set up the stove and camping gas on a little concrete porch and cooked some beans and stew. We'd picked up a couple of Mocafs at the bar.

The inside of the house was warm, friendly, lived-in. A generous library of paperbacks rested on rock and plank shelves. A friendly note: "If you take one, please leave one—thanks."

I slept on a cot in the larger bedroom next to an open window facing the river. You could hear the swift current swirling against the bank. Early in the morning the frogs and crickets quit and the mosquitoes came, their frenzied, high-pitched drone drowning all other sounds. A swarm of vampires they were, and with a mechanical thoroughness they probed for the slightest tear or stretch in the net. I felt quickly for the loose ends and tightened the net down under the mattress, being careful not otherwise to touch it, since they bite at the slightest point of contact. At first light the mosquitoes vanished, their drone replaced by the clucking and crowing of the principal's chickens. Oddly, my companion had slept in the room at the end of the hall, not 40 feet away, and likewise at an open window, but with no net, and she had only one or two bites.

I made coffee and savored the rich dank smoke from a smoldering trunk on the river bank where someone had burned away high grass and a few trees with it. Two bank fishermen were throwing lines into the river from beneath dateless palms. It was a sultry, humid morning.

Pavica was a coffee plantation run by M. Bichet. He had been there 25 years. His wife and children waved at us from the porch of the old plantation house, she in a long calico dress and the towheaded kids running about in native clothing. Some 50 African workers were in the yard waiting to get paid. He said the price of coffee would stay high until April, 1979, when it would fall. He was wrong.

All along the road now were acres and acres of coffee, bananas and rice. The Chinese had come ten years ago to teach rice harvesting. They'd built levees and paddies in the lowlands. The results were bumper rice crops for several years. But then the Chinese and the Emperor (then President-For-Life) Bokassa had a falling-out, and they left. The paddies had gone to seed.

The night before the falls, we stayed at Kempe at the Catholic mission. My companion knew one of the sisters, and she provided us with bunks and a shower for a small fee. That night on the way back from eating mantioc in the village we took the wrong path around the mountain. By chance we came to the hut of the mayor. He gave us his son and a lantern, and the boy guided us back to the mission. Singing was coming from the chapel, and we stood at the door and listened to a choir of some twenty white-frocked twelve-year-olds. I have rarely heard such superb exaltation.

The Twin Falls at Kempe on the Kotto River look deceptively inviting. One sees them first from the narrow, dilapidated bridge at a distance of some 500 yards. There are two narrow chutes: a single falls on the left about 100 feet high and, on the right, a series of six, the first perhaps 60 feet and the others half that. Just east of the bridge are tracks which lead out to a shalelike shelf overlooking the right, or east, falls. One can stand at the edge and touch the water as it curls over. Behind the falls is a wide deep pool of dark reddish green water.

"You must have swum here lots, passing by . . ."

"No, never."

"Never even wanted to?"

"Yeah, every time. But the Swiss girl . . . this is where the Swiss girl went over."

She had mentioned it earlier and I had forgotten.

134

They had driven their Bedford up over there (she pointed toward the jeep) and stopped to eat lunch. A bunch of them decided to go swimming. Evidently, she swam out to the middle (I followed a phantom swimmer from the rocks) and became caught in the current. They said she was a good swimmer and that she struggled well with the current, moving sideways to get clear but she couldn't quite make it back in time. Some of them ran to the edge of the falls but she was too far out . . . Last year her parents had come down on the anniversary to see where it happened.

"They were nice people, I heard. I did not meet them."

As she talked, the spray from the falls gently touched our faces, wet our hair. I got a book and looked for a place to sit and read. My companion looked into the water, meditating.

At the falls we attracted the inevitable crowd of children. One, who ventured too close to the ledge, slipped and fell. Fortunately, he was able to grab hold of a root or he would have plunged into the falls. None of his mates moved to help him, although there was a likely rescue perch. Suddenly, a rock of considerable size struck the ledge. I couldn't tell whether one of the children had thrown it or it was only a delayed fall from the rock slide. In any event, the lad had soon scrambled expertly to the top and rejoined his companions. His hands and knees were a bit skinned, but he seemed intact.

An African teacher I had met in Bassangoua said that a child would sometimes go over the falls. Recently one had survived such an accident. But they have almost no chance once they get in over their heads. In spite of living in a land of rivers, few Africans ever learn to swim. The pool below the falls is a favorite place for local women who beat their clothing on the rocks. According to the teacher, the women claim the "falls spirit" gets the children.

In Bangassou there were hand-lettered posters on trees along the road: a witch doctor from Zaire was giving a public demonstration at the Bar du Singe (Monkey Bar). At 3:30 p.m., the appointed time, there was a large crowd, but the owner refused to start before the mayor arrived, and when he had not come by 6:00, the witch doctor took a canoe back across the river to Zaire. To start an event without the mayor or chief would be a grave breach of protocol. Why he refused to come or send word to start without him was anybody's guess.

My companion invited me to stay at the Peace Corps house. Her roommate, a male volunteer, had not yet returned from a visit to a neighboring town. I was given a small room to one side. The house was one of those concrete and plaster houses built in the late 1950s or early 1960s by the colonial administration. It had been wired for electricity but the wiring had since been removed. The village had never had power, but a private generator had been used at one time. Behind it was a similar but smaller house inhabited by Africans.

Late that afternoon, for the first time, I began seeing ominous flashes of lightning over the Congo rain forests to the south. I hoped it was only the normal lightning that flashes through evening cloud covers over jungles everywhere. Yet I wondered whether the heavy rains had already begun which would swell dormant creeks to flood, wash out bridges overnight and make roads impassable. It had been my original plan to get at least as far as Kisangani by mid-March. Hence, I was running over a month behind. Of course, no one seriously expects to adhere to a rigid timetable in Africa anywhere north of the Zambezi.

The ferry across the Ubangi at Bangassou consisted of three twenty-foot-long metal riverboats joined by a subplatform of 50-gallon drums. Over this was a wooden platform or matting. It could carry a large truck or two smaller vehicles at one time. When not running, it remained on the Zaire side. The river was about an eighth of a mile wide.

Inside a straw and concrete gazebo on the Bangassou side was a bar that sold Mocaf and a beer from Zaire called Primus. Primus in taste was superior to Mocaf and came in a bottle twice as large. A relatively light, smooth brew, it cost 50 CFA more per bottle.

The gazebo bar was a kind of luncheon club for local honchos, such as the son of the village chief and the school principal. Sometimes they were joined by the Peace Corps volunteers and one or two other Europeans that happened to be in town.

One could spend an afternoon sitting in the gazebo watching driftwood float by and talking to the pirogue boys who would play and hustle customers among the natives returning to Zaire from the market in Bangassou. Sometimes people at Ndu, on the Zaire side, came over to shop. There was little traffic in the other direction, since beyond Ndu there was nothing but forest.

About a quarter of a mile from the bank was the customs house. Scores of elephant tusks, the weight of each written on it in red crayon, were stacked outside. Just inside the door was another, smaller stack. The elephants are poached in Zaire and the tusks are smuggled across the river at night at Bangassou. From here they are shipped by truck to Bangui, from which they are flown to Paris. No effort is made by authorities of the empire to impede their importation. Indeed, the Emperor Bokassa himself is the monopoly licensee. Nor is there any serious enforcement in Zaire.

The four or five stores in Bangassou were run by former colonial merchants, or their widows, who elected to stay on after independence. There was one Greek family. The general stores were stocked with packets of dried milk, macaroni, Nescafe and, for those who could afford it, tins of Argentine canned beef. As always, the beef came in two sizes: a square red can with a picture of a healthy black cow and a rectangular tin with a picture of the meat in a casserole. The meat in the picture of the casserole did not resemble the meat in the tin. It was, however, good to vary one's mantioc-potato-and-rice diet from time to time, even with coarse beef. The stores also stocked 150-franc sacks of spaghetti. There was a bakery which baked bread once or twice a week.

Majestic shade trees planted by the colonial administration in the '20s and '30s gave the town a cool, plantation atmosphere. The trees were white-waisted with thick coats of worm paint and fungicide.

The primary school was top-heavy with older students—some in their

30s. Who goes to school is determined by local politics. If you know somebody, you can stay in school for years even though you're failing. One has an advantage being a student, since one can avoid conscription into the army, and in many instances a small allowance is paid. The priority for hard-to-get funds is staff and teacher comfort. For example, a lounge and bar costing 40,000 CFA (approximately $160) had just been installed. That money could have bought quite a few textbooks.

The usual fare to cross the river by dugout was 25 CFA—50 both ways. After some haggling, this price was agreed. The ferry captain was on deck, drunk on Primus. His first question, before I could speak, was why I had not brought him more beer from the gazebo. He said the price of the ferry was 1,000 CFA plus two and a half gallons of kerosene and that I would also have to provide a twelve-volt battery to start the engine. I was thinking what it would be like lugging my battery down to the river and across in one of these pirogues. Regarding the kerosene, although ostensibly it was for running the engine, this particular crossing only took about half a gallon—at the most. The captain, of course, would sell the remainder. I thanked him, and called for the boy to come with the dugout.

When the pirogue pushed off I saw that we had become three—the second boy larger than the first and quite stout. No one said anything until we reached midstream. Suddenly, the pirogue lost momentum and limped into the current.

"You pay now," the newcomer said.

"Pay what?" I asked.

"300 CFA," he replied.

"That is no good," I said. "Price 50 CFA."

"No. 300."

The ferry landing was quickly disappearing. These guys were serious. I figured I had better think fast or I would be joining the hippos.

"Okay, 300," I said, "but not until we reach the bank. The money is in the jeep."

They looked at each other. They hadn't thought about that one.

"Okay—we go to bank. Then you get 300 CFA."

"Okay," I said.

When I tossed him the two 25-CFA pieces I made a careful note of him and his canoe. It would not be wise to ride with him again.

There was a small gravel bar upstream from the ferry landing where my Peace Corps companion occasionally went to swim and bathe. She would take a pirogue from the landing. The boatman had to be careful or he would hang up in the shallows on the downstream side.

We went up one afternoon, and, when we got to the island, the boatman waited just offshore in still water while my friend bathed and I read and caught some sun.

The boatman, she said, was a friend of a boy who had been eaten by a hippopotamus. A mile or so further upstream is a slow, deep pool where the boatmen rest. The hippo must have been there when the boy floated in in his pirogue. The animal knocked over the canoe and grabbed the boy, and that was it. The canoe was found washed ashore downstream. I didn't think hippos ate people, though it is known that they will attack if angry or frightened. This was a common river story throughout Central Africa, and I am sure that it was sometimes more than apocryphal. There were no hippos in the river then, but the canoe boys said there were quite a few later on in the rainy season.

Later that afternoon, after washing my mess gear at the Peace Corps house, I walked out on the back porch and set it out to dry. Without warning I was set upon by a nest of giant forest wasps and stung several times. They were a dull reddish-brown and almost double the size of any I had previously seen. I had jarred their nest when I opened the door. A student who was visiting at the time told me that the wasps, particularly their larvae, made excellent fish bait. This was interesting, because in Arkansas, fishermen also use wasps and hornet larvae as bait.

The next morning, in a Land Rover with two Italians I'd met at the customs house, I went to the immigration office. Already there were two five-ton Bedford trucks, each with about 25 people, mostly British and Commonwealth students. One belonged to Encounter Overland, a London tour group which runs between Nairobi and London. This one had been on the road about eight weeks out of Nairobi.

The advertised duration of an "encounter" is sixteen weeks, although with breakdowns and border delays it may last up to twenty. The ages of the passengers vary, but the average is about 25. Many northward-bound passengers are Australians and New Zealanders who have worked for a year or two in South Africa or Rhodesia to earn their passage and European travel money.

Northbound overlanders who have worked in South Africa must obtain new passports or remove the pages of the South African visa stamps from their old ones. Although Rhodesian officials will provide a looseleaf visa, the South Africans won't. The result is that one is barred automatically from all Black African countries except Botswana and Malawi (both of which have economic relations with Pretoria). European and American businessmen get special passports from their state departments for Rhodesian and South African travel—thus avoiding the problem altogether. For an overland traveler, however, it can be a nuisance. The problem is overcome by having the South African visa stamped on a supplementary passport page which can be "lost." Less convenient are lost passports which take weeks to replace at the next embassy.

The other Bedford, from London, was a private venture of Terry Williamson's, an old traveler of Africa and South America who had been leading overland expeditions for years. His group had been on the road about eleven weeks.

Bedford travelers share cooking, cleaning and other chores. Usually two or three will share the duty for a day. That means buying, cleaning and cooking the food, scrounging firewood and building a fire, and washing up.

Half of the provisions are bought along the road: bananas, pineapples, all fresh vegetables. Water is obtained at each main town before departing, some twenty plastic five-gallon jugs of it. Water is rarely taken from streams because of bilharzia (the slowly fatal worm common in Central Africa), typhoid fever and the usual host of tropical diseases. Depending upon where it is obtained, the water is then purified with halazone or other tablets.

The Italians and I had agreed to split the crossing fee. I would furnish the required half jerry can of gasoline, and they would provide their battery. We found the ferry on the Bangassou side already started by a northbound truck, saving the Italians the task of removing their battery. I tendered the can of gasoline which the ferryman promptly emptied into his tank. But half a can, we learned, was not enough. Each vehicle was required to make such a contribution of gasoline, in spite of shared passage. (The Italians had insisted on paying for half the fuel.) There was a heated discussion on the way over, and when we reached the other side, the Italians rolled up their windows and zoomed off onto the bank. About halfway up they got stuck, and there was a shaky moment as the captain and crew chased after them, shaking their fists and brandishing crowbars. Fortunately, the shorter of the two Italians jumped out and pushed, and they escaped. I had considered accepting their invitation to travel on with them. But they were in too big of a hurry, trying to make Uganda (for God knows what reason) by May 1.

This was the time of the so-called "Shaba War," a civil war over local tribal grievances but supported by the Soviet-backed regime in Angola in an attempt to separate the copper-rich province (formerly Katanga) from Zaire. It occurs every eight to ten years, a cyclical blood-letting. This particular flare-up was not a guerilla war but rather an armed conventional attack from Angola. The Zaire army had at first fled, and the war seemed lost. The French, however, had then flown in elite Moroccan paratroopers who had been able to turn the tide. Eventually the Zairois had rallied and helped repel the invaders.

In April of 1977, however, the war was still in progress, and I expected to see a conspicuous military presence—truckloads of troops, patrols, and police barriers. Yet the dramatic calm of the forest seemed to forbid such mundane activities as war.

There was a dramatic change not only in the foliage at the river but in the people of the forest as well. Their mannerisms, appearance and response to strangers became less reserved and more assertive. Some were downright aggressive, and occasionally they would curse and make threatening gestures as I drove past. I could not help but think that their hostility was the result of some real or imagined injury perpetrated by a recent traveler.

When I first saw the stranded white Mercedes caravan I did not know that it was Chris and Windy, a young English couple I had met in Tamanrasset. They had made it all this way with their cumbersome vehicle, only to lose a wheel bearing some 60 miles into the forest. Somehow they had managed to creep back here to the landing. From Bangassou Chris had wired his father in England to send the necessary parts. Two weeks later the parts had come to Bangui. After a further two-week delay they arrived here. Unfortunately, some components were missing and the process had to be repeated. Chris had gone personally to Bangui to handle the communication and to be at the airport when the gear came.

Windy did not mind staying behind. Accompanied by an impossible Irish setter named Tosca—who wandered off with anyone who took a fancy to him—she had become a kind of big sister to the boat boys and children of Ndu village who hung out on the bank. She knew most of their names and which ones could be counted upon for certain things. For instance, one eager lad would go to the market for her across the river in his pirogue. Another would buy beer at the gazebo and bring back bread from the pantry there. She had free transportation whenever she wanted to go shopping herself in Bangassou and visit an old African woman whom she had befriended downriver. She had been there barely a month but it seemed as if she were already a permanent part of the community.

I camped just up the bank and Windy invited me over for dinner. We brought each other up to date on our adventures during the three months since Tamanrasset and speculated on what lay ahead in Zaire.

That night I began to feel a deeper, closer kinship with the forest, not explained by the mere novelty of being there. I had arrived gradually over several thousands of miles of desert and savannah and to a great extent had discounted any sense of adventure. Whatever the source of the feeling, it was certainly a commanding one that I had only felt twice before—in Vietnam and, much later, in the Bocas del Toro of Panama.

CHAPTER IX

McMath at the Equator, eastern Zaire.

Just before dusk, the southbound Bedford came across on the ferry. It made the bank with no trouble and soon the crew was clattering about making camp. The smell of fresh coffee and smoke from their fires blended with the chatter of frogs and crickets in the early night.

Terry Williamson invited me over for a cup. He talked briefly about his previous crossings and some overland trips he had made in South America. We swapped what little information we had on the roads and the war. We had both heard that the war was going badly for Mobutu's government and it was rumored that all borders might soon be closed. We had also heard at Bangui of a warning broadcast for the Zaire people to be on the lookout for mercenaries moving into the country from the north. This would surely make us targets of intense scrutiny.

To add to our concern, the rainy season was about to begin. The Italians had spoken of bridges washed out less than 50 miles into the jungle.* Even here the road was a mere rutted track broken with mudholes. Toward the end of the evening we agreed to travel together, at least as far as Bongo on the Velle River, some 125 miles. Thus began a month-long relationship with 25 stalwart travelers across one of the most desolate passages of the journey. They offered me a hearty companionship, and I provided them with an out-riding vehicle which was able to range far ahead of their cumbersome Bedford. I began carrying one or two of them with me that first afternoon, and these rides they eagerly looked forward to as a relief from the monotony and discomfort of the truck.

Among the crew of the Bedford was a young Scottish naturalist, Nigel Hunterston, who had a scout's ability to spot the faintest animal track or broken twig or to locate a superbly camouflaged bird after only two or three calls. Indeed, he was an expert bird caller. Also aboard was Sidney Jeffers, a

---

*A brief note here regarding the word "jungle." There are those who reserve it strictly for those Asian and Amazonian woodlands where the vegetation grows in at least three discernable layers or canopies. I won't quarrel with them, except to say that I have seen both these and the rain forests of Zaire and the Ivory Coast, and to me there is no practical difference between them. Each is dense, lush, teeming with life and normally impossible to penetrate without a machete. My treatment of the term, therefore, is not so strict.

young Jamaican black who had been studying in London, which he now considered home. Sidney was, without doubt, the most well-read and articulate of the crew. He was also an ideal traveling companion, pulling far more than his share of the load of chores and trail duties, and always doing so pleasantly. Nigel and Sid became my most frequent outriders.

The northern province of Zaire is the country's most sparsely populated and unpoliced region. The dominant tribe is the Azande. They get along rather peacefully with their neighbors, the Ngabaandi and the Nzakara; at least they have in recent years. Each tribe inhabits both sides of the Ubangi River: the Azande and Ngabaandi primarily in Zaire, the Nzakara in the Empire.

These tribes share the distinction of being the furthest-removed citizens from their respective capitals. They have no schools, built-up roads, hospitals (other than the missions) or other public services. Their only government contacts are with the tax collector and the police—both of whom they avoid. These are the African people least reached by international aid, which is administered under the control of Bangui and Kinshasa.

Local tribal leaders in Zaire are usually members of the "revolutionary" party of Mobutu Sese Seko. They proudly wear a little red and green party badge with Mobutu's picture in the center.

At the border river village of Ndu I observed that the people numbered about 200 and lived in a series of dirt-floored, rectangular, mud and straw huts. Some were round, with rock at the base. Crops of mantioc, bananas and peanuts sprouted in small patches in the forest, each tended by an individual family. The earth on the immediate periphery of the village was caked and sterile from overgrazing by the goats, and the villagers had found it necessary to burn into the forest to uncover fertile land for planting. Such fires had devastated hundreds of nearby acres, rendering the least-charred trees suitable only as firewood.

Some land is cut clear without burning. This is done with axes made of stone and iron. These vary widely in make—some double-edged, others only single-edged with a hammer-end opposite. The stones appear to have been carefully selected and individually fastened in much the same manner as those on axes found at Olorgesailie and other Stone Age sites in East Africa.

We found the ferry ten kilometers east of Monga at sunset. We would have had time to cross before dark, but we found no crew. The ferry was a raft of heavy, almost submerged, logs lashed with strips of discarded planks. It lay in a still pool near the landing, just outside a swift current.

(Several years before, some people in a Land Rover had refused to wait for the crew and attempted to pole across themselves. Captured by the current, they had been carried through rapids to the far side, where they had been stranded aground for several days. Such an example discouraged us from making a similar attempt.)

Traditionally, a ferry captain assembles his crew by drumbeat. If this

A "pothole" in the road to Kisangani, Zaire.

summons sounds in late afternoon, the crew will not respond until the following morning. Since the captain was nowhere in sight, we walked back to Ndu in an attempt to muster a crew. The villagers told us the captain would come in the morning. We camped at the landing, attracting before dusk a larger-than-usual crowd of Africans, some of whom ventured annoyingly close to our tools and camping equipment.

(The sudden encampment of 25 Westerners is a natural curiosity to any African. The closer to dusk they are attracted, the less of a nuisance they are, for when darkness finally arrives, they quickly melt away. I don't recall a crowd ever coming after dark, not even if we were quite near a village and making a great deal of noise.)

An hour after dawn the crew assembled and began poling the vehicles across individually, the ferry groaning under the weight. The proud captain walked the deck in a wide-brimmed straw hat, his Mobutu button glistening in the sun. A drummer beat a rhythmic cadence to which he chanted a river-crossing song. At the end of each verse his mates responded in a resonant chorus that reverberated over the water.

Between the crossing at Ndu and Kisangani lie 450 miles of some of the most wretched roads in Africa. The rainfall is greater than virtually anywhere else on the continent, and the rust-red humus, which can grip tires like molasses, renders the forest floor an expanse of troughs, pits and sluices, the depths of which one learns only by venturing into them.

There are hundreds of sloughs and creeks, each bridged by a motley assortment of logs at varying stages of decay. Many of the logs are simply trees wasted and felled by fire or old age. These weakened logs are very dangerous and must be carefully inspected.

Also dangerous are the inevitable holes between the logs. For a small-based, narrow-wheeled vehicle like my own, this was especially a problem. The customary procedure is for the passenger to get out and inspect the bridge. He first checks the logs themselves to make sure they are not rotten or broken. This is best done by jumping and bouncing on them. Usually there will be six or eight logs, one or two of them of questionable strength. The problem, of course, is to select two sturdy logs which the wheels can safely roll on for the distance of the bridge. Next, the passenger checks the spacing between the logs.

As elemental as this may sound, we would have ignored it at our peril. Several times, we found only two good logs, which either were too far apart for my wheels to straddle or perfectly situated at the beginning but diverged before they reached the other side. We would have to decide in these instances whether to risk driving on one good log and one bad one or to reinforce the bridge with another log or two, whereupon I would use my winch to pull in the bridge's logs or retrieve nearby poles from the forest. Only once did I pick one that was too weak, but the channel was only a few feet deep and I was somehow able to climb up the opposite bank before it completely broke.

Although the shotgun passenger checks the bridge first, the driver, in

146

the end, must make the decision. Whenever there was the slightest doubt, I always got out and personally checked both the timbers and the alignment of the wheels. My best shotgun rider was Mary Edmonston, an Australian with whom I became very good friends. She had spent a good deal of time in the Outback and had quite a bit of experience in rugged terrain.

Toward noon the third day out of Bangassou Nigel and I, who were leading the others by several miles, came to a bridge with a small game trail leading off upstream. We decided to stop, Nigel thinking the place auspicious for bird watching. We had seen a covey of splendid yellow-orange birds fly into a shaft of sunlight which hit the ground 100 yards up the trail, indicating a clearing. I pulled clear of the ruts so the Bedford, would be able to pass. Just then the truck was too far away to hear, but before too much longer it would be grunting and crashing its way toward the bridge. Nigel gathered his camera gear, and we headed up the trail.

The clearing turned out to be only a bank at the bend in the creek. There were no birds in sight. We came to a pool of quite stagnant water; it was, nevertheless, the watering place for scores of animals, whose fresh tracks could be seen in the loose, dry earth.

Somewhere in the forest a Tinker bird sounded and Nigel repeated its cry precisely. It called out again, more clearly this time. Nigel waited for a moment, then responded.

"I'll bring him to those branches," he said, pointing just over our heads.

Once again the bird cried to us, and Nigel answered, quickly this time. In a moment we saw a flash of yellow wings in the branches. The bird did not call again but sat there as Nigel photographed it, its head tilting from side to side, then arching up inquisitively as if to ask just why we had interrupted its afternoon.

Ten minutes down the road we heard another call—this one very low and guttural. It was a Hornbill—a kind of redheaded crow. Nigel, well ahead now, motioned for me to freeze and then answered the caw. In no time we heard a stereophonic reply: there were two of them. The Scot repeated his answer, and out they came, more cautiously than had the Tinker bird. They circled overhead, giving us plenty of berth. They finally alit, high in the branches. Nigel shook his head after trying the zoom lens. He called to them again, but they responded with silence. He called again. Nothing.

Just then, something not six feet away caught my eye. Slithering down a limb was a chubby puff adder, one of the most perfectly camouflaged of all African snakes and one of the most poisonous. It had dark orange and brown skin with faded geometric shapes, which would blend perfectly with the olive-orange floor of the forest. As quickly as he had caught my eye, he disappeared from view. I picked up a stick, eased over to the end of the branch and poked at it cautiously. Nothing. Turning aside some vines, I discovered a hole several inches wide. He could have disappeared into that with no problem, I thought. Just then I was startled by the call of the Hornbills, high in the trees. I didn't dare look up, but Nigel was filming away.

We mounted the bank and worked our way slowly back down the stream bed, this time using the trail. Halfway back we heard the Bedford. We could tell it was at the bridge because the sound of its engine suddenly died away. We knew that Terry and Jim, the driver, would be out checking the log and wheel alignment. After a few moments, the motor revved again, and they crossed with a rush. The sound of the engine receded into the forest. We were puzzled to hear several long impatient blasts on the horn and then silence.

Ten minutes later when we drove over the rise beyond the bridge, we met some of our companions walking towards us.

"What's up?" I asked.

"Trees in the road," someone replied.

Africans sometimes fell trees across the road, finding it easier to chop them up there than in the underbrush. This was the source of our consternation, for across the road lay two great iroko trees and between them worked four African choppers.

To the left was a solid wall of forest; to the right was a twenty-degree slope which had been strip-burned and cut and now bristled with scores of ankle-high sapling stubs. The only ways to get through were to dig out the stubs, or to help the Africans log the trees, which would be much quicker. So we went to work.

The four African choppers had stopped working when the Bedford came. They had been drinking home brew, and the one who appeared to be their leader was quite inebriated. He offered his calabash all around, but none of us accepted it. I could tell that Terry had already had a heated exchange with him.

We had arrived at their lunch hour. To substantiate this, the chief produced a shiny chrome wristwatch which read 12:10. I knew better than to interfere with a working man's lunch hour. But I persuaded them to leave us their primitive iron axes.

In shifts of four-on-four we began cutting. I drove the jeep ahead of the Bedford and anchored my rear hitch to its front axle. As a limb was cut almost in two, I would hook it to the cable and try to winch it away. We cut and winched for a couple of hours, and although we had moved a lot of timber, we still had a long way to go. Naturally, all this was a circus for the score of children who came up from the neighboring forest to watch—their little bellies swollen from their pure starch diet of worthless mantioc. While getting at some tackle in a tool box I found two chocolate bars. I tried to distribute them evenly but found it impossible. I should have known by then not to give *cadeaux* until just as I was leaving. Soon I was beseiged.

Next, the thunderstorm that had been threatening us since late in the morning let go. Everyone dashed for cover except the two Aussies, who continued chopping as if nothing had happened. I was finally embarrassed into joining them, and soon we were playing in the mud like kids. The rain was terribly cold, and we were hardly efficient.

Winching can be a hazardous business, both to the operator and the bystander. It is best to clear everyone from the radius of the cable and for the operator to stand behind a sapling or some other protective shield. Fortunately, the winch, a Ramsey Electric, never failed, and although it reached its tug limit several times it never slipped, and the cable never frayed or broke. Naturally there was little we could do to control the curious bush children; as soon as we had shooed them away, they would come right back again.

Finally, a gent with a green and red Mobutu badge came by on a bicycle and, as it was now well past any reasonable lunch "hour," I asked him if he could muster the African crew. Not only did he refuse, but when we had cleared the last log and I took a picture of our handiwork with my Instamatic, he threatened to have me arrested for photographing a "military installation."

It was 5:00 when we had finally cleared the last debris, five hours of work for which I should have billed the Zaire Highway Department—especially since it appeared that the Mobutu character was a road official. We loaded up both vehicles and were preparing to leave when the man with the badge came up to press his complaint about my photograph. It was late, and we were very tired and did not wish to argue. So I gunned my engine and shouted to my companions, "Follow me!" In the mirror I saw Jim charge the Bedford in behind, the high branches scraping his roof. We were away.

Campsites are difficult to find and even more difficult to set up on by flashlight. Ordinarily we would have stopped and set up camp an hour before dark. But this time we decided to push on through, so as to put a little distance between us and the man with the badge and cover at least a few miles for the day.

Mary Edmonston, the group's blithe spirit and self-coronated "Queen of Australia," was riding with me. We gradually increased our lead over the others. The storm had been heavier than we had thought; fifteen miles further, the road became so muddy that we had to go into low-range four-wheel drive. The Bedford was now far behind, and as it was dusk, it would be absurd to return through all that mud to look for it.

Finally we saw a small village ahead. We could stop there and sleep in the jeep—difficult, but with the front seats bent forward you could achieve a fairly comfortable curled-up position, even for two people. We got out and stretched.

"Ça va, monsieur?"

I was momentarily startled, not having seen anyone. I turned and saw a young man carrying a satchel and two schoolbooks, one of which was entitled *Geographie du Monde: l'Europe* (World Geography: Europe).

"Are you a student here?" I asked him.

"Not here, at Bongo."

"What do you do here?"

"Visiting relatives. What do you do?"

"We are going to Kisangani."

The road ahead was very bad, he said. It was dangerous to drive it at night. Bridges were under water: we might easily drive right into a river. An old man in a faded T-shirt stood next to him, nodding agreeably at everything the student said. As we talked it began again to rain and they retreated to the inadequate shelter of a mangrove tree along with a half-dozen children.

"Is there a place we can stay the night?" I asked the student.

"Yes, this house, here," he volunteered, pointing to a house standing by itself off to our left. The woman who lived there had gone to the next village to visit relatives, he said. At the student's command the children fled through the mud and, after a moment, returned with a tall man who introduced himself as the chief. He and the student took us to the house. It had a wooden frame, a thatched roof and a dirt floor. It was retangular-shaped and divided into three rooms. The chief broke a small lock on the door to let us in. Protocol seemed to forbid all but a mild protest from us, which he firmly waved away.

The house was dry and well kept. In the kitchen was a waist-high chopping table and a square iron stove which straddled a hole for the fire. There was a smoke hole in the ceiling directly overhead. On the stove were two formidable iron pots and a skillet. Hanging from the post supporting the roof was a long strand of garlic which, with the lived-in dirt smell, created in the damp air a pleasant, musky odor. From wall pegs hung assorted gourds and two rusty wide-bladed knives, the cutting edges of which had been finely sharpened. Behind the kitchen were a bin full of ripening tomatoes and two bounteous stalks of green bananas. Our mystery hostess was scrupulously tidy. It was obvious that the floor had been freshly swept with a switch broom which stood in the corner of the entryway.

We lit a couple of candles and, with a pot from my mess kit, boiled water. Mary measured out some rice and I peeled a half-dozen small potatoes, which we added to a can of green peas and our last tin of beef stew. We had both fallen into the African habit of mixing rice and potatoes. Dinner was soon ready, and a mighty good one it was.

We discussed the day's events and how heavy the rain had been. We knew we were still 400 miles out of Kisangani, with more of the same roads in between. We tried to find this little village on our map, but it was not marked. Still we were able, from the odometer, to place our approximate position: we had come only 23 miles since crossing the ferry at Monga.

I went out to take a look at the jeep, and when I came back Mary was already asleep. After a cup of coffee, I strung the mosquito net so that it protected us both from aerial attack as well as from the scores of crawlers that had suddenly materialized on the dirt floor. I had to tuck it in pretty tightly and weigh it down with our boots.

The wind whistled up in the rafters, and it began to get cooler. After making sure the door was closed and propped to with a pole, I turned in. It felt good to lie there and listen to the wind and rain and night noises. Funny how they always seem to get louder when you put out the light.

I was just about to doze off when suddenly I heard what sounded like someone coming into the house with an armload of parcels. After awhile it stopped, and I heard instead a soft scraping sound, rather like someone brushing off a coat. This was followed by a series of crackling, popping noises, like someone wadding up a cellophane bag or chewing a raw carrot with his mouth open. I thought that surely our hostess had returned and was having her dinner. She was not yet aware of our presence and I was thinking of something appropriate to say: *how terribly grateful... you sure it's no bother....* Perhaps she was a witch doctor and that's why her house was so

150

set off by itself. She would not, in that case, be amused to find intruders. Maybe she knew about us already and was having a little snack while she pondered what to do with us.

Then it occurred to me that there was no light, no fire . . . not even a candle. The first thing an African woman does is light her fire. But the noise resumed. Strange for her to make so much noise—sounds like those of a big . . . I grabbed my flashlight with one hand and a boot with the other. As I rolled out from under the mosquito net, I knocked over the camping stove. Quickly I switched on the light.

Then I saw them: two big cold eyes reflecting the light. A rat the size of an overgrown possum swaggered into the kitchen and disappeared. I found that the bottom of the back kitchen wall had a hole, obviously cut away as a person might do for a dog or cat.

The next morning I looked in Nigel's guide to the animals of East and Central Africa and found that what we had seen was indeed a rat, a Great White Rat—the kind the Africans keep as a pet and frequently eat as a delicacy. I was glad that I had not killed it.

It occurred to me that both my encounters with what I had thought were dangerous animals that day were only imagined drama on my part. There had never been the slightest danger. Both the puff adder and the giant rat had simply ignored me and gone about their business. Africa was teaching me one of its basic lessons: life proceeds here in a normal, disinterested way. Adventure is an alien concept.

The rest of our party arrived before we were ready the next morning. They had camped about two miles back. We waved them on and spent a quarter-hour thanking our friends. I left several tins of food in the kitchen together with, inadvertently, my tent poles. (The night crawlers had finally become such pests that we had spread out the tent as a ground cover.)

It was at about this time that many of us began to suffer from festering sores and boils. I developed two on my left hand that simply refused to heal. It seemed as if the slightest bruise or scratch would give rise to a running canker that not only failed to abate with medication but would overnight multiply into others.

Such wounds are common among the native population. The indigenous humidity and heavy concentration of bacteria inhibit healing. The best treatment is antibiotic powder, but even that is only protective: it does not hasten healing. Some of my companions developed cankers that were not only painful but depressing to look at. Yet covering them only made them worse.

The butterflies were rivaled for diversity by the moths which appeared nightly, about an hour after dark, and increased in number and size as evening wore on. Nigel and his brother, Robert, collected scores of these insects, which were particularly attracted to our camping lights—sometimes in such numbers that the lights were all but obscured. I told my companions about the hordes of moths which had risen from the forest in the northern Empire the night I had run over the "CBC."

It was north of Mondo one afternoon that Mary Edmonston spotted a large troop of baboons, over forty of them. Baboons soon became so common, however, that we took no notice of them unless they were very close.

Although it prefers vegetation, the baboon is omnivorous, and his tough social hierarchy and rigid troop discipline make him an invincible predator of smaller animals and assure his defense from the big cats and hyenas. Baboons avoid people and can be dangerous if surprised or threatened by them. At the turn of the century, there were more baboons in Africa than there were people.

(One day much later, in the Transvaal, I was talking with an old Afrikaner about garbage pickup service. "How do you keep the baboons out of the garbage over there?" he asked, referring to my home. When I told him we had no baboons in Arkansas—in America for that matter—he was shocked. "I'll be," he said. "I thought they were everywhere, like dogs and cats.")

Some African farmers lose whole crops to this pest alone. So crafty is the ape that he will ignore an empty-handed farmer but flee the corn patch if the farmer has a spear or gun. The farmer's wife is likewise ignored—unless, of course, she is armed.

Second only to man, the baboon is the most "successful" primate, in that it has not declined in number over the past 10,000 years. The primate as a life form has passed its heyday and is chewing its way quietly into extinction, except, that is, for the baboon. And perhaps man.

My giving rides to alternate members of the Bedford crew proved to be a most satisfactory arrangement. It was good for each of them to get a side trip from time to time, and I thoroughly enjoyed the company. Although we were traveling in convoy, the jeep was much more mobile and flexible than the heavy truck and was able to go ahead or lag behind by several miles. Our understanding was that the passengers of one vehicle would not launch a search for the other until a separation of several hours. Although this routine would have been undesirable in the desert, here where there was only one principal rut road through dense forest—passable side trails were few—it gave each of us flexibility and freedom from constant worry about keeping up.

Although most ferries in Zaire are officially free, there is, as we have seen, a requirement that some fuel and a battery be supplied to run the boat. At Buta we actually had to force our way onto the vessel.

We had been forewarned by a northbound traveler in Bangassou to expect a shakedown for from 50 to 100 dollars and an equally exorbitant amount of petrol. Sure enough, as the boat approached the bank, the crew waved other traffic around us. We were then told that if we wished to pass we would have to pay extra. Our only alternative to a confrontation was to wait hours, perhaps days, to reason with the ferry's captain. Since his service is a public one and he is legally bound to carry all traffic, we felt we had the right to board. When we did so, the captain refused to cross—in spite of gathering local traffic on the far shore. The local police chief finally came down and chewed us out. He also chastised the captain, but we were "fined" an extra half-can of fuel.

Through this area there are several short-line, narrow-gauge railroads which had been built by the Belgians to carry bananas, pineapples and other produce from their plantations to barge landings on the Ubangi's tributaries. Wherever they cross the road, there is a barrier and block house. An old African invariably comes to the door and waves as you pass. The trains still run, but as there are problems with spare parts, much is now shipped by truck in the dry season. In the rainy season, railroad breakdowns result in the spoilage of a large portion of the crops.

As in the Empire and southern Chad, we encountered the usual rain barriers, although they were less frequent due to the smaller amount of traffic. Small four-wheel drive vehicles could pass provided they were not too heavily loaded. Commercial vehicles were, without exception, detained. As the Bedford was a borderline case, we sometimes found it necessary to negotiate—at times with a small fee.

We crossed on two more ferries—each without incident—before reaching Kisangani, six days out of Bangassou. We entered the city by a bridge over the waterfall of the Congo River. Just below the bridge thundered rapids of olive-red forest water which plunged into the falls. Above us was an elevated public park planted with lush green grass and a variety of vines and flowers. We could walk out to the point and stand just above the falls, facing the rapids, head-on. At the foot of the falls were wicker-like, cone-shaped fish traps of various sizes woven out of long, limber sticks. These cages faced into the falls so that any fish tugged into the rapids had a good chance of being captured.

Later, I took the trail around to the base of the falls to watch men fishing with throw lines while they watched their traps. I asked one of them, in bad French, how his luck was running. He replied in perfect English, "Quite well, thanks." He was, as it turned out, a professor of physics at Kisangani University. His two fellow fishermen were students of his.

About ten years before, beginning about five miles northeast of the bridge, the road had been blacktopped. Many rains—and no repairs—later, it had become a gauntlet of pot-holes. The roadbed of one street had caved in, leaving a hole twenty feet deep.

Kisangani (formerly Stanleyville, after the *New York Herald* reporter-explorer who found Dr. Livingstone) was the largest town between Kano and Nairobi. Most of its colonial-style wooden buildings had been built in the '30s and '40s, although there were a few recent concrete and glass structures in the center of town. One early hotel which had not been remodeled was the single-story Hotel Olympia. Like many of the others, its wood was rotting and mildewed, its paint long since chipped away. But the original decor was there, and its advantage for overland travelers was twofold: it was cheap (rooms for four dollars a night) and secure (you could camp in the big enclosed garden out back). Kisangani was no exception to the general rule of large African cities: it was full of thieves. I tied down everything and locked it in my jeep.

I took one of the four-dollar rooms. It had a shower—the first hot water I'd had since N'djamena—and a fairly comfortable cot. As it was a double room, Terry took the other cot. We shared the shower with our companions and, reluctantly, with the 23 members of an Encounter Overland group which had just arrived in another Bedford.

The Hotel Olympia had moderately priced, tasty African food. We could have ordered just about any native dish, as well as several European entrées. *Capitaine* was still the local staple, and I had grown so fond of it (as well as fried plantain and rice) that I rarely ordered the more expensive continental cuisine.

The Hotel Olympia was run by a Greek couple in their early 50s. Back in Beni, near the Ugandan border, they had once been quite wealthy, owning nearly half the town. At first they had avoided expropriation, but as the Mobutu government had expanded its socialist program to the distant provinces, they had lost their holdings. With what little they were allowed to take with them, they had left Zaire for Greece in 1973. Two years later they had come back, under a new program to attract former colonials as managers and instructors—usually to serve on their former property. This couple had not returned to Beni, however, but to Kisangani, to manage the Olympia, one of their last acquisitions prior to expropriation.

Compensation for most third-world holdings is paid in local currency— in this case, *Zaires*. (The official rate was .85 *Zaire* to one U.S. dollar; the local black-market rate was between 1.7 and 2.25 *Zaire* for the dollar, depending upon who did the trading. In London and Zurich the rate varied between five and eight *Zaire* for the dollar.) Compensation was to have taken place over a period of thirty years, although payments of late had tended to fall further and further behind schedule.

When I visited the lady who managed the Olympia, I found that the government was six months in arrears to her and her husband. She looked exasperated and fatigued. On her desk were pictures of her four daughters, each married and with a family of her own. She sighed, gently touching the picture of the youngest. A proud Greek bridegroom stood at her side. This picture had been taken following their wedding in Athens. They lived in Canada now, my hostess said. She'd seen them last year at the family reunion in Piraeus.

The girls had all grown up in the old colonial home at Beni, she continued. From a drawer she produced an early family picture. In the background was the colonial homestead.

"It's all gone now," she said. "Plumbing ripped out, windows broken. . . ." Some native had occupied it for a while after expropriation, she said, but no one lived there now. She had heard that the property had been acquired by a government official but no restoration had begun.

The office was in a closet down a long corridor which led from the kitchen. She—or her husband—would be there from 7:00 in the morning until midnight. She was weary with constantly having to supervise the employees. They were mostly bush migrants who had been hired through the local bureaucracy. It was impossible to fire one. The Africans who had worked for them before expropriation had disappeared without leaving a trace.

Her tales of disappointment and frustration continued for an hour. Listening to her, I was unable to understand why they had returned. Perhaps it was because Zaïre was the only home they had ever known. Or perhaps because there were many Greeks in Kisangani—almost as many as there were Belgians.* Together they ran most of the hotels and many of the shops, and a number of young Greeks were purchasing agents for local companies.

No discussion of Kisangani would be complete without some mention of the two crucial transactions one cannot avoid there: changing money and buying fuel.

As noted, the government's official opinion of its currency's value was greater than the market's. This is true for all African countries except South Africa and the CFA nations, the currency of which is backed by the Bank of France.

The black market is, of course, illegal and I don't recommend it. If you get caught you can go to an African jail (not a pleasant *sejour*) or pay a heavy fine. Besides, if you are a guest in a country you should abide by its rules; black marketeering can threaten a country's economy. The small amount traded

---

*Although the Belgian colonial administration in mid-century was one of the continent's most benign, the rule of Leopold II, for whom the country had been a personal fiefdom, had been ruthless: "... Leopold's rule was mercilessly exploitative. How much money he made out of the Congo, after his investment began to pay off, no man can know. He had to borrow large sums at first. Certainly he became one of the richest men in the world. As early as 1885 a decree made all 'vacant land' in the Congo the property of the estate, i.e., Leopold. This meant, in effect any land the white man wanted. Natives were simply pushed out into the bush. Rubber and ivory, the two chief objects of value in the Congo at that time, became state monopolies, and the government gained 'an absolute proprietary right over nearly the whole country.' In 1896 came the creation (by secret decree) of the *Domaine de la couronne*, which gave Leopold special additional rights over not less than 112,000 square miles of territory, an area almost as big as Poland. But this was not all. The most heinous and ghastly atrocities ever to accompany the 'development' of a primitive area by a presumably civilized power occurred. The appetite of Leopold's agents for rubber and ivory grew steadily more voracious and insatiable. African workers were made to fill quotas, and if they failed to bring in the required amount of rubber and ivory they were mutilated or shot... Competent authorities say that the population of the Congo was about 20,000,000 in 1900; today (1955) it is 12,000,000. Leopold's regime is believed to have cost, in all, between five and eight *million* lives... Most horrible was the practice of mutilation. If an African boy did not satisfy his bosses, a hand or foot—sometimes both—were cut off ... To prove their efficiency in this business, the bosses of labor gangs brought into their superiors baskets full of human hands. The right hand was always favored. To preserve them in the humid climate, they were sometimes smoked." (John Gunther, *Inside Africa Today* [New York: Harper & Brothers, 1955], pp. 656-657.)

by foreigners, however, is dwarfed by the sums illegally converted by government officials who do so at two or three times the black-market rate on European markets. A goodly portion of the funds which corrupt officials trade in these markets is bribe money deposited by multi-national corporations into numbered Swiss bank accounts.

The people who run the black market that travelers see, however, are small businessmen who need dollars to replenish sparse inventories of basic consumer goods and spare parts. Additionally, expropriated Europeans still in the country and those here on contract work, both of whom have a portion of their salary paid in *Zaires,* seek convertible currency to deposit in their home bank accounts. In East Africa, these merchants and expropriated owners are usually East Asians.

Once having obtained convertible currency, there are a variety of ways to get it out of the country. One is to outfit baggage with a false liner and have a friend carry it on what purports to be a business trip. Most people find this a bit difficult to arrange, however, so they resort to sending a little at a time in the mail to friends overseas. Mail is, of course, pilfered, but a thin personal letter with a ten-dollar bill is less likely to be bothered than a fat parcel.

To thwart black-market dealings by travelers, officials require them to fill out a currency declaration form upon entering a country. Border officials then count the money to see if all has been declared. If it hasn't, the balance is confiscatable. I say "confiscatable" because I talked to several overlanders who had accidentally (they said) underdeclared and had suffered only a lecture and a warning. A Zairois I met had not been so lucky: returning on leave from his job in Bangui, he had neglected to declare 25,000 CFA ($100) and the entire amount—a month's pay—had been confiscated.

The forms are checked and your money counted again when you exit the country. In between, you are supposed to keep a record of every dollar you've exchanged on a form you can only get at the bank. As a practical matter, many people simply declare up to what they expect they won't need while in the country. A modest amount (say $50) is then changed at the bank so that they will have at least one official slip to show at the next frontier. This, of course, necessitates carrying large quantities of cash, since the process has to be repeated in each country.

It is wise to declare traveler's checks since they are not acceptable by black marketeers anyway. (They used to be, until some enterprising tourists came up with the idea of reporting their checks stolen after they left the country, thus invalidating the checks and getting a refund.) I was less daring than most and dutifully plodded to the bank to exchange my precious dollars at the official rate.

To buy fuel, however, I was forced into *le marche noir.* And since the seller accepted my dollars at a most favorable rate, I, too, became a profiteer.

There are some half-dozen gas stations in Kisangani, none of which ever has gas except immediately after the fuel barge has arrived from Kinshasa, after a three-week trip up the Congo River. But I learned quickly that if one needs it badly enough to pay the price, it can be found. Government and bank officials will buy up drums of fuel right at the barge dock. Additionally, officials of "Petrol Zaire," the local distributor, withhold emergency rations from the market which they later release at their discretion. When the pumps go dry, this hoarded fuel can bring up to six times the pump price of .57 *Zaire* per liter (at four dollars a gallon—no bargain!).

My first day in Kisangani, I checked out all the gas stations. Everywhere the scene was the same: empty grease racks and storerooms. A single young African watchman would sit listening to rock music on his transistor. Before I could ask, the lad would shrug:

"*Pas d'essence* (No gas).*"

The next morning I again made the rounds and, at the Shell station on Mobutu Sese Seko Avenue, discovered a crowd of at least 100 shouting and shoving toward a lone attendant who was stoically attempting to fill one jerry can at a time. Some fuel had indeed arrived—5000 liters the night before—but the limit was one can per customer, and I needed the equivalent of sixteen cans to make Goma. As I continued to watch the mêlée, a burly truck driver in a red T-shirt waded through the crowd and seized the nozzle from the bewildered attendant. No sooner had he begun filling his can than the *patron* (boss) ran from the office waving his hands: "*C'est fini. . . .* Stop!" That was it. No more gas. Grumbling, the mob began drifting away. I wondered why the fuel had not been rationed out, twenty liters at a time to each vehicle as they drove by in orderly succession. But even the impressive policeman sitting in the office talking to the *patron* had made no attempt at organization.

Continuing my hopeless search for fuel, I returned to the office of Petrol Zaire only to find it closed with a hand-lettered sign: "*Pas d'essence jusqu'a le peniche* (No gas until the barge comes)"—which would be another two weeks, according to the people at the Olympia. I returned to the hotel, determined to relax and enjoy my *sejour* in Kisangani, even if it turned out to be a month longer than I'd expected.

Just past the bridge above the falls were two primitive ivory shops. Outside, scores of craftsmen and apprentices carved away on work tables and in the shade of trees. There was little variety in the individual pieces, all seemingly made by apprentices of varying talent trained by the same artisan in the same style. There were war and wedding tusks with village friezes, natural tusks (plain except for a small head carved at the base), several varieties of miniature animals and people, and large ceremonial African heads, which are the most expensive pieces. Their primitive appearance reveals that they are locally carved, not flown to Hong Kong as is much of the far-more-expensive Kenya ivory.

Most of us would have bought something if the prices had been somewhat lower, although others were deterred by the knowledge that they would be contributing to the slaughter of elephants.

Several of us did trade clothing for small ivory trinkets. The hottest things a Westerner could trade here were blue jeans and T-shirts. Some overlanders I met had added to their provisions a bale or two of old jeans. They only thing in greater demand was a wristwatch. I always had to lock my Seiko in my cash box before going to trade, in order to keep it out of the bargaining.

157

The bar at the Olympia opened at six every evening and everyone who had a car—or a friend who did—seemed to be there to order a Primus. Functionaries sat on the terrace or in the dining room, and the working people stood at the bar. The night my Bedford friends found enough diesel to get to Goma we had a farewell party at the Olympia. I had still had no luck purchasing gasoline and was thus obliged to remain behind.

After several rounds of cheer, we decided to go for a final bowling game, at the Cafe du Sport. The alley was a 50-foot, rickety platform with hand-carved pins and homemade balls—most of which had only one hole about halfway through the ball, which, although made of hardwood, looked and felt like a petrified coconut shell. There was an old waiter named Mekimba who would run back into the pit as soon as someone would step up to bowl. He would gingerly retrieve each ball and return it along a ramshackle sluice, which was made of several hollow logs divided lengthwise and placed end to end at just the right angle to carry the ball back to the players. Watching this contraption work was half the fun of bowling. It was customary that anyone could immediately join a game in progress. This last night, we wound up playing with regular customers (some quite in their cups, which made every throw a game in itself). We did manage to keep a fairly accurate side score and, as usual, the Australians insisted that the losers (my team) buy the beer.

Most Zairois rarely see their country's big game since most animals live in restricted game parks over in the plains, or in dense rain forests far from the nearest village. Thus, they have adopted the Western expedient of the zoo. One would think that in a land of such great animals as Africa has, man would be incapable of the atrocities of European and American zoos. This is, unfortunately, not the case.

The *jardin zoologique* at Kisangani was in a high, wooded area above the falls, offering one of the most striking views in the country. I discovered there cages stuffed with monkeys, cats and lesser beasts, all doomed to a life of torture from lack of exercise and the random cruelties of native children who harassed and stoned them with impunity. Two great eagles sat in an aviary six feet square. They looked like scurvied chickens, their head and tail feathers shriveled to the bone.

Perhaps the grossest single example of custodial cruelty I have ever seen was a magnificent python whose snout had been crushed to a bloody pulp from its repeated lunges at the children who tittered with his every crash.

The children who frequent the zoo also go down to the river bank to beg and pilfer. There were only two couples of us, and I was mildly concerned for our safety. The children were not directly menacing but contented themselves by circling the Land Cruiser stealthily at a distance of 50 to 100 feet. They went up to it only when we had left it. They were as curious as children anywhere. Their presence, however, was motivated by more than mere curiosity or playful idleness. I do not doubt for a moment that they would have seized and run with anything left unattended or that they would have broken into the vehicle if they had not known we were watching them. At one point, I left a bunch of bananas on the hood while I looked inside for some film. One of the children immediately grabbed it and ran. I could only shrug and scold him, his teeth bared in a grin of conquest 50 feet away as he shared the booty with his mates.

Kisangani, like most African cities, has thousands of homeless waifs who band together to forage and plunder—as much for something to do as to eat. Irrespective of the obvious advantages of bringing industrialism to Africa, most of its people only participate in it indirectly, as scavengers. These children are among them, and their numbers are staggering.

When the Bedford had finally gone the Olympia was strangely silent. Luckily, five New Zealanders in an oversized Land Rover arrived that afternoon. We hit it off, and before long they were telling me how beautiful it was down under. They invited me to their tent for dinner, and afterward, I took them to the Cafe du Sport, where we bowled and talked about the South Pacific.

I don't suppose that I have ever met an unfriendly Australian or New Zealander. These people seem always to be big-hearted and friendly. And they are generous to a fault: it's impossible to buy one a beer, except if you lose—as you will—at his game of darts or bowling.

The next afternoon, a wiry little fellow whom I had met at the wharf the week before came to the Olympia. He said he had 50 gallons of super which he had been allotted by virtue of his position as vice-president of the local bank. He wanted 250 *Zaire* (three dollars per gallon).

"Too much," I told him.

"We can talk later," he said. Would I like to see it?

As the New Zealanders were also looking for fuel, I asked them along.

We drove out along the blacktopped road toward Beni, heading northeasterly along the river, then through an unexpectedly tidy subdivision. We came to a neat little mud-frame house along a street of others just like it.

Four children ran up to meet us. Our host patted their heads. One of them was about six and toted two six-shooters and wore a red cowboy hat. He drew and "fired" on us, then spun his pistols backward into the holsters. The others were quiet and well behaved. There was a new Peugeot station wagon in the yard. Flagstone steps led to the door. A coiffured woman's head appeared in the window, which a pink curtain subsequently covered. Moments later the door was opened, and a handsome, if matronly, woman in a blue housecoat called for the children to come in. They obeyed, except for the cowboy, who was then towed in by his sister. The woman was mildly scolding them as she closed the door. The rest of the neighborhood was by then alerted to our presence, and the yard soon filled with curious parents and tykes.

The drum of super (ethyl) gasoline was cached in a shed to the side of the house. Its cap was rusted and took a good deal of effort to open with a wrench and hammer. I had only a small plastic siphoning hose with which it would have taken us hours to transfer the gasoline, so we lifted the drum onto a stack of rocks above a ditch. A bully neighbor held the funnel and jerry can, and the New Zealanders tilted the drum. It was very heavy, and they strained mightily. Before I could negotiate a price, I had to satisfy myself that the gasoline was not contaminated with water or debris. I poured the jerry can into my regular tank, which was dry, and started the engine. After a few anxious turns, she kicked off and ran smoothly. I made a five-mile run: no coughs, no knocks. The gasoline was fine. The horror stories one hears (ruined motors, breakdowns due to water-gas) makes one cautious to a fault. Even at the pump I always held a filter between the nozzle and the tank.

After much haggling, I was only able to get the price down to 200 *Zaire* (about $2.50 per gallon). I did not know it then, but I would need the last fumes to make Goma.

Mural on house near Bangassou, Central African Empire.

Aïn-Salah ("God go with you") at dusk from the great emptiness of the Algerian Sahara.

Street kichen, Bobo-Dioulasso, Upper Volta.

The Hoggar Mountains of the deep Sahara, as seen from Assekrem, Algeria.

Villager builds a thatched hut, central Chad, near Lai.

Sara village, southcentral Chad, near Mondou.

McMath at Victoria Falls—"the mist that thunders"—Zambia. At flood stage, over 175 million gallons of water a minute plunge over the falls.

Market scene, Matameye, Niger.

Chapter X

There are rapids in the Bulu River just above the bridge at Epulu. There, on the riverbank, I found that the undergrowth had been neatly cut away for 180 acres, leaving only the giant silver trees of the forest and a pebbled footpath winding through them. This area is called the Station du Capture d'Epulu. There are several half-acre enclosures near the entrance to the park. At the time I was there, admission cost one *Zaire* and included the services of one of the dozen or so guards who loitered by the guardhouse.

In the first enclosure, just beyond the gate, grazed a pair of ecarpi—an astonishing animal which appears to be half giraffe, half zebra. The ecarpi has an unmistakable giraffe's head, yet its lower shoulders, flanks and legs are striped black and white like a zebra's. Because it serves as a refuge for this rapidly disappearing species, the Epulu station is informally known as "the ecarpi park."

The Belgians had stocked this station in the mid-'50s with a number of large regional species, including lions, leopards, gorillas (both the mountain and lowland varieties), chimpanzees, and several kinds of monkeys. An assortment of rare snakes had inhabited ground cages near the gate. During the civil war which followed independence in the early '60s, however, the park was attacked and its rangers and animals killed. Most of the cages have since been grown over by jungle. Those that remain visible are rusted through, the hatches open, bars bent or missing.

My guide insisted on showing me what I thought was an empty ground cage. I couldn't understand why he was leading me to it until he pointed with his walking stick to a magnificent puff adder, even larger than the one I had seen earlier in the creekbed. The snake was perfectly camouflaged against the yellow-orange of the fallen leaves.

Passing a small clearing, we came upon a column of army ants, each reddish brown and about a half-inch long. The guide crushed their leader with his boot, whereupon the column fell into disorder. Their confusion did not, however, stay their aggression, for several of them climbed onto my legs where they clung like leeches and had to be removed individually, a most painful process. I thought how inconvenient it would be to stumble into a whole nest of them. Jokingly I asked my guide if there were any truth to those hackneyed torture stories in which the victim is tied down over one. He smiled wanly and shook his head—an oddly ambiguous response, I thought. At length, I thanked him and returned to my tent, which I had pitched in a meadow overlooking the rapids. I made coffee and sat on the straw stool and meditated upon the lush green morning.

At Epulu I began to see the Pygmies. These "people of the forest" have more steadfastly rejected outside influence than perhaps all other Africans, including the Masai of the Serengeti and the Tuareg. Perhaps this is due to their isolation in the rain forest, which both camouflages them and provides them with shelter. It is also due to their dogged self-sufficiency. They can find edible herbs and roots where no one else would think to look, and their hunters are among the best.

For the most part the Pygmies resisted the predations of the slave traders as well as Leopold's wicked regime. They have also resisted efforts by the Zaire national government to politicize them. Their one link with the outside world is this tenuous trail along which a few of them sell their tiny rawhide drums and tortoise-shell mandolins.

About six kilometers behind the park into the forest is a Pygmy village. No outsiders go there without an invitation. The morning I spent at the park, however, a score of the Pygmy women and children had walked down the trail to the river bank just above the bridge. They were shy at first, but became less wary the longer I remained at the edge of the clearing. Eventually, I was able to get some pictures, but to my regret, they did not turn out. I was told that these Pygmies had grown accustomed to seeing foreigners; my Bedford companions had in fact made the trek to their village.

Around 10:30 that morning I continued towards the east. As I mounted the long hill into the village of Mambassa, I came upon the Bedford. They had had engine trouble and had taken a day at Epulu for rest and repairs. They were most fatigued, and their sores were multiplying. Normally hearty and rambunctious of a morning, they had grown jaded, wan and cantankerous. Our reunion was cheerful but subdued.

Just before the village of Komanda, the Ituri River is swift and narrow. Mary Edmonston was riding with me when we reached the old iron bridge. As we were well ahead of the Bedford, we pulled over on the far bank and stopped after we crossed the bridge.

The trail down to the river led through dense undergrowth, and we began to follow it. We had gone about 400 yards when suddenly it appeared as if we had entered an aviary. Hundreds, perhaps thousands, of every species of bird seemed to be gathered as if for a convention in this forest niche. We watched them for a long time, and when we moved on, they seemed to take no notice of us at all.

Just beyond a small clearing we reached the river and found, strung out over some rapids, two of those conical stickwoven fish traps facing into the current with only about a fifteen-degree arc protruding above the water. Inside the closest one to the bank were several frying-pan-sized fish.

163

Returning to the jeep, we drove up the ridge and experienced one of the most abrupt and dramatic changes in topography since the Sahara. Out of the dense rain forst there suddenly arose great bowl-like hills, with soft, easy-rolling meadows of thick blue grass. In twenty minutes we had reached the village of Komanda and were looking over the green hills of Africa toward the great Ruwenzori range of Uganda, its snow-capped Margherita Peak just visible through the distant mist. We could have turned left at Beni to drive into these "Mountains of the Moon," and it was hard to resist their allure. But Uganda was at the time a most perilous place. Indeed, it was at Beni that we first met some Ugandan refugees, mostly young men, whose tales of atrocity and malaise confirmed all that we had heard of the evil Amin Dada.

Beginning just south of Beni and continuing for some 150 miles to the village of Kayna-Bayonga one traverses the green hills of Africa in all their splendor along the western ridge of the Great Rift Valley. The hills are, in fact, cultivated terraces—gardens of maize, melons, coffee and tea, cultivated initially by the Belgians in the early 1900s. Handsome stone and hardwood homes with fifteen-foot ceilings—or at least their remnants—can be seen every dozen miles or so. It is truly remarkable how well preserved the foundations of these structures are when everything movable inside them has been looted or destroyed, every window broken, the plumbing ripped out, the exquisite paneling and cabinets chopped up for firewood. Amid the rubble one occasionally sees a family inscription and date on a concrete floor.

The Africans who reside on the property rarely live in the houses themselves but in huts or lean-tos alongside. When I asked one what he used the house for, he pointed proudly to the rafters. There in the beams was a beehive and a swarm through which one could climb to the second story, which housed several goats, one of which was a nanny badly in need of milking. She was chained to a section of pipe that extended from a beige commode still in place. The bathroom had apparently been installed in the 1950s. The bird's-egg blue tile and the shower curtain rod were still affixed to the wall, as was the medicine cabinet, although the mirror had been smashed. There was an ancient Gillete safety razor rusting on the top shelf. I wondered how that had escaped pilferage. In the ceiling were sockets for electric light fixtures, some with wires protruding. The generator was still in its shed out back, rusted away.

This colonial home was some twenty miles from the one before it and about ten miles from the next one down the road. It was on the top of the highest hill in the area and there was a large stand of timber which came right up to the garden. The garden—or rather, what was once the garden, as it had long since gone to seed—was a series of semi-circular, terraced plots which led up to where the lawn had been. This estate had been a cattle farm as had the neighboring ones. According to the Africans who were there, the farms belonged to a government official from Kinshasa who came out occasionally to inspect them.

Between Beni and Bukavu, on the south shore of Lake Kivu, I visited six of these expropriated estates. With the exception of one still lived on by the wife of the original owner, they were in approximately the same condition as the one just described.

One evening we camped along a narrow, grassy ravine below a modest homestead, occupied by a young agronomy graduate from Kisangani and his wife. They had fixed the doors and windows, and the wife had begun a small garden. Behind the house a hill rose at an abrupt 30 degrees. This was a tea plantation, the original terraces of which had eroded into one another. Scrub brush was growing among the tea plants. You could see where the young farmer had begun clearing away the brush and pruning the plants along the bottom tiers.

It was necessary for us to climb the hill for firewood, and the farmer directed us to a thicket near the crest. He gathered an armload and followed us back to camp. His wife offered us some of her pineapples, which we politely refused.

There was a brook nearby, where we bathed and washed our clothing. As dusk fell, the crowd of adults and children that had gathered to watch us began quickly to melt away until, at dark, not one remained, although there was still good visibility from the moonlight and our fire.

Continuing toward our destination of Goma, late the following afternoon, we arrived at the hamlet of Kayna-Bayonga, at the end of the ridge. To the northwest we could still see the rain forest from which we had climbed two days before. We made a camp on a promontory by the charred ruins of another Belgian homestead. The valley directly below us was blanketed by a thick, spongy fog that concealed its depth. Over the forest collected a bank of dark clouds, in which an electrical storm fired incessant flashes of lightning. It must have been far away, that storm, because we never heard its thunder.

At dawn the next morning, I watched as the fog below us lifted with the sunrise and dissipated into streaks of mist. The floor of the valley was deeper than I had imagined, nesting a village at the confluence of two streams. We saw smoke arising from fires there and a second column of smoke from another village, hidden from view behind a hill beyond the first. I wondered whether the people who lived in the furthest village knew any of the people who lived in the one directly below, and if any of them knew any of the people who lived up here.

Beyond Kayna-Bayonga we descended into the plains of the Great Rift Valley. There were a number of earth haulers and trucks working on the road—the first major road construction I had seen since Nigeria. They were building the road from Rwindi, the central station of the Virunga Game Park, up the mountain to Kayna-Bayonga.

The valley runs for several thousand miles from Lake Malawi in southern Africa through Ethiopia into southern Yemen in the north. It is the result of massive faulting in the earth's crust over millions of years. Some of the troughs in the fault are very deep. They are filled with water and are known today, south to north, as Lakes Malawi, Tanganyika, Idi Amin Dada, Mobutu Sese Seko, Victoria and Rudolph. A number of lesser lakes lie in between.

The valley's mild temperature, abundance of water, and vegetation made it in prehistoric times the range of hundreds of species of herbivores, of which the most abundant modern descendants are the wildebeest, gazelle, and zebra. These animals provide food for a host of predators, the most successful of which are the hyena, the big cats, and man.

At the foot of the mountain we saw grazing the first of what were to become vast herds of antelope and gazelle. Not far away, in a marsh to the east, wallowed 22 well-nourished hippopotami. While several of the others approached the hippos from downwind for photographs, Sidney and Nigel stalked them along the bank of the narrow stream which fed the marsh. Sensing something awry, the lead bull snorted defiantly and opened his huge jaws and slashed about in the air. The others replied with lesser grunts and moved more closely together in their communal huddle, each with its head resting on the shoulders of the next one in front. Then one of the women spied three lionesses prowling the perimeter of a herd of antelope, and we followed them with our field glasses for half an hour until they disappeared in the high grass.

CHAPTER XI

The cable-ferry boatmen who were to transport us across the Rutsuru had been drinking heavily and could not pull the cable without the help of the passengers. When we arrived they might have stayed on the far shore had it not been for the Ugandan Land Rover that suddenly appeared with four important-looking people in khaki. The ferry hurried across, with the four passengers doing most of the pulling. The Land Rover sped away as the ferry was being secured to its moorings.

Sidney and I were second in the queue. An aged Peugeot station wagon laden with fruit and vegetables and children was ahead of us. Only later did we see that the eight forlorn women on the levee also belonged with it. The Peugeot was just about to board when another Land Rover, this one from Rwindi, churned up the west bank in a cloud of dust. Inside were four Swiss tourists accompanied by an African park ranger in what looked like the uniform of a Boy Scoutmaster.

The ranger waved back the Peugeot and commandeered the ferry. They were breaking in line, but the Scoutmaster was impressive with all those medals and his .45 Colt. I wasn't about to argue. All we could do was cross with them to make sure that the ferry returned. By the time we reached mid-stream, it was obvious that Sid and I were doing all of the pulling. (The Swiss were chattering in the back seat. They only smiled condescendingly when we greeted them. They never dismounted.) The Scoutmaster strolled the deck like a commodore.

(We had left the Bedford at Rwindi—or they, rather, had left us. Because a bridge on the main road to Goma was washed out, the big truck had been forced to return to Kayna-Bayonga and attempt the back road. The Rutsuru ferry had a two-ton limit, so only smaller traffic could come this way. The road to the ferry had been a series of interconnected game trails in eastern Virunga Park. It had taken us three hours to get here. Only twenty miles ahead lay the Ugandan border, at the village of Ishasha. This would be as close as we would go to that unhappy land.

It was odd that with all of that road construction and ranger activity no one had warned us that the bridge was out. That meant that we had had to drive all the way down to Rwindi, wasting precious fuel. Once at Rwindi, I had had no choice but to take the shorter route via the ferry since I had already calculated that I was already 30 miles short of enough fuel to make Goma. I had asked Sidney if he wanted to go with me, and he had quickly accepted. Hopefully we would meet the others at Goma. But they, too, were short of fuel.)

Once we had put the Swiss and their guide ashore we pulled back to the west bank. The river was worse than I had feared, its current a surging, muddy flood that shoved against the starboard side. The crew only feigned at pulling. They'd passed their bottle around again before pushing off, and their breath reeked with liquor.

When we returned to the west bank our hands were blistered. The Peugeot boarded and the captain motioned for me to follow. I did, setting the brake and descending to help pull again. I had worn my muleskin work gloves for the first few minutes of the previous trip but had taken them off when I saw that they only slipped on the grease of the cable. When the crew chief saw that I was not wearing them, he demanded to use them himself. I knew he would get no traction and that they would only slip on the cable for him also, but it was amusing, in spite of my blistering hands, to watch him straining at his burden as he pretended to be pulling his share of the load.

"Hey, look at that water, man." Sid pointed—wide-eyed. I walked over and saw that we were in real trouble. The water level had risen so that the river was exactly flush with the top of the pontoon hull. The weight of both vehicles was proving too much, and if we did not hurry, the river would surge into the hull and the ferry would sink.

The captain now saw the danger and stopped his clowning and banter and exhorted the others to pull. I knew that none of them could swim in their condition and that, if we capsized, their combat boots would surely drag them to the bottom.

Sid and I were pulling valiantly on the seemingly dead weight. It was like one of those escape nightmares you have as a child. But just as the water was beginning to bleed over into the hull, we canted slightly upstream, following the slack of the cable into the current at some 30 degrees. This reduced the drag and enabled us just barely to make it across.

Sid and I quickly agreed that we had earned the five *Zaires* we would normally pay as toll. Before the crew had a chance to collect it, we packed in and bounded away up the levee. The chief was so shaken that Sid had even managed to get my gloves back, slipping them off as they shook hands.

The road followed a game trail across a dry marsh flat. It was poorly marked, and we had to guess at successive junctions of meandering tracks. Twice I made compass sightings.

The area was teeming with wildlife. Antelope and zebra were in abundance, and a herd of twenty elephants grazed in high grass near the road. Suddenly Sid hit my shoulder and said in a low voice, "Lion." Sure enough, a handsome lion was sitting in the shade not twenty feet away. He gazed at us distractedly. Sid took a photo, and we continued to watch the cat for several minutes.

By now, it was close to 4:00 p.m. Ishasha was, I calculated, twenty miles to the east. I was disturbed from my logistics when Sid said again, "Lion." This time it was a lioness, much bigger than the male. She was out 100 yards, but as she was lying directly in the sun, no photograph was possible.

We drove on and were passing through a ravine when the engine began missing. It backfired rapidly and then died. Maybe it was only the condensor, I thought, which could be quickly replaced; if it was the distributor, the lions were going to have neighbors for the night. I got out of the jeep.

I got out the spark-plug wrench and pulled out a hot No. 6: there was the problem—dirty spark plugs. I hadn't cleaned them since Bangui, 2000 miles back. "Damn!" I knew I should have been doing that at least every 500 miles.

Just then we heard a car: it was the Peugeot from the ferry, loaded to the last onion. People were hanging out of the windows and one door was open. The driver made no move to stop, and we did not flag him down. We hoped our only problem was the dirty plugs. Half an hour later I gave her a try: sure enough, on the second turn she kicked off and away we were.

The Ugandan border post at Ishasha was quiet. Relations between Zaire and Uganda were cordial, and there was no visible military contingent on either side. At the edge of town was a small lodge next to an empty gas station. According to the attendant, there had been no fuel there for weeks, although most of eastern Zaire's fuel comes through here (from Kenya's port of Mombasa via Kampala). We decided to try to make Rutshuru where the Michelin map indicated a Catholic mission. Perhaps they would spare a jerry can of gas.

We found two priests at Rutshuru who were glad to have company and gave us a warm welcome. They were having dinner and cheerfully set two extra places, inquiring anxiously about conditions to the northeast. They were surprised to hear that we had seen no military activity and had been stopped only once for a road check since Kisangani. They were skeptical about our friends' making it on the back road. The Goma mission had reported the road impassable.

"By the way," asked the older priest, "how did you get across the Rutshuru? I thought the ferry had sunk."

We told them of our experience.

"*Mon Dieu,*" he said. "That thing sank last month with two Land Rovers. They're only supposed to take one vehicle at a time, you know. . . ."

Later, over coffee in the den, we browsed through a fine French and English library and a wide collection of jazz and Bach with which we were serenaded at breakfast by the Sansui stereo.

There was a third priest, who kept to himself and smiled and nodded only when addressed. He had served in Uganda before coming here and still had friends there. When the conversation turned to Idi Amin he told us quietly that the news accounts were not exaggerated. There were, indeed, many worse atrocities than those which had been reported. During the years immediately following independence, he said, tribalism had been much less of a problem in Uganda than elsewhere—for example, in Kenya. The priest said that he had tried to communicate directly with colleagues in Uganda, but "one must be very careful with what one says in a letter." He had not received a reply to his letters for over three months.

The priests told us about the volcano Nyirangongo, above Goma, some 50 miles away. They said that when it was active they could see the reflection of its fire against clouds in the night sky. The volcano had erupted the previous December 23rd and devastated the entire northern section of Goma, killing over a thousand people. The fathers had heard the rumbling for several days during the eruption; the display of lava and fire was, they said, "unearthly."

Our hosts did not know where we could find fuel. We had asked a store manager in town, who had none (or so he said). The mission had several barrels of spare fuel for their own vehicles, but as few and unpredictable as deliveries were, they had to hold on to it. We did not even ask.

We were each given a guest cabin, simply but comfortably furnished. The next morning, to the strains of Bach, we breakfasted and said goodbye.

Twenty miles outside of Goma, on a stretch of steep, uphill grade, the gas gauge sat on zero. Miraculously, there were enough fumes to get us to the summit of the lower ridge of Nyirangongo, where we were able to look down on the Rift Valley's most beautiful lake, Kivu, with Goma nestled like a tiny gem in its northwest bay.

The rim of the volcano was high and to our right. The slope was strewn with the remains of the December holocaust: a charcoal-grey field of cold lava, like the rapids of an escaped river suddenly frozen in full fury. The volcano had since become dormant.

I cut off the engine and we coasted the eight kilometers down into Goma. Following some Shell signs, we arrived at the station and coasted into line ahead of a friendly Australian couple in a Land Rover. It was 11:45 a.m. Fifteen minutes later, we were full and the station was closed. That afternoon a notice was posted that there was no more fuel. That station did not reopen during the five days we were there.

Goma is the forwarding depot for food, petrol and sundries coming from Kenya, through Uganda, to the remote lake provinces of eastern Zaire. The large town on the south coast, Bukavu, depends on this lifeline for its fuel. One need only look at the map to see why Zaire's Mobutu maintains friendly relations with Uganda's Amin.*

South of Goma we found some tracks leading to the lake and on a small peninsula located a campsite and set up the tent. We built a fire, made coffee, and watched women from the nearby village draw water from the lake and slap clean their clothes on the bank.

When we returned to town we met the Encounter Bedford. They confirmed the priests' description of the back road. Dozens of vehicles (mostly trucks) they said, were hopelessly mired in the mud. Many had had to be pushed aside so the Bedford could pass. Some of the drivers had no food or water. In one instance they had had to completely unload a log truck

---

*Zaire is also on friendly terms with South Africa and Rhodesia since most of its copper now goes by rail across southern Africa to Durban and Port Elizabeth. The Angola railroad has been closed by the continuing civil war there.

so that it could be pushed out of a hole. The driver had then deliberately allowed the truck to roll into the next hole, blocking the road again. It was obvious that he would have kept that up all day. Somebody forcibly took the wheel and steered the truck off to one side on the next push. "The chap had the cheek to expect that we should reload his logs!" one said.

Many of the trucks were stalled because they had no batteries: it is customary in Africa to depend upon passersby to restart one's engine. Many vehicles carry no spare tires or other parts. A flooded road can be a real disaster.

At dusk that first night on the lake, my eye caught a flash in the mountains to the south. Looking more closely with the field glasses, I discovered the freshly erupted volcano, Herakunta, hardly three weeks old. In apparent slow motion, great slags of lava were being hurled out of the ground. Occasionally, its rhythm would be interrupted by a particularly massive shot that would soar far down the mountain, leaving a trail of settling cinders. It hardly seemed that it could be approached on foot to within 200 meters, as a park ranger in town had said that afternoon.

But Sid and I and some twenty from the Bedford decided to make the climb. We arrived an hour late, and there was a hustle in the guide's voice as he led off. He was, you could tell, a seasoned mountain man, although a scrappily dressed soldier. He carried a heavily oiled Springfield .03 rifle, the bolt of which remained open the entire time. Except for a single round of ammunition (which he carried in his left hand), his only other equipment was a small canteen of water.

After a cakewalk through a banana and pineapple grove, we entered a menacing thicket of brambles and thorns, which slowly gave way to open, rocky hillside interspersed with saplings. The ground was strewn with sharp, angular chunks of lava that cut painfully into the sides of our boots. Several of the climbers wore sneakers and had a most difficult time of it.

The hike lasted over six hours, with but a single rest stop of about twenty minutes at 2:00. We hiked single file and for a time maintained our original order of march. However, with more and more sore feet and undone packs, there developed an accordion effect (exacerbated by the guide's pace, which was much too quick for unconditioned climbers). I saw what was happening early on and managed to stay right behind him in order to keep a more even pace.

When we had not reached our destination, or seen any sign that we were near it, by 3:15, I thought that perhaps we had taken the wrong path. Then, from just over the next rise came what sounded like the air burst of a 155 howitzer round. As we climbed higher, the explosions became louder, though at times they were muffled when we were in a draw or behind a ridge. Gradually, we were able to hear the crashes that followed each explosion by several seconds as the red-hot slag slid down the base of the cone. After a particularly loud explosion there would be a longer delay and the crash would sound much nearer.

Finally, about 4:00, we came to a slope just opposite the cone, about 250 to 300 yards away. The cone was about 200 feet high and I would estimate it to have been a quarter-mile in circumference at its base. The volcano was a relatively small one—a mere fissure compared to the enormous Nyiran-gongo. The top, or mouth, of the volcano was partially split so that you could see the fiery cauldron frothing within. It was easy to see how primitive peoples would think these things alive, with souls of their own. As if to warn us against taking it for granted, its deceptively steady rhythm would suddenly be interrupted by a terrific churning crunch, following which a bargeload of slag would be hurled into the forest.

As we reached the campsite it began to rain, a slow, even downpour. At first this was refreshing, but when we stopped moving it became miserable. Our campsite consisted of a dozen or so flimsy lean-tos from previous expeditions. When I had located a relatively dry one, Sid and I set up my light Alpine plastic tent under it so that we could lie slightly uphill out of the rain and watch the volcano. Carolyn joined us and together we scrounged about for dry grass for matting.

As it became darker, the eruptions increased in intensity. The smoke billowed straight up hundreds of feet before being caught by the wind. The air had the faint smell of sulphur, but it was not as pungent as I had suspected it would be. More than once during the night, a chunk of lava landed in the forest only feet from our lean-to, hissing as it vaporized the wet leaves. Most of the slag, however, slid down the surface of the cone to smolder at the bottom before turning cold. I suppose that it was inevitable that two of the more daredevil Australians would climb down there to light their cigars. One of them even left his trousers out to dry overnight.

Among our party were a half-dozen porters, hired at five *Zaires* each by some of the Bedford people to carry their gear, which included packs and sleeping bags as well as two jerry cans of water and a smaller can of kerosene for fire-making. For this, however, the Africans simply followed the old scout practice of retrieving dry kindling from under fallen logs. Within a very few minutes, they had a fire that warmed the lean-to but didn't smoke it up. A narrow improvised flue let the smoke escape. There they huddled snuggly before a big black kettle fetched from a nearby cache, while the rest of us thrashed about looking for shelter and firewood. We eventually borrowed coals from their fire to start our own.

I slept little, waking occasionally to walk about. The camp was silent except for the volcano. We were like mythological voyagers camped at the gates of Hell.

The climb down the next morning took but two and a half hours. It was a warm, dry day, but we felt punishment to our feet from the hard, knotty lava much more acutely than we had the day before. Happily, two of the Bedford crew who had remained behind had tea ready when we arrived.

Sid and I drove back to the peninsula at the end of the lake and resumed possession of our campsite. Later that afternoon, our companions arrived with their own horror stories of the back road from Kayna-Bayonga.

That night I again fell asleep watching the explosions of Herakunta. I was aware that it had not been all that long since our planet's first men stared in wonder at Kivu's enigmatic volcanoes.

CHAPTER XII

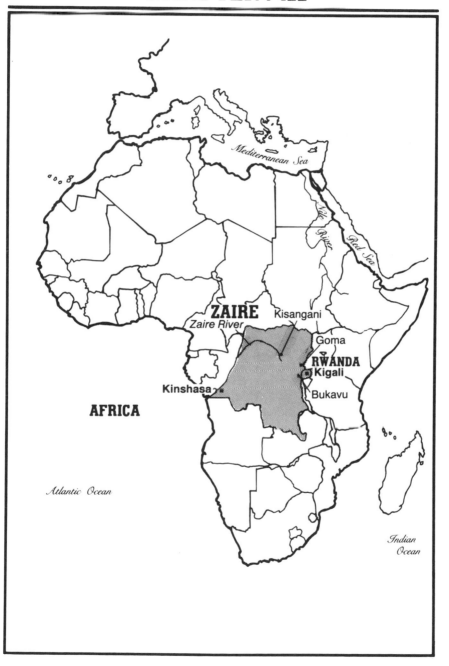

Mediterranean Sea

Nile River

Red Sea

ZAIRE Kisangani

Zaire River

Goma

RWANDA
Kigali

Kinshasa

Bukavu

AFRICA

Atlantic Ocean

Indian Ocean

After three days' rest I again felt like moving on. According to the map, I could either drive directly into Rwanda from Goma or proceed south to the far end of the lake and have a try at finding the elusive mountain gorilla.

Although once the lord of the forest, this titan primate has been reduced to foraging for a living in two tiny redoubts of Lake Kivu's mountain rain forest. One, Kiushi Biega, is in Zaire. The other is in Rwanda, across the lake. Although both are officially protected by government decree, they are constantly raided by native poachers. Heads and paws bring high prices in Europe, and most zoos will pay a princely sum for a live infant.

I decided to head south. My Bedford companions, having also hiked to Herakunta, met to decide which direction they would take. The 100-kilometer road down the lake was known to be treacherous, and they barely had enough diesel to make Kigali, not allowing for side trips or detours. But they decided to risk it.

The west coast of Lake Kivu had the same rich, fertile farmland we had seen north of Goma. As before, the specialty crop was tea and the trees along the bank were contour-terraced in the rich soil of the hillsides, right down to the lake itself.

Each plantation we passed seemed to have a distinct character and, although most of them had been expropriated, a few Belgians remained as managers or life owners. I briefly visited two of them, each with an elegant 1930s ranch-style home with self-contained generator, radio shack, pink and blue tile, and stainless-steel plumbing—some of the first available anywhere in Africa. The second home I visited was on a small plantation, about 1000 acres. The widow of the man who had founded the plantation in 1923 still ran it. She had gone to Goma to the doctor and I did not see her, but her manager, an old African who had been there for the entire life of the estate, showed me around. He was 75 years old, and he and his wife had both been born there before whites had settled the region. His sons and their families worked the place with him now. The widow, unable to venture into the fields, depended upon the old man to supervise the work.

She and her husband had raised six children, all of them long since married and settled in Europe or America. Their photographs papered the walls of the living and drawing rooms, which contained quaintly inappropriate eighteenth-century French furniture. The floors were littered with worn Persian rugs; the walls smelled of cedar. In one corner, facing the lake, was a stately mahogany secretary's desk. Wide French windows opened onto a garden lush with roses and a collection of local flora. From the drawing room window was a panoramic view of the lake. The full colors of the flowers and the aggressive jungle green of the hillside harmonized with the ice-blue water of the lake. Bees droned among the flowers and the air was heavy with the scent of roses. The caretaker's naked children wrestled in the grass.

We camped just off the road near the plantation. By mid-afternoon the following day, we reached the foot of Kiushi Biega, twenty kilometers north of Bukavu. We camped in a quinine orchard, several of us actually stringing our tents between pairs of the more solid fruit trees. After dinner, Terry, Wyn Jones, and I drove the ten kilometers up the mountain to the ranger station to see if we could enter the park to look for gorillas. The guard told us to be there the next morning at 8:00 sharp.

Wyn, an amiable Welsh farmer and car dealer, about 29, had taken off a year from the family business to make this trek. He was the "favorite uncle" of the Bedford group.

That night I had the misfortune of stepping in not one but two hills of giant ants. Crawling out of the tent to make a late visit to the woods, I suddenly felt them crawling and stinging their way up my legs. I charged out of the orchard and tore off my clothes. It took fifteen minutes to pluck the clinging devils off, one at a time. Hopping mad, I poured a pint of gas into a fruit can and headed back to seek my revenge. I had poured about half of the fuel on their nest when, to my dismay, I once again felt something funny. Looking down, I was standing in an even bigger nest. I again danced about like a wild man, this time ripping my trousers as I pulled them off. After that, I gave up and slept in the jeep.

The *pistiers* (trackers), two barefoot old men, dismounted from the rear of the jeep. Three soldiers, who were also rangers, sat in the front talking and smoking. One of them had an M-1 carbine. The other two were unarmed, except for the elaborately carved walking stick the lieutenant carried. He had an empty .45 holster on a web belt.

The *pistiers* stood silently off to one side awaiting the order to proceed. Each carried a machete in the manner of all bush people—not in a sheath or scabbard as soldiers and Europeans do, but in his right hand, the hilt cupped so that the cutting edge rested lightly against his wrist and forearm.

When we were ready, the lieutenant motioned and the *pistiers* set out on a trail which was hidden at the side of the road by high grass. We followed a narrow cut for some 50 yards, then we came to a track which remained clearly marked for a quarter-mile. We walked at a steady pace, the *pistiers* leading the way. They obviously had performed these services many times, for they went quietly about their task, listening and looking along the side of the trail for telltale signs of the animal they were paid to track.

I was at the head of the column, close to the older tracker. He was short, not stocky but indisputably solid. His bare feet were calloused and gnarled.

The formidable musculature of his calves carried him along with the grace of a *danceur*. The younger man was taller and he moved on ahead as the point. He held up his hand and the column stopped. Somewhere overhead fluttered a bird, unseen. The lieutenant pointed off to the left of the trail where the growth had been mashed down quite recently.

"*Gorilles*," he whispered. "*Ils etainent deja ici ce matin* (They were already here this morning)."

But the animals had entered the road here, not left it. So we went on, everyone very quiet now, our first eager whispers having died away. The point halted again and sawed the air with his open palm to the left: they had returned to the brush here. We approached the spot slowly. The undergrowth was much thicker and very damp, and you could see the trail clearly. The animals had broken twigs and branches as they walked, so that for some 40 feet into the forest, their trail was clearly marked with freshly exposed pulp.

The trackers moved into the brush, hacking a narrow passage with their machetes. The smell of the damp leaves and freshly cut brush mingled with the intoxicating aroma of unknown flowers. Our clothing was by now drenched from the wet leaves. In the distance we heard a long roll of thunder, and the lieutenant said it would be raining soon. We continued for an hour, up and down one ridge after another, halting occasionally to follow the intent gaze of one of the *pistiers*, then resuming our march.

"Pssst!" the lead tracker sternly signaled us to be quiet. He smiled broadly and pointed into a stand of trees up the hill to the left. Standing in a thicket, browsing calmly, was a female gorilla. She observed us with curiosity, not alarm. With my binoculars I could discern a half-dozen other gorillas in nearby trees.

We had been watching for half an hour when a young male began to pant rapidly and bounded playfully to the ground. One by one the others followed and strode in front of us, not twenty feet away. The female, who was larger than the others, stood motionless while they passed. From a tree further up the ridge came a high-pitched shriek, whereupon another large female descended. On her back was an infant, the size of a small puppy.

Then we heard a great roar from far to our left. All activity stopped, even the playing of the young male. There was another roar, then a crash, followed by intermittent roaring and crashing until, suddenly, there he was: Muchamuka, at 650 pounds, the largest gorilla known to exist. His body was silver-grey, with just a faint charcoal streak along his flanks. He hulked from the undergrowth toward the elder *pistier*.

We had been told not to flee if a gorilla charged us, but to stand and look past him. To run might stir him actually to attack. To look directly into his eyes might convey a threat. It was important to remember that although the animals were naturally withdrawn to the point of timidity, a dominant male such as Muchamuka, if his position or territory is threatened, can and will attack.

We now looked on with both fear and anticipation. Suddenly, the animal beat his chest and, with a rapid succession of defiant roars, charged to what seemed barely a foot of the old tracker. It was all the rest of us could do to stand our ground—that the *pistier* did not even blench was the supreme tribute to his professionalism.

True to what we had been told to expect, the ape gave the tracker a long, admonitory glance, then turned and strutted to the nearest tree and slowly ascended—all the while keeping a cold eye in our direction. Halfway up, he paused and let out another roar, whereupon all of the grounded gorillas hastened to the trees. The mother bounded up the trunk of a sapling, her baby clutching her hackles.

It soon began to rain, and our binoculars and cameras quickly clouded over. The plastic bags we had brought along to protect the lenses were ineffective. In any event, there was little to photograph in the cold downpour. Smarter than we, our subjects had snuggled out of sight in the thick leaves to abide the storm. After half an hour, even those of us who had thought to bring rain gear were drenched.

Just as we decided to hike out, Muchamuka climbed down and everyone's interest temporarily returned. The bully took his time, as if delighting in harrassing these undignified interlopers. Finally, he stood for a long moment against the backdrop of the tree, then turned and stalked into the forest.

Bukavu sits high on the green banks above Lake Kivu and somehow blends into the forest so that you are there before you realize it. Although it is the largest town on the lake, there is only a small harbor for the two or three ferries that ply to Kibuye in Rwanda and to Goma to the north. They run once a week when they are loaded.

Because there is no rail outlet or all-weather road from Lake Kivu to the outside world, its traffic is strictly local. Bukavu handles most of that— largely tea, coffee and fish in addition to Primus beer. There are scores of small pirogues. and a few motor launches belonging to local fishermen.

Sprawled along the high bank of the lake is a long market where meat and fish, and a wider variety of vegetables than in any market I'd seen since Bangui, could be purchased. Perhaps this is because most of the produce is for local consumption, and little is exported. Along the bank of the lake was a labyrinth of stalls selling green and red peppers, onions, giant catfish, several types of yams and ground roots, and, of course, potatoes. Among the available fruits were passion fruit, pawpaw, pineapple, banana, a kind of knotty green apple, and several sweet wild berries.

Merchants in the Bukavu market were brisk but friendly in their dealings. I immediately noticed that the normal market custom of idle young men hanging about was not followed here. Customers made their purchases and moved on. The air was full of sweet fragrances of flowers and the smoke from fires where women were cooking peanuts and making a kind of tortilla of bananas and red peppers. There were, of course, pans full of frying plantain and mealie meal and rice. I was surprised that I did not see any mantioc. A Peace Corps volunteer I met later said that the people here eat very little of it, preferring potatoes and yams instead.

After buying fruit and vegetables, we crossed the river into Rwanda at

Cyangugu. Rwanda is one of the two former German colonies (Burundi is the other) taken over by Belgium after World War I and administered as part of the Belgian Congo. They were actually part of Tanganyika but, because of their geographic and tribal grouping, were deemed more convenient for the Belgians to administer than the British who took Tanganyika.

It was 90 miles from Cyangugu to Kibuye along the eastern rim of Lake Kivu. The road was a goat trail of basketball-sized boulders and three-foot-deep potholes. Washouts cut across it at regular intervals. The trace itself led up and down the volcanic mountains of the lake—now verdant with tea and lush grass and occasional patches of potatoes, cabbages, and maize. At times the grade exceeded fifteen degrees.

The drive up took two days, but the weather was cool. I had begun feeling the need for a slower pace than the Bedford had set and decided to leave my friends in Bukavu. Since we chose to proceed to Kigali at the same time, however, we were inevitably together. At the Rwandese border I asked Mary, the Australian, to ride with me.

Kibuye was a dust- and wind-blown shanty town, except for the old stone mission, a veritable cathedral, high on the bluffs above an inlet from the lake. The mission had been built from native rock and wood by the village's first Belgian priest. It resembled a medieval palace.

Mary and I were so weary of the wretched potholed road that when the mission's Scottish sister, Rosalie, told us of the guest house on the shore at the bottom of the town, we immediately decided to stay. The house was spacious and tidy. Facing the lake was a narrow porch where I set up the camp stove. There was even a hot-water bath—if you asked the houseboy to connect the electric water heater. The power came from a generator at an army camp at the top of the hill. It was cut off at 10:00 after a three-flash warning five minutes before the hour.

After dinner we hiked back up to the mission and had a long visit with Sister Rosalie. She conducted us on a tour of the cathedral's vocational school for girls, of which she was headmistress. From the steps we watched the sun settle behind the green hills and shower orange and purple hues across the blue-green water of the lake—the blue soft in the twilight, like a coral sea.

CHAPTER XIII

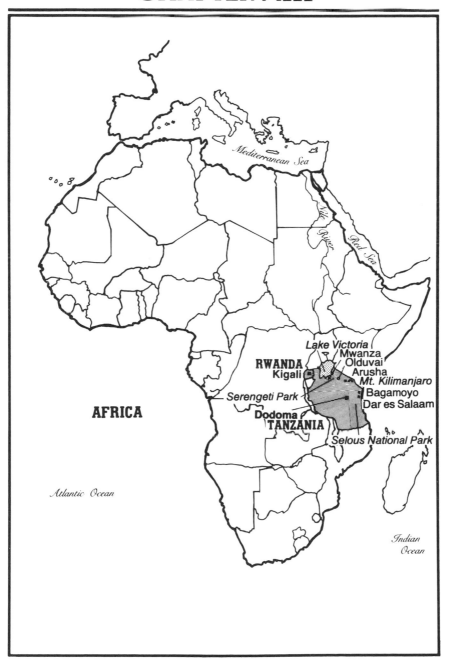

Mediterranean Sea

Nile River

Red Sea

Lake Victoria
Mwanza
Olduvai
Arusha
Mt. Kilimanjaro
Bagamoyo
Dar es Salaam

RWANDA
Kigali

Serengeti Park

AFRICA

Dodoma
TANZANIA

Selous National Park

Atlantic Ocean

Indian Ocean

Kigali was teeming with thieves. Many were Ugandan refugees who had no other source of income. Local Indian merchants, however, said that there were also among them many Rwandese who had been unable to find work in the city and could not return to their homes in the mountains. Whatever the reason, a vehicle was an understood mark. Bystanders quickly edged close to feel and pry at the doors and windows—even before the passengers dismounted. Twice after having gone for coffee, I returned to find the right wind vent forced open. On the first such occasion my Instamatic, a wrench and a screwdriver (carelessly left in the glove compartment) were gone. I evidently surprised the thief, for as I walked over to the rig a strapping young African darted away, his arms bent as if clutching loose objects.

With so many thieves, camping was impossible, and there were no moderately priced hotels. I finally found a small clean room at the Presbyterian youth center for the equivalent of three dollars a night. The young people, some twenty of them, were mostly students from the bush. The staff were students and received a salary from the church for keeping and cleaning the building. Exhausted in spite of my two-day respite at Kibuye, I became very depressed. I was fending this off one afternoon by writing, when from the next room came the soft harmony of a choir. I listened for a good while, then rose and walked down the corridor and peeked in through the slightly open door. There were only five of them, but they sounded like twenty. I returned to my notebook, my loneliness and melancholy somewhat relieved.

One young man with whom I talked at the center was a Ugandan refugee whose entire family (father, mother, four brothers and two sisters) had been arrested by one of Amin's terror squads. He was about twenty. He had returned from a neighboring village to find his home deserted, the cooking fire still burning. A neighbor told him the police were looking for him. He had hidden in the forest, making his way by night to the border and finally slipping into Rwanda. It had been three years, and he had heard nothing of his family's fate.

The family of a tradesman's helper I met in the vegetable market was, according to the Indian merchant, beheaded and their heads placed on stakes in the village as an example to others.*

It rained virtually the entire three days I was in Kigali. I was having compression problems (fearing a defective valve) but at the small Toyota dealership found a savvy Dutch mechanic. He assured me that my problem was due only to the abnormally high altitude for which the valves had been set and that normal compression would return on my descent into Tanzania. Pressed for time, the Dutchman referred me to the garage of an Indian, Manjit Sing, for body work. There I repaired the horn, which had been jarred loose and fallen into the engine. Sing next spent a half-hour securing the roof rack, which had become a wobbly nuisance and upon which I had long since ceased carrying anything but light personal effects. Sing charged me nothing for his hour's work. When I insisted, he absolutely refused, saying that it was the least he could do for someone who had come so far.

The seasonal rains were earlier and heavier than usual. Sing told me that I would be lucky to get through western Tanzania to Mwanza, since many bridges were reportedly washed out. One driver had become stranded in a flood which completely submerged his truck. He had had to abandon it to save his life.

It had at that time been raining for twelve hours straight in Kigali. The hall in the Presbyterian center was a half-inch deep in water from the broken window.

I was up before sunrise the next morning. The rain had stopped briefly and there was some visibility. I had parked the Toyota right up next to the church—back in—at the direction of the old guard. He slept on the ground on the other side of the hedgerow that separated the church from the residence. He had a six-foot corrugated iron shed as shelter, which was just big enough to keep him dry. With him was a ferocious wolflike dog. Given the high number of practicing thieves in Kigali, I did not envy him his job. He and a companion told me how they had carefully protected my vehicle during the night. I showed my appreciation by tipping them a dollar.

I had breakfast at the Hotel Mille Collines, where I tried to cash a check at the only bank that was open. While eating a surprisingly cheap two-dollar breakfast I met two United Nations food-aid officials with disgust and ennui written on their faces. These normally restrained bureaucrats (from whom such emotions do not easily escape) did not cease bending my ear. It was stupid, they said, to spend scarce funds to fly in food to a country which should be exporting it. The distribution of food was not only stymied by an ineffective bureaucracy, but a great deal was stolen by officials. They too had seen the bags of American grain for sale in the local market in Kigali as well as other African markets. They recounted numerous instances of the failure of farmers to pursue, once taught, simple techniques which would increase their production.

---

*It is difficult to decide which of these atrocity stories are true. On several occasions I would read the lurid details of an atrocity in the local press but find it unreported in the British or American papers. One such that played for days in the South African tabloids was of the beheading of three Americans caught with prostitutes in a Kampala Hotel. To the best of my knowledge, the story was never reported by the American or British press.

The road was blacktopped to within twenty miles of the Rusumu Falls on the Kegera River border with Tanzania. Where the surface ended, the terrain suddenly rushed downhill to make up in twenty miles the previous 500 miles of ascent from Lake Kivu. As I descended, I looked down upon the mud flats and scrub brush of western Tanzania. In spite of the rains, the Kegera seemed to be low and its falls modest.

The Rwandese immigration officer was selling Tanzanian shillings in the middle of the bridge. Although it was illegal on his part, and the Tanzanians watched with binoculars from the post on their side, I bought some from him. When they asked how much I had purchased, I answered truthfully: 285 shillings.* When I was told I would have to forfeit the money, I protested on the grounds that they knew that he was trading as if he were an official banker. The inspector at length relented, and I was allowed to go with only a warning.

For the next twenty miles I saw not a single dwelling or vehicle. The road narrowed to a wet, red-clay track which at times all but disappeared. It had rained heavily the night before, and there were no individual vehicle tracks to be seen. Up and down the roller-coaster landscape I continued until, suddenly, down the next hill I saw water surging across the road. It was a rising river, swirling with eddies and whirlpools sucking down and disgorging drifting debris.

A boy hailed me from the bank: "Okay, you go okay like this—" He motioned to the right, then abruptly left, with the back of his hand. I was not convinced; I shook my head. He smiled a great reassuring smile, removed his sandals, rolled up his trouser legs, and waded out into the stream, motioning that I should follow behind him. The water remained at mid-calf for a few yards, then abruptly he sank to his knees. Smiling, he beckoned again. A gaggle of children appeared on the far shore and behind them blurred a splotch of color which resolved into a group of women. They too were still, watching. I advanced, cautiously, stopping at the edge of the water when I remembered I hadn't shifted into four-wheel drive. I dismounted and locked the hubs.

Back in, I shifted into low ratio and drove into the river. The machine growled, and as I shifted into second a wake of muddy water churned up behind me. I could feel the pressure of the current above the running board. After a sudden dip, the jeep slowed as if it were going to stall, then regained its power and climbed the bank to dry ground.

It was 4:15 p. m. and getting dark when I reached the village of Rulenge. I wanted to push on toward Mwanza, the main Tanzanian port of Lake Victoria, still 430 kilometers away. I decided to try to make Biharamulu that night, another 30 kilometers. Although there were several more fords indicated on the map, I had renewed confidence in the vehicle's ability to handle them.

---

*At the time the official exchange rate was twelve shillings to one U.S. dollar. The black-market rate was eighteen to twenty shillings to the dollar.

184

Ten kilometers further on, I met the first vehicle I'd seen since entering Tanzania. It was a small red Peugeot panel truck loaded with road workers. I asked about the road ahead.

"Very bad flooding—long washout ahead," said the driver, an Indian. "We had to turn back, but you can make it." In the headlights I studied the map and calculated that it was another twenty miles to the next village, Kyakahura. I thanked the men and continued on my way.

I didn't see the water until it was too late, striking it just as my foot hit the brake. I must have been doing at least 40 and great sheets of brown water churned out from either side of the jeep. It fishtailed and skidded to a stop, headlights shining into a thick fog.

I sat for minutes, dazed. How far I had hurtled into the river I did not know—nor did I know in which direction the road lay. I was sitting at an angle, the water in front almost up to the lights. Fortunately, I had my seat belt fastened. I left the lights on, took a flashlight from under the seat and climbed up through the window. The water was just above the running board, so I dared not open the door. The engine was dead, but I didn't want to try to start it until I was ready to go and knew exactly which direction to take. I jumped. The current was quite strong, but it was not quite so deep as I had feared—about knee-high. The lights made a strange glow in the fog.

It was important to feel the bottom slowly with my feet, else I might have stepped off into a hole and lost my footing. Five, ten, twenty paces now I crept along with the flashlight, seeing nothing but a few clumps of shrubs here and there. My headlights were now barely visible.

After another 30 feet I finally reached the bank, keeping the receding lights all the while in view. I made my way slowly downstream, deciding to risk losing the headlights, which I did. After another 50 yards I came to the road. Turning left, I followed it as it submerged into the water, and shortly the headlights reappeared. Approaching the jeep, I saw that I had gone about ten feet off the road into about four feet of water. If only the jeep would start, I felt that I could back out. Carefully, I waded out and climbed aboard.

The jeep started on the first try. Shifting down into low ratio and into reverse I backed onto the road, then quickly aimed between two clumps of trees which were swaying gently in the current. I knew they lay on either side of the roadbed. Moments later I had mounted the bank.

Needless to say, I drove much more carefully after that. Finally, at 10:30, I came to the Finnish Pentecostal mission at Biharamulu. The young director and his wife were eager for conversation. I was the first overlander they had had from Zaire in many months. They were especially anxious about the war in Shaba Province, where they had a mission. I, of course, could tell them only what I had heard from others. The woman prepared a good supper of meat and rice, and we talked until very late.

The room to which I was assigned was next door to that of two Finnish geologists who had been searching (unsuccessfully, they said) for minerals in the Westlake district. The following morning at breakfast we swapped road information. The geologists insisted that there was even worse flooding between Geita and the Lake Victoria ferry at Busisi. The road, they said, was completely blocked by a bus that had partly fallen off the bridge into the river. Traffic was backed up for miles. My only hope would be to drive into the river in four-wheel drive and attempt to cross and regain firm ground without getting stuck. They strongly advised against it, saying that several other vehicles had tried and failed, becoming irretrievably stranded.

The mission's primary task was to care for expectant mothers and some 60 infants, many of them orphans. The director and his wife had two very small children—one two years old and the other six months. Their tour of service was for three years, although she had flown home for the birth of their latest child. This seemed to be the usual practice among missionary couples in the region.

I left with the key to my room in my pocket. On reaching Geita I passed a woman in a Volkswagen with two small children traveling west. I asked her if she could see to it that the mission got the key, to which she agreed. She was the wife of a British teacher at Geita.

For twenty miles, the road remained bumpy but passable. Then, suddenly, I came upon the wreck of which the Finns had warned me. A long old public bus, resembling a spent beetle, had tried to go around an eight-foot washout. Its weight had caused an even greater breakaway, and it had fallen head-on so that its rear stuck up at a 30-degree angle. For three days, traffic had been blocked while drivers of other vehicles and a small army team from the Geita post had attempted to raise the bus's front end enough to give the rear wheels traction.

The queue was over a mile long in both directions. Tempers had long since abated, and most of the motorists were making do in good spirits. Some had even spread blankets and were picnicking when I arrived. In addition to the motorists, several hundred local people had come out to watch. But they, in contrast to the motorists, were a sullen lot. Their vacant, menacing stares chilled me. Their eyes seemed to say: "I know you not, I care not for you. You are only what is happening now. If you need help, I will not help you. But if I can, I will steal what you have. If you are stranded it is nothing to me. . . ."

I drove to the head of the line to take a look myself at the wreck and to reconnoiter a bypass. When I reached the washout, I dismounted and walked down the bank. The water was gushing through the narrow but widening gap where the bus had fallen. The bus was supported by planks of wood and three spare tires laid up under the chassis. The short Indian driver of a waiting lorry, who had organized the excavation, said that it would be several hours before they would be ready to try to pull it out. I waded out into the stream to plot a potential route down the bank—some twelve feet— through the mud and marsh to the other side.

The marsh was full of reeds two to six feet high and lay about 50 feet further along the river from the bank. The mud between it and the bottom of the bank would be the problem—not the water or the river bottom itself. I would have to lighten up as much as possible. I returned to the Toyota and began removing my gear. As I did not trust the crowd, I chained it together. I had just secured the last jerry can when the Indian called that they were ready. He told me not to try the marsh but to await the pull-out effort, since once the bus was clear I would be positioned to go first.

As we were talking, a Land Rover charged up. The driver, a government interior official, made a quick survey of the scene, then drove off the bank into the river on the path I had just scouted. When he hit the mud he sank all four wheels spinning uselessly. But just when it seemed he was stuck, his wheels began to inch forward. In another few seconds he reached firm ground and was grinding up the bank on the far side. I knew I could make it if he could.

Just then, however, the towing bus sounded his horn and backed into position alongside my jeep. A sergeant gruffly ordered me out of the way. The Indian helped me replace my gear.

With both buses spinning in reverse, the stuck one rolled back, engine revving, horn sounding triumphantly. The Indian rapidly motioned me upstream and around the break. I knew it was now or never, since the first truck that tried to cross would get stuck too, and the pull-out process would have to be repeated. I gave it full throttle and plunged into the cut. At first I thought I had it made, but just then I slipped sideways and became stuck. I quickly alternated between reverse and forward but without success. I could feel the mounting pressure of the current against the door. The water rose until it was within six inches of the open window, yet somehow, miraculously, the motor kept running. I could hear the strange muffled dribbling of the tailpipe and the exaggerated groan of the engine. It was at that moment that I saw in their most stunning coldness the vacant sharklike stares of the people on the bank. They had all clustered greedily as if to watch some freak spectacle like a public hanging or the death throes of a wounded animal. Although I had been many times the object of such stares, this was the first time I had read in them the anticipation of my own demise.

Then in their midst appeared the little Indian. He shoved first one, then another, until he had marshalled a dozen laborers, which he herded into the water. Behind him, the sergeant and two of his men also jumped in to push. "Reverse," shouted the sergeant. I obeyed. Then forward. The sergeant stopped and plucked from beneath my front wheels a limb at least six inches in diameter. Forward again. This time she plowed straight on, and as I gained the road I received a generous applause from four young people in an open Land Rover. The crowd, however, did not applaud but milled about, deprived and disappointed.

I thanked the sergeant and the two soldiers and called to the little Indian and the others who were still in the river. They waved and smiled. I then mustered my shaking knees into the jeep and drove away. Not three miles down the road I came upon the Land Rover that had made the downstream pass. Its roof was barely visible some 25 feet out in the water from the road. The driver had attempted to go around a stalled chicken truck. The water was much deeper than it appeared.

Feeling relieved and grateful, I stopped for a young woman who gave the palm-down hitchhiker's sign. It turned out, however, to be her boyfriend who needed the ride. He sprang from a bush nearby, jumping up and down, grinning. He almost forgot his sack of clothes. It took ten minutes to

187

rearrange the gear that I had piled up in the shotgun seat.

Providence must have urged me to have our seat belts fastened, since two miles further on, we hit a two-foot pothole. The shock broke two leaves of both rear springs and the bolts on both sides of the roof rack—sending it hurtling through the air for 100 yards and damaging it beyond repair. I hoped the old farmer to whose hut we carried it (rather than leave it for the crowd of scavengers) would be able to sell it for scrap.

I stopped at a roadside stall and ate my fill of hard-boiled eggs, fried plantain and skewered beef. Thus refreshed, I arrived at about 4:30 that afternoon at the ferry village of Busisi. I parked the jeep at the head of the ferry line at the bottom of the hamlet and walked up the hill. On three sides, deep blue water lapped against rolling green hills studded with white granite slags, like discards from some primeval Stonehenge. I found the town beer hall, where a loudspeaker affixed to the door blared a scratchy number by Thembi, the East African rock star. Somebody ordered me a bottle of Kilimanjaro beer and there came onto the machine a New Orleans trumpet blues piece from way back: "Black and Blue." I felt the cool sensual heat of the late afternoon sun on my face and watched its yellow-gold reflection wrinkle in the blue lake. Far in the distance a knotty, cotton-grey cloud drifted over the lake carrying with it an incessant display of lightning—a miniature minstrel of a thunderstorm. Yet I could not hear the thunder. Eight months after just entering Africa, I had reached the shore of Lake Victoria.

There was an hour's wait for the ferry. At first I remained on the porch of the bar catching the sun and the guffaws of clients entering the bar. (I was never able to get used to the primitive custom of laughing directly into the face of someone strange—as often happened to me with my red beard and scruffy attire.) I visited in the back room with a stout, kindly gentleman, about 60, and his hefty teenage girlfriend. They planned to be married soon, she said. He rolled his eyes and winked at me. There were eight large Kili empties on the table. I drank my second beer very slowly. It was cold but a bit tinny, I thought.

There were at least 40 people in that little place, half of them older fellows and young women. Somebody offered to find a ladyfriend for me, but just then the ferry whistle sounded. I chug-a-lugged the rest of the Kili, said goodbye amidst peals of renewed laughter at my expense, and raced down to the Toyota. It was first in line, and the queue of overloaded Peugeot vans and chicken trucks behind it had begun to sound their horns with a fury.

The ferry was a bright red new one which reminded me of the Star ferries of Kowloon in Hong Kong. I climbed to the observation deck and watched the growing electrical storm to the southeast. The cloud I had seen earlier seemed to have rendezvoused with a dozen others, each with its own self-contained lightning display. Opposite the storm, in the west, the sun had disappeared over the horizon, leaving soft golden rays to play upon the blue lake and the green granite hills. Against the oncoming storm, the effect was exquisitely surreal.

Mwanza is the commercial capital of northwestern Tanzania. Normally, ferries run twice a week to Kisumu, the main Kenyan lake port and, of course, to Entebbe, the port for Kampala, the Ugandan capital. In May of 1977, however, the Kenyan border was still closed and all trade links, including shipping, between the two countries had been suspended since February. This was President Julius Nyerere's retaliation for the withdrawal by Kenya from participation in East African Airways, a division of the East African community, a kind of trade union between the three former East African British colonies.*

The joint airline had been profitable only on its Kenyan routes—largely because of international tourist flights to Nairobi. Unprofitable regional routes in Tanzania and Uganda had thus been subsidized by Kenya. Tanzania acknowledged this but claimed that most of the major sites the tourists came to see were in Tanzania (the Serengeti, Ngorongoro Crater and Mount Kilimanjaro, for example) and it was merely convenient that Nairobi and not Dar es Salaam was the port of entry. The dispute had eventually resulted in the breakdown of the community.

There was also a history of bitter personal enmity between Dr. Nyerere and Kenyan President Jomo Kenyatta. This doubtless stemmed from rivalry for regional power, yet it must have been exacerbated by the fact that the economic policies of the two countries were the most divergent of any two neighbors on the continent. Kenya, the former "pet" of the British empire, had been heavily colonized and subsidized. Every town of any size at independence in 1962 could boast a paved road or railroad line or both. A European system of public utilities was handed over intact to the new government. Since independence, Kenya had pursued a course of virtually unbridled capitalism. Most top technical and managerial positions in industry and commerce were filled by whites—some ex-colonials, but mostly British and American people on two-year service contracts.

Despite its constitution and parliament, the government was in fact under the more or less benign personal dictatorship of Kenyatta, or, since he was virtually senile, an oligarchy headed by his wife, Mama Endima, her immediate family and a few very wealthy Kenyan businessmen. Though criticism by the press of routine government actions was tolerated, no criticism of Kenyatta, his wife or her family was permitted. Little meaningful opposition to these persons appeared in the parliament, and when it did, detention under the so-called Preventive Detention Act was the result. Members of the parliament had even been arrested on the floor of the house—as were the Deputy Speaker Mr. John Marie Seroney and Mr. Martin Shikuku in October of 1975.**

Tanzania, on the other hand, was one of the United Nations' twenty

---

*Again, I use the term "colony" to include territories, protectorates, mandates, etc., where power was in fact being exercised by a European state.
**Amnesty International Report, 1977.

poorest nations. It was absolutely dependent on grants-in-aid and development loans from the various international institutions and economic powers. Tanzania was not a widely settled colony. Deemed a protectorate, Tanganyika—as it was then known—had been seized from the Germans in 1914 in a swift naval operation at Bagamoyo and Dar es Salaam. British sovereignty was formalized by the League of Nations in 1920.

Most investment in the colony was limited to Dar es Salaam and to the large coffee and peanut plantations up in the north between Arusha and the Kenyan border. Mount Kilimanjaro—and its coffee—had been deleted from Kenya at the whim of Queen Victoria, who awarded it to her cousin, Kaiser Wilhelm II, as a birthday present in 1901. When the British had seized Tanganyika, they left Kili alone.

The British had added to the old German railroad line from Arusha to Bagamoyo and Dar by building a line from both Mwanza and Kigoma on Lakes Victoria and Tanganyika. They had also added a spur to the Nairobi-Mombasa line. The Chinese had just completed their marathon rail project connecting Lusaka, Zambia, with Dar, thus giving service to the sparsely populated south. Each of these three railroads—the German, the British and the Chinese—ran on different gauge tracks so that the rolling stock was not interchangeable. Indeed, the Chinese terminal in Dar was ten miles from the old British depot; yet there was no connection between the two lines.

Tanzania's roads are the worst of any country through which I traveled. The red clay soil in the west is molded by rain into disastrous potholes and crevices. The black cotton soil of the Serengeti, when wet, is impossible to navigate even in a jeep. I doubt that a tank could go through it. There are three hardtopped roads in the country: the southwestern route, connecting Dar with Lusaka (1500 hundred miles of virtually uninterrupted tar); Nairobi to Arusha; and Tonga to Arusha and Dar. There are no paved roads in the interior except for occasional dabs of potholed blacktop in and around larger towns.

Politics in Tanzania is frequently called "brotherly African socialism" or *ugamaa*. The government is run by Dr. Nyerere's Socialist Party. It is hard to describe exactly what Dr. Nyerere is. He is certainly the most powerful man in the country, but I hesitate to call him a dictator—although he surely wields autocratic power. The press is controlled, dissent is not tolerated, and opponents are jailed. According to Amnesty International, in 1977 there were between 1000 and 1500 political prisoners in the country, including 37 sentenced in Zanzibar for treason in connection with the 1972 assassination of Sheik Abeid Karume, President of the Zanzibar Revolutionary Council.* According to Amnesty International, torture, deprivation of food and family visits and improper medical attention are common practices.

Dr. Nyerere, however, was the only African chief of state who publicly shared the prestige and pomp of office with his next-in-command: the two vice-presidents' pictures hung equally with Nyerere's in public places. Dr. Nyerere also had no private villa, no Swiss chalet or harem of European

---

*Tanganyika merged with Zanzibar in 1964 to form Tanzania, although Zanzibar still maintains a great deal of local autonomy.

prostitutes—perquisites frequently enjoyed by African chiefs of state. His attempt at socialism had not fared well as the result of the usual third-world problems of ignorance and corruption, and also because of the flat refusal of some tribes to give up their traditional homelands or nomadic territories for a sedentary, collective existence in the government's new so-called "ugamaa villages" or communes.

Among the most stubborn holdouts were the Masai, nomads of the Serengeti,* who did not consider themselves Kenyan or Tanzanian. They would cross the border back and forth at will, living for a time in each country. Lately, because of the extended drought which had killed large numbers of their cattle, some of the Masai had submitted to resettlement. Most, however, still refused. These tenacious nomads might appear without warning virtually anywhere in the plains.

It was at Mwanza that I first fully appreciated that I was in East Africa. Everywhere there was talk of the border closing and of Kenyan politics, of game poaching in the Serengeti, of Idi Amin Dada (greatly admired by ordinary Tanzanians even though in a recent piqued moment against Dr. Nyerere he had had one of his planes bomb the Mwanza police station) and, of course, the latest prices on the black market.

The Tanzanian shilling is on official par with the Kenyan shilling: that is, eight shillings to the dollar. That rate is pretty much accepted worldwide for the Kenyan currency, but Tanzania's is so inflated that on the London market it had recently stood at 35 or 40 shillings to the dollar. On the local black market, it was selling at 18 or 20 shillings to the dollar. Many persons trading on the black market were East Indians** whose property had been expropriated. They were forbidden to export any currency—neither savings, profits, nor money received in payment for their expropriated properties, a condition tantamount to outright confiscation. This, the Indians claimed, forced them to protect themselves in the black market.

There are thousands of such people, many of them third- and fourth-generation Tanzanians, who claim to have suffered unfairly and who seek convertible currency to deposit abroad. This is usually done by mail and in small amounts (ten to twenty dollars) to relatives in India or England in business-logo envelopes.

Other persons, blacks as well as Indians, want convertible currency to purchase household appliances, spare parts and other consumer goods which will only be sold for hard (convertible) currency—not Tanzanian shillings. Ironically, Kenyan shillings are usually accepted.

---

*The Kenyan name for its part of the Serengeti is the Masai Maru Preserve. There are no patrols or permanent markers on the border and only one dirt road, which is often closed.

**Some, descendants of straw bosses and civil servants imported from India by the British, to supervise the blacks and administer the colony. In the '20s and '30s, many outright immigrants had come from India and Pakistan to set up small businesses.

The New Mwanza Hotel had a relatively cheap single room—six dollars—with shower. It also had a permanent night watchman for the parking lot, which left me at ease. Upstairs on the second floor was the local bar.

It was 7:00 when I clocked in. I had a hot shower and repaired to the bar, where I fell into conversation with Jalou Kadi and his friend, Forts, young Indian businessmen who had just opened a new garage. They also ran a single Land Rover safari service into the Serengeti. Their few safari customers—mostly German tourists—came from Dar. Occasionally they would book a group of British or American businessmen, but that was rare. Jalou's father had immigrated from India in 1948. The rest of the family had followed two years later. The family integrated very quickly into the thriving East Asian community here, and as a child Jalou had watched the last great construction spree by local Indian businessmen. Most of Mwanza's buildings, factories, and homes had been built between 1935 and 1955 by its Indian families. Mwanza had at that time been known as an oasis for East Indians, because of its cool lake climate, good business, and the community's relative freedom from interference by the colonial government in Dar.

Jalou insisted on taking me on a tour of the city, pointing out as we walked various buildings, two of them quite beautiful: the Khoja Shia Mosque (1953), and the Ladha Meghji Indian Public Library (1935), with its sizable collection of both Hindi and English literature. We were greeted on the street by a number of his Indian friends, all of whom spoke fluent English.

Indian children attend private schools through the equivalent of the twelfth grade, and many go to universities in India or Britain. Neatly scrubbed and dressed in their blue-and-white school uniforms, Indian youngsters make an uneasy contrast to the hundreds of idle African youths loitering in the streets and markets of the town.

Jalou was especially proud of the new German-Israeli hospital at Mwanza, constructed on the hill overlooking the town. It has a capacity of over 500 patients and boasts two modern operating rooms. Theoretically it services the entire western region, but rural roads are so bad that, in practice, most patients come from the Mwanza area. I visited one of the operating rooms and talked with a Tanzanian doctor who had just performed a tonsillectomy. I also met several of the hospital's administrative staff. They were almost entirely dependent on German and Israeli funds, one said, although the government planned to fund the 1978 fiscal year. Small unpublicized Israeli projects such as this are found throughout Black Africa, even in countries officially hostile to Israel.

Near the hotel was the New Rose Restaurant ("Daily servings 7:00 a.m. to 11:00 p.m.") where, for thirteen shillings, I got some excellent chicken curry, a fresh green salad and a mug of tea. In true African fashion, the tea had been mixed with powdered milk and oversweetened so that I could barely taste the tea. But it was hot and good. The place was full of workers on their way to the late shift at the local canning factory and security guards on break.

Luckily, there was a decent Toyota dealership in Mwanza. Their chief mechanic gave me priority over four local police vans and all of the damage was quickly repaired: two new leaves put in each rear spring, trailer hitch rewelded, right front signal light mounted and repaired, rear view mirror (which had been stolen) replaced, and the horn which had fallen down inside the engine mount bolted back into position. Unfortunately the big affable welder managed to sever two of the retaining bolts on the spare gas tank. This was to prove almost disastrous.

During the Mwanza days I relaxed and wandered around the little town. The people were not used to tourists and would frequently stop me and ask where I was from. Especially curious were young Indians, and when they learned I was an American they were most disappointed that I was not from Texas or California (a common reaction).

In speaking here with young Africans I was again surprised at how little English they knew compared to the knowledge of French among the people of western Africa. I set about trying to learn some basic Swahili but was discouraged when I learned that even Swahili is not universally known and that it is frequently necessary to speak a person's own tribal language in order to communicate. (For example, Dr. Mary Leakey always spoke to her African workers in Mkumba, their tribal language.)

My friends of the Bedford arrived while I was there, and some of them came to the hotel for coffee and conversation. It was good to see them in such high spirits again.

Because I had lost my vaccination certificate and Tanzanian customs declaration form, it was necessary that I report to the local police. You risk a lot of trouble (possibly even a fine or a heavy tax on what some official thinks lost goods are worth) if you show up at the border without the form. In its place, all you need is the official police-theft or lost-property report form. The same principle applies, strangely, for vaccination certificates or for any other official document.

Because I had no further use for them, I sold my aluminum ladders and the heavy desert sand tracks to Jalou for his new garage. I threw in a box of spare parts (such as rubber tubes and funnels) which had also outlived their usefulness. Most of this equipment was for desert emergencies and was now only extra weight.

One afternoon after a visit to the hospital on the hill I tried to return to town on a ridge road with a grand view of Lake Victoria. For half an hour, I stopped and surveyed the coast and town with my binoculars. Oblivious to all but the splendid view, I drove around into a dead end which, I saw too late, was a military compound. I had not seen the sign which said "Prohibited Entry." I was immediately surrounded and ordered to get out. The rig was thoroughly searched. I was thankful I didn't have a camera. After lengthy interrogation, I was gruffly escorted back to the main road by three Land Rovers bristling with rifles and machine guns.

CHAPTER XIV

Mediterranean Sea

Nile River

Red Sea

Lake Victoria
Mwanza
Olduvai
Arusha
Mt. Kilimanjaro
TANZANIA
Bagamoyo
Serengeti Park
Dar es Salaam
Dodoma

AFRICA

Selous National Park

Atlantic Ocean

Indian Ocean

I left Mwanza one fine morning and drove northeast along Lake Victoria to Nyahanga, planning to enter Serengeti Park at the southwest gate. With me was an Australian hitchhiker, Lucy, who had been three months down the Nile, then through northern Zaire to bypass Uganda. About ten kilometers north of Ushasha we turned onto a choppy red-earth road. I do not remember striking a particularly heavy pothole, but there was a sudden drag on the rear of the jeep accompanied by an awful scraping noise. Then came the ominous smell of escaping gasoline. Bounding out, I saw that the spare gas tank had collapsed into the road and was bent under the rear axle. It was barely attached by a single twisted bolt, the other bolts having been cleanly severed by the welder's torch. Fuel was gushing through the fuel line aperture. Clasping my hand over the hole I called for Lucy to bring jerry cans. Fortunately all except two were empty. As I held the damaged tank off the ground, a young African in the crowd that had gathered crawled underneath and knocked away the lingering bolt with the hammer. He and I then tipped the tank as Lucy passed four jerry cans beneath it. Luckily, the road just here was quite muddy, for had there been rocks, sparks from the dragging tank would have ignited the gasoline and blown us to bits. Although I was furious, I was thankful that the welder had only cut the bolts and not torched into the tank itself.

Ten kilometers further on we missed a turn and came to an enormous stone lodge. Although May is normally an active tourist month, the place was empty except for four teenagers, children of white diplomats in Dar. The superintendent said the Kenya-Tanzania border closing had been disastrous for their business. The main road, he said, was closed. Impossible to pass. Bridge out. Detour now flooded. A park Land Rover had stalled in there yesterday. There was also danger of snakes. (We had seen a great black cobra whip across in front of us that morning north of Nyahanga.) Snakes are normally no problem, but the flooding had disturbed them. There were many black mambas, he said, the continent's deadliest snake. We thanked him and returned to the crossroads.

Five kilometers further a single branch lay across the road—the African signal for "road closed ahead." The tracks to the left seemed to be a detour. We followed them and drove smack into a flooded marsh, the water swirling above the running boards. The open space between the trees had to be the

Kabibo, the Olduvai camp cook.

road. Yet there were occasionally other open spaces: we had to choose and keep moving.

I shifted into low ratio and kept the gas pedal on the floor. Suddenly the road dropped into what had been a clearing. A hut lay upended, swaying in the current, its conical top caught by a branch. Movement slowed to a crawl, although the tires were spinning under full power. Slowly the vehicle inched across the hole—the water now less than a foot below the windows and swirling with incredible force.

My mind darted through the unpleasant scenario of swimming out among the snakes. Yet the engine never stalled, and although it coughed ominously a dozen times, we navigated through this seemingly endless marsh like some intrepid amphibious craft which, I suppose, we had become. After fishtailing, rocking and continuously slugging ahead, we eventually came to the riverbed itself, achieving an almost normal speed on the gravel bottom. When we had climbed the far bank and joined the road again, we shouted and gave each other a big hug, so relieved were we to be out of there.

The ranger at the northwest gate of the park had just closed it for the night when we arrived. The only other tourists had been the Dutch that morning. The ranger pointed at the sign which read, "No Entry After 6:00."

It was 6:15. We told him we were only going to Seronera Lodge, that we had no other place to stay since he had told us it would be unlawful to camp in the open. I did not intend to drive back through that marsh.

He finally relented and let us in. Our late arrival was fortuitous, since our first impressions of the Serengeti were formed at dusk. Within moments we began seeing giraffe, hyenas, zebra . . . virtually a full menagerie of herbivores and small predators. The animals were close to the road but seemed oblivious to us. We drove slowly, stopping often to listen to night sounds and stargaze. We were soon able to see only those animals that came into the headlights, but these included several elephants and a herd of some twenty cape buffalo.

After some difficulty we found the lodge and we approached a concrete camping dormitory built by two Chicago philanthropists in the 1950s. We were the only guests. Driving back to the employee cook shack, we talked the cook into warming up some leftovers for us. A shift of rangers was there for coffee.

Although we were led to believe that the dormitory was included in the 120-shilling park entrance fee, there was an additional rental of 30 shillings per person, not including sheets, toilet or running water. The dorm had army cots but no mattresses. We would have preferred to camp, but that, of course, was forbidden.

As we drove out onto the plains the next morning at dawn we were surrounded by herds of migrating wildebeests, zebras, Thompson's gazelles, and wild hogs. The scene was comparable to that depicted in paintings of migrating American buffalo in the early nineteenth century.

As far as the eye could see from one horizon to the other, animals were walking, loping, trotting toward the north. That we could witness such an event in solitude in 1977 was as difficult to believe as the event itself. Yet we were totally alone: during the day we saw no other persons except the rangers at the gate.

We came to a series of knolls which cropped up unexpectedly from the floor of the plains and provided superb observation points. With the field glasses, I picked out pairs of female lions following herds of wildebeest. I waited for an attack, but none came. I did not realize then that lions normally kill only at night—although they follow the herds even during the day. Strangely, the herds seem to know when the lions are and are not hunting, and if not, will continue to graze nonchalantly with a lioness in full view.

Just east of an elevation called Lion Hill we came upon two magnificent male lions sitting so close to the road that their paws protruded into it. One had a great shaggy mane; the other was maneless except for a tuft down the back of his neck. They were vexed by hosts of lion flies—great fat brown flies that roll and tumble through their victim's fur and are apparently inescapable. The lions seemed to have resigned themselves to these pests and appeared to be otherwise resting contentedly, their long pink tongues hanging down as they panted like two amiable dogs. We were, however, not deceived; they were barely five feet from the right door, and Lucy was ready to roll up her window on short notice. We observed them for over half an hour. Their only movement was when the maneless one suddenly

198

lumbered away from us to sit on the other side of his more imposing comrade.

From the map, I knew that I was now very near to one of the key objectives of my trip, Olduvai Gorge. An ancient lake that rose and fell repeatedly over several million years had had a long stretch of its shoreline exactly where the gorge cuts through the earth. The gorge has been cut out gradually over the past 100,000 years by the big, seasonally dry creek that runs through it, and by faulting of the earth's surface.

Successive generations of hominids (advanced primates, among whom are ourselves and our immediate ancestors) had inhabited the lakeshore. Their bones and the bones of other animals not carried off by predators or scavengers had become buried by sediment and preserved. As the gorge sinks down through these sediments, the bones—now fossilized—are revealed.

The person responsible for exploring and analyzing this mother lode of paleontology was Dr. Mary D. Leakey, the widow of the late Dr. Louis S. B. Leakey.

I had been a freshman at the University of Arkansas in the fall of 1959 when I read of Mary Leakey's discovery of the skull of *Zinjanthropus* (East Africa Man). The animal was a hominid, thought by many at the time to be man's ancestor. It has since been determined that he was only a distant cousin, a species never in our direct line of descent, and that he eventually became extinct. However, in spite of his disappointing geneology, his being discovered had been crucial to paleoanthropology, since it stimulated worldwide interest in the Olduvai project, attracting funding from the *National Geographic* and making overnight celebrities of the Leakeys. With star billing on the American lecture circuit, they have since been able to raise millions of dollars for fossil research.

For years I had read articles by and about the Leakeys in the *National Geographic* and the general press. As a young Marine in San Diego I had attended one of Dr. Louis Leakey's lectures at a local college. Afterward, when I told him I planned one day to travel across Africa, he insisted that I would be welcome at Olduvai.

Before leaving Mwanza, Lucy had agreed that in the event I decided to tarry here, she would hitch another ride to Nairobi from Ngorongoro. I had hoped to find work at Olduvai, but I had no idea what my prospects were or whether, in view of the border situation, the Leakey camp was even open.

The cutoff leading to Olduvai is easily missed. Indeed, we had unsuccessfully tried two sidetracks before coming to its nondescript dirt trail marked only by a hand-lettered sign. We drove three miles down the trail, arriving finally at an empty guard shack. To the left the trail continued into the gorge. The depth at the dry riverbed was some 200 feet. A mile further down stream, beneath high red bluffs, it was twice that.

At the bottom of the gorge we surveyed the riverbed and the irregular canyon walls, some sections of them appertaining to others 100 feet above, from which they had been faulted. We drove across into the south gorge, which branches off from the main gorge at this point. The road became even narrower and led up a precipitous slope at fifteen degrees. A kilometer further, we came to a compound of tin-roofed huts. Some Africans were sitting around a fire. We told them we wanted to see the various dig sites, whereupon their foreman told us the gorge had been closed to visitors since the closing of the border in February. Nevertheless, he would take us on a private tour. He introduced himself as Absalom. He got in and I drove as he directed. The first site, called DK, was about three miles up the gorge, down an even steeper incline. In view of the rain clouds which had begun to form, I had reservations about driving down the loose dirt slope, but Absalom insisted there was no problem. (I later learned that there was a short foot path down to the site just past the workers' compound.)

The Site DK has been dated at 1.8 million years. Part of the site is covered by a small concrete building. Inside, the floor is divided in two: to the left are what appear to be the remnants of four stacks of rocks which a sign says were the supports of a four-pole shelter. To the right is a rich collection of bones and rock tools. Both the supports and the tools are *in situ*, i.e., right where they were found.

Outside the building, excavation of the site continues, recently spurred by the discovery—by Absalom himself—of a portion of a hominid skull dated at about 1.75 million years.

Although there are some 50 official dig sites in the gorge, only two or three are worked at a time—years sometimes elapsing between a site's designation and actual digging. A site is designated when an impressive bone or tool is found there. Not all sites are worked for hominid bones—indeed, most bones found at most of the sites are bones of animals who shared the country with the hominids.

The gorge is some 30 miles long and, according to Mary Leakey, though it has been walked over scores of times by the Leakeys and their workers, there is so much material yet to be found that it would take many scientists many lifetimes to find it all, much less analyze it.

While we were looking at the bones and tools, it began to rain. From the clouds it was obvious that a considerable downpour was imminent. I decided I had to climb the grade right away, or we would not be able to get out. The red soil had turned into slippery mud. I put both Lucy and Absalom out in the rain to lighten the load. Absalom suggested that we return to his compound and wait out the storm. As we drove in, I said to Lucy how nice it would be to have hot tea. No sooner had I spoken than Absalom hastened to the cook shed. In minutes he came out and motioned us inside. The temperature had fallen ten or fifteen degrees, and it was getting chilly. One of the other men brought in some wood, and soon there was a warm fire in the potbellied stove. Then came the tea—as always, generously mixed with milk and terribly presweetened. Still, it was delicious.

These men, we learned, were all Tanzanians, about twelve in number, who worked directly for the Department of Antiquities in Dar in liaison with (but independent of) Dr. Leakey. The chief foreman was named Maringo.

In addition, there were some twenty Mkumba tribesmen—all Kenyans—brought in and trained directly by the Leakeys. They were under the direct control of Mary Leakey and constituted her main working force.

Most of the Mkumbas lived in Dr. Leakey's compound in their own barracks, although several lived here with the Tanzanians. Dr. Leakey's compound, with its two tall windmill generators, could be seen from the ridge. The road up there was closed: no visitors allowed. When I pressed him on this, Absalom said he would ask Dr. Leakey. When he returned, the answer was no. I was very disappointed, but well understood her need for privacy.

Absalom and the others talked freely, telling us of their latest finds, how the workers are trained on the job, and about their home villages. When we asked about the Masai, Absalom produced a handsome spear, which he tried to sell to us for 200 shillings.

When the rain let up, we drove back across the gorge—the river was now running—to the guard shack and the small museum. There was an impressive collection of fossils, one of which, the skull of a giant horned giraffe, dominated the gallery. There was an excellent cutaway color plan of the various layers of gorge sediment, together with a geological time chart.

Driving Absalom back to the camp, we discovered that the river had swollen to a dozen times its previous size so that it now covered the width of the gorge floor. It was impossible to cross in the jeep, but Absalom deftly picked his way over on some slippery rocks. He had been a good guide—well worth the 50 shillings he demanded as his fee. On the way out we noticed thick patches of the wild sisal which gives the gorge its name: *olduvai,* the Masai name for the thorny green cactus-type plant.

It was 4:00 when we regained the main road. In the distance loomed an imposing cloud-capped mountain that I knew from the map to be Ngorongoro Crater. It had been a good afternoon, but it had gone too quickly. I had an empty feeling. I had really wanted to meet Mary Leakey and try my luck at getting a job.

The road continued for another five miles over the plains and then started up the crater. It was steep but firm, considering the rain. The slopes and ridges were now banked with fat-petaled sunflowers in exquisite shades of yellow—from bright gold to vanilla. In another five miles, we came to a gap in the south wall where a precarious trail cut down to the crater floor. It was just past sunset in a lingering purple twilight.

We entered the gap and stopped in a meadow of sunflowers. As the engine died we heard overhead swarms of millions of bees. They were finished with their day's work among the sunflowers and were high-flying above the crater as if in celebration of their labor. The sound was hypnotic, weird, like a celestial choir holding on a single note. As if provoked by these alien sirens, the sun seemed to be struggling to rise again beyond the eastern rim. Then it became apparent that the lake on the crater floor was reflecting the light in the clouds, which were in turn reflecting it back at us: a simultaneous dawn and sunset.

Turning around, we drove back through the gap, and the road became a morass of black cotton mud. We passed several trucks which had become hopelessly mired. A tourist van from Arusha lay on its side, barely visible in the muck. It was dark, but in the thick fog the headlights were virtually useless. I picked my way along by flashing them and was for a time somewhat successful in clinging to the uphill shoulder where there were still patches of grass. This was my first encounter with black cotton soil—the notorious quick mud of which Dr. Louis Leakey had so often written as stymying his work in the Serengeti. At the small Olduvai museum are photos taken in the 1930s of an entire safari stuck in it.

Suddenly, ahead on the shoulder I saw two men trotting at a smart pace. Each was carrying a rifle and motioning for us to stop. They were soaked and muddy. I asked what they wanted and they replied, "*Simba, simba.* You take us to lodge."

"That means 'lion,' *simba* does," Lucy said. "I wonder what he's trying to say."

"Yes, lions," the older one repeated. "We go with you?"

I politely explained the obvious—that we had absolutely no room—and asked him what he meant by "lions." "Lions now," he replied, pointing down to the left in the dark.

I had no doubt that these guys were hustling a ride to the village. They figured tourists would love the adventure of saving them from the lions. Just then there was a roar from somewhere down where he had pointed. It was followed quickly by two others.

"*Simba* . . . lion . . ." the soldier said, this time with a broad but nervous grin. "We walk in front of jeep," he said, pointing to the front.

I had no problem with that. I told them that we would drive slowly enough for them to stay with us. The windshield wipers began grating on the glass and I realized that the rain had stopped. The soldiers resumed their trot, keeping just in front of us and always in the headlights. I was afraid that one of them might fall and discharge his weapon.

A quarter-mile further on, the jeep began sliding uncontrollably toward the left edge of the road on a steep downhill grade. All we could do was ride it out. Inches from where we stopped, there was nothing but darkness as the slope fell away into the crater.

We had gone about three kilometers when we saw dead ahead of us, over a rise, a Land Rover half sunk in the mud and completely blocking the road. Its lights flashed several times, and a tall woman, obviously a Westerner, scrambled out of the driver's door and ran towards us.

"Hi! I'm in trouble. Can you help me?" she asked in an unmistakable American accent.

She was Robin McKinney, 23, a recent prehistory graduate who was working with Mary Leakey at Olduvai. She said that she and Stephen, Mrs. Leakey's foreman, had come to the crater lodge that morning for supplies and mail. They had waited until 6:00 for a telegram from Nairobi. Among their supplies was 150 pounds of fresh meat. When it was obvious that they were stuck, Stephen had set out to the village, some three miles back, for help. He had been gone but a few minutes when she heard the lions. Remembering the raw meat, she had become quite concerned. As we talked, the roars came again, closer, much closer than before.

I unlatched my winch cover and hooked the cable to her front bumper. It was no use. There was no anchor for the chain, so the winch only pulled the jeep downhill. Next I tried towing her backward with the chain, but that too was useless. The grade was too steep, and she was firmly stuck. Then I tried driving around to pull from below, but that was impossible to do without crushing the sides of both vehicles. There was a bypass trail through the grass up the hill—which they should have taken rather than drive straight into the pit. I was unable to back up, so I tried a 90-degree turn, whereupon I myself became completely stuck. The jeep sat crossways with each set of wheels firmly mired in a rut. There was a small tree some 50 feet up the bank, and I was just preparing to winch out on it when vehicle lights appeared toward the village. It was Mike Mehlman, whom Stephen had managed to hail just as he was leaving his hut.

Mike jokingly referred to himself as the resident American archaeologist of Ngorongoro. He had been there almost three years on a grant from the Leakey Foundation and the University of Illinois. He was doing some research on a Stone Age tribe who had lived in the area.

Mike turned onto the bypass from below and drove up flush with me. I then winched free on his axle, drove behind Robin and pulled her out with my chain. After a good deal of splashing about in the mud and peals of relieved laughter, we drove to the bar at Ngorongoro Crater Lodge and, over bottles of cold Kili, told each other our stories and swapped yarns. The *maitre d' hotel* was kind enough to reopen his restaurant, and the chef came from the village to cook an outstanding steak dinner for his first customers in a week.

Robin said she'd flown to Nairobi as a tourist and then decided to stay. She'd landed a job with a Kenyan weekly doing feature interviews and had come out to do one on Mary Leakey. When Mary learned that she had majored in prehistory at Princeton, she offered her a job as girl Friday. Robin accepted and had been out here for over a month exploring the gorge, looking for fossils and helping around the place, chiefly by identifying boxes of previously collected fossils according to anatomy (leg, wing, rib) and species. (Dating of fossils is done only tentatively, by ascertaining the layer in which the bone is found. Precise dating, when required, is done by carbon-14 and potassium-argon tests in England and the States.) Robin was from Santa Fe, where she had been a reporter on the *New Mexican,* a daily formerly owned by her father.

Mike Mehlman's work had begun as a doctoral project on late Stone Age man in the Serengeti. Although most of his field work was done in Olduvai Gorge and at Lake Eyasi, he was required to reside at Ngorongoro. Since he was a naturalist too, this was like throwing Br'er Rabbit into the briar patch. Mike had eventually been given permission to enter any part of the crater by Land Rover at any time. (Access is normally restricted to park vehicles and then only to designated "safe" areas.) He also had carte-blanche use of all park facilities, such as they were, and was on excellent terms with the park superintendent and the chief of police.

Seeing that we were stranded, the lodge manager kindly provided us with free lodging. Our rooms, as well as the lodge bar, looked out over the crater. When the weather is clear, one can see down for miles. On a clear night, the stars and the lingering sunset are spectacular. Unfortunately, it was cloudy during most of our stay—a swirling mist of fog and rain. It is said that once it even snowed lightly at Ngorongoro. In just one hour, between sunset and dark, the temperature dropped 25 degrees—the most dramatic fall I'd experienced since being in the Sahara.

Ngorongoro village consists of four tiny enclaves: Crater Lodge (until recently a private venture); the government's Park Lodge, a formerly private stone and wood restaurant three miles to the east; the police headquarters (two large office shacks); and some twenty 1950s-style corrugated iron cabins for the officers and their families. This area is a mile west on the main road. The park headquarters itself is at the gas station about two miles up the mountain on a side road. There is a small airstrip about three miles west of the police headquarters.

The three to six miles of road which connect these settlements are frequently impassable—sometimes for days—following a heavy rain. With a few hours of direct sunlight, however, the mud hardens and even a car can pass, although the road is very rough.

The rain continued until the following morning. Robin did not want to get stuck again but was in a hurry to return to Olduvai, fearing that Dr. Leakey would think she had tarried. Stephen and Mike, however, advised against her trying the mud that morning. The several stranded vehicles we had seen were still stuck and an army tow truck had overturned, blocking the road. Some Swiss tourists from Arusha had had to abandon their Land Rover. To kill time until we could see how the afternoon weather looked, Robin suggested we walk down to the government lodge. Luckily, Lucy had been able to get a ride in a truck to Arusha right away that morning. As I recounted my disappointment at failing to meet Dr. Leakey, Robin said she would introduce me if I would return with her and Stephen.

The area around the lodge was not altogether safe. In April of 1976, an American woman returning to her room at Crater Lodge had been attacked and gored to death by a Cape buffalo. These beasts roam right up to the lodge compound—usually in herds but sometimes singly, when they are most dangerous. I had seen several of them start into the trees the night before, as we had driven up. A pride of lions lived nearby and fed on the gazelle and an occasional old buffalo. Although the lions ranged down into the crater, they tended to headquarter up here near the village. The leopard were more secretive, resting well camouflaged by day in the trees under the cliffs of the steeper slopes of the crater and feeding at night. It was forbidden to walk about alone beyond the immediate vicinity of one of the facilities. Walking on the road was permitted, though there were signs all along it warning of the danger of wild animals.

The Masai, of course, are not bound by these rules, although they are not stupid and at night tend to remain inside their compounds. Several months earlier, a Masai had been attacked and mauled by a leopard on the trail below the government lodge. The big cats, however, are rarely a danger. It is

McMath with Stephen, the Olduvai foreman, on the road to Ngorongoro, Tanzania.

the ubiquitous Cape buffalo against which one must constantly beware: a lone bull will immediately attack if he feels at all threatened.

Our three-mile walk was otherwise uneventful except for an incessant serenade by a chorus of hornbills and tinker birds. The only attack *we* sustained was by a swarm of bees as we entered the lodge (which was open but unattended). They divebombed us from hives overhead. I got two nasty stings on the left shoulder through my shirt. Passing through the lodge hall, we slid back the glass doors to the patio and stepped onto the balcony. There again I was attacked by the bees. Robin, for some reason, was not bothered by them.

Halfway back to the lodge Mike drove up in his Land Rover. Would we like to see the crater? He was taking the afternoon off and wanted to go down himself. The road descended behind the government lodge. It took a long curve, then a series of steep dips. Considering the rain, it was in good shape. Toward the bottom, we sighted a herd of Cape buffalo and, off to the right, several elephants. It was a clean, fresh afternoon after the rain.

The depth of the crater is far greater than it appears from the lodge at the top. As you descend, the depth is accentuated by the curving away of the crater rim in both directions. Against the slope, the foliage is as thick as any in a Congo rain forest. It is there that the leopards live, holing up by day in trees and rock crevices and prowling down into the crater by night.

Mike was chatting away, telling us the history of the crater, its various animals and their patterns of feeding. We were told to be on the lookout for Lisa, his "pet" cheetah. She had been taken when her mother was killed by poachers and raised at Olduvai. Later she was released into the crater, but with a collar so that tourists would not be alarmed when she approached their picnic tables (there is a small spot near the lake for picnics). There had been no tourists in several months, and Mike feared Lisa might have gone to seek human company elsewhere. She was certainly not welcome by the Masai, one of whom had speared her when he caught her chasing his goats.

Off to the left now were a half-dozen more elephants, one, a very young calf that clung close to its mother. They were foraging near the lake, about a quarter of a mile away.

Mike was still talking when we came to a deep mud sump dead ahead in the road. Off to the left was a short bypass, but I didn't think to mention it. Mike missed the turn, and in seconds we were stuck.

We rocked and pushed and sat on the hood. Nothing worked: the tires only sank deeper. We had no tools—only a short, wide-mouthed shovel, worse than useless. We spread out, searching first for the few available rocks, then simply gravel, to throw into the mud behind the tires. We hoped we could build up a small base for traction. After half an hour Mike gave it a try. Nothing. We tried again, this time using a feed sack full of gravel scraped up with our bare hands. After filling in the tracks for ten feet or so, we tried, again without success.

Our only hope, we finally realized, lay with another vehicle. Perhaps we could signal an SOS to the lodges above. We could see both of them, high on the crater rim. I unscrewed the left rear-view mirror from the hood and, using the day's last twenty minutes of sunlight, flashed an SOS alternately to each one. We knew that the lodge workers rarely looked down into the crater and that even if they did, and saw the signal, they would probably not know what it meant.

At 5:00 p.m., the sun vanished behind the crater rim, and with it, our signal. It was barely an hour before dark. Water was no problem (Mike's two-quart water bags were full) but we had no food or blankets. It was going to get pretty miserable before morning on the hard floor in the back of the Land Rover.

It was Sunday afternoon, the middle of a three-day holiday. There were no tourists, and even the park garage was closed; private vehicles, even if there were any, were forbidden to enter. Worse, no one knew where we were or was likely to realize we were missing. We had no schedule and no place to be at any certain time. Maybe in a few days, Mary would worry and come looking, or maybe Stephen—yes, Stephen and Jooma, Mike's house-boy. Mike remembered he had said something to Jooma that morning about how it might be a good afternoon to drive into the crater but he had talked about a lot of things to Jooma and, besides, he frequently left the house for several days without telling Jooma where he was going. We would probably have to walk back up the mountain the way we had come in—but it was too late to try that tonight.

The herd of buffalo had come closer while we were talking. The lead bull pawed the ground and raced about with his snout raised, nostrils flaring, and ears flopped down. He stared at us for a indeterminable moment. Then he turned away, to our relief.

There was not much tidying up that could be done. We would just have to crawl in the back and lie down as best we could. Mike had only the T-shirt he was wearing. I had a jacket, and Robin wore a sweatshirt.

Just then Mike said, "Hey, I think I heard something."

We listened. I heard nothing.

"Yeah, I'm sure," he said. "It's gears shifting. It's a car."

I climbed onto the hood, looked all around and told him that I couldn't see or hear a damn thing. Nor could Robin. Indeed, the only interruption of the twilight silence was the rustling of the tall brown grass in the breeze.

"No, I hear it. There, there it is. It looks like a Toyota!"

I caught a movement far off, against a rise. "Hey, you're right!" I shouted.

In the next few seconds we waved, shouted, flashed headlights and blew the horn. I even took the motor repair light out and swung it while Robin touched it to the battery. Yet it seemed as if our rescuers were going to drive away without seeing us. Frustrated, we ceased our antics. Then, as we were moping, the car came back—they had merely taken a bypass around another mudhole. A flash of their headlights told us they had seen us.

Five minutes later, we were greeted by the park superintendent and his assistant. They had been fishing in a hippo pond near an old German home-stead several miles away and were on their way home. They had planned to go out by the far side—which leads up to the gap where Lucy and I had stopped the day before. But the superintendent decided at the last minute to check on the road, so they had driven this way.

They were unable to pull us out with their chain, so deeply stuck were we. Finally we persuaded them to let us return in the morning with my Land Cruiser and winch. We were three happy people—and even Mike's embarrassment at being pulled out by his "boss" soon abated.

The next morning I returned with Mike, Stephen and Jooma in the Toyota. Since there were no trees nearby, I drove the heavy tent stake into the solid earth and anchored the chain to it. This was exactly the leverage we needed, and in seconds the Land Rover pulled free. I winched straight ahead, through the hole, rather than attempt a backup through the muck of the day before. There was a sucking snap as the mud finally let go of the rear wheels. Our excavation took place within a stone's throw of a lioness and her four day-old cubs.

Afterward, we drove over to a pond where a rambunctious hippopotamus swam and dived, seemingly for our benefit. Although I had seen many previously, this was the first time I'd ever seen one submerge for over half an hour. I did not know they could stay under for so long.

When we returned to the lodge, we found that Robin had hitched to Olduvai with the Swiss. Stephen loaded the meat from the freezer into the Land Rover, and I followed him the 30 kilometers back to the gorge.

CHAPTER XV

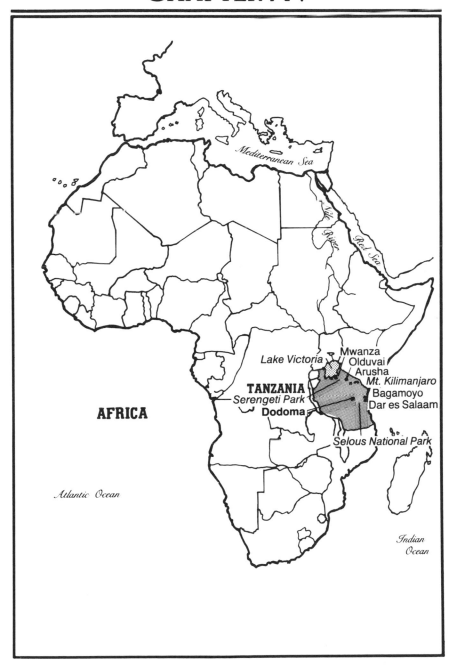

Mediterranean Sea

Nile River

Red Sea

Lake Victoria

Mwanza
Olduvai
Arusha

TANZANIA

Mt. Kilimanjaro
Bagamoyo
Dar es Salaam

Serengeti Park

AFRICA

Dodoma

Selous National Park

Atlantic Ocean

Indian Ocean

Dr. Leakey was standing on the steps of the lodge as we drove into the thorn-bush compound of Olduvai Camp. Mike had scrawled his own letter of introduction and had given me two jerry cans of gasoline to repay some he'd borrowed from her earlier that week.

Robin had returned in time to alert Dr. Leakey to the arrival of an "unexpected guest." Mary, as she told me to call her, was most gracious, thanking me for rescuing her workers. I told her if it hadn't been for Mike we would still be stuck. She smiled and asked how I'd enjoyed Mike's exclusive tour of the crater. We all had a good laugh at that. Mary and Mike were good neighbors. She had helped him get started with his work and occasionally consulted with him. Speaking of neighbors, Mary's next closest, Patty Moehlman, was there with her friend Leo, a young Dutch photographer. She was studying jackals, and Leo was filming cheetahs at Ndutu in the camp of the eminent wildlife photographer, Hugo Van Lawick.

Patty, from Indiana via Texas, had spent the last three years in the Serengeti studying the jackal, an ubiquitous little scavenger often more wily and tenacious than the hyena. She and Leo were just leaving for the 35-kilometer trip to Ndutu. When they had gone, Mary asked me to sit down and offered me tea. How long had I been traveling? Had I had any trouble in Zaire? Was the Sahara difficult?

"Louis and I always wanted to make that drive, the other way—to London—but we never did. We sailed once up through the Red Sea. *That* was a scenic trip." I had wanted to see Egypt and the Sudan myself, I said. Maybe next time.

Louis B. Leakey had been my hero—one of the few that had withstood the test of time since my first free-reading days at Sheridan Junior High.

Mary Leakey came across right away as pleasant but direct—the kind of person that didn't enjoy aimless polite chatter. She expected conversation to be informative or not at all. She worked hard days and expected those around her to do the same and keep quiet. I instinctively made myself at home, knowing that only relaxed guests who took care of themselves were welcome.

There was a large library, roughly divided into natural and earth science and popular fiction, several hundred paperbacks ranging from Agatha Christie mysteries (Mary's favorite) to James Bond. There were a few hardbacks, including some histories of science (*The Piltdown Scandal*, for example) and *War and Peace*. These, and the volumes on natural science, were kept in a special glass bookcase on the terrace. There were a number of classic reference materials, works by herself or her husband and distinguished colleagues, and certain texts dealing with the geology of the gorge, including the Texan Richard Hay's classic, *Geology of Olduvai Gorge*. Other prominent volumes were Ewer, *The Ethology of Mammals*; Wood, *The Evolution of Early Man*; Biship and Miller, *Calibration of Hominid Evolution*; Tobias and Leakey, *Olduvai Gorge 1951- 1961*; Oakley, *Frameworks for Dating Fossil Man*; Napier, *Hand-Book of Living Primates*; Chaplin, *The Study of Animal Bones from Archaeological Sites*; J.E.G. Sutton, *The Archaeology of the Highlands of Kenya*; and a tattered old French dictionary. Wedged between these primary works were a dozen or so first editions of peripheral writings inscribed by their authors.

The cook, Kabibo, soon helped me place my things into the small one-room cabin next to the lodge. A second cabin, further down, was Robin's. Mary lived in a roundavel, a circular hut constructed from poles and thatched with bamboolike plains grass. The roundavel had a porch all around it, on which were stacked various boxes of equipment. The windows were barred and meshed—and with good reason: Mary kept four Dalmatian hounds, white with black spots save one, Black Dog, who was her favorite. Each had its own special wicker basket and matting.

The year before, Black Dog had survived an attack by a pride of young lions up at the Tanzanian workers' camp. The lions killed and ate his brother and later killed a Masai shepherd boy who had attempted to protect his goats. Park rangers and sharpshooters came afterward, but the lions had gone. Later they were found in another area of the park, rich with game. The shooters killed zebra for them for a week or two, until they began themselves to stalk the herds. No thought was given to killing the lions once they had left the gorge. It was thought that they had been expelled by the adults of their natal pride. Such lions are as dangerous as old or wounded ones: not knowing how to hunt, they will attack stock and man.

Leopard are not as common, preferring areas where the game is less migratory: such as Ndutu or Ngorongoro Crater. Nevertheless, they do appear, and when one does, it can be disastrous. Dog meat is perhaps the leopard's favorite; he will forsake even easily taken goat for it. It is said that a leopard will kill a man to eat his dog.

But at that time, lions were the menace. Several prides, following the northward game migration, were hunting in the gorge each evening.

At 1:30 that first night, I had been reading and just dozed off. Mary and Robin were long asleep. Suddenly, I was awakened by a deep, bellowing roar like those I'd heard up on the crater. There was a moment of silence and then another series of roars. They were only just the other side of the thorn-bush fence. The roars continued for some fifteen or twenty minutes, while the lions methodically circled the camp, then drifted below into the gorge. The last roars came from some distance away and were barely audible. I had felt safe inside the compound until the next morning, when Mary told me what had happened to Black Dog and his brother.

"If they really want to come in, those thorns won't stop them," she said. I realized then why she had iron bars on her windows.

Mary lives virtually alone in the plains. No other Europeans are permitted permanent residence. Among the native population, only the nomadic Masai are allowed to live out in the park and, except for the photographers and an occasional scientist at Ndutu, and a Catholic mission at Indolyn on Lake Eyasi, there are no other residents. Mike is at Ngorongoro, but that can be three hours—or worse—on a bad road, and besides, he is usually out in the field.

Mary stays in touch with the outside world by radio—a standard transceiver set that goes through Nairobi Central when there is no interference and not too much local traffic. For the past few days she had been trying to get through to ask about her daughter-in-law, Valerie (wife of son Philip), who was going to Canada for an operation. Obliterating static, from the storm clouds which had brought Kenya's worst floods in 25 years, was frustrating her efforts. She had been unable to even raise the central operator. Although the second night of my visit she was able to get a response, there was still too much static for him to place the call. The following night she finally got through.

The front of the lodge is open and faces Ngorongoro. The crater almost always wears a cap of grey clouds. Except for the mountain and its dormant sister volcanoes the terrain is flat. The only constant sound is the wind. From time to time the wind will bring the scent of a passing herd of wildebeest, and the Dalmatians will growl. Sometimes it carries the musk odor of a predator, and they will leap into a frenzy. So it was at dusk my second day.

I had been tinkering with my engine. Mary was working at her desk in the office next to the porch and Robin was next door in the lab. Suddenly, the Dalmatians bounded from the porch and advanced toward the gate, hackles raised. The gate was shut, but I could see beyond it the unmistakable movement of slinking yellow fur. *Lion*, I thought, remembering last night's roars. Mary was off the porch now. "Grab them, grab the dogs," she yelled. The servants dropped what they were doing and ran from all corners of the compound. By then I had the binoculars and saw what I was certain to be a lion or leopard.

"Cheetah! Cheetah!" she screamed. "It'll rip them to shreds."

The men had now collared all but Black Dog, who was already at the gate.

"Get him! Get Black Dog!" Mary was beside herself. Kabibo finally did, just as the dog crouched to leap the fence. The Dalmatians were locked in the office, still yelping madly, while Mary and David, another of the workers, jumped into the Peugeot van and drove through the gate. I followed them with the binoculars, then tried to pick up the cat again, but it had disappeared. Around and around the compound Mary drove, stirring a wake of dust and honking her horn. Surely this would frighten it away.

She had just returned through the gate when the animal bounded onto the porch.

"Cheetah!" called one of the men. It was crouched, tail curling back and forth. It was much too small to be a lion. I would have thought it was a leopard but for its long spindly legs.

212

"Lisa!" Mary shouted. She was suddenly ecstatic. I looked closer, and sure enough, the cat had a brown leather collar just as Mike had said. Mary was stroking the animal's neck. "She came back. Eighteen months and she came back. She remembers me!"

Lisa was emaciated and infested with lion flies. We rolled her over on her back in the dirt and began picking them off, one at a time, squeezing them as we would fat ticks. Otherwise, they would rebound onto Lisa, or the dogs, or us.

"They're a bloody nuisance, those. Don't let them escape, or they'll be all over us." Mary was adamant. I soon saw that squeezing them was inefficient so began putting them in a can for burning.

The dogs were still growling in the lab, but the bedlam had subsided. Black Dog alone was insistent. The cheetah sprang from the porch and paraded around the yard. Returning to Mary, it rubbed its back on her leg, purring like a big pet tabby.

Lisa remained for a time, gorging herself on bowls of milk and a mixture of meat and dog food. At dark, however, she disappeared. Two small genet cats came and sneaked along the porch to retrieve their customary ration of bananas. Genets sometimes follow in the trace of a hunting cheetah or other predator in hopes of scavenging a free meal from the pickings. These genets were frequent guests but had not been seen in several nights.

Later, over Kabibo's succulent roast of lamb and squash, we discussed Lisa's future. Mary was afraid the animal might be killed by the Masai if she were returned to the crater. She would be safer and happier in a place where she could have human contact as well as a wide hunting range. Since Leo was working with cheetahs and Ndutu was full of small game, that seemed like the perfect place. Would I go to Ndutu and ask Leo if he would take her? It was an excellent chance to travel some back trails of the Serengeti, and I immediately said that I would be delighted.

The next morning, Kabibo brought morning tea half an hour early, at 5:45. It was good, this custom of morning tea. It got you going an hour before breakfast. I was to do some of my best reading in the hour between Kabibo's first knock with the jittery tray of tea service and his call to breakfast at 7:15.

This morning, however, I was on the porch right away—I wanted to look again at Ndutu on the map and plot it on the compass—returning again to my earlier habit of plotting all directions off the main road. Although Ngorongoro (visible for 40 miles) gave you a constant point of general reference, it was good to know where you were in your immediate vicinity.

Mary and Robin were also up early and we soon were having soft-boiled eggs and thick Canadian-style bacon. Edward would be my guide, she said. He was one of only two men whom she let groom and exercise the Dalmatians. He was, I was to find, a much better groom than guide.

The trip to Ndutu took just under two hours. We backtracked for twenty minutes on the road to Seronera, then turned north toward the Kenyan border. Everywhere around us darted and cantered dust-raising herds of zebra, gazelle and wildebeest. Soon we came to some nearly obliterated tracks leading west, marked only by a rickety hand-lettered sign that read, "Ndutu Game Camp: 15 K." Just as we turned, Edward called my attention to four lionesses nonchalantly trailing a herd of wildebeest.

When we reached Ndutu, we found that the lake had risen over the road. We circled several miles around the lake to locate a suitable ford.

Van Lawick's camp consisted of a dozen tents, all in a neat military row. Out back rusted a vintage Land Cruiser. A dignified gentleman sat in a lawn chair reading a magazine. He looked up and smiled warmly as we drove up: "Glad to have company. Sit a spell."

We introduced ourselves. "Hugo," he insisted.

Leo and Patty had gone to Seronera to look for leopards and wouldn't be back for several days. Would I care to leave a message? I said that I would and told him the story of Lisa. No, he wouldn't mind if the cheetah came, he said, but he would reserve the right to send her back if she became too playful, since his seven-year-old son was coming from England to spend the summer.

He insisted that I stay for tea (and as the day wore on, lunch, and finally, afternoon tea).

"New here, aren't you?" he asked. I could tell he meant it kindly.

"Yes, just a few days. Drove in overland. Sahara, Zaire, all that." We talked a lot about overland traveling—sand, mud, wars, running out of gas, spare parts—he'd driven the continent a great deal.

Before long I was the kid asking all those "have you ever/ what's the biggest" questions. He was relaxed, enjoying the role.

Most dangerous: Cape buffalo, by a long shot. Once he was filming some lions at rest, a rather routine day. Just as he began packing up to go, he spotted a lone Cape buffalo trotting toward the pride, but downwind and out of sight behind some rocks. Neither the lions nor the buffalo knew the other was there. The buffalo rounded the rocks and quickly picked up his enemies' scent, whereupon he snorted and charged. The lions lazed contentedly, unawares.

"He wasn't twenty feet away and coming at a good forty miles an hour," said Hugo. Then the first lion saw him and sprang, and then the others bolted in all directions.

"What a sight that was. He gave one old lion a really good chase but of course they all outran him."

Another lion story: one day he found a leopard lounging away the afternoon in a small tree. He set up in a well-camouflaged position and was filming when several lionesses on the hunt passed directly beneath the leopard's tree. Among them were three cubs tumbling close to their mothers. A few yards from the tree they entered high grass and momentarily disappeared. When they returned, the cubs were not with them. Hugo knew, he said, what was going to happen. The lionesses—still unaware of the leopard—began stalking a herd of Thompson's gazelle about a quarter of a mile away. The leopard waited until they had disappeared, then crept down the tree and out toward the grass. Methodically, for over half an hour, it crawled back and forth searching for the cubs—raising its head every now and then in the direction of the hunt. Hugo was pulling for the cubs but feared the worst when he heard snarls and frantic rustling. Not long afterward, the lionesses returned. Smelling them, the leopard bounded back to his tree. They sauntered into the grass and in moments reappeared with all three cubs intact. It had been a narrow escape.

I told him about the cobra Lucy and I had seen near the west gate. "They are all around but you seldom see them," he said. "They want to avoid you as much as you do them." One day just recently, he had been sitting here doing nothing in particular when he heard the "awfullest squawking" at the camp's bird tray. That day the birds had hardly touched the tidbits put out for them by the campers. All of a sudden there was a terrible commotion, like a dispute about to come to blows.

"I looked over and there was one lone hornbill." The bird must have been disturbed, he said, by all the noise, for he suddenly flew up and as he did, just a fraction of an inch behind him, a cobra shot through the air. "I mean it just missed him. I grabbed a stick but by the time I got over there it had disappeared."

You can frequently tell where they are, he said, by the sudden chatter of the birds over in some part of the grass. "Of course, as you can see, the grass is so high and thick, you would never find them—even if you wanted to, which I don't particularly. . . ."

The camp was an ideal setup, two miles from the tourist lodge (which never had much business anyway) and just above the marshland of the little lake. "We see everything here in the course of a week," Hugo said.

It was late and I needed to be getting back. Hugo and I shook hands and he invited me out for a few days if and when I got back from Nairobi. I had told him I might try to get a job over at Mary's. Edward had run up to the lodge to visit a friend and buy cigarettes. It took 40 minutes to locate him, and it was after dark when we returned to Olduvai.

That night Kabibo served fried calf liver. Towards the end of the meal Mary began talking about her summer projects. Chief among them was the excavation of a site called Laetolil* out near Lake Eyasi, about 30 miles from Olduvai. She and her husband had found the Laetolil beds back in the 1930s, but until the summer of 1975, no one had excavated them. They lay in solid volcanic rock, but to get out to them one had to drive through 30 miles of chuckholes, thorn bushes and black cotton mud.

Because of the mud, the only time the site could be worked was in the dry summer months—July through October. The year before, they had tried to mark a passable trail, but it had been washed away by the subsequent rains. The road would have to be rebuilt. Her youngest son, Philip, had supervised the previous project, but this year he was tied up planting on his vegetable farm near Nairobi. In addition to the road, it would be necessary to construct a temporary camp, including a cook shack and huts for the various workers.

---

*The spelling—and thus the pronunciation—was changed to *Laetoli* (lie-toe-lee) by the Tanzanian government in 1979.

What exactly was the importance of the site to her work? It was there that she had discovered the remains of several primate skulls which had been dated at between 3.2 and 3.6 million years B.P. (before present). Whether these primates were hominid or ancestral to man was still speculative. The scant anatomical evidence available seemed to place them as ancestral to most of the later forms which are now generally considered to be, if not our ancestors, at least our distant cousins. These latter—*Australopithecus, Homo habilis* and *Homo erectus*—beings who lived from 1.8 million to 500 thousand years ago, were as distant in time from the Laetolil primate as we are from the earliest of them.

In 1975, her work at Laetolil had almost been completed when she came upon a creekbed which had cut down into an ancient game trail of the same era as the primate skulls. Fossilized in the trail (now the creekbed) were scores of discernable footprints of the animals that had walked it. Among these were tracks of giant herbivores, for example, *Dinotherium* (the great-tusked ancestor of the mammoth and today's elephant) and a much smaller equine-type creature, ancestral to the horse.

There were many other prints, some yet to be identified. Among the unidentified were five very clear prints made by something that walked upright, for nothing except a bipedal creature could have made tracks like those. The only such animal of which there was any evidence at that place and time were the primates whose skulls Mary had found. Now, she wished to excavate further along the bank in hopes of uncovering other prints and of making casts and additional measurements. Of special significance was that the prints, if they were indeed those of the primate, would give scientists an idea not only of the animal's foot and body size, but, inferentially, of its bone and muscle structure as well. Since the prints were more or less in a straight line and not side by side it could be inferred that their author, though bipedal, had not yet fully developed the swiveled gait of the later hominids.

I had to confess that my last scientific training had been in an under-graduate course at Fayetteville called "Physical Science" fifteen years ago. Still, I would be willing to do any yeoman's work for a few weeks for room and board and a chance to roam the Serengeti. She pointedly asked how serious I was. I told her "quite," that I'd be delighted to undertake whatever she had in mind.

"I think you could be a great deal of help to me," she said. She asked how long I had, and I told her at least a month, perhaps longer, that my only concern was making the Cape of Good Hope in September.

Mary Leakey's concern was the one needling everyone at that time who lived in Tanzania but had a family or business in Kenya: the border closing. No transit was allowed residents of either country. Although Mary was an exceptional case—working as she did under the Tanzanian Department of Antiquities and having her own private office at the Kenyan National Museum in Nairobi—she still had to get special permission to travel back and forth, even to transport the necessary supplies for the Laetolil project. She hoped to be permitted to fly to Nairobi with her cousin the following week. Whether she could then return with the equipment would depend upon the authorities in Dar.

I was planning to leave the next morning for a short stay at Nairobi, but at Mary's urging, I decided to stay over another day and investigate some nearby fossil sites with Robin and Stephen. Stephen took me to Site DK, where I observed his men about the painstaking task of excavation and sifting. They were digging in the area where Absalom had recovered the portion of the skull of *Homo habilis*. Although the fossil had apparently come from near the bottom of a large overburden of earth protruding from the gorge wall, it was essential that their excavation begin at the top of the bank (some ten feet above the floor) and proceed downward toward the point of recovery. The reason for this was that the skull might have simply washed down to the level where it was found—the rest of the bones remaining in the original level. If they just started digging where it lay, they might miss its level of origin, and in the process scramble bones and artifacts of distinct periods hundreds of thousands of years apart. The process is, therefore, almost maddeningly time consuming.

First, a grid is laid out according to standard archaeological practice. The grid is three-dimensional, so that the resting place of each fossil or tool fragment found can be pinpointed with exact coordinates. Strings are placed at convenient distances to mark base lines. Diggers work with a kind of narrow cement scalpel, scraping dirt from a specific quadrant as they keep a hawkeye out for the tiniest scrap of evidence, which is carefully collected and put into a jar marked for that quadrant. Next they carry the dirt over to a sand sifter, where all four men sift by gently running their hands through the soil. Evidence thus obtained is sometimes double that previously found by sight.

As a further safeguard, the soil already sifted from each quadrant is kept in a separately marked pile and can be sifted once again on command from Dr. Leakey. Each night, Stephen certifies the results, checks that they are properly marked as to coordinates and quadrant and carries them to her.

From time to time, several crews may be working simultaneously on as many sites. This is especially true in the summer months when extra help (usually British and American graduate students) is available. But supervision of these people is a problem. Although most are talented and eager young people, they have no practical field experience. The time necessary to train and oversee them is considerable. Mary prefers to use the Mkumba, who she knows will stick strictly to the tasks for which she has trained them, although they too require careful supervision. She is fortunate in having in Stephen an exemplary foreman.

Once a site has been set up and digging is underway, Mary will inspect it only periodically unless something significant is found. Of course, she carefully monitors the soil samples and their quadrants.

We stayed out at Site DK until just before dark. On the way back, Stephen and I jumped two sleek cheetahs stalking a herd of Grant's gazelle. We spoke of Lisa, who had not returned since the first night.

217

The next morning I thanked Mary for her hospitality and said goodbye. She gave me several letters and parcels for her office at the National Museum in Nairobi. I would let her secretary know where I was staying and she would call me when and if Mary arrived the following week.

I spent the night in Arusha at the New Arusha Hotel after a long day's drive with Jooma, Mike's houseboy, over the crater and through the coffee plantations on the eastern side. (I had left some equipment with Mike at Ngorongoro, and when I had gone to pick it up, Jooma had asked if he could hitch as far as Arusha.)

The next day, a Friday, I crossed the border at Mamanga with no difficulty. It was terribly overcast to the east, and I did not see Mount Kilimanjaro, although I kept a constant lookout. The immigration authorities were amazed that I had entered the country from Rwanda. The roads in the west were now closed because of the flooding, they said. I looked at the vehicle registry and saw that except for Williams' Bedford, I was the only overland vehicle crossing to Kenya in weeks. Only vehicles registered outside of east Africa or those carrying selected persons on official business could pass. There was a long line of tearful people being denied permission to visit their families in Nairobi.

An American couple crossing from Kenya in their Maryland-registered Land Rover were having money-changing problems, since the border officials wouldn't accept Kenyan shillings as payment for Tanzanian visas. They had nothing else, and there was no bank. When I came up, they asked if I would change money with them, but the immigration officer warned me not to do so—an illegal transaction, he said. After I was cleared to pass I gave them the twenty Tanzanian shillings they needed.

I did not see a single vehicle for the next hour, as I crossed the Amboseli Game Preserve. Some twenty miles the other side of the border, I descended a hill and almost collided head-on with four graceful cheetahs idling in the middle of the road.

I was unprepared, 150 miles later, for the sight of what could have been an American freeway: the Kenyan National A-5—the trunk road to the port of Mombasa. At 6:19 p.m., May 20, 1977, I passed a standard green and white highway sign that read, matter of factly, "Nairobi City Limit."

CHAPTER XVI

Mediterranean Sea

Nile River

Red Sea

Mount Kenya

Aberdare National Park

Nairobi

Lake Victoria

Milindi
Mombasa

KENYA

AFRICA

Atlantic Ocean

Indian Ocean

Nairobi was the most modern city, except for Abidjan, that I visited north of the Zambezi. Driving in, I had the impression I was back in London, the main streets all intersecting in neat British roundabouts. Perhaps its utterly British character was due to its having been founded as a supply depot in 1905 during construction of the Mombasa-to-Kampala railroad. There had been no previous settlement there.

I had been told to take the first right after the third roundabout and look for the Norfolk Hotel. I was there in ten minutes. At first glance it appeared to be yet another of those posh, sterile tourist hotels that I had so far successfully avoided. Nairobi had its share of these, but the Norfolk was an exception. For gentility, tradition, and service, it ranked in my mind with the old Canadian Pacific's Banff Springs and Colorado Springs's Broadmoor. The style was British colonial, circa 1900: one story, high ceilings, heavy wooden beams. The exterior was a kind of adaptive Tudor. Of course, it had been expanded and modernized. There was an informal grill on the patio where one could eat until midnight. It was not a big hotel—small, really, by American standards—and I soon knew most of the desk clerks, stewards and waiters by name. Its famous Lord Delamere Bar was the traditional watering hole for Westerners, most of whom would drop in at least once during the week.

One wall of the bar had been painted with elaborate but satirical English hunting scenes from the 1920s. Adjacent were frescoes of colonial Nairobi of the same period. The characters were straight out of Rudyard Kipling, their facial expressions and attire cleverly exaggerated to absurdity. The African who painted them, now an octogenerian, still tended bar as Waiter Emeritus, and it was considered top honor to be waited on by him.

One of their few cheap rooms (ten dollars) was vacant, and I took it. It faced on the inside courtyard just above the kitchen and an aviary. There were interesting morning noises and the community shower was at the end of the hall, but the regular rooms were $40 per day, and, for a savings of $30, I could handle minor inconveniences. In addition, the hotel was only a five-minute walk from the museum.

Out on the little balcony, I wrote cards and letters to the 90-odd folk who in the last six months had written me c/o U.S. Embassy, Nairobi, Kenya. The embassy, of course, had long since arranged for such stragglers' mail to be held by the post office at *Poste Restante.* I had enough mail to read for three days and I read each one very slowly, savoring this first contact with home and friends. Other than the mail I read with relish the *Herald Tribune,* the *Times* and *Le Monde.* I hadn't seen a current major newspaper since Paris.

When I had stopped at Ngorongoro, Mike Melhman had given me his list of "must" attractions in Nairobi—chiefly restaurants and watering holes. He had also given me the name of his good friend, a New Mexican anthropologist named Tom Wilson and his ladyfriend, Rowan Lindley. While quaffing a bottle of Guiness at the hotel bar that first night, I noticed a fellow American at a neighboring table with a very lovely English lady. I introduced myself and they asked me to join them. When, after a few moments, he said that he was from New Mexico and was teaching anthropology at the University of Nairobi, I knew that he must be Tom Wilson and said so. When I also knew of Rowan, they were doubly shocked. I reviewed for them the events of the previous week and we all had a good laugh over our getting stuck in the crater. We became the best of friends, and Tom and Rowan introduced me to Nairobi.

To meet the real folk of Nairobi, you have to go to their places. Contrary to the local white myth, I did not find Kenyan working people as a whole heavy drinkers, at least not those I met and visited with. They seemed to go home early and spend a lot of time with their families. There has emerged, nonetheless, a Western youth culture, a hell-raising set whose night spots are legion. They tend to headquarter at the Starlight Club opposite the Pan African Hotel or at the New Florida Bar, an ultramodern disco-in-the-round that sits over a garage on Koinage Street virtually in the center of town. At 5:00, when I took my morning jog in the central park, the place would invariably be still booming and jumping, the vibrations shaking store windows six blocks away.

A little more subdued (but more socially active) establishment was the Star, a combination bar and beer garden surrounded by an eight-foot-high fence topped with barbed wire (to dissuade patrons from evading the two-dollar cover charge). The place is peaceful before 10:00 and you can sit in the beer garden and enjoy quiet conversation with your friends. Toward 10:00, however, the band starts, the crowd swells and the action begins. Single ladies in Nairobi tend to be more socially aggressive than their Western counterparts. I would find myself tugged first this way, then that to the tables of competing lovelies. Dancing is almost mandatory and, being a shy dancer, I was somewhat handicapped. Nevertheless, I soon learned that, as in the States, the larger the crowd and the later the hour, the less one regrets his failures at Junior Cotillion.

After collecting my mail at the post office, I had the feeling some of it was missing. It was. In spite of embassy policy to send mail back to *Post Restante,* there was another bundle half as large as the first awaiting me in the consular section. The embassy staff and employees in Nairobi were the most courteous I dealt with on the entire trip. They carefully searched for mail and messages and took mine for others without complaint. Because I had had all my correspondence forwarded to me there, they put in a lot of time on my behalf.

I had some money wired from my U.S. bank account to the main branch of the Standard Bank of Nairobi. I wanted to purchase traveler's checks but first had to convert all my wired dollars to shillings, then purchase the checks. That way the bank got a double commission. It amounted to almost three percent, quite a rip-off. On the back of each traveler's check they rubber-stamped a gratuitous little notice: "Valid throughout the world except in Rhodesia and South Africa." (That gave me a bit of a worry when I later noticed it at the Rhodesian border. But the officer only smiled and cashed the check. Traveler's checks can be negotiated anywhere and such limitations have no effect.)

After mail and money, the first order of business was a complete checkout of the Toyota. The dirty, greasy spare gas tank which I had been carrying in the back since the Serengeti had to be bolted back in place. Fortunately, the local Toyota dealership had an excellent garage, and this and other minor repairs and replacements were handily made. I should note that the only flat tire I had sustained the entire 8,000 miles I'd driven since Algiers was in Arusha—a nail picked up in the street. The tires (Dunlop, All Terrain) were superb.

The University of Nairobi is just up and across the street from the Norfolk. Tom would occasionally come over for lunch. One day he suggested we go to Olorgesailie, an early Stone Age site discovered and excavated in 1942 and 1943 by Louis and Mary Leakey.

We drove out in the jeep the next morning, a Saturday. We took the road to Magadi, a sulphur mining town on Lake Natron. The entire road and the site itself lie in one of the most dramatic segments of the Great Rift Valley. Enormous ridges rise precipitously on either side as they did hundreds of thousands of years ago when early man roamed and temporarily resided in the area. The Olorgesailie site was littered with Acheulean hand-axe blades when the Leakeys stumbled onto it. It is still the richest Acheulean site known. A built-up wooden walkway leads around most of the site where the stone tools were made and abandoned by late *Homo erectus* over 400,000 years ago. Of particular interest is a grotto which was used for butchering large animals, including great baboons. Skulls of the latter were opened, obviously to get at the brains.

We spent the entire day roaming the area, then drove to Lake Natron to take a look at its lone sulphur plant—weird in its solitude on the primeval landscape.

I found that the class "C" New Avenue Hotel across from the post office served the best and cheapest breakfast in town: all the eggs I wanted, thick slices of bacon, sausage, and hot cereal, for ten shillings (compared to 25 at the Norfolk and other first-class tourist hotels). The two New Avenue waiters, Wilson Apwapo and Francis Omolo, became my good friends and

222

saw to it that I was always well served. The bar through which I had to walk to get to the dining room reeked of spilled beer, dirty glasses and mildewed carpet, but once I got past that, I had a hearty breakfast.

Seemingly every other business in Nairobi is a souvenir shop. Most of the inventory consists of wood and ivory carvings of animals. The wood carvings and the poorer-quality ivory carvings are produced in factories or workshops in Pumwani, a slum section of town, where they are turned out by the thousands. Ivory prices are not high, they are beyond exorbitant. A fist-sized elephant costs 1200 shillings ($150). The quality of the finished work has lately been immeasurably improved by air-freighting raw tusks to Hong Kong, where they are worked by Chinese artisans and returned to be sold as African art.

This flying around of ivory is interesting because the only legal sources of ivory are elephants destroyed by accident, illness or old age. A dealer told me that at least a planeload of tusks is flown to Hong Kong every month. "There sure must be a lot of sick elephants up there in the Samburu," this fellow told me. Most of these animals are, of course, poached.

The East African Wildlife Society has estimated that at the present death rate, Kenya will have no elephants in ten years. The rhinoceros, whose horn is powdered into an aphrodisiac, is also waning. Other game, such as zebras, are killed for their skins but are not yet on the endangered-species list.

How can so many elephants be killed and so much ivory transported in the face of stringent laws against it? The answer is corruption: corruption at the highest level of government. Armed park rangers and police regularly hunt down and kill small-time Somali poachers but do nothing to halt the large-scale operations of Kikuyu poachers operating in the same areas. Customs agents turn a blind eye to the cargoes of Hong Kong-bound ivory freighters—not to mention tourists leaving with phony certificates of origin, or none at all. Any criticism of top government officials in this or any other regard is quickly stifled. One may decry this general lack of enforcement but one member of Parliament who pointed his finger directly at a relative of Mrs. Kenyatta was found eaten by hyenas. Others, as previously noted, have been arrested even on the floor of the house and jailed.

In June of 1977, with great fanfare, the government decreed an end to big-game hunting. Conservationists in America and Europe rejoiced. The poachers did too, because the professional hunters had been their only effective competitors in the field. Most arrests of poachers had come only after information was supplied by professional hunters. Organized hunting safaris—for which the tourist-hunter pays a considerable license fee— destroy only a fraction of the game which succumbs naturally to disease and predation. Poachers, on the other hand, destroy many times the number which die naturally. The last hope for the game now is the efforts of private agencies such as the East African Wildlife Society and the World Wildlife Fund. Requirements such as the United States law which prohibits importation of products from endangered species without a certificate of origin are helpful, but can easily be circumvented by corrupt officials issuing false certificates.

One last word concerning the killing of wild animals: some farmers have

223

a legitimate grievance against some animals, particularly elephants, who destroy crops by trampling or eating them, or both. It is difficult to condemn a farmer who kills in order to protect his fields. Unfortunately, some farmers are also poachers who use this excuse to bag anything that moves.

Among the letters Mary had given me was a personal note of introduction to her son Richard, the curator of the National Museum of Kenya. I had expressed an interest in browsing through the library and fossil collection. We had a good visit and he gave me a pass to the library and museum facilities. Richard is the second Leakey son and the one who followed his father as both curator and celebrity on the American lecture circuit. He regularly appears at the National Geographic headquarters in Washington, D.C. and Leakey Foundation lectures in California. His field work is presently concentrated at Lake Rudolph (decreed "Turkana" by President Kenyatta) in northern Kenya and Ethiopia. This has tended to shift attention to that area of the Rift Valley as an even earlier habitat of man than Olduvai. A skull he found in 1972 has been tentatively dated at 3.4 million years—although some have placed it as more recent, around 2.6 million years B.P.

Other finds which fall into the same time frame have been made by his teams, as well as those of French and American sponsorship. Although the various teams maintain liaison with each other (and all work out of the museum here), there is a certain friendly rivalry among them which occasionally becomes quite intense.

This same spirited rivalry is seen in the mother-son relationship. Mary's position is that the earlier Olduvai hominid predates those of the Turkana and northern area. The Laetolil fossils go a long way towards substantiating that, but since exact dating has yet to be done on the Turkana finds, no definite conclusion can be made.* What everyone will admit to is the strong possibility that there was a lot of roaming up and down the valley for millions of years and, depending on the luck of the find, one fossil will appear today to be the more remote, only to be replaced tomorrow by another.

It is important to realize that many of the fossils found belong not to man's ancestors, but to his distant cousins, i.e., to sidelines that may have even thrived alongside his ancestors but which eventually became extinct. As mentioned earlier, there is considerable disagreement over which of the three "species" (*Australopithecus, Homo habilis* and *Homo erectus*) found out here was ancestral to man. Some say all were, some say only *erectus*, and others say both *habilis* and *erectus*, in that order (*habilis* becoming *erectus*).

The museum is certainly the most efficiently run in Africa. It houses the largest prehistory collection on the continent and ranks behind only the British Museum, the Smithsonian, and the Musée de l'Homme in the world. Its collection of marine life (illustrated by the renowned wildlife artist Joy

---

*Olduvai Gorge—indeed the entire Serengeti—is Mary's private preserve, since it is in Tanzania and she is the only permanently authorized resident archaeologist there.

Anderson) is surely unsurpassed. The section on Kenyan history and culture is a model one, excelled only by the National Museum of Niger in Niamey. The Kenya Museum does not seem to be oriented toward general public service but more toward research. School children are brought through on tours and the exhibits are open to all, but I never witnessed the eager, almost festive, use of the facility by the public that I saw daily in Niamey.

Under construction and almost completed was the L.S.B. Leakey Center for Primate Research. A vast auditorium and classroom complex, this would house not only Leakey's fossil collection but also his library and support equipment. It is financed by the Leakey Foundation.

I spent, all told, a good twenty days in the museum and library reading up on the latest finds and making notes on the fossils as well as the region's culture and history. It was a great help to me both as a traveler and as an amateur student of prehistory.

One afternoon in the street outside the New Stanley Hotel, I saw three haggard young men with backpacks who looked familiar. Approaching them, I spoke and then recognized them as having been in Mwanza several weeks before. They were an American and two Australians, and they really looked beat. I asked them where they had been, and they said Uganda.

They had spent a worried but uneventful week until the night before they were to catch the bus back to the Kenyan border. The police had come to the Catholic mission in Kampala where they were staying and arrested them. Somehow, the priest had succeeded in getting the police to leave them at the church while they went to check with their chief. They had spent an uneasy night waiting for the police to return. The next morning they had left at 7:00 for the bus, when the police returned and found that they were not at the mission. The police had come to the station, dragged them off the bus and detained them for three days in a local prison. They feared that the priest was in trouble for their having left but had been unable to return to talk to him. Finally, they had been taken to the border and expelled. No reason for their detention had been given. They were very hungry and I gave them directions to a good cheap restaurant on Koinage Street.

While I was in Nairobi, there were several in a long series of audacious stickups. A gang of hoods, about ten of them, would suddenly burst into a restaurant around 10:00 or 11:00 at night, close the doors, and collect everything from earrings to cash. In the classic style, everyone was made to sit with his hands on the table and then drop his contribution into the sack as it came around. Most embarrassing for the government, one Saturday night the gang robbed the Casino restaurant and gambling hall and made off with a half-million dollars. The last I heard, none of the gang had been captured.

All the major restaurants and night clubs had steel grating installed, which was opened for patrons just as they entered and quickly closed behind them. At least two armed guards stood outside with rifles and flashlights, both to deter robbers and to signal to the public that the places were open but protected.

Tom generously offered me the use of a spare room in his apartment to store my heavier gear—the steel boxes, trunk, spare tire and jerry cans. This relieved me from worry about theft since, although the Norfolk had a well-guarded parking lot, it is never a good idea to leave gear like that for an extended time in your car. While theft is a problem in Nairobi (including bold-daylight car-window smashing) it is not as pervasive as in other large African cities. Much of this is doubtless due to the excellent police force modeled on—indeed carried over from—the British colonial police. The officers patrol on foot in smart khaki tropical uniforms. Their training is tough, and many candidates fail to finish.

The first week in June I checked out of the Norfolk and drove up to Aberdare National Park. For two weeks I had seen the daily tally of rhino, elephant and other game sightings on the Treetops board in the hotel lobby and had decided to go see for myself.

Treetops is the oldest and most famous of a number of luxurious game lodges built next to water holes, the edges of which have been heavily salted to attract the animals. The lodges are sumptuous, chalet-style motels with dining rooms and snack grills. They are partially camouflaged and sound-proofed, however, so that the animals will not be frightened away. Treetops itself was actually a blind built in the heights of trees across the pond from the present facility. Before it burned down in the late '50s it was already one of Kenya's top tourist attractions. A plaque on the roof of the new lodge tells you that Queen Elizabeth became queen there in 1952. (Her father had died that night in England while she was on tour.)

The present lodge is a massive structure built on telephone poles some 30 feet from the ground. Each room has a window opening out onto the water hole or the woods out back. Guests are warned not to open the windows until after dark, lest they be robbed by the troop of baboons which live there. One woman had recently ignored the warning and been severely bitten when she sought to retrieve a pair of shoes from one of these bandits. After dark, however, the baboons perch in the distant trees, and nothing else, save an occasional mongoose or a genet cat, will climb the poles to the lodge. At dawn the baboons are back again, monkeyshining for the tourists on the roof. It is strictly forbidden to feed them.

One goes to Treetops by reservation, preferably placed by a Nairobi hotel. This I did and was told to be at Outspan Lodge in Nyeri by noon. My ticket was 200 shillings ($25), which included three meals and the night's lodging. We left our vehicles at the Outspan Lodge and were driven in two vans to Treetops.

A white hunter, who appeared to be about 70 and carried a .300 magnum, accompanied us. The route out is about fifteen miles, half on paved highway and the rest on a dirt road that winds through some small truck farms to Aberdare Park gate. The lodge is about three miles inside the gate. The trail leading to it branches off of the main road where a sign reads, "No vehicles beyond this point." We dismounted and the white hunter briefed us on safety: we were to walk slowly behind him and remain silent. If an animal attacked, he would kill it.

He may have been a great white hunter but he didn't seem to be too enthusiastic on this day. He carried the weapon as one might a squirrel gun, nonchalantly crooked in his left arm, bolt open, gabbing with one of the tourists. Of course, we all knew that the hunter was part of the adventure scenario. Yet, as we walked into the clearing between the gate and the lodge, there were a dozen Cape buffalo licking salt not twenty feet from us. Several stopped licking and stared at us but made no threatening moves. Aside from the buffalo, we could see several waterbuck and a wart hog. As each guest reached the foot of the wooden ladder, he breathed easier and mounted quickly toward the open hatch above. Later I saw the catering van and kitchen crew down there shouting and bustling about, and none of the animals appeared in the least bit disturbed.

The bar was a handsome mixture of native wood and had a long backbar. Everything was available, from ginger ale to Drambuie. Deep leather lounge chairs and sofas offered us comfortable seats and a panoramic view. Waiters hurried back and forth, trays and glasses tinkling. Outside, a few more buffalo came up, swelling their number to 30. There was another wart hog. The waterbuck had left.

We were led individually to our assigned rooms and warned again about the baboons. Most people went up onto the roof or observation deck right away. The baboons were there too, anticipating the disobedient lady in the pink pantsuit who fed one a portion of her sandwich. The animal wolfed down the morsel and lunged for the remainder. Startled, the lady withdrew her hand. Snarling into her face, he wrenched the sandwich away. Had she held on, she would have been attacked. The next morning, she was still shaking from the experience.

My room looked out back into the woods where the only view was of the now-treed baboons. Around 4:00 the clouds that had been covering Mount Kenya in the distance momentarily lifted, revealing its snow-capped peaks and plunging glacier. A half hour before dusk, the hunter turned on the outside floodlights. By then a half-dozen elephants had joined the buffalo. When the elephants approached an area, the buffalo would quickly retreat. I didn't know buffalo could be so compliant, but those elephants were awfully big.

Suddenly someone shouted, "Rhino!" and a lady squealed, "Look at the baby." Sure enough, on the far side of the pond a no-nonsense mother rhinoceros waddled towards us. Scurrying along beside her was a tiny bull calf. She took her time, but as she proceeded, the buffalo quickly cleared her path, faster even than they had done for the elephants.

Our hunter by this time had joined the more refreshed guests at the head of the bar and was holding forth about the good ole days in "Keen-yah." When he saw the rhinoceros he told us about the time his truck had been attacked by a big male, who had bent a fender down on the tire so that the vehicle couldn't move. That had been at noon, and the rhino stayed until dark, glaring at them from 30 feet away. Even after dark, when they fixed it by flashlight with a crowbar, they weren't sure that he wasn't still lurking somewhere nearby.

The elephants seemed to enjoy hogging as such terrain as they could. We watched as one young bull began rushing some buffalo that had crept back to a less-than-respectable distance. He would charge right up to where a buffalo was licking contentedly, and the buffalo would buck away, shaking his head disgustedly. The elephant would then urinate on the spot. In fact, each time an elephant would displace another animal he would urinate extensively on the place it had been. Whether he was only relieving himself, being ornery, or scenting his territory, the hunter didn't know.

As we talked, the mother rhino came up in front of the bar and began licking at the mud just vacated by the buffalo. The calf wandered off a bit and found his own place. Suddenly the young elephant rushed at her: but Mrs. Rhinoceros was not frightened—neither was she amused. When she didn't budge after another feint, the bully turned and began walking back toward his family. No sooner had he exposed his flank than she gave it a good jab with her horn. That sent him howling to his mother—a funny sight since he was almost as big as she.

The next visitor was even more interesting. The water hole was now quite crowded with elephants and buffalo and scores of pigs and deer. Mrs. Rhinoceros and calf were minding their own business, having moved to the left edge of the clearing. Suddenly, she snorted and shook her head as if she'd been stung. Stamping the ground, she whirled in a tight little circle. Then one of the children shouted, "Hey look, another rhino." And there was indeed another rhinoceros—a Mr. Rhinoceros this time. He was all the way on the right side of the pond, but she had already smelled him and obviously was not pleased. She wheeled toward him, pushing assorted buffalo and a forest hog out of the way. It looked as if she might attack, but just when she reached him, they both stopped and she began pawing the ground and snorting—as to give him a good scolding. This went on for a minute, following which the newcomer turned and skulked away. From then on, he kept a good distance from her and the calf, confining himself to the far side of the hole. At least a half-dozen times mother and calf walked to a distant corner of the clearing, paused for a while, then returned to the choice salt lick in front of the bar. She never scolded the male again but he moved himself well out of her way each time she traveled.

Black rhinos, which these were, are notorious loners, pairing only briefly during the mating season. On the contrary, the rare white rhino (found only in Uganda and Rhodesia) lives in herds of up to a dozen. Because there were only a handful of them at the hole the entire evening, it was easier to keep track of the individual rhinos than the other animals.

The house keeps a scorecard of animals sighted. I kept a separate one, which showed fewer animals since I went to bed around 2:00. My own list:

elephants	22
rhinos	6
waterbuck	10
wart hogs	12

forest hogs	6
hyenas	2
mongoose	2
genet cats	3
Cape buffalo	50 (and stopped counting)

There were no large cats in the area. Lions live far away in the plains with the migratory herds of zebra and wildebeest. Very rarely, a leopard might come up early in the morning. The hunter told us that two months previously, a leopard had killed a waterbuck right there in front of the bar at around 4:00 a.m. The afternoon of her visit in 1952, Queen (then Princess) Elizabeth had seen a male waterbuck charge and kill another.

The hunter said that hyenas would stalk and kill an old bull or a young calf at the hole. He had previously watched some hyenas select an old bull and chase it around the hole, until it fell, whereupon they devoured it alive. "Strangest thing," he said. "Once the victim's been selected, he knows it's all over and you can tell it. The other buffalo know too and they treat him like a pariah. They stay completely away." As hyenas chase a victim they nip at its legs and flanks. They especially try to bite into the belly and expose the intestines, thus hastening its loss of blood and energy until the animal falls.

Although I saw thousands of animals in the Serengeti and other big parks, nowhere did I see so many large herbivores close up as at Treetops and, the following night, at the Ark. The Ark is a somewhat more commodious ground-level game lodge only a few miles from Treetops across Aberdare Park. Some say you see more game there, although this night there was only a small herd of Cape buffalo, half a dozen elephants, and a single rhinoceros. There were, however, over 30 identifiable species of birds which came for the seed thrown out by the Ark's hunter.

When game comes to the Ark, you can join it by going down into the dungeon, a concrete bunker with wide, open slots which extend in a six-foot radius from the base of the lodge. While I was down in the dungeon, a young bull elephant was turned upon by a sour old buffalo he had been pestering with mock charges. Like the rhino the night before, the buffalo gored his aggressor in the flank and was thereafter left in peace.

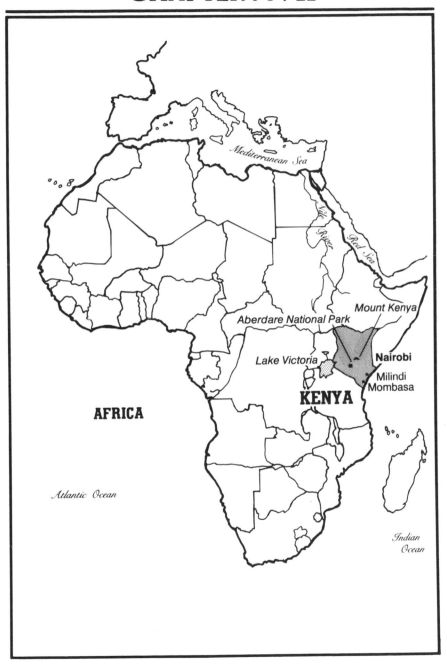

Mediterranean Sea

Nile River

Red Sea

Mount Kenya

Aberdare National Park

Lake Victoria

Nairobi

Milindi
Mombasa

KENYA

AFRICA

Atlantic Ocean

Indian
Ocean

His name was Dune-go: of the Kikuyu tribe, 45 years old, twice-married, twice-widowed, the father of five children, porter and guide for climbers of Mount Kenya, Africa's second highest peak.

Even carrying my 50-pound pack, he was as sprightly as a teenage athlete. I was making it, but struggling. For Dune-go, it was a Sunday stroll.

The guide shack where I picked him up was halfway to the park gate. The clerk at the lodge had said it would be conspicuous, but it wasn't and I drove right on by. By the time I backtracked ten miles and found him, it was 10:30.

I had packed two pairs of ski socks, an extra pair of jeans, a wool sweater, two tins of Exeter-brand Argentine corned beef, two small tins of canned Kenya peas, two loaves of brown bread, eight chocolate bars, a tin of Nescafe, a spoon, a knife, a can opener, a sleeping bag, and the poncho liner. Dune-go carried a bag of mealie meal and some hardtack.

I would have preferred to climb alone, but the regulations required a guide. You could not even pass the gate without one. The loose mud was as resistant to climbing as melting snow. Neither the black cotton soil of Ngorongoro nor the sharp slag of the Herakoonta volcano was as formidable. From the base of the mountain to the last ranger station where we had parked the jeep and begun climbing, there was a thick piney wood. Near the station, this was replaced by a mountain rain forest of hulking trees hung with thick, grey-green moss.

We'd climbed only ten minutes when Dune-go pointed to fresh tracks: "Buffalo," he said. A ranger had recently been attacked by one just up the trail. He stopped and pointed again: "Elephant." I hadn't known they lived this high (13,000 feet). Evidently, the same herds tended to remain on the mountain, rarely descending to the plains. There were also rhino and leopard tracks—quite a few of the latter. Leopards hole up in small caves in the higher ledges and at night feed on plump rock hyraxes, with which the mountain teems. These little creatures—looking like chipmunks infected with giantism—are about the same size as a small muskrat. Hyraxes are trusting of man and you can approach to within a yard of two of them before they scamper away. With their grey coats, they are well camouflaged against the rocks so that you will be amongst a whole family of them before you know they are there. Oddly, the hyrax is the elephant's closest relative. They, and a species of field mouse, appeared to be the only mammals living in the

232

damp, rocky fields below the glacier. They are certainly the most plentiful. During one rest stop alone, I counted 35 of them.

Halfway, we stopped to rest beneath a 100-foot-high outcrop. The temperature had dropped from a balmy 80 degrees at the lodge to a windy 50 here. For the past hour, clouds had enveloped the mountain, and now the mist waxed occasionally into rain, limiting visibility to 100 yards. My hands became numb with cold and, having neglected to bring gloves, I pulled a pair of old ski socks over them. They were soon soaked. Dune-go needed no gloves, not even a jacket. He wore only a thin brown sweater and a faded beret. He seemed to thrive in the miserable damp climate.

Soon the tree line abruptly receded, leaving not a single eccentric fir. Replacing the trees as the dominant vegetation were some peculiar alpine shrubs, red pulpy-stemmed rock plants. Around 5:30 we arrived at the Booking Hut, the overnight climber's shelter. This was a rickety one-room shack with a tin roof. There were two small single windows, the top panes of which were shattered. The place was surrounded by hyraxes, some of whom had obviously been inside the hut through the broken windows.

Chest-high was a wooden platform a quarter-inch thick, which covered half of the room and upon which were spread four thin sleeping sponges. The shack provided a break against the wind but not much protection against the night cold, which was already beginning to nip at our wet feet. Dune-go was visibly perturbed that I had not brought camping gas. When he saw that there was none in the hut, he insisted that we continue on to the rescue lodge —fifteen minutes up the mountain, he said. I told him that it was OK with me, but I didn't want to hike up there then have to come all the way back down after dark. He said he thought we could stay, that the rangers were his friends and would have food and hot tea for us. I'd resigned myself to the cold corned beef, but the thought of a fire and hot tea renewed my strength, and 35 minutes later Dune-go was knocking at the door of the rescue hut, a solid wooden cabin built on a concrete foundation on a slight elevation beneath the glacier. Inside was one large room with six double bunks which took up half of the space.

The two men (actually rescue-unit soldiers, not rangers) had been up there for 25 days of a 30-day shift. One of them, a corporal, had been trained in mountain rescue in Austria, the other by an Austrian team on Mount Kilimanjaro. Their job was casualty evacuation, but they also took wind, temperature and snowfall-depth readings as well. Communication with park headquarters, far below, was executed by means of a standard military dispatcher transceiver backed by an ancient U.S. Army PRC 25, which the corporal tested spontaneously from time to time. A Sony AM/FM clearly received Nairobi's rock station.

The soldiers were indeed Dune-go's pals. That was a good sign, for I thus assumed that they would graciously take care of our food and shelter requirements. They brewed up some hot African milk-tea and showed me where to hang my wet socks and shoes to dry. Dune-go and I crowded around the potbellied stove, our hands stretched toward the fire.

It was dark when, an hour later, I went out to take a look around. The wind was higher and the mist-rain well nigh freezing. When I came back inside, I could tell they had been talking about me by the way they fell silent and batted their eyes. Dune-go finally spoke: "They say this place not for tourists. We have to go back to Booking Hut."

"That's too bad," I said. "It's awfully late. You don't think they'd let us stay just tonight? We'll leave early in the morning."

The corporal spoke enough English to understand the gist of what I had said. "No. Boss come, we get in trouble," he replied.

I told him no boss, nobody, would come up here at night in this weather, and we'd be gone before dawn. Dune-go translated this into Swahili. They talked for a good while then Dune-go said, "How much you pay to stay?"

I had figured it would get around to that. I thought for a while, shaking my head.

"Ten shillings," I said. I was starting off low. Dune-go relayed that and there was an incredulous smile on the corporal's face. They talked.

"Twenty-five," Dune-go said. "They cook us dinner too. Twenty-five shilling." I had been afraid they night say 100, so I replied "Twenty last price." This was beginning to resemble Marrakech.

"Okay, twenty," said the corporal, not waiting for the translation.

"Fine," I said. "But you'll have to wait until we get down for the money, since it is all in the jeep. I'll give it to Dune-go and he can get it to you later."

At first this was not acceptable, but after Dune-go promised to act as agent in good faith, they finally agreed.

Dinner was beef jerky and rice and mealie meal, a heaping bowlful, but I was still hungry and added half a tin of corned beef to the last of my mealie. More tea was boiled, and we sipped it and listened to the corporal show off his English by reading some passages from a bad 1950s British novel. Outside, the wind was loud. Dune-go said there would probably be a snowstorm up on the glacier in the morning.

Normally, the climb takes three days. You climb here to the base of the glacier the first day, spend a day resting, and complete the climb the following day. I was really beat, since the air was so thin and I had not been that high for well over a year. But it was a fitful night, the corporal reading the novel endlessly in my dreams.

Mount Kenya is 17,058 feet high, after Kilimanjaro (19,340 feet) the highest in Africa. Our climb was to be to the smaller of three summits, the only one accessible without ropes and professional gear.

We left the rescue hut at 5:40 the next morning and walked down a hump into a flat marshy basin below the hut. The marsh is fed by the freshet that becomes Naro Maru River. Looking up I saw its source: the Great Kenya Glacier, a massive shelf of blue-white ice that seemed to hang suspended in midair at the top of the draw. It was still early, just after first light, when we came to the goat trail which wound up from the basin floor to the gravel ridge alongside the ice. It took half an hour to climb it.

"Fifteen thousand feet here," Dune-go said, when we had finally reached the ridge and could look out and down on the glacier. I was beginning to feel unacclimated and exhausted from my fitful sleep. The last of the corned beef and some mealie had made a sparse breakfast. Yet the real problem, I knew, was that I was simply out of shape. My wind, normally kept deep by fifteen miles of jogging a week, was incredibly short after six months on the road.

We began an over-fifteen-degree ascent on the loose gravel surface, climbing zigzag fashion and keeping our footing by staying next to the few firmly anchored boulders. Some of these were deceptive and gave way at the slightest pressure, plunging down onto the ice.

Dune-go climbed further and further ahead. The idea was to climb ten or twelve feet, rest, then climb again. Although I started out doing up to twenty feet, by the time we got near the top of the first ridge I was barely doing five before resting. Dune-go had stopped by then and was taking in the view— such as it was, for the clouds had now settled into a thick soup through which nothing was visible beyond the peaks, which themselves were soon lost in a punishing snowstorm. It was not so much the snow that frustrated us, but the wind which lashed with such frenzy that even Dune-go grimaced at the cold. He had borrowed a pair of gloves from the corporal. My ski socks were again wet and frozen, but as long as I didn't remove them, my hands could stand it. Thus we continued our grueling slow-motion ascent. I've never regretted not being in shape more than I did that day. Finally, at 10:00, we reached the Austrian Hut, an overnight lodge for professional climbers who tackle the main peaks. The storm was by then a blizzard, and we were truly grateful for the shelter of the hut. None of its windows were broken, and after we had stomped about and slapped ourselves for twenty minutes, the air became warm enough to mist the panes. I had never imagined that I would experience a snowstorm virtually on the equator.

Dune-go absolutely vetoed my half-hearted suggestion that we climb the remaining 300 feet to the low summit, and I must admit that I did not press the point.

We were back at the rescue hut at 12:30. The soldiers had prepared their mealie-and-rice lunch, and they shared it with us, displaying all the while a good-natured contempt at our defeat and scoffing at the severity of the storm. I let Dune-go lay it all on me. I must have looked funny to them with the icicles still clinging to my beard.

The hike down was not enjoyable. My legs were wobbly with fatigue, and the endless muddy slopes were an ordeal to navigate. Still, by 4:30 we had made the station and were on our way back to the lodge. Dune-go's fee was 60 shillings. I gave him 100, plus the twenty for the soldiers. His wife was waiting for us at the guide shack.

Back at the Naro Maru Lodge I ate a hearty supper and took another walk along the river, still a mere stream. It was stocked with trout for the length of the lodge property. Lower down, about a mile, it was partially diverted by a culvert into a small English country pond. An elderly warden in the habit of a Kentish squire collected fees from would-be fishermen. A carefully hand-lettered sign limited the sizes of hooks that could be used, fish that could be kept, and dress that could be worn ("no bathing trunks or loud attire"). The lower half of the pond was marked "off limits." A yapping terrier was helping with the enforcement. Two guests in khaki shorts were fly-casting as their wives observed stiffly from lawn chairs nearby. One of the fishermen wandered too near the prohibited area and the mutt ran out and nipped at him. The fisherman retreated silently down the bank. The wives said nothing.

Chapter XVIII

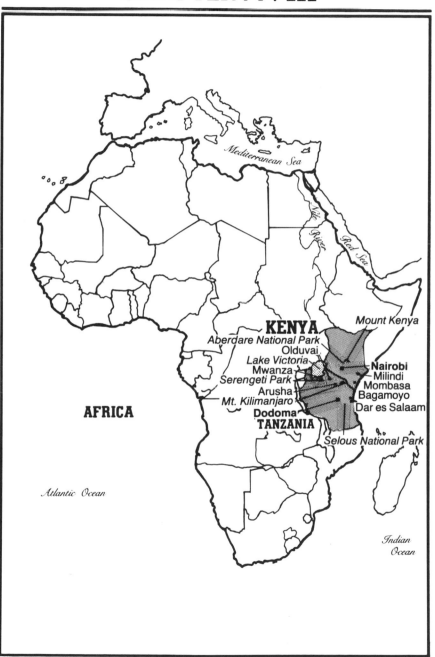

Mediterranean Sea

Nile River

Red Sea

KENYA

Mount Kenya

Aberdare National Park

Olduvai

Lake Victoria

Mwanza

Nairobi

Milindi

Serengeti Park

Mombasa

Arusha

Bagamoyo

Mt. Kilimanjaro

Dar es Salaam

AFRICA

Dodoma

TANZANIA

Selous National Park

Atlantic Ocean

Indian Ocean

McMath with Mary Leakey at Laetolil Base Camp, Tanzania.

When I returned to Nairobi the following afternoon, there was a message at the hotel to call Dr. Leakey. She said she had received permission from the Interior Ministry in Dar to bring the equipment down and wanted to start the Laetolil project as soon as possible. Did I still intend to help? Yes, I told her. How about starting the fifteenth? Fine. I had to get the Toyota roof patched at Specialized Molding, the only fiberglass menders in town. (It had been raining through the holes formerly occupied by the bolts of the lost roof rack.) She was going back to Olduvai the next day in her van with some new men and food supplies. Could I bring the rest of the supplies? I said I would.

She was also anxious to get back since she had left no one in charge. Robin McKinney had flown back to the States, so she no longer had that help. She would use the meantime to finish a chapter in her book on the Gorge's history.

The Bedford we were to use to haul supplies from Olduvai to Laetolil was being used just then by her son, Philip, on his farm. It wouldn't be available for another couple of weeks, but that would give us time to get the road built and the site cleared.

The next day Hazel, Mary's secretary, brought 70 pounds of meat (for Mike Mehlman) and some snakebite medicine over and put it in the hotel refrigerator, where it stayed until I was ready to go. (The chef was a mite perturbed to find cobra antivenin on the shelf with his custard pies.)

With the roof patched and some new cassettes for the player I loaded the groceries (including six twenty-pound sacks of dog food) and made Ngorongoro by 8:00 p.m., a leisurely twelve-hour drive, counting a two-hour lunch stop in Arusha. The Tanzania customs officials thought I might be smuggling the dog food, but I showed them a letter Dr. Leakey had written on her Olduvai logo, and they waved me through. "How is Mama Leakey?" the chief asked, referring to Mary in the familiar manner of those Africans who know her.

I became worried that Mike's meat might spoil. It had already begun to thaw out on the floorboard. Luckily, a chunk of ice from an Indian restaurant in Arusha saved it through the afternoon.

Just south of Longido, the clouds partially lifted to the east and I saw Mount Kilimanjaro for the first time. It was still somewhat obscured, so I stopped and used my field glasses. It was silent where I stopped, there being neither traffic nor animals nearby. I wanted very much to climb Kili and resolved to do so sometime. There are guided climbs from Marangu, taking four days, minimum; it is better to take six or seven. Several of the Bedford group I had seen in Nairobi had climbed it and they said it was a slow, easy pace except for the last 300 feet. From there only a handful made it to the top. With my experience on Mount Kenya, I could understand.

I stayed overnight at the Crater Lodge, stowing the meat in their fridge when I learned that Mike had not yet returned to his cabin. I left a note on his door. In the morning the manager gave me Mary's mail on the way out.

I arrived at Olduvai about noon, unloaded the gear and read a recent *Nature* article on the Laetolil project. Mary produced several old maps and a low-resolution satellite photo for my orientation.

My job, Mary repeated, was to plan and mark a single passable trail to the site and then put up the camp. Washed-out bridges and fords would have to be rebuilt and potholes filled. I would have all the help I needed from Stephen and his twenty men.

I moved my things back into Guest Cabin No. 1. Kabibo made the bed and strung the mosquito net. There weren't many mosquitoes, but occasionally, early in the morning, several would attack. The only other nuisance was a nest of red wasps in the eaves who occasionally flew down to reconnoiter their unexpected guest.

Between the two guest cabins was a canvas-bag shower stall. Kabibo would fill the bag with hot water at the kitchen and carry it to the stall and hang it up. When he thought it had cooled enough, he would call. We had to be careful, however, or we would still be scalded. Rinsing thoroughly was also important since, in the dry air, soap adhered to our skin and itched maddeningly.

The privy was in the back of the compound, behind Mary's roundeval. A path led behind the lodge, then parallel to the guest cabins: another one led from her place. At the head of the path, before you turned left to enter the outhouse, there was a short wooden tripod and board on one side of which was faintly carved "VACANT" and on the other side "IN USE." It was important to arrange the proper signal. A small library there consisted of old *Time* magazines and mystery novels.

About 40 feet from the outhouse were two electricity-generating windmills which had been contributed by a firm from Texas. Only one was necessary to charge the high voltage batteries kept locked in the hardware shed behind the lodge. The door was painted with a skull and crossbones over which was written in red, "HITARI—DANGER." Only Kabibo had the key. There were also drums of distilled water and chemicals used in connection with the lab work. In a high wind it would be necessary to feather the windmills; otherwise they would run wild and strip their gears. Usually, though, one was running all the time and I could hear it up there whirring and creaking at night. That was frequently the only thing I could hear, except for the wind and the occasional roar of a lion down in the gorge.

240

Sometimes at night I would walk about the compound and look at the brilliant sky and listen to the windmill. There was a primeval, surreal feeling about the place. The night sky in the Serengeti was cold, direct, brilliant. Even in the darkness of a new moon, one could faintly see the outlines of Ngorongoro and her sister volcanoes. In the full moon there was a luster from the fringe of the crater's inevitable cloud cover, and somehow one seemed to hear more rustlings and snorts and muffled screams from out on the plains. One such night I stood out by the gate for an hour, listening to the roars of lions stalking below in the gorge and the answering yaps of a jackal that seemed to mock them.

Edward was in charge of the Dalmatians—before any of his other duties, which were helping Kabibo in the kitchen and occasionally pitching in when an extra hand was needed at the digs. But the dogs came first. He carefully brushed and groomed them, pulling off lion flies and ticks and doctoring their sores. Once a day, usually early in the morning just as Kabibo was brewing morning tea in the cook shack, Edward would jog down to Mary's cabin where the hounds were whining and yapping in anticipation. Mary would then release them and Edward's task was to make sure that they did not leap the front fence and rush out into the plains. First, he would leash Jenny, the oldest and the leader, so that the others would not stray too far. As soon as he had her tied, he would race like a deer for the gate, the dogs all jumping and bounding around him, and the five of them would sprint down the road toward the gorge and out of sight.

Occasionally, the dogs would be out of the cabin and gone before he could catch them. This would rouse Mary into a frenzy and the whole camp would turn to looking for the Dalmatians. The dangers were lions and cheetahs, especially in the summer when the females were cubbing. The Dalmatians, knowing no fear, would give chase to anything, including a lioness with cubs. One morning when Mary let them out early after a rain, they yelped with delight at the fresh scents and were off before the hapless Edward could reach them. Scolding him mercilessly, Mary summoned me from my cabin, and all morning we drove up and down the rim of the gorge. Stopping, we would scan the plains with our field glasses, but all in vain. The men meanwhile dispersed through the gorge, calling the dogs like so many Arkansas fox hunters.

At noon, just as we had given up hope, three of the dogs, exhausted and covered with lion flies and assorted pricklies, dragged in through the front gate from the south gorge, the one place no one had looked. But Black Dog was not among them. The lion flies seemed to betray their activities. The old dog had a small gash behind one ear. It wasn't deep but it looked like a claw scratch of some kind.

"I'm afraid Black Dog might not come back," Mary said.

I drove out about a mile, past the grassy area used as an airstrip and was just turning back when I saw him. He was covered with fat flies and limping badly, dragging his left hind paw. Otherwise, he was intact.

"Domestic animals out here are an invitation to disaster," Mary said once when I asked her if they had ever kept horses. (The terrain was perfect for riding.) She gets a lot of enjoyment from the Dalmatians—they are her

241

resident family. But she knows it is only a matter of time until she loses one of them.

The first afternoon, after I had secured my gear in the cabin, I told her I would like to drive out as far as possible along the old Laetolil trail. The sooner we could get started building the road the better, but first I wanted to get an idea of the terrain. She and David and I drove in the Toyota along the back trail to the main road. The trail ran due south from Olduvai base camp about three and a half miles. It was not normally used and its intersection with the road was almost hidden. At the main road we turned left and crossed the almost-washed-out low-water bridge. Some 300 yards further on we turned right onto the plains and began following a faintly marked track that soon disappeared. This was the Laetolil road, unused now for nine months. Even when it was being used, it was so poorly marked that each vehicle seemed to make a new track every trip. Many drivers became hopelessly lost and a lot of valuable man-hours were wasted. Additionally, there were punishing potholes made mostly by fox and jackal for lairs and, of course, washouts.

We drove eleven miles through the plains, taking care to avoid clusters of inch-long wait-a-bit thorns, which collect in the best tires and puncture their tubes when least expected. Finally we came to an impassable forest of neck-high scrub brush, all grown up over the past nine months. Mary was surprised at how quickly it had reclaimed the road.

It was on the return leg of this trip that I first really appreciated the significance of the gorge. Going out, the terrain rose slowly until we reached the ridge above the Laetolil beds. On the way back, going downhill, we were able to have an almost cross-section view of the top of the gorge. Clearly visible were the two quartz inselbergs, the source of the tools of the early men who had lived here. They rise out of the otherwise flat plains to the west of the gorge, which had been the center of the old lake. The hills, in other words, had been islands when the lake was full.

Of course, the water level varied, and access to the islands was easier when it was down. All along the crests of these hills were strewn thousands of eroded scraps of quartz, just as there had been 2,000,000 years ago. Although most of the topography of the Serengeti has changed since then (the gorge for example, is only about 100,000 years old), the two inselbergs have remained virtually the same. There, hominids would gather rocks to take back with them to their lakeshore camps for fashioning into primitive scrapers and choppers, chipping one against the other until suitable edges would break away.

To the right, the northeast, lay Ngorongoro Crater; below and to the northwest, the shallow depression which holds the present lake, which is really a kind of year-round marsh and the receptacle for the river that runs through the gorge and for other seasonally dry streams in the area.

The potholes were deep and hidden, and Mary got bounced around quite a bit. She rode in the back of the jeep, having given the passenger seat to David, the Mkumba she had taken along for tracking. Frequently he would have to get out and physically scout the trail, so obliterated had it become by the rains and the hooves of the migrating herds. The project, Mary said, would begin around July 15th. That would give us three or four weeks to finish the road.

The following morning after breakfast, I drove with Stephen and three men to the low-water bridge. By 10:00 we had filled the washout with gravel and fist-sized rocks from the dry streambed so that the surface was flush with the natural dip of the road. We spread on a coat of red clay from a nearby deposit and then drove up and began marking the Laetolil trail. We did this by stacking a set of two piles of stones about two feet high on each side of the road every few hundred yards, so that a driver would always be able to see the next set (preferably the next *two* sets) of markers. These were later dabbed with lime wash, which ultimately wound up all over our clothing and vehicles.

Driving back and forth through the plains was a dusty business, the worst since Chad. I was careful to keep the air filter blown out and the three clutch-brake fluid jars filled. It was more efficient to split the weight between the two jeeps. Accordingly, I would carry most of the supplies (food, lime, tools) and two men, and Stephen would carry the other six men. He was the only one of the workers permitted to drive.

Each day at noon we would break for an hour and a half for lunch. By 11:30, two of the men would have found a shade tree and built a small cooking fire. By noon the big black pot of mealie mush or rice stew would be boiling. A balanced meal was considered to be rice, mealie, potatoes and fried pinto beans, together with the tortilla-like bread called *japati*. I began to put on weight eating this, so I started bringing along a can of corned beef and some mixed vegetables. Kabibo would pack this for me in a big red picnic box—much too large for the meager rations inside. Sometimes he would supply me with some fresh fruit (usually a slice of pawpaw or pineapple). Mostly, though, he just threw in the tins and some bread and a can opener. The second week I began packing my own lunch.

Sometimes while we were eating lunch the Masai would come up— particularly young shepherd boys if we stopped near their flocks. Almost without exception, the children's eyes would be infected with the cursed glaucoma, sometimes in a very advanced stage. They would tilt their little heads back and to the side so that they could see us. When the pain came or the eye itched from the swarm of flies they carried with them, they would rub their eyes, aggravating the swelling and bringing tears and yellow pus. Once I gave two apparent two-year-olds some eye salve and showed them how to apply it. I do not think I was very successful, for two days later, when we had stopped a bit further on, these same two appeared and asked for other gifts. There was no sign of the salve or of its having been used.

One morning on the way out, a herd of wildebeest scattered to our left. We had seen few of these the past week, most having migrated on to the north. Stephen was leading by about a quarter of a mile. I could only see his dust. Suddenly, to his right a great lion bounded away and slunk under

243

McMath haggles with two Masai warriors over the price of a goat for the Laetolil camp pot. The price was ten pounds of sugar and a pocket knife.

some brush. He was about 300 feet from the road and could yet be seen and must have known it. When the Land Rover had passed, he attempted to cross the road again but no sooner was he committed than he saw the jeep. Again he raced back to the brush. Stephen, who had not seen the lion until after he had passed it, turned around to have a look. I followed him, and in a few moments we were facing down a handsome lioness, clearly perturbed at having been separated from the herd she was following. She played at retreating into the gorge which was just at her rear but finally decided to hold her ground. She knew we would soon tire of her and leave, which we did.

At almost the same place several evenings later we drove upon a cheetah with two cubs standing over a freshly killed Thompson's gazelle. The cheetah tried to carry away the prey but it was too heavy, so she fled without it, her cubs scurrying behind her. When one straggled, she pounced back and picked it up by the scruff of the neck in her mouth and carried it to the safety of some shrubs, from where she peered back at us. The gazelle must have just been brought down, as it was still in its death throes. It appeared that she had broken its neck.

Throughout the 30-mile stretch from Olduvai to the Laetolil bed we would see herds of up to a dozen giraffe. The females were foaling, and baby giraffes would frequently spring out of the brush and run to the sides of their mothers as we passed. Older brothers and sisters would occasionally run alongside for a mile or more.

My favorite animals were a herd of great eland who clustered in a meadow halfway to the site. The place was out of the wind at the head of a draw with a small spring. With their great antlers they looked like prehistoric elk, to which they are, I understand, related.

We would reach Olduvai camp around 5:00, an hour or so before dark. Of course, as we went further and further away, we would return later. The extra distance increased our chances of sighting game. One night I saw and observed for fully ten minutes the rare golden cat, which normally lives in the mountains and is almost never seen this low. It looks almost like an American mountain lion or cougar but is much smaller. Mary was understandably skeptical, but I was certain after looking at several photographs of them.

My one big disappointment was not finding a leopard. Although they thrive in Ngorongoro (and the chief reason for reinforcing Mary's Leitolil cabin with corrugated iron and chicken wire was to protect the dogs against them), I did not see or hear a leopard, to know it, the entire trip.

Late afternoon at Olduvai brought me some special moments. After a hard day's work I would sit on the lodge wall and have a beer and feel the mysterious stillness of sunset in the Serengeti. For respite I could read one of the mysteries in the paperback library or, occasionally, a current seller, such as *Roots*. It was interesting to read that particular book in such a place.

The weather was dry, but electrical storms could be seen some evenings towards Kenya in the north. We had to contact Nairobi by radio in order to hasten the lorry, with its vegetables and fruit and other sundries, on its way. After several attempts I was finally able one night to raise the central operator, who phoned Hazel at home. I relayed to her the shopping list and Mary's concern about the Bedford. The connection was so terrible that we had to use phonetic spelling.

A few evenings later, while walking out by the gate after dinner, I heard someone fall and cry out. Racing back to the steps of the lodge, I found that Mary had fallen on the steps and twisted her ankle. Kabibo, Edward and I carried her to her cabin. The ankle swelled during the night and became very painful to her. It seemed to be broken, but she said it felt more like a pulled ligament than a fracture. She soaked it in hot water and a kind of epsom salt, but to no avail. The swelling appeared to abate after the third day, but when she walked to the lab and around the lodge for an hour it became worse than ever and she was forced back to bed in great pain. That afternoon I sent Stephen to Endolyn, the small Catholic mission for the Masai on Lake Eyasi, to get some codeine and request a stop of the Flying Doctor. Fortunately, a doctor was scheduled to fly his fortnightly circuit the next day, a Thursday.

The next morning I stayed behind when the men went out. Around 10:00 the plane flew low overhead, wings dipping, to signal he was landing and for transportation to the camp. I got in the jeep, drove out to the landing strip and watched his approach. The landing was a perfect one. The pilot remained seated but the doctor climbed out, a stocky, smiling Austrian with curly grey hair, bronzed skin and a bristling white moustache. He waved as he walked behind the tail, which was painted with a Rotary Club wheel and the legend: "Flying Doctor, A service of Rotary International."

He had been in the Serengeti for two years. He climbed in the jeep, and I drove him to Mary's hut. When I returned half an hour later, he had placed her in an elastic splint, snug and secure but removable for soaking. He ordered her to rest it for at least another week and left some pain medicine. The entire visit took less than half an hour. Soon, he was again airborne, winging his way toward Ndutu, his next stop.

The men began preparing the straw thatch for the Laetolil huts. It had been stacked in sheaves in the compound under tarpaulins when the camp was dismantled the previous September. Stacked to one side were the poles for the workers' tents and corrugated iron sheets used to build the kitchen and roof the huts.

The Bedford finally drove in one night but its generator had gone out and it took ten men pushing to start it. I was unable to learn from Yoka, the driver, why he hadn't fixed it in Nairobi before leaving, or at least in Arusha where they had spent the night. A stalled vehicle in the field is worse than useless and often dangerous. We did get it running, and in two trips the following day, all the building gear was hauled to the campsite at Laetolil— not without two breakdowns, each fortunately on a hill. The first, which was due to a clogged fuel line, left the truck stalled in a meadow just west of the south gorge. Yoka and Lucas, his assistant, went through the standard African procedure of opening the carburetor and the fuel tank and huffing and blowing until they had blown out the debris. While this was in progress, a swarm of bees suddenly descended. There were so many that they appeared as a dark cloud. They flew just inches off of the ground; some lit on the truck and on the grass but seemed to studiously avoid us. The men barely seemed to recognize that they were there, which was reassuring, for they remained at least twenty minutes. The incessant hum was like that heard earlier in the gap at Ngorongoro Crater. When they moved on, they did so quickly and were gone in less than a minute.

For the first time since Morocco, I had cassette tapes for the radio-player. I had bought them from a discount shop in Nairobi. Among them were some Chopin études, Mozart's Symphony No. 40 in D, and Brahms's Concerto for Violin in D. I also had Beethoven's Fifth Piano Concerto and a collection of arias from Italian operas. Listening to good music while driving alone through the Serengeti reopened to me a dimension of happiness and relaxation I hadn't known for many months. I had grown quite accustomed to being without social diversions, Western food, music, a bath every day, a radio. But while I reveled in the Spartan exuberance of the open road, I

246

Paul, one of the Mkumba crew (right), with a young Masai warrior. Laetolil Base Camp, Tanzania.

longed occasionally for a grip of culture, of intellect. The music and my conversations with Dr. Leakey gave me this.

Because of her foot, Mary was unable to walk even the 50 yards to the lodge, so she stayed in her cabin and Kabibo served her meals there. I ate alone at the dining table on the porch. I would drop by briefly before driving out with the men in the morning to learn if there were any special instructions. At night, after we came back from the field, I would go by and have a beer and discuss the day's progress. Sometimes these visits lasted several hours, interrupted only by the evening meal.

Mary would hold forth on various aspects of prehistory and her Olduvai work. We discussed present-day Africa and its people's responses to life's problems, particularly old age and death. She observed that as uncivilized as many of the practices of Black Africa appeared to Westerners, Africans suffered relatively few of the anxieties of industrial societies. We agreed, though, that this was quickly changing.

One night I asked her it if were true that the Masai abandoned their old people on the plains to be eaten by the hyenas. It was true, she said, recalling an afternoon many years before when she had come upon an old man with a group of warriors. The old man was very weak but was pleading with them not to leave him. There was nothing she could do there, but she drove to Ngorongoro and reported it to the park superintendent who sent some officers to investigate. They were unable, however, to find the warriors or the old man. Several days later his body, or what was left of it, was discovered by a game warden not far away, eaten by hyenas.

Once they become unable to provide for themselves, only very important elders—such as chiefs or magic men—are permitted to live out their lives with the tribe until they die a natural death. Being nomadic, the tribe is frequently unable to procure enough food for its productive members and children, much less for a contingent of unproductive old persons who can barely keep up with the migration. The old ones know that it is coming, though, and there is a kind of ceremony connected with it and everybody has his last say, including the one being abandoned if he (or she) is able to talk. Although the Tanzanian government has halted the practice among the Masai it has settled in its ugamaa villages, the abandonment of old persons continues out in the plains.

While the men were unstacking and retying the straw one afternoon, one of them suddenly cried out, "Cobra!" He had picked up a stick and was walking slowly toward a small sapling and pointing. Immediately, the other men dropped their bundles and ran toward the tree, stopping on the way to pick up rocks and sticks. They surrounded the tree as if performing some ceremonial rite, weapons at the ready, their eyes transfixed.

I could see the snake as I approached. Its head reared, it was darting quickly first to one side of the tree then to the other, only to be beaten back again. It was dark brown, almost black, and well camouflaged against the dry grass. Whenever it paused it became almost invisible. Then, in a flash, it would lunge to escape in another direction. "Mamba, not cobra," David said. Just then, the snake darted between two of the men and disappeared into a clump of grass. Someone followed it and cried out that it had gone into a hole. Paul ran to the cook hut for hot water and, using a piece of corrugated iron as a funnel, he now poured it, scalding, into the hole. Joseph Masavo, the taller of the two Josephs, began digging up the ground with his pick. Then David shouted that he had found the exit hole about ten feet away. They all gathered there, weapons poised, but the snake didn't appear.

By then Mary had driven over in her van. "Fire," she ordered in

Mkumba. "Get some kerosene and light a fire in the hole." Again, using the corrugated iron as a funnel, David poured a quart of kerosene down the hole and lit it. A bright orange flame shot out, then slowly settled and began to smoke as everyone began thrashing the ground with his stick. Suddenly, Joseph pried the snake, singed and angry, out of its burrow. It was still very much alive and struck out savagely. A slender, knotty-headed snake, it measured four and a half feet—not particularly long, but quite sufficient: the black mamba is the world's deadliest snake, with only one known survivor of a full bite—a snake handler who had already been taking antivenin. When the men had killed it I took their picture holding it aloft in triumph.

Snakes did from time to time creep up at the lodge, usually to snatch the birds who fed on the bread and seeds Mary put out in the pans under the shade tree by the porch. The bosses of this menagerie were two magnificent white-naped blackbirds who roamed at leisure about the compound, although they roosted several miles away in a cleft in the gorge. After this particular episode, Mary said that she had sensed something was wrong: "The birds had been squabbling and fussing so for the past several days. I should have known they were talking about a snake."

It was Saturday afternoon, and the men were off for the weekend. Mike Mehlman was preparing to leave for two months' fieldwork at Mongola on the other side of Lake Eyasi, and I wanted to see him before he left. So I drove up to Ngorongoro.

I found Mike eagerly packing the last of his equipment. He was glad to be returning to the field after six months at the village. After tea, we drove up to the crater lodge for dinner and by great coincidence met an old college friend of Mike's, Peter Schmidt.

Peter, his wife, Jane, and their two sons, Luke and Adam, were on their way out after working a year on an Iron Age site near the western shore of Lake Victoria, near the Rwanda and Uganda borders. The site was remarkable in that the civilization that had been there had begun to produce moderately tempered steel around 700 A.D., a formidable achievement. Trying to pin down exactly who these people had been and what had become of them was a most difficult task. They had certainly been the most advanced culture to live in the area. He hoped to publish some preliminary findings soon at Brown University in Rhode Island, to which he was returning in the fall. Luke and Adam were spunky, intrepid little men. They had lived and worked alongside their parents at various dig sites, each with his regular chores. When Adam learned that I had traveled through the Sahara he asked so many intelligent questions you would have thought he was with the CIA. When I tried to exaggerate with a tall tale or two about slave catchers and magic carpets, he would have none of it.

I stayed overnight at Mike's cabin and, next morning, helped load his camping and fossil-prospecting gear—tentpoles, tent, sifting screens, rods, two drums of gasoline, two drums of water, a half-dozen crates for rocks and bone samples, sponge bedding, pots, pans, etc.—onto a five-ton truck, which was five times too large for what he had. The crew was not very helpful. The driver kept going to sleep and the men—six of them—watched while Mike and I did most of the loading.

Since Mary's truck was at that time over a week past due, she suggested that I buy some fresh vegetables at Gibbs Plantation, about fifteen miles east of the crater. The manager was Mike's friend, Per, an impeccable Norwegian, who was serving dinner for a party of Dutch tourists. The plantation, several thousand acres of rich land, was losing money in spite of the highest coffee prices in history. (The government takes all the coffee at artificially low prices set years ago and none can be sold elsewhere.)

Although the farm was legally permitted to remain in the hands of the owners—Australians then away on vacation—it had been, for all practical purposes, confiscated with the owners remaining merely as managers. To raise extra cash, they had built a few rooms for tourists but, with the border closed, there was little business.

We were invited to have dinner after the guests had been served (Per good-naturedly remarking that Mike always seemed to arrive just in time). There was an excellent beef-and-chicken curry with spices. This was supplemented, *au choix*, by a tray of peach, mangrove and pear chutney, several kinds of fruits, shredded coconut, brown sugar and crushed elderberries.

While we were eating, one of Per's men stuffed a feed sack full of produce for Olduvai: two kilos each of Chinese squash, cabbage, rhubarb, turnips, greens and carrots and one kilo of green peppers. The bill for all that was 34 Tanzanian shillings (about four dollars). He carefully made out the ticket and put it in an envelope. Mike ordered about twice as much for his camp at Lake Eyasi.

Per next took us on a tour of the pantry and kitchen. It was one of the richest larders I have ever seen: dried beef, hams and sausages hanging from the ceiling, bins of fresh vegetables of every variety, an array of butcher knives and general cutlery, cooking pots and churns of butter and separate ovens for baking breads and pastries.

The plantation house itself looked to be one of those 1930s "early modern" colonial ranch houses I had seen remnants of in Zaire: large brick fireplaces, great panoramic glass windows, simply but spaciously furnished, a terraced brick patio and porch: solid, functional, comfortable, elegant.

Kabibo was happy to have the vegetables. He knew that we had grown weary the past few days of rice and potatoes. When the truck came the following Thursday, we had enough for an army. The vegetables were kept in the pantry, just off the terrace, where there was a small gas refrigerator and a gas stove and several cartons of provisions, including a case of Kilimanjaro beer that I had had Stephen purchase for me on an earlier trip to Ngorongoro. (Everyone provides his own spirits at Olduvai.)

Stephen had returned to Ngorongoro (to the makeshift but oddly efficient park garage there) with the camp's Land Rover, which now had a broken drive shaft. The vehicle had been plagued with breakdowns, most recently a snapped rear spring hasp. We had chained the spring to the axle, and Stephen had just managed to nurse it back to Olduvai. The rest of the crew—nine of them that day—returned with me in, and on, my Toyota.

250

By July 4th, a week after the visit of the Flying Doctor, Mary was doing considerably better. She asked that I park the Peugeot next to her cabin so that she could drive it back and forth the 50 yards to the lodge and sound the horn in case of an emergency. Gradually, she was able to get around on a pair of crutches I'd brought back from a second trip to the photographers' camp at Ndutu.

Edward had come along again, this time to scout our way from Ndutu to Laetolil over a little-used back trail. Unfortunately, Edward had traveled it only once, and that many years before. We soon became lost in a forest of white thorn trees. Every few yards my guide would hop out with his machete to clear a path through the thorns. Eventually, we came to a double-peaked inselberg about 300 feet high. Climbing up for a reconnaissance, I surprised a troop of baboons who fled down the opposite slope in a comic charge. The rock was similar to the two quartz islands west of Olduvai, although its stones were larger and appeared to be more granitelike. From the summit I could see Ngorongoro and the other volcanoes and the shallow lake beneath them. Then, from below, Edward signaled that he had found the tracks again.

As it turned out, he was mistaken. Still, a mile further on we hit some ancient tracks, which we followed for another six miles until we came to what looked suspiciously like the Garusi riverbed (the seasonally dry creek that runs through Laetolil), a trail of black-grey volcanic rock along a twisted gulch. It wasn't the river, though. We bounced along for a couple miles when Edward suddenly said, "This way, now." But his voice was uncertain. We drove up the bank and found ourselves in a sea of hard-dried black cotton soil. The ground was weathered and furrowed into choppy waves, gnarled by the wind and migrating herds. It resembled nothing so much as Sahel wasteland in the nether reaches of Niger. Driving was so rough we could have churned butter. I gruffly ordered Edward on ahead to see if he could find the tracks (which lay two miles to the south, I later learned from Mary). I watched through the field glasses as his green shorts and white shirt became a mirage on the horizon. I couldn't see the volcanoes to guide by so I drove as straight as possible, using vaguely distinguishable patches of terrain. About a half-hour later I hit the tracks and found Edward standing there waiting. In less than half a mile we came to a rhino skull atop a six-foot pole on which Stephen had scrawled in pencil: "Camp this way."

Laetolil camp was now taking shape. The mess hut had been reversed from the year before so that the open entryway faced down wind. The mess hut was also a work and reading shelter, but the year before, the cold wind had scattered papers and chilled workers. (The temperature at Laetolil was ten to fifteen degrees colder than at Olduvai.) Although the campsite was in a rare stand of trees, it was at the head of a draw and caught the full force of the northeasterly wind.

Deebo, the carpenter, had put up two staff huts as well as Mary's and was already working on the storeroom. This had to be built securely because it

Deebo, McMath's Ndutu guide, stands at the gate to Olduvai Camp, Tanzania.

housed not only fossil and tool finds but also provisions—especially sugar, which had a strange way of disappearing almost as soon as it was brought down. (Mary suspected—accurately, it turned out—that it was being traded by the workers to the local Masai for spears and knives.)

I had been sleeping snugly but comfortably in a small one-man tent that was just big enough to drape a mosquito net. The men were bunked in the large workers' tent, except for tall Joseph, who was nursing a toothache on codeine tablets in Mary's hut. He had jarred a front tooth loose while riding in the back of my jeep, so I felt a bit responsible.

Although the men were officially off on Saturday afternoon and Sundays, they frequently used the time to search the creekbeds and gravel banks for fossils. An award of 300 shillings each was paid for hominid bones. Lesser sums were paid for other finds.

At night the men would build their own fire, separate from the cook's and from my own. It was in a clearing behind some shrubs which had been left deliberately uncut so as to provide a barrier of privacy between their end of the compound and that used by the Europeans. They would sit around the fire in their T-shirts and shorts, sometimes even shirtless, in the cold night air. Their ability to withstand the cold was astonishing. I was only just comfortable in a medium sweater and a flight jacket. They had sweaters and jackets which they had brought down from Olduvai, but they never wore them while I was there. Joseph Masovo had an AM/FM transistor radio with which he was able to pick up Swahili broadcasts from Nairobi and Dar. They rarely listened to the English-language station in Nairobi except for rock music, preferring African pop and chants.

Paul Mancilla became my valet. There is no other word to describe the sudden, unexpected attention which I received from him. He pitched my tent and hung the mosquito net and brought me morning tea and, later, coffee. He saw to it that the chair and table in my room at Olduvai were on the first truckload down and that one of the camp's two big paraffin lamps was on my table at dusk. Later in the evening, when it turned cold, he would move it inside the mess hut. There I would read and write up my journal until he brought dinner. Paul was also the camp cook, Kabibo's unofficial apprentice.

Mary good-naturedly chided that he had pretentions. "He cooks everything in a gallon of grease," she said. "I wouldn't touch it." Whatever he was, Paul was certainly consistent. A typical dinner would consist of deep-fried sweet green onions with deep-fried mashed potatoes and deep-fried bacon, light bread with Blueband margarine (made in Nigeria). Alongside would be two big sweet slices of fresh pineapple and, of course, plenty of *japati* cakes. Sometimes there was corned beef and peas or a can of tuna. All this he kept in the big red picnic box along with jars of mustard, jam, honey and other condiments, such as mangrove chutney, which I had carried along earlier when preparing my own lunch. When he served dinner, Paul would put the picnic box down beside the table.

It took just under three weeks to complete the road and get the building gear transferred to Laetolil camp. We spent fully half of that time cutting scrub brush and weeds that had grown over the old tracks the past nine months. The rest of the time we collected boulders from the gorge and nearby plains and stacked them on the road as markers. It was good hard labor, the likes of which I had not done in months.

The road out to the fossil site, a mile and a quarter from camp, had grown up in weeds and thorns which would take several days' chopping to clear. Beyond, the road passed through a black cotton marsh, and to our dismay, we saw that a herd of elephants had tramped down it, leaving prints over a foot deep. One hole actually measured twenty inches. These tracks, now dried as solid as rock, continued for a quarter mile and had to be filled in, painstakingly, by pick and shovel. Joseph Masovo, Daniel (a quiet, hard worker who was my best man with a machete) and I did it in three days. We had no rocks or loose dirt to use as filler so we had to pack the depressions with neighboring soil dislodged with picks. Joseph finally took over this "human rock crusher" detail while Daniel and I carried and tamped.

The low-water rock bridge crossing the creek to the gravel banks and fossil site was washed out; it took a day to rebuild. The rocks had to be carried from 30 yards downstream. Finally, the road completed, all that remained was to have Deebo build a shelter on the bank next to the site.

The afternoon we discovered the elephant tracks in the road, Joseph led us to the fossil tracks and playfully stalked down the streambed in those of the giant *Dinotherium,* ancestor of the elephant, mammoth and mastodon. Then he showed us the "mystery tracks." As Mary had described, they appeared to be the prints of a small child. Of course, they were not *prints* as such, but tracks—depressions in the general shape of the foot that had made them. Mary wanted to excavate further into the bed with the hope that a less-weathered section might contain still clearer tracks or even prints themselves.

Further up the creek bed, above a small dry brush-clogged waterfall, I saw two footlike depressions that, with a little imagination, could have been those of Big Foot. Mary acidly replied to my enthusiastic find by saying, "So you've seen the *yeti* have you?" Whatever they were, they were not clear enough to permit informed speculation. That is, no fossil remains had been found nearby that could account for their originator.

Laetolil had its share of snakes. While we were filling the elephant tracks we flushed two black mambas. At the camp, Joseph Masovo found a five-foot-long puff adder crawling along the wall of one of the staff huts. Later that same day, Paul reported seeing a cobra in the thicket next to the staff privy. It was a cardinal rule of camp—both here and at Olduvai—that one never walked at night without a flashlight. Snakes seem to find outhouses attractive places to visit, and there had been some surprises over the years.

The small wood that borders Laetolil camp on three sides is a sanctuary for birds. Their calls blended with the whistles of the Masai shepherd boys and the bells and lowings of their cattle. At one time or another I personally observed many different species at Laetolil. Among the more common were: the tinker, tropical boubou, D'arnauds barbet, and the hornbill. Most useful was John G. Williams's *Field Guide to the Birds of East and Central Africa* (London: Collins, 1963).

The Masai were never, of course, far away. They grazed their cattle in the lush meadows that joined the Laetolil beds for several miles and collected them at night in their circular corrals. The trail to and from their fields passed just north of our camp. The young men would occasionally wander into camp, bringing with them hosts of flies which lingered long after the men had gone. You could always tell when they were around because of the flies. They were amiable and curious and loved to touch the jeep and make faces at themselves in the rear-view mirror. They particularly liked looking through the binoculars and were fascinated by the camera, demanding to have their pictures taken. One discovered how he could make things small by looking through the wrong end of the binoculars, and his comrades each had to have a go also. The men enjoyed the Masai both for their entertaining diversion as well as for the company they provided.

Although fierce-looking, the Masai are among the most gregarious of all Africans toward strangers. They are also deft traders. As mentioned, the men traded camp provisions with them in exchange for their colorful knives and spears, which fetched high prices in Nairobi.

On two occasions, four young warriors gave demonstrations of their spear-throwing prowess. Paul deposited an empty carton some twenty feet away on a berm. Each warrior in turn threw three spears through the center within an inch of the dollar-sized blue label. They next posed for pictures in menacing stances (as did the other men). They then strutted and chanted

Puff adder killed by Joseph Masovo (standing) in the workers' hut at Laetolil Base Camp, Tanzania.

through a fearsome battle dance. Each one, in addition to his six-foot spear and bowie-style hunting knife, carried a shiny metal pail full of their staple soup of milk, curds and cattle blood. One insisted that I share this concoction in return for some chocolate I had given him. I was able to escape only because the truck arrived at that moment and diverted his attention. I later photographed this same fellow posing in a pair of my old sunglasses.

Not infrequently Mary would send her men on errands for the Masai, with whom she maintained a most neighborly relationship. (As they roam the entire gorge and plains, it is good to be on friendly terms with them.) Once she even diverted our badly needed truck for a whole day to haul their goats to a new camp. On another occasion Stephen carried two sick Masai in the Land Rover from Laetolil to the mission hospital at Endolyn. One chief would usually stay close to the Olduvai base camp and, whenever he needed a favor, come and stand for hours at the gate with two or three warriors. So it was with the truck, which he needed while Mary was in bed with her broken ankle. He stood there silently for two days, although she sent word she couldn't see him until she was well and that Stephen would handle anything he needed. Still, he refused to leave. I supposed that he knew that the use of the truck was a pretty important favor to ask. Finally, he put the matter to Stephen, who got "Mama" Leakey's OK.

One afternoon the chief of the Laetolil tribe came with a delegation to sell us a cow. A shepherd boy led the animal in the background. I told him he would have to deal with Mama Leakey, that she would be down in another ten days or so. She was quite surprised when I told her about it later: "He wouldn't even sell us a goat last year," she laughed. "Times must be getting pretty bad."

Mary was a hard-working, no-nonsense scientist. She worked from the moment she finished breakfast until dark, except for a half-hour lunch break and two teas—one at 11:00 in the morning, the other at about 5:00 in the afternoon—of about twenty minutes' duration each.

The daily schedule revolved around these teas and meals—which, of course, depended upon Kabibo's punctuality. Toward that end, Mary provided him with a "Tiny Ben" standard alarm clock, which she kept synchronized with her watch. The alarm was set an hour before each meal and fifteen minutes before each tea, which were supposed to be served as follows:

Morning tea	0600
Breakfast	0715
Mid-morning tea	1100
Lunch	1300
Afternoon tea	1700
Supper	2000

Needless to say, punctuality was not the rule, but in general, meals and tea were served within a quarter-hour of their appointed times. As long as Kabibo prepared exactly the dishes Mary had taught him, the results were reasonable. But the slightest deviation courted trouble, if not disaster. As a minor example, I liked toast with my eggs; Mary didn't. It took him two weeks to get the toast ready at the same time as the eggs.

The Olduvai Masai chief waits to talk with Dr. Leakey at the camp gate. He wanted Stephen to truck his cattle in the Bedford to a better grazing range. Dr. Leakey, as always, complied.

McMath with some of the Mkumba crew. Laetolil Base Camp, Tanzania.

During one of our evening chats I asked Mary whether there was any social or political significance in learning man's origins. She replied, puffing on one of her Havana cigars, that she was an archaeologist, not a philosopher, or a politician, but that *she* couldn't see any possible significance at all and people were silly to attach any to it. Robert Ardrey, she said, was a good journalist but "his speculations are rubbish." She disagreed with his finding, for example, that man is a predisposed killer, a kind of naturally selected murderer. Moreover, she disputed his assertion that a majority (or even a sizable number) of the fractured hominid fossil skulls Ardrey cites in support of his theory had been bashed in by other hominids so that they could eat the brains.

While territoriality is a valid concept, she said, there is a certain natural religion among all animals that transcends mere respect for territory and pecking order and enables them to get along—with each other and with other species. Man has, she said, created metaphysics in an attempt to define and accomplish the same thing institutionally; yet he also has the same natural religion.

Each of the Mkumba had a family in Kenya whom he was unable to visit because of the closed border. He might obtain an emergency exit permit but then might not be allowed to return to Tanzania. To make matters worse, mail service between the two countries had been interrupted during their dispute. When the men learned that I would be going to Nairobi soon, they each wrote a letter (or had Stephen write one for them) and gave it to me to post.

One afternoon I went with Stephen to Site JK, located near the top of the northwest gorge wall and dated at about 450,000 years B.P. It is attributed to *Homo erectus*. JK had clearly not been a living site: no shelter, tools or bones had been found there. What was it then, if anything? Stephen asked me if I knew. I said, yes, it had been a salt mine. He said that, indeed, was the tentative conclusion.

The site is a twenty-square-foot bed of holes, some of them very large and craterlike, about two feet in diameter and eight to ten inches deep. Adjacent to each large hole are several smaller ones. The holes are not, of course, still intact; entire sides have eroded. Yet the overall site is sufficiently intact that one can easily see its similarity to the salt-mining pits at Teggidan-Tessoum, Bilma, and other sites in the Sahara of northern Niger. The very nature of such an activity would seem to necessitate a socially organized, sedentary population specializing in one phase of food production. Although it is not impossible that this was only a "communal lick" for whomever came along, that would be highly unlikely, given the state of repair and maintenance necessary for such an operation. Heretofore, the earliest known salt mines are dated at about 10,000 years B.P. I told Mary about the Sahara mines and referred her to the book *Sahara*, by Rene Gardi and to Mike Foster in Agadez.

Northwest of Olduvai Gorge on the Michelin map is the designation "Shifting Sands." These are two sand dunes about three miles apart on the open plain which were first seen "leaving" the southern edge of Lake Natron, some 25 miles away, almost 30 years ago. At some 30 feet high, they are not large dunes, but they are unique for the Serengeti. As a part of her meteorological and other observations in the area, Mary regularly measures their movement.

With the road built and marked and the camp up, my tour of duty at Olduvai was about done. I had told Mary that I would stay as long as I was useful but that there was not much left that I could do. She was a fine lady to work for. She gave me complete authority and left me alone to do the job. We respected each other's privacy and got on well personally. On several occasions she told me that she was pleased with the work that had been done and wished that I could stay on and manage the camp for the rest of the year. I must confess that I was really tempted. Still, not being a scientist, there was a limit to how effective I could be once she and the other paleontologists were on hand and the men were working directly for them. Besides, my goal was to reach the Cape. I wanted to get there by the first of September—and after that I knew that I would have a lot of writing to do.

Mary had not yet been out to Laetolil because of her ankle. I wanted her to inspect the road and campsite so that anything she didn't like could be straightened out before I left. Finally, on the third Saturday in July, she said she felt up to the trip. We drove out in her van. I had feared it would be too shaky a ride for her but was surprised that the Peugeot rode much more smoothly than either the Land Rover or the Toyota. She was quite satisfied with the work, and after visiting the fossil footprints and supervising a few minor alterations, we returned to Olduvai.

The next morning I said goodbye and drove to Nairobi. Before I left she expressed her thanks and again encouraged me to stay on through the fall. Again, it was hard not to accept. I had grown very attached to Olduvai and had begun to harmonize my own with its gentle but disciplined routine.

CHAPTER XIX

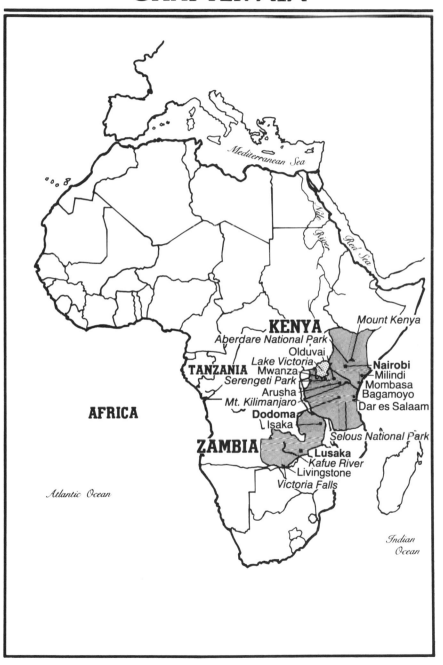

AFRICA

Atlantic Ocean

Mediterranean Sea

Nile River

Red Sea

KENYA

Mount Kenya

Aberdare National Park

Olduvai

Lake Victoria

TANZANIA

Mwanza

Nairobi

Milindi

Serengeti Park

Mombasa

Arusha

Bagamoyo

Mt. Kilimanjaro

Dar es Salaam

Dodoma

Isaka

Selous National Park

ZAMBIA

Lusaka

Kafue River

Livingstone

Victoria Falls

Indian Ocean

Back in Nairobi I found Tom Wilson holed up, putting the finishing touches on an anthology for the September Pan-African Congress on Prehistory. The Leakeys had begun the quadrennial meetings in 1948.

Tom had just received a research grant to study medieval Arab settlements on the island of Lamu. Rowan had happily managed a transfer to the secondary school there, which was in need of a new math teacher.

I spent most of the following week in the museum library and managed to have a couple of long visits with Richard Leakey. In addition to preparing for the congress he was busy collating fossils from a recent expedition to Lake Rudolph. He was interested in the progress at Laetolil and in his mother's condition. I told him that Mary was already up and about and hoped to come to Nairobi in a few days.

One afternoon while jogging in the park I met Helene Mathery, a teacher from Grenoble down visiting a hometown friend, Marie Josie Rey. Marie Josie was *directrice* of the Art and Film section of the French Cultural Center. Helene was also going to the coast, so we decided to go together.

The highway between Nairobi and the port of Mombasa was a grinding industrial turnpike—the busiest stretch of road I'd driven since Algiers. It was too narrow for safe two-way traffic; each passing truck had to take a part of the shoulder.

We departed on a Sunday, and hundreds of families were out for the afternoon. Freight was moving too: in the 300 miles to the coast, we "guestimated" 290 heavy trucks, each trailing a sooty plume of diesel exhaust. Visibility was zero for a good distance behind one of these and to pass we would literally be taking our life in our hands. So we had the choice between a steady gassing of diesel fumes or suffocating heat with the windows rolled up.

The terrain alternated between semi-desert and parched plains of dry brown grass. For 100 miles, we passed through Tsavo National Park, infamous for the pride of man-eating lions that had terrorized Indian railway workers in the early 1900s.

We bought gas and ate spaghetti at a truck stop where a dozen petrol tankers crowded the narrow parking lot, some of them extending onto the

262

highway. The spaghetti was cold but reasonably good, and there was lots of it. There was also fresh Mombasa rockfish and prawns, which were what most of the truck drivers were eating, along with generous helpings of mealie-and-rice mush.

We had been steered to a beach lodge north of Mombasa by Marie Josie. It was a quiet, rundown place with a folksy fishnet bar, wallpapered with faded clippings and snapshots from the '40s of colonial cricket champs and Big Ones that didn't get away. Above the nets, a vintage ceiling fan barely rotated. Facing the ocean was a red-tile patio with rusty tables and deck chairs strung with cobwebs under mildewed awnings. Between the patio and the sea was a thin stand of palms.

After dinner we walked down to the beach. The water was at low tide and only lakelike ripples washed the sand, the surf having retreated a mile away to the coral reef. The reef broke up the surf except very early in the morning when the tide broke loose and heaved up into the palms. By dawn it had again retreated to the reef. Overhead a mild, steady easterly paraded, one squall after another, the downpours interrupted by moments of peekaboo sunshine.

A reticent just-married Peace Corps couple were in the bar the first night. They had been working in Zaire (south of Kisangani) and were taking a three-month honeymoon before returning to their village. The husband had wanted to see the Kenya Reef, considered by divers to be one of the world's most spectacular—equal to the Great Barrier Reef of Australia and the Caribbean one off Belize.

A London accountant, about 30, and his wife and two children were there—fresh out of Zambia after seven years. He had worked with a bank and then a copper company. He was "beyond disgust or disillusion," he said. "There just is no way the country can function as an organized economy without European management." Even with European help, he saw nothing but difficult times ahead, including default on the country's international debt. It would be a mistake, he claimed, to ascribe Zambia's problems to the Rhodesian war. The real causes, he said, were "mismanagement, laziness and corruption." When it had been northern Rhodesia, Zambia was the largest food exporter in southern Africa. Now, fifteen years after independence, it has to import half of its food.

Fort Jesus was the first permanent European structure in East Africa, built by the Portuguese in 1520. It looks exactly like its medieval counterparts in Europe—a massive castle built on a slight peninsula at the entrance to a harbor. Each successive occupant has added a wall, warehouse or magazine, so that it is truly a melange of colonial history, all the way up to the mid-twentieth century.

The wait for European reinforcements was a long one in the early days. One young Portuguese soldier whiled away his time drawing pictures of the anticipated ships—frescoes of sixteenth-century galleons—recently found in a hidden inner wall. Also on display were guns, anchors, ballast and booty from a score of men-of-war and merchantmen sunk in the bay.

In the Arab city next to the fort we followed crooked streets with tall old houses and terraced gardens which seemed to thrust almost naturally out of the bay.

Walking behind the fruit and vegetable stalls of the central market, we entered a certain small street, where the air was heavy with the odors of spices and incense. We followed the aroma to a small shop which over-flowed with fennel seeds, beetle nut, dried coconut and *mukhvas* (a mixture of nuts and sunflower seeds eaten as a kind of *digestif*). There was paprika, saffron, mace, cinnamon, cumin and an entire shelf of special teas and curry spices. On a counter were jars of pachoule and musk. Inside an ornamented cedar case were ginger, cloves, black pepper, nutmeg, Kenya tea, Kenya coffee, cayenne pepper, bay leaves, rice, pilan, anise, and pickled masala.

Helene bought a packet of *mukhvas,* which we munched with our coffee on the terrace of the Castle Hotel while watching the traffic on Klindini Road. Up and down the road and its immediate side streets were signs betraying again the ethnic mixture of East Africa: Khandwalla & Co., Sadrou's Auto Stores, Abdulla & Sons, Shakoor's Household, Penny Electronics, Reddy Kilowatt: The East African Power & Lighting Co., Ltd.

The second morning, while walking along the beach, we saw a fisherman crabbing in the shallows. We hailed him and asked how much he would charge to row us out to the reef. Forty shillings, he said. That was too much: How about twenty? I helped Helene climb into the dugout and shimmied in after her. The canoe was anchored in waist-high water so that there was a good deal of splashing about. When we were settled and dutifully hunkered low in our places, he rowed out, taking a quarter of an hour. The tide was low, and we roamed about over the sharp coral looking at starfish and minia-ture purple conches and a variety of shells. Schools of pan-sized shoal fish darted here and there in deep fissures in the reef. One chunky rock bass was stranded in a tide pool.

"Where is the best fishing?" I asked him on the way back.

"Milindi best," he replied. "Good fish inside reef."

Milindi's Driftwood Lodge was a cluster of roundavels with high, thatched ceilings separated from one another by thick stands of palms. In front of the roundavels was the bar and restaurant. The lodge lay above a short white beach with a heavy surf. Such a surf was rare along this tract, but here there was a gap in the reef.

Walking south along the beach early in the morning, we spied a battered launch. When it was near I waved to the three fishermen and pointed to us, to them and then out to sea. They smiled and motioned that they under-stood and headed in to the beach.

They were going some eight to twelve miles to the south to fish with throw lines inside the reef. Since the shoals to the south can only be crossed at high tide, they fish until three or four in the afternoon. When the tide comes up again, then return across the shoals. If they didn't hurry, they would miss the tide.

How much for us to hitch along with them? 200 shillings. We said we would pay 50. No, they said, 150. We ran back up to the cabin and got our sunglasses and a canteen of water. From the top of the beach, we could see the boat bobbing in the surf like a toy, impossible to steer, the worn cylinders ca-punk, ca-punking. The men pulled Helene over the gunwale and I swung up behind. A light-skinned Chinese half-caste with a faded Muslim skull cap sat in the bow tying lines.

The captain held out a pack of Rooster cigarettes. His wide-brimmed straw hat had a fancy tied black band. The tasseled ends snapped in the breeze. He motioned me up amidships, keeping Helene there in the stern. The boat weaved as if by instinct above the fissures of the coral bottom, which was now but a few feet below the water line. Sometimes the fissure was barely wide enough for the boat. I listened for the thud that would indicate that we had struck the reef, but it never came. Our course was guided by a succession of prominent rocks lying just off shore and the estuaries of small streams.

The tiller was tarred and greasy from the diesel fumes which sputtered out to port from the exhaust. They were blown straight back on top of us. Helene's muumuu was soon hopelessly smudged, as was my shirt. We followed the coastline for an hour, the captain occasionally letting Helene steer. From time to time he would gesture with his hand to correct her drift.

Another half an hour and all at once, the captain gave the signal to turn in toward the reef. As Helene obeyed, the coral bottom quickly rose to meet us with splendid displays of green, copper and gold. The captain deftly lifted the cover off of the "engine room," a low rickety shed which housed the source of all that soot and noise. The ca-punking slowed to strained heaves and then quit. There was no sound but the surf and the light thump-thump-thump of the waves on the barnacled hull as the men prepared their lines. We were about a half-mile from shore, I judged, and about 200 yards from the reef.

The captain took out three "spools" (three chips of wood nailed into small double crosses) around each of which was wound some 100 feet of nylon line. From a coffee can he removed three crappie-sized hooks which he tied to the lines. Next, he dipped into a pail and removed the bait: a pulpy fillet of squid, which he cut into quarter-inch strips about six inches long. Before threading the strip onto the hook, he slapped it repeatedly with the blade of his knife on the gunwale until it was spongy. He then baited the hook until the eye and the prong of the hook were covered, leaving a tail about four inches long.

Winding up, he flung the apparatus some 50 feet aft and let it settle. He released the sinker, a four-inch bolt, which dragged in another 30 feet, whereupon he tugged and played the line for a moment before slip-knotting it to an oar lock. He repeated the procedure for each line until everyone had a fistful of nylon ready to jerk and wind. It was important, he said, to hold the line so that the bolt just touched the bottom—that way you could feel a bite immediately.

The captain's little brother quickly hooked one and began pulling it in, hand over hand, feeding the line onto the deck beneath his feet until his catch was thrashing alongside. It was a four- or five-pound yellow fish, the same species which constituted the bulk of our catch. The little brother was pleased. He lit a Rooster and exhaled the smoke with a grin. Before the day was out he had accounted for better than half our catch. As Helene and I failed to master the quick reflexive pull, we lost a good many of our strikes (though, I must say, she did considerably better than I).

Occasionally whole schools of yellow fish and rock carp would pass along the trough and each of us would hook one. These were exhilarating moments, especially for Helene, who had never fished before. By mid-afternoon the small hold was stacked with fish, a *very* good catch according to the captain.

They had another hole or two they would like to try, he said, and we might as well since the tide would not be high enough to go back across the shallows before 4:30. He started the motor and we ca-punked for twenty minutes back to the north. I could tell he wasn't quite sure of the exact place, as he made several passes. Finally he killed the engine and we drifted.

Helene's was the first hook in, and the captain had only begun to slap the squid bait for the next one when she gave a cry and began to struggle mightily with her line. She fought for twenty minutes, until the fish finally came alongside: a 35-pound rock carp, the largest of our catch and, according to the captain, the largest they'd caught there in some time. Helene was exuberant.

The three men worked rhythmically together as a team, each performing a separate task: the captain cut bait, the "Chinese" threw and retrieved, and Little Brother did the poling with one of the two ten-foot poles they kept lying along the port side.

As it drew near 4:00, the captain ordered in all lines and we struck south for another hole. But this time only the captain fished: a throw line with three short triple-pronged hooks. He stood on the bow and tossed out 30 feet or so, retrieving the line with very quick, jerking motions. Each throw hooked one, sometimes two rainbow-colored sunfish, about hand-sized. When he had a dozen or so of these flopping on deck, he started the motor and we headed south again, then turned almost into the reef.

Suddenly, he stood up and, cutting the motor, pointed into the water. Here and there, floating just beneath the surface, were small white blobs of flesh: squid! He had already baited a sunfish onto one of the lines, and no sooner had the bait hit the water than the first squid shot for it, clenching the sunfish with its tentacles. As the captain pulled it alongside, he handed the line to his brother, who by then had baited another. Again they repeated the procedure. Within fifteen minutes they had pulled in a dozen two- to three-pound squid, plenty of juicy fillets for tomorrow's bait. The brother pitched them into the hold with the fish to protect them from the harsh sunlight which, by now, had had its effects on our exposed arms and faces.

In the time it took to catch the squid, the tide had risen so that the depth of the water had almost trebled. Riding the incoming tide we made it back to Milindi beach in only 45 minutes, less than half the time it had taken us to go out in the morning. The giant rock carp (which we kept) made almost two meals for us and the dozen or so other people at the lodge.

The Big Catch—from throw-line fishing off Kenya Coast near Milindi. McMath is pictured with Helene Mathery and their guide.

Kenya coast from Milindi north is desert beach. Except for an occasional small fishing village, there is only one settlement, Kipini. Beginning in the twelfth century Arab slave traders and merchants established communities along here, from Somalia to Zanzibar. It is said that the most picturesque of these now-deserted outposts is on the island of Lamu. I did not drive to Lamu but visited instead the forest-covered ruins of Geti just south of Milindi.

Geti has been dated at between the twelfth and fifteenth centuries, which was the time of Lamu's heyday. Indeed, there is speculation that Geti had eventually been sacked and destroyed by Lamu-based pirates or rival slave traders. The site has been carefully excavated under expert British supervision to reveal temples, butcheries, storerooms, and houses—all of heavy stone which was cleverly sculptured and terraced. The city stretches for

267

scores of acres, and just to stroll through it requires the better part of a day.

While the north coast may be desolate, the 120-mile coast between Milindi and Tiwi, some twenty miles south of Mombasa, could be in Florida. This is the so-called "sun strip" of east Africa, one of Kenya's chief tourist attractions. In the high seasons, from August to September and from February to May, it is difficult to find accommodations. The tourists are mostly British and German, although there are a number of Americans.

We spent our last day walking through the ruins at Geti and drove back to Mombasa that afternoon. Helene had to catch the 6:00 train to Nairobi. She was going spelunking with a contingent of French teachers the following afternoon in Amboseli Park.

That night I took the ferry to the south shore of Mombasa Bay and drove until I had passed all the billboards advertising casinos and motels and ponytailed white girls water skiing. I found a muddy rut road leading to the ocean through the silent village of Mushinda, about twenty miles north of the Tanzanian border. There was a fisherman's camp near the beach, and dogs began barking as I drove past it. Someone came out of a hut and raised a lantern, then went back inside. I killed the headlights and drove on in the moonlight until I came to a small cliff that emptied onto a half-moon beach.

On the far side of the beach was a hut which looked abandoned, though I couldn't tell for sure. There was a clump of palms whipping in the wind out on the tip of the little bay beyond the hut. The moon began fading behind the clouds, peeked briefly out again, then disappeared for the night. These were squall clouds, but they were moving too high and fast for rain before morning. I turned the jeep around and faced it back up the road for a fast getaway in high-ratio four. I then eased it back behind the wall of the cliff so anybody would have to be right up on it to see it. I found a soft tuft of grass behind some scrub brush and a little bit sheltered from the wind, spread out a blanket and put the sleeping bag on top. The air was warm and humid in spite of the wind, so I slept on top of the sleeping bag with only the poncho liner for cover.

I must have been very tired for I didn't waken until 8:00, when a dog—possibly one from the fisherman's camp—poked his cold nose in my face. Overcoming the shock, I lay against the rock outcrop and surveyed the beach. It was obviously going to rain before too much longer because the clouds had ceased racing and were beginning to coalesce. After visiting my left front tire, the dog trotted down to the beach, sniffed around the hut, then disappeared into the palms. I saw that the hut was not abandoned but was used to store canoes, and also fish, until they could be dried outside in the sun on mats and racks set up for that purpose. After climbing down to the beach and inspecting the hut, I saw an old wooden house on the cliff just up from my camp. There were some weathered stone steps, almost washed away. I made my way up them and found the house bolted and shuttered. A faded hand-lettered sign on the front door read, "Club Members Should Refrain From." The rest of the sign was gone.

When I got back to the jeep it had begun to rain. I stowed the sleeping gear and drove out to the highway. I was hungry but there was no mangrove or banana stand in the village. I did find a general store a few miles down where I spent the last of my Kenya shillings on a can of corned beef and two tins of Nescafe.

I drove the last twenty miles to the border at Lunga Lunga, a shanty town. Its one bar had a pot of sugar-tea on its third morning boil. I talked the young man into boiling some fresh water and broke open one of the tins of Nescafe. The rain was over now, and it was a fresh, sweet-smelling traveling day. While I drank my coffee, only some clucking chickens broke the morning silence.

Again, I was the only foreigner to cross the border in weeks. I had feared that I might not be allowed in without a visa, but when the immigration officer saw my *carnet de passage*, he issued a visa without comment.

The two pairs of blue jeans I had worn since the Sahara were all but finished. Each had been stitched three times—in Abidjan, Mwanza, and Nairobi—each job worse than the last. As I drove south along the red-dirt coastal road I passed through the village of Katribukata (which is my own phonetic translation). Sitting on a porch of his mud house and surrounded by clients and children was a tailor, treadling away at one of those old Singer sewing machines seen in every African market. The sign out front advertised "Mending, Repairs, Good Work."

There was a banana and mangrove stand next door tended by an old man who served me some tea with a biting, cinnamonlike spice while I waited my turn. I think the tailor advanced me ahead of some regulars, for in no time he was painstakingly cross-stitching the first pair of jeans (he had no patch material). He worked on them for almost an hour and a half, during which I sat and visited with the old tea vendor and a playful crowd of curious raga-muffins. It was not every day that a whitey stopped there, especially an ugly one with a long red beard.

As I sat there taking in the village, thinking how much it reminded me of so many villages across so many miles, a woman came along the road with two young girls, about fourteen and ten. On their heads each carried a bundle of wood and what looked like giant brown peapods but were a kind of east African forest leaf that burns well when dried. The woman walked to the corner of the house and heaved her bundle onto a stack. Hearing the fall of the pods, I again realized that the burden is carried by African women from the time they are children. The ten-year-old's load was almost as heavy as her mother's, which was surely 60 pounds.

When she had deposited her wood, the ten-year-old picked up a chubby infant that had fallen on the porch and carried him, spread-eagled and squalling, hitched on her waist. When he continued to cry, the mother—the tailor's wife, I now realized—reached down and scooped him up in her arms, giving me a wary glance as she did so. Carrying the infant, she began busying herself about the yard and porch. Occasionally she spoke grumpily with her husband as he rocked the treadle and chatted with the customers I had preempted. The old tea vendor—he must have been about 80—was having a run on mangroves as more and more curious children congregated to stare at me and the jeep. A fat red and black rooster darted out and pecked savagely at some gravel, where two scrawny hens without tail feathers had been ranging. A tot, having made sure he was unobserved by authority, hurled a stick at the rooster, dispersing all three chickens in a flurry of cackles. The boy grinned at me triumphantly, looked quickly around to confirm his anonymity, then skipped after some fellows.

I was beginning to realize that I had not really slept well the night before on the cliff, and that my fatigue had slowed my metabolism so that my perspective seemed momentarily and pleasingly synchronized with that of the villagers. I watched the vanquished chickens return cautiously to their pecking. Funny how this particular village seemed that morning to become Everyvillage. I seemed to slip into the stream of consciousness of the people and found myself within the supposition that I was but another villager waiting on the tailor. Without knowing the slightest whos and whiches of the passersby I felt nevertheless that I knew them all.

The fee was fifteen shillings for the jeans but I handed him twenty. The stitches looked secure enough to get me to the Cape—although I turned out to be wrong, and the knees were soon tattered once again.

Dar es Salaam: the name means "haven (or port) of peace" in Arabic. For many centuries it was a minor Arab trading post. The Germans had had a small settlement here, but until 1891, their colonial capital had been at the missionary/slave port of Bagamoyo. They moved it to Dar because of its superior harbor. I decided it would be best to stay on the beach at Kunduchi, about twelve miles north. It was 9:30 when I got there, only to find there was no free beach—it was occupied by an industrial area and several giant tourist hotels. Fatigued, I checked the prices at the Kunduchi Beach Hotel, found them exorbitant and took a room: 150 shillings a day (twenty dollars if you cash your money at the bank, which I did). The only thing African about the place was a floor show of native dancers, a duty group of snake charmers and drummers who put on quite a good two-hour performance on the patio outside the dining room. Once again I felt like I was in Miami Beach or Honolulu—except that there was no surf and the beaches were polluted from a recent oil spill and assorted building scrap from the industrial area.

There was, however, a parking lot patrolled by soldiers with rifles. I left the rig there and hitched the twelve miles into town on a gravel truck. The wind blew dust into my face as I stood on the load behind the cab, drawing double takes from pedestrians.

The driver let me off in the southwest part of town, a sprawling market district. I wandered through a maze of stalls in which cabinetmakers and chattering apprentices were busily sawing and chiseling sweet-smelling lumber into tables and chests of drawers.

At the end of the cabinet mart I entered a dingy side street, where I found a series of sparsely stocked Indian clothing shops with an occasional watch salesman sandwiched in between. At the end of the second such street was a concrete market building that looked like an unfinished football stadium. There was a bookshop stocked with official government propaganda (in English and Swahili), including the autobiography of Julius Nyerere, *Das*

270

Capital and the latest agricultural plan. On a table were assorted year-old *Time* and *Newsweek* magazines and some British pulp novels.

Asking directions repeatedly, I eventually found the business district, a quarter of diverging side streets with grey, unkempt, three- to five-story office buildings built mostly in the '30s and '50s:

1950
Batashi Building
Estate of Sheikh Ali Bin Said

1956
Swastik
Bhuvan

1931
Mani Bhuvan

1948
The DK Popat Building

The streets tended to be almost, but not quite, parallel so that two of them would diverge slightly to sandwich in another. Once, when I attempted to return to a given point I found upon my arrival that the old street had disappeared and a new one had taken its place.

I retraced my steps to a mosque, where, finally, a taxi driver directed me to the harbor. Soon I was standing at the entrance to the old post-office building, looking out at a dozen offloading European freighters. Above me on the wall was the World War I "Honor Roll" with some hundred names, among them the following:

Head Coolies:
Quamar Din
Nan Koo
Bahadurali
Bhola
Failirmohd
Said Mohd (906)
Said Mohd (959)

Workmen:
Abdullah

Bhisty:
Bastiao
Mendoza

In spite of its seedy appearance (or perhaps because of it) Dar has greater character than Nairobi. This is due also to the neutral, almost disdainful attitude towards tourists of *ugamaa*. Whereas in Kenya tourists are sought after, catered to and hustled at every turn, here they are quietly tolerated. Not that the people are unkind to foreigners, for they are not. But there is a distance, almost aloofness, especially among the better educated, students, civil servants, and local merchants. That is in sharp contrast to the solicitous, rambunctious commercialism of Kenya.

Almost all business, especially tourism, is in government hands. Some small private firms still exist but they are strictly controlled. There are no sleek promotional campaigns as in Kenya. Advertising is virtually non-existent: there are no billboards or wall posters. In every one of the Indian clothing and sundry shops there is now a black partner or co-manager along with at least one black employee for every Asian one. These were initially trainees, but many now have full partner status. The word "partner" implies ownership; since these businesses are so tightly controlled (some have been taken over outright), "co-manager" is probably the better term.

Newspapers in Tanzania are dominated by government propaganda and exhortations to produce. Even the reporting of normal events, such as marriages and births, frequently takes on a political overtone. Advertisements are conspicuously absent from the papers.

Asians in Dar are especially fearful of talking alone with Europeans. There have been accusations of currency black marketing, and some Indian merchants have been prosecuted. Some young Asians will nevertheless approach warily to ask if you have dollars or marks to change. "Cash only," they warn. "No traveler's checks." As mentioned before, such trading is illegal, and in spite of the artificial official rate, it is advisable to change at a bank.

While Dar, being a superb natural harbor, is more accessible to the world than is Nairobi (and most other Third World capitals), the Nyerere government was building a new capital at Dodoma, nearly 500 miles inland over stretches of seasonally impassable roads. The official reasons for the change were that Dodoma is more centrally located, both geographically and politically, and that Dar was the colonial capital.

The old German officers' club in the center of the harbor was remodeled by the British into the Dar es Salaam Club. It served as the colonial community's dance hall and supper club. The ballroom was built over 500 foot-high springs.

The Dar Club is now the government's Hotel Training School, supervised by Franz Van Stein, a master pastry chef attached to the Dutch Embassy Aid section. Franz and his students were in the process of building a bakery with multiple ovens and a butchery and smokehouse.

Meals were served by uniformed student waiters on fresh embroidered tablecloths with fine linen napkins. The settings were composed of polished silver and monogrammed Dar Club crockery. The fare was first class, while the prices were barely above what I might have paid at a street restaurant: twenty shillings (about $2.50) for a lunch of celery soup, green salad, roast beef with rice in a special cream sauce, carrots or squash, Chinese cabbage, and a truly superb Dutch pastry for dessert. Most of the clientele (it was open, but not advertised, to the public) were senior government servants and European residents. But a goodly number of students were also there.

When I told Franz of my accommodation problem, he happily replied that he had a spare room in the old hotel over the club (now a student dorm). I told him I would be very much obliged. The price (about 40 shillings a day) included breakfast—and it was a fourth of what I was paying at the Kunduchi Beach. It was a big room with high ceilings and an old four-bladed fan that turned just enough to circulate the air without causing an uncomfortable draft. The room opened onto a roof terrace bordered by the leafy branches of great old shade trees through which one could see the harbor and scores of beached dhows undergoing reparations.

For several days, I roamed Dar and read Jane Goodall's *In the Shadow of Man* on the HTS roof. The book is about the chimpanzees she lived with and studied for some ten years at Gombe Stream over on Lake Tanganyika.

One morning at breakfast, six strong older women with ruddy, outdoor complexions, two stout young women, and a girl came into the dining room. They were Pentecostal missionaries, all of them Swedes except for their leader and the girl, who were Americans. They spoke sparingly, in Swahili and English, and with reserve—rugged, competent, no-nonsense—except for the young girl who was visibly nervous and had been crying.

I struck up a conversation and learned that they had come in from their mission just north of Kigoma to get the girl, a new recruit. They had met her yesterday at the airport and were going to ride back today in the Land Rover. They complained light-heartedly of the bad roads. As we were talking, the girl excused herself and walked out onto the patio.

"She's pretty homesick," one of the Swedish ladies said. "They all are at first," the leader responded, "but she'll get over it when her work begins."

I asked her what their work consisted of. "Saving souls, son, saving souls. Oh, we try to teach them sewing and home economics—you know, things useful in the home and like that," the woman said.

She was from Chicago and had been at the mission for 27 years. I asked if there were many wild animals nearby and whether they were ever any threat. "No, no wild animals, except a kind of big cat that looks like maybe a fox." She must have meant a genet cat but I did not say so. To my surprise they were only about twenty miles as the crow flies from Gombe Stream but did not know that there were chimpanzees there. Nor had any of them ever heard of Mrs. Goodall. I gave them a small donation for supplies.

Late the third afternoon I met two German girls who had come on a three-week holiday. The Hotel Training School bar was closed until 8:00 so one of the Germans suggested the Rex Hotel and Clock Tower. On our way there we became lost and wound up on a side street facing a bright red and green neon sign:

ZANZIBAR

A long corridor led to three large consecutive rooms teeming with noisy patrons and smoke. In the front an aged Wurlitzer crooned the latest hits:

Kwela Mfana
Taxi Jive
    by Themby

Mlenda Akii En Dewa
Mlenda Akii En Dewa
    by Mwanch Hassan

273

Vijana
Kipato Sina
Maj Wetu Mai
   by KK of Zambia

A hand-lettered notice taped on the jukebox read: "Listen to the newest numbers from the best jukebox in town."

We squeezed into a booth on the patio with a couple of well-imbibed civil servants and a girlfriend of one of them. The lady had grown tired of her date and was making eyes at his companion. They had stacked a dozen Kili empties on the table (U.S. college style). I ordered a round, but before she would get them, the barmaid demanded the 21-shilling payment in advance. On the roof two black and white tabby cats looked down on the scene with disgust. Although it seemed impossible to do so, someone managed to turn up the Wurlitzer even higher. As we downed our brew and prepared to leave, we saw that the girlfriend had switched partners and a dispute was in progress.

Resuming our search for the Rex and Clock Tower, we turned down Jamburi Street and saw a well-dressed gentlemen step onto the sidewalk from two swinging doors. The sign overhead read, "Cameo Bar." It was clean and the closest thing to a pub in sight. There was no music, only subdued conversation. It had an arcade and courtyard out back. Across the courtyard was the Cameo Asian Cinema, which was half full of patrons watching one of those Eastern soap operas in which all the acting takes place in one room with each actor taking his turn at posturing through the sequence of melodramatic humor—deceit, suspicion, envy, anger, fear, admiration—then miming the opposites while another actor took up the dialogue.

In the center of the bar was a single card table around which sat three Indians and a very tall African wearing a white turban. They were playing cards, although I was unable to discover the game. The African appeared to be winning. Two adolescent boys stood behind the oldest Indian, who boasted a white beard. The small backbar was stocked with quality Scotch whiskey and Gordon's gin plus the usual Dunkan's blend and Kili beer on tap.

My German friends having decided to continue on to the Clock Tower, two young Africans, one of them an Arab half-caste, sat down in their places. They were from Zanzibar. The Arab was a customs agent for the Zanzibar government, checking cargo and passengers on the erratic ferry boats before they embarked from Dar. (In spite of its union with Tanzania in April of 1964, Zanzibar maintains virtually complete internal independence, including its own customs and excise taxes.) The other young man was a taxi driver.

They had schooled together, completing the sixth form (equivalent to the American twelfth grade). The customs youth said he had taken chemistry, physics and biology from Indian professors. The taxi driver had had an American English teacher in elementary school—one of a small American community on the island prior to the January 1964 revolution.

274

There are no Americans there now, other than a part-time deputy consul. The customs boy said he would like to go to Kuwait to join his uncle and older brothers. The wages were ten times higher there than in Dar, he said. He had been waiting for two years for an exit visa but felt it would be forthcoming shortly. When I asked him if he wanted someday to return to Tanzania, he said, emphatically, "No!" They were interested in America and amazed that our chief use of millet in Arkansas (a major food crop here) was for feeding wild ducks.

I finally found the Rex Hotel. The grill had decent steak and chips, and on the wall was a wide variety of African wall art. The restaurants and bars in Dar had more of this than I'd seen anywhere since Zaire.

On February 24, 1874, Dr. David Livingstone's native porters deposited his body at the mission church in Bagamoyo, 35 miles north of Dar es Salaam. They had removed and carefully buried the viscera, then dried the body by exposure to the sun and salt for fourteen days. They then wrapped it in bark and carried it for more than nine months across 1500 miles of jungle, swamp and savannah.

Bagamoyo*—"Here I lay down my heart"—was for hundreds of years the chief port to the Arab slave market on Zanzibar, just twenty miles off the coast. The slaves would be shipped in dhows from Zanzibar to ports in the Red Sea and Persian Gulf or sold to Portuguese traders for shipment to Europe and America. Captured blacks, mostly young males and adolescent girls, would be marched in chains to Bagamoyo across the "trail of tears" from their villages near Lake Tanganyika, where they had been captured by the Arabs and their native henchmen. Those who could not keep up were mutilated, killed outright or left chained to die. These unfortunates were frequently "rescued" by local tribes and resold to another caravan after being fattened up.

Bagamoyo was the site in 1868 of the first Christian mission on the mainland of East Africa. A church was completed in 1872 by the predominantly French Fathers of the Holy Spirit (*Peres du St. Espirit*) who had come here from Zanzibar, where they had already built a mission under an agreement with the Sultan there. They quickly began to use Bagamoyo as a base of operations inland in the race with other Catholic orders and the Protestants.

The Fathers of the Holy Spirit raised money to rescue some of the captives as they were chained together on the beach. With their efforts and those of missionary-explorer Livingstone and others, the slave trade was officially outlawed by Britain in June of 1873. From then on, at least as a regular seagoing commercial venture, slavery was no longer viable. The result was that Bagamoyo slowly diminished in importance in favor of Dar, to which the Germans moved the colonial capital in 1891.

But it was to Bagamoyo, in the winter of 1874, that his loyal native guides and colleagues Shuma and Susi and some 60 other African porters carried

---

*Known to the Arabs as Kaole, the ruins of which can be seen just south of town. They are in the Lamu-Geida style, thirteenth- to sixteenth-century Zenj Empire.

the body of the man most responsible for the abolition of slavery and the opening of Africa to the Western world.

The road to Bagamoyo was paved only twelve miles, to just beyond the cutoff to the luxury hotels at Kunduchi Beach. The remaining 33 miles was plagued with potholes, indicating the relative importance of Bagamoyo to *ugamaa*. Indeed, upon arrival I found the town pretty much as it had been when the Germans left, with the exception of a few gas pumps in front of the general store. The three-story customs house still sat right up on the beach where it had originally been built. Next to it, all that remained of the warehouse was a checkerboard network of rusted iron pilings protruding from a primitive concrete foundation. These pilings are the basis for a local myth that slaves were chained there awaiting shipment.

Just a few hundred yards north, and fortuitously hidden from the view of the customs house in a gentle curve in the shoreline, were a score of dhows and outriggers. Most were beached, but a few were close in under sail. At the top of the beach was a makeshift market of sorts, where two big fires were covered with cooking pots. The tasty smell of frying fish and plantain filled the air. On strips of straw matting, fishermen were sorting their morning's catch. A very large woman was grinding mealie or rice, and a dozen children laughed and played around her.

Walking back to the customs house and over the beach trail to the village, I saw that the doors of the houses were each splendidly ornamented— carved doubtlessly by individual craftsmen after the style of the Lamu Island doors so well preserved at the National Museum in Kenya. What totem or talisman a design portrayed seemed lost to the occupants, who were not Arabs and seemed not to have lived there very long.

From the village living area it was a mile-and-a-half walk up the north beach to the palm-lined mission compound. The compound was dominated by an imposing neo-Gothic church of reef coral built in 1915. Just behind it and to the right was the whitewashed original chapel with its high belfry. The chapel was the only remnant of the 1872 church of the *Peres du St. Espirit*. There was a brief plaque on the open door commemorating Livingstone's return. Behind the present church was a small museum with a fair number of relics and copies of newspaper articles.

The surf at Bagamoyo was uninterrupted by reef or commercial harbor and was therefore full, clean and splendid. On the south end of the village, past the police station, the road led down to the beach and the shabby but clean Hotel and Bar Bagamoyo Beach. Always in Africa these two words, "hotel" and "bar," unless the contrary is clearly expressed, invariably intimate a rickety assemblage of timbers and plaster with possibly a hard-surfaced floor. Such was the Bagamoyo Beach. The bar icebox was full of cold Kili beer, and the kitchen's pot boiled with fish soup and rice. The fish was terribly small and bony, so that by the time you finished chewing it and spitting out the bones, you had lost half of it. It was delicious, though, and I joined in with a dozen locals and three Peace Corps volunteers from Zaire. They had ridden the Chinese railroad up from Lusaka and were full of stories. When the maitre d' said that the hotel was full, they insisted that I stay with them. The girl had been stationed in Bukavu and loved Lake Kivu as much as I.

That night I lay awake, listening to the surf, long after my companions had fallen asleep. Occasionally, over the sound of the water, I could hear Africans who had lingered up the beach at the bar.

Up at daybreak, I left my share of the tab on the table and drove back to Dar. I checked out of the HTS with Franz and filled both gas tanks. Remembering that I had wanted to see the Chinese railroad station before leaving, I drove out south of town. After six miles, I thought I'd missed it, when on the left I saw an enormous concrete stadiumlike building with an empty parking lot. I parked conspicuously and went in.

My footsteps echoed in the almost-empty building. Two tellers' windows were open, and a short line of native women stood at each. I wanted to see the locomotive and rolling stock, but the doors leading to the platforms were closed. Overhead, hanging from the second story catwalk, a schedule indicated there was a train every three days to Lusaka at 9:00 a.m., but the date of the next departure was not listed. I walked back outside and around the edge of the building, jumping as I did the narrow gutter, and climbed the grassy bank beside the platforms. There was one train—a diesel, with a red star and black Chinese characters painted just beneath the windows. Two Chinese in grey-blue uniforms and black caps stood talking to each other by the engine.

Off to the right was a bunkhouse in front of which were huddled some 40 workers. When they saw me they fell silent. I smiled, then saw they were looking past me. As I turned to see what they were staring at, I was grabbed by a soldier in khaki toting a submachine gun. I was in real trouble. A wily, officious functionary in civilian clothes briskly ordered me to follow him.

"You know you have broken the law and must be punished," he said over his shoulder as the soldier squeezed my arm until it hurt. "What are you doing here? Don't you know this is a restricted area?"

I seemed to have bad luck with trains. Once, many years before, while hitchhiking through Central America, I had taken a banana train from Guatemala into El Salvador. It was just after the "soccer war" in which, in a dispute over a football match, El Salvador had invaded Honduras. I was arrested as an Honduran spy of Irish descent and held, trussed and blindfolded, in a boxcar for two days. I am convinced that it was only because I had been riding with a boy whose father was a high government official that I was spared a terrible fate. He and his father came on the third morning and obtained my release.

We went up to an office on the second floor where, in a tiny room off to one side, I was immediately surrounded by eight idle khaki-clad guards (each with a pistol and two with machine guns). The functionary sat in a secretary's swivel chair and clasped his hands behind his head: "Well, well, don't you know you're not supposed to go roaming about through defense installations?"

I told him I didn't know the railroad station was a defense installation.

"Where are your papers, your papers?" I told him they were in the jeep, which was parked out front. "Why do you not carry your passport with you?" I told him I didn't want to lose it, that I didn't carry my papers with me everywhere because chances were I could lose them or have them stolen.

"But the law says that you must carry at all times your papers, your passport." I didn't want to argue so I nodded my head.

The door to the small room had been closed; no one else seemed to notice the suffocating heat and body odor. Each set of beady eyes was coldly fixed on me as the soldiers pressed in as close as possible—some of them actually touching me with their trouser legs. I was made to sit in front of the interrogating officer on a straight-backed metal chair.

The officer was insecure but obviously sensed the possibility of a major event in his career. The armpits of his suit coat were wet with sweat, as was his collar. He loosened his tie.

"You know it, espionage, it is capital offense; you can be shot?"

I earnestly assured him that I was only a stupid tourist who liked trains. At this, the soldiers pressed even closer. None of them spoke, but out in the hall I could hear the excited staccato babble of high-pitched voices talking about the captured spy.

There was an authoritative knock at the door. "Come in," my interrogator shouted. An officer in khaki with heavy insignia came in and everyone stood at attention. I started to get up but a big hand grabbed my shoulder and shoved me back down into the chair.

The officer very calmly repeated most of the questions I had already been asked by his subordinate. Finally, he said, "Go out to your vehicle and get your papers."

I obeyed, winding my way through a network of doors and hallways to the upper lobby. I didn't look back as I descended the stairs, but I knew one of the machine gunners was hawking my every move. Out at the jeep I felt rather subversive as I worked the combination lock on the safe box. Of course, if they had taken time to inspect my gear, they would have seen that I was really an overland traveler—as was also evident from all the visas in my passport. But such people sometimes don't take time. They will throw the book at you, then rearrange the evidence to justify what they did, if it turns out later that they were wrong.

As the lock came open and I pulled out the box, I remembered the Instamatic on the front seat under some shirts. "Better leave it," I thought. "Just let it be. If they want to search the car, maybe they'll just think it funny that it was there and not carefully put away." I was never more frightened than when I thought how close I had come to taking a few snapshots of the trains.

Back up in the interrogation room I went carefully over my route down from Morocco: Algiers, Chad, Zaire. . . They were just about half convinced that I was indeed only a tourist when the commandant asked why I was driving a military vehicle. The soldiers murmured to themselves and stared at me more sullenly than ever. I said that I was traveling as lightly as possible. He didn't seen particularly impressed. I was placed under double guard in the outer office for an hour. I don't mind saying I was quite concerned. Finally, the commander emerged and closed the door softly behind him.

"You're free to go now," he said, handing me my passport. "Do not be so careless in the future as to enter a defense installation."

I assured him that I would not.

Wanting to put a little distance between me and the Dar railroad army before they changed their minds, I quickly headed out of town. For the first few miles the road passed through the flat marshy countryside of Selous National Park. Wallowing hippos were as common as hogs in Iowa, and scores of elephants grazed within feet of the road. At one point, traffic was stopped for a quarter of a mile by a mother rhinoceros and her calf, who stood in the middle of the highway.

Feeling the straight open road for the first time in months was like a shot of adrenalin. I am a lover of forest trails and desert tracks, but on those you have to drive hard and keep ever so vigilant. On a highway, all you do is let the wind blow in your face and watch the country go by.

I was in no great hurry, now that I had left the railroad army far behind—although there was a rifleman on every bridge or trestle of the tracks that paralleled the road. So I eased up to 40 and just let it sit there. Remembering the cassettes, I put one on, a medley of Italian arias.

Irunga is a railroad crossroads as well as the cutoff for the dirt road to Dodoma, the new capital. Driving up there a ways the next morning, I could see why the diplomatic corps in Dar had been dismayed when they heard about the move. I stayed at the Railway Hotel and left at dawn. The only thing remarkable about Irunga was the food at the hotel dining room. Except for Franz's Hotel Training School, it was the best since Nairobi.

Zambian immigration and customs were in a chicken-wire-meshed Quonset hut. An officious lieutenant demanded to count my traveler's checks. There was $700 worth, but twice he counted only 600, so I agreed. (It was not his job to check currency, but that of the customs agent.) I was then passed on to the customs officer who asked me the same question. "Six hundred dollars, according to your friend there," I said. This one counted $700 and threatened to confiscate $100 of them. It took half an hour before I was finally passed, with a warning against false declarations. Zambian immigration was the only one north of the Zambezi to demand a current health certificate as a condition of entry.

CHAPTER XX

Beginning at the border and continuing to the Zambezi, the Zambian countryside is, for the most part, gently rolling woodland that might be North American hardwood forest. The highway was in much better condition than it had been in Tanzania, and I eased my speed up to 55 mph. The forest slipped by, and the sun settled into a red-orange glow, then faded away into night.

I drove on for two and a half hours without seeing another vehicle. The loneliness was a bit chilling since the highway was so straight and well paved. On each side, the forest came right up to the narrow shoulder. The road seemed to lead nowhere, and except for an occasional old tire or grease patch there was no sign that anyone had ever traveled it. When I stopped, as I did occasionally to stretch and listen to the darkness, the din of the crickets and their accomplices felt strangely menacing. On the Michelin map was a village called Isaka, with a lodging notation. I felt I must have somehow overshot it. I had been told at the border not to camp off-road on pain of a 100 *kwatcha* ($140) fine and possibly being kidnapped by rebels. I was told instead to stay at the government guest house for travelers in Isaka and other larger villages.

I had about decided to take the risk and set up the tent when, suddenly, over a hill, a pair of headlights swerved into my lane and it seemed as if a collision were unavoidable. I braked and veered left, and at the last second my assailant, a truck, swerved into the yard of what I saw was a small grey chapel with a cantilevered belfry. I pulled in behind the truck, ready to protest, when I was stayed by singing. As the dust cleared, I saw some 30 young people sitting on a load of straw. The boys were dressed in short-sleeved sport shirts, and the girls wore colorful cotton dresses. A tall lad stood on the tailgate, directing. He held in his hand a familiar red hymnal. I killed the headlights and listened.

> *Amazing Grace, how sweet the sound*
> *that saved a wretch like me*
> *I once was lost*
> *But now I'm found*
> *Was blind but now I see . . .*

It was a Wesleyan youth group on a hayride.

With the help of my brother Methodists, I backtracked ten miles and found the almost-hidden Isaka cutoff. It was a small town about four miles off the road. Upon inquiry in a noisy bar (which had rooms by the hour), I found my way to the guest house: one and a half *kwatcha* (officially about $2.50) a night. It was a tidy lodge with rooms for a dozen guests. While there was a kitchen, presided over by a kindly native cook, we were required to provide our own food. I broke out some corned beef and black-eyed peas, which the cook heated and served in the small dining room.

Janette, an English girl, had taken the Chinese railroad to Dar to collect her new Peugeot, thereby avoiding duty and excise taxes. She and her German companion, Heidi, had been working in Lusaka for several years as secretaries to Europeans managing local firms. As we shared our tinned provisions, a stout, ferociously bearded gentleman joined us: Pelle, a Dane, who was the chief truancy officer for the Zambian juvenile court.

"I spend most of my time chasing violators back up in the forests near their home villages," he said. "Of course, when we punish them [usually a public thrashing] I have one of my native co-workers do the beating. The last thing we want are charges of neo-colonial racism."

One would think the mere thought of the formidable Pelle chasing him through the forest would be enough to stay even the most incorrigible truant.

Serenje was the next night's ville. It was on a bad dirt road about five miles off the highway. The day's driving was largely uneventful, again a long straight highway with hundreds of square miles of wilderness scrub brush and hardwoods. It was well into the southern fall, almost winter, and the trees and brush exuded pastel oranges and yellows.

The government guest house at Serenje was smaller but otherwise a copy of the one at Isaka. In the center of this village was a bar with no name which observed the strict national drinking hours, 5:30 p.m. to 7:30 p.m. It sold only beer, the local Pilsner, but patrons began queuing heavily by 5:00, and by 5:30 there was a mob on the porch.

Janette and Heidi, from the night before, joined me, and we took a table at the rear. The place had some unusual murals. One depicted a desperate swimmer about to be devoured from behind by a crocodile. In another, a hunter and his dog sat by the fire at the mouth of a cave; in the next panel the dog and his master (close behind with a spear) were chasing a rabbit. On the wall opposite, a bell-bottomed dandy and his miniskirted lady were dancing, rock style, while a friend in the adjoining panel chug-a-lugged a beer.

There was a sustained, festive roar as women and children visited here and there among the tables of drinking men. The stocky, balding owner and a lissome barmaid in a black-checked yellow blouse (which she took great care to protect from spillage) rushed to fill the orders of impatient patrons. With less than an hour of drinking time to go (it was now 6:30), the drinking was serious indeed. The barmaid seemed to be especially attentive to a young man in a polka-dot blue shirt. The polka dots were of a luminescent green material that reflected even through the fog of tobacco smoke.

Two adolescent girls, holding hands, pretended to be teased by the playful catcalls from a table of boisterous young men. An old gentleman forcefully pecked his way to the bar with his cane and, when seen by the barman, was promptly served ahead of the others.

As the harried barmaid began to ignore him, the high-bouncing polka dot caught sight of Janette and Heidi and came to our table to bum cigarettes. Heidi obliged and in no time had other requests from a number of other customers.

"Sorry, no more," Heidi said as she crumpled the packet.

We ate dinner at the local government vacation house at the far end of town. The house was evidently a recreational center for Lusaka employees, about twenty of whom had just arrived. The bath was next-door to the kitchen, and vacationers in towels came and went through the dining room while we ate.

Dinner, I had thought, might be portions of the mysterious red hunks of meat that three stewards were quickly carving and heaving onto old newspapers for storage in a warm refrigerator. We were, however, served thick mealie meal, rice and cooked cabbage and tomatoes, generous helpings of tiny dried minnowlike lake fish, and loaves of hot maize-flour bread. There was of course the ubiquitous pitcher of super-sweetened milk-tea. The small sardine-sized fish were imported from Lake Tanganyika, according to the steward. They were dried there on the shore in the sun, shipped to Dar on the old British rail line, then to Lusaka on the Chinese railroad.

My second arrest of the week came the next morning, and I was certain that this time I was in for a long stay in a bush jail, or worse. Covering the walls of this little town were government propaganda posters exhorting citizens to "help the police protect the revolution: report suspicious persons." Others encouraged the population to support President Kaunda's "political humanism" and otherwise extolled the virtues of "His excellency, Dr. Kenneth Kaunda, our great and wise president." Another one said, "A bomber is a killer. Are you his next target?" Whatever its ostensible message, the impact of each slogan was to make any stranger suspect, particularly red-bearded ones.

I was up early and jogged about two miles down a side road near the lodge. When I got back I took a cold sink bath, loaded my gear and sat at the wheel writing up my log. I had just finished describing the political posters and their admonitions when I felt a tap on my shoulder. A cop in mufti and a short, stocky gent in khaki and Sam Browne stood alongside. The tall one asked what I was writing, and I said I was keeping a diary. He said that he had had a report of a suspicious person running and walking around town, then coming back to write something in a book. He then told the short one to seize the two notebooks there on the seat and ordered me to produce my passport. Of course, this was locked in the strong box which had to be opened in plain view, whereupon everything was confiscated, including the wallet with my driver's license, cash and credit cards.

I was ordered into the pickup truck between them, and off we drove, the big one driving—not, as I quickly noticed, toward the police station, which was just a few hundred yards away. Continuing down the side road for about ten minutes, we finally pulled into the yard of a house that belonged, I surmised, to their chief. He wasn't home, so we drove on for several miles, passing the place where I had turned around jogging. No one said anything. About two miles further on we turned off onto a trail and stopped. The two of them spoke in their tribal language, whereupon the driver abruptly turned the truck around, and we headed back into town. I don't think the speedometer fell below 50. It was a rough ride.

At the police station I was led to a windowless room and made to sit in a straight, wooden chair. My hands and feet were handcuffed by the short one. A sergeant began asking questions while turning through my passport.

"When did you leave Kenya?" he asked.

I tried to remember the exact date but couldn't. I said, "Around the twentieth, but I'm not quite sure."

"Do you always travel alone?"

"No, I—[here I hesitated but knew the answer was on its way] I am traveling with the two British girls. They left early because they have been having car trouble. I am following them in case they break down."

He hesitated and looked at the others. There were a half-dozen of them by then.

"What if you break down?" he asked.

"Oh, I never do. I can take care of myself," I said.

"What government do you work for?" came a voice from the door. From his insignia, he was obviously the chief.

An aide took his briefcase. An important official for such a small place, I thought. I told him that I was a traveler and that I had a proper passport and a visa for his country and that I was minding my own business.

"You will only answer the questions," said the sergeant.

"What is your government?" the chief asked again.

"I'm an American citizen," I said. "I don't work for them, though. I'm an overland traveler. I'll show you where I've come from and where I am going." I started with Morocco.

"He was writing in his book . . ." The big guy held up the journals. He said that he had had a report of a suspicious person walking around town.

"What were you writing?" asked the chief.

"I told him"—nodding toward the tall guard—"I was keeping a daily journal of my travels and that was what I was doing when the man arrested me."

There was a discussion out of my hearing. Finally the chief came over. "You say you were only writing a diary?" he said.

"Yes," I replied.

"We will see. Read us what it is you wrote."

The tall one who had arrested me handed me the two books. I opened the one I had been writing in to the last written page. While I was doing this, the chief told the sergeant to unlock the handcuffs. I started reading where I had described the bar paintings and the town generally.

When I had gone about two pages the chief said, "That's enough. Now show me where you came from." I knew he meant my route from Morocco so I drew a map. He then began asking friendly questions and talking about a friend of his that had visited Zaire not long before. At length he told me I was free to go and ordered the tall one to drive me back to the lodge, although it was only a short walk.

I did not stop in Lusaka, except to try to call Jeff Care, an old classmate from the London School of Economics, who was with the Ministry of Justice. The city looked more like a west-Texas ranch town than an African capital. It loomed off the wooded flats like an out-of-place movie set. A dozen or so recently constructed banks and hotels dominated a drab skyline. Along the wide, windy streets, I subconsciously waited for a tumbleweed to roll past. There was the usual noisy traffic of taxis, though there were far fewer than I had expected for a town of this size. A number of Fords and Plymouths, models from the '50 and '60s, were in evidence.

Not being in the mood for another dirty city, and unable to locate my friend, I drove on, camping for the night on the banks of the Kafue River. Later I drove back up to Kafue Tavern where the men from the shift changes at the local chemical plant congregated. One young man at the bar said he had been selected a year ago to attend a computer programming course in London but had been unable to do so because he could not afford to bribe the chief of his natal village to verify his birth.

Up at 3:00 a.m., I decided to get an early start and again drove for an hour and a half without seeing another vehicle. Just before 5:00, I stopped on a hill to watch the dawn and to boil water for my morning coffee. I was now pleasantly accustomed to the soft autumn woodland. There were, as before, random thickets of scrub brush, vines and thorns, but the greater part of the forest was open and consisted of leafy, dispersed hardwoods.

A little after 3:00, I drove through Livingstone. The town was wide-streeted and uncommonly tidy. There was a modern drugstore and a shingle-roofed bank and several smart, new, compact office buildings. The streets were paved, and there was a commercial bustle in the air I had not seen since Dar. A good many of the customers were white—farmers come to town a'Saturday in vintage Land Rovers. Just beyond the town, a wide, slow-running river appeared. It appeared to be a shallow, lazy river, studded with boulders and small islands just out from the bank. (I saw later how these made the river seem much smaller than it really was.) Perhaps what I was about to see was enhanced by the fact that the town, the highway, the woods—indeed, the river itself—were all so pleasantly nondescript.

I turned onto the shoulder, and when I stopped the engine, I heard Victoria Falls for the first time. It was like a constant peal of thunder, wavering in tone. Far downstream, beyond the largest island, puffs of what looked like white smoke were billowing hundreds of feet into the air:

> The falls are singularly formed. They are simply the whole mass
> of the Zambesi waters rushing into a fissure or rent made right
> across the bed of the river. In other falls we have usually a great

change of level both in the bed of the river and in the adjacent country, and after the leap the river is not much different from what it was above the falls; but here, the river flowing rapidly among numerous islands and from 800 to 1000 yards wide, meets a rent in its bed, at least 100 feet deep and at right angles with its course, or nearly due east and west, leaps into it and becomes boiling white mass at the bottom ten or twelve yards broad.
—from *Livingstone's Private Journals, 1851-1853* (London: I. Schapera, 1960).

But Livingstone was such a conservative observer that he underestimated both the width and the depth of the falls *by more than half.*

Livingstone named the falls Victoria after his queen. They are the world's most massive and three times the height of those at Niagara. The average volume of water over the falls is 50 million gallons per minute. On a commemorative plaque the recorded maximum was stated to be 150 million gallons; according to John Gunter, it was 169 million gallons.

I drove to the Rainbow Inn, a cluster of roundavels set back in the woods 100 yards or so from the bank, just above the falls. From a trail along the side of the river, I was even more impressed by the suddenness of the falls— since, again, the river above them was not particularly impressive. The water was infested with crocodiles and there were signs warning away would-be swimmers. From time to time an elephant or two would wade out to an island and feed on the lush foliage, all to himself. The trees teemed with vervet monkeys, unabashed thieves and quite dangerous if cornered or refused further booty once fed. About a mile up from the falls themselves, hippos basked in shallow marshes adjacent to the fenced-in Livingstone Game Park.

Upon reaching the point of fall, one looks down into the chasm and sees that as fast as the river plunges the mist rises—great wafting puffs of it, so high and incessant that it has created in the immediate vicinity a rain forest to replace the regional hardwoods. The rain forest on the Zambia side is lorded over by a pesky troop of baboons who brook no interference from either of the other two indigenous primates: the vervet monkeys and man.

One cannot fully appreciate the magnitude of these falls until he has walked around in front of them and reviewed them face-on from the bluff opposite which forms a peninsula from each bank almost to midstream. They are, in fact, a freak of nature, owing their existence to the unlikely combination of two highly unlikely events: first, the abrupt change in the course of the Zambezi from a southerly route that, in the Miocene, flowed into the Limpopo, some 500 miles to the south; and, second, the forcing of the resultant channel over a rock plateau, the end of which had been opened by dramatic faulting of the earth's surface.

The most spectacular events at the falls are its rainbows. They are full, rich in color and, at one point on the old iron footbridge, can be seen in full circle. I can attest to having seen all but perhaps two degrees of a full 360-degree circle of a rainbow looking to the southeast.

Most spectacular to me was the full lunar rainbow seen after 11:00 on two consecutive nights, August 2 and 3, 1977. On each occasion I was with David and Sara Whould, a British math teacher in Malawi and his wife. The colors were exquisite pastels—very light and elusive but quite constant nevertheless. The first night we had just walked down to the falls from our roundavels when the floodlights playing on them were cut, so that the only light remaining was that of the moon.

The second night I followed the rainbow out across the footbridge to the island (a rocky knoll that is really an extension of the peninsula) in the center of the river on the Zambian side. The mist was cold, and I was thoroughly soaked before I could cross. Below, the roar was so loud and sustained as to threaten not only my hearing but my equilibrium as well. But from the island the colors of the rainbow were fuller and richer than ever.

Each morning the Whoulds and I would walk together to the falls and return to my hut for coffee. One morning Sara said she felt that there was something sinister about the almost hypnotic lure of the water, as if it were beckoning you closer, inviting you down into its depths. She noted apprehensively that there was no rail or barrier between the slippery, mucky bank of the promontory and the fault. We wondered how many people had been lured too close.

The railroad bridge over the gorge just down from the falls was built in 1905. Its site had been personally selected by Cecil Rhodes, the wizard and dynamo of South African development, who planned that the railroad should run from Cape Town to Cairo. He died at the age of 50 without seeing that particular dream become a reality. Still, he did get the railroad up into northern Rhodesia, and eventually, a spur was extended into Zaire.

It was interesting, Sara said, that there appeared to be no records of ritual sacrifice or witchcraft associated with the falls. She had done a good bit of reading on the subject, as well as other aspects of local anthropology. She had visited a number of archaeological sites and had been invited to work on one in northern Malawi in the coming year. Her particular interest was in the Nyau cult of the Chewa tribe of eastern Zambia and Malawi—a secret male society whose members masquerade as animals in bizarre costumes made of feathers, maize and sisal. They perform rites of spell casting and exorcism and appear *en masse* at various annual festivals. Marathon dances, ostensibly closed to foreigners on pain of death, are said to attain a frenzy unrivaled in aboriginal choreography. With regard to the tribes inhabiting the immediate area of the falls, the Lozi (from whom comes the name "Mosi-Oa-Tunya" —The Mist That Thunders) were dominant when Livingstone first arrived.

Before light each morning I would walk down to the observation point just flush with the north-south line of the fault. There I could catch the first light of dawn as it played onto the mist and brought up the rainbow. The fault line is, of course, not straight. Its irregularity, plus the billowing mist, normally makes it impossible to see more than three or four chutes away. While walking out along the bluff beyond the footbridge you lose all visual contact with the land. Indeed, it was easy for me to imagine not falls, but a behemoth surf such as that at Makupu or Wiamea Bay in Hawaii. At the end of the island bluff is the narrow (barely 50 feet) river channel itself. I would hesitate to estimate the speed and force of the water but it is certainly equal to that of the Green-Colorado at its most furious.

Downstream on the Zambian side is a whirlpool called the Boiling Pot, in which all this water churns suddenly upstream against itself in one last defiant gesture before hurrying on through the gorge beneath Rhodes's bridge. The gorge is roughly a series of triple Zs, each leg of each Z being a previous fall site, replaced later by the next as the river carved its bed upstream. On the Rhodesian end, just two chutes out, you can see where the water has begun cutting the next falls.

Although you can walk out to the end of the island on the Zambian side, the Rhodesian land's end (called Danger Point) is a place of sudden death. Two young Canadian women with backpacks were murdered there in 1974 by guerilla sharpshooters firing from across the river. Since then, no one goes out there—although, strangely, there is no barrier or even a warning not to do so.

The border was officially closed (Zambia had by this time declared war on Rhodesia), and Zambia had complained of lost revenues as a result. But what was surely one of the most unusual states of belligerency in the history of warfare existed. Each afternoon around 4:00, a freight train of some dozen cars was backed onto the falls bridge by a Rhodesian locomotive. The next morning these cars were gone, replaced by others. The cars were mostly flat cars or gondolas and were covered with tarpaulins, carefully tied down to impede both car and cargo identification. (It was generally acknowledged, though, that the cars contained coal for Zambia's copper trains.) My attention was first drawn to this when, the second morning after my arrival, I saw the change in the cars from the afternoon before. That night at dark, I walked near the customs house and watched the switch engine make the change. (The official Zambian position was that the cars were bound for Zaire, to be returned with copper ore destined for Durban, the South African port. Zaire had a shipment agreement with South Africa.)

According to the waiters at the Rainbow restaurant there were frequently a half-dozen switches an evening. "This is a big game," the head waiter said. "They play over there and we play over here. The trains, they just keep moving." According to four white farmers and their wives, with whom I had lunch later at the Hotel Mosi-Oa-Tunya, about twice a week a convoy of semitrailer trucks, some refrigerated, would arrive from South Africa. The license plates were changed just behind the customs house when they crossed the bridge. They were then driven to Lusaka to be unloaded. On their return their regular plates were replaced before they crossed to the Rhodesian side. No one was able to give a reliable estimate of the volume of this trade, but a United Nations official with whom I talked in Cape Town said that it was Zambia's lifeline. It was common knowledge that this trade was going on—and with Botswana and Mozambique as well. Indeed, Rhodesia operates Botswana's railroad with Rhodesian employees and rolling stock—just as South Africa operates Mozambique's rail system and her harbor at Lourenco Marques.

The combined population of Rhodesia's Front Line enemies is 35 million (42 million if one counts the 7 million Rhodesian blacks from whom the

United Front guerillas claim 90 percent allegiance). Rhodesia's adult white population is 130,000 and falling.

Rhodesia's land area is 390,000 square kilometers. Zambia's alone is 752,000. The combined land area of the Front Line coalition is 4,200,000 square kilometers.

Rhodesia has been cut off officially from the mainstream of world commerce since the 1970 UN embargo. Although initially evaded, the embargo has recently been enforced by Western nations whose own recessions and trade deficits have made it more convenient to obey. The Front Line nations (including the United Front guerillas) have received billions of dollars in economic and military aid from Western and Communist governments, international institutions and charitable organizations.

These facts must be mentioned (in spite of their use in racist propaganda) because they are true, and because no honest report of the conditions in this unhappy corner of our planet could be made without them. They reveal that fifteen years of official independence and billions of dollars of aid have not even begun to achieve economic self-sufficiency for these so-called independent nations. The African is still, in other words, dependent upon the European—even, as in this instance, his declared military enemy—for survival.

When one considers the growing number of African youths leaving the countryside for the cities in search of jobs, the capacity of the agricultural base must be even more diminished. Worse, most of these immigrants go from rural subsistence to urban dependence in cities where there are few subsistence jobs and almost none that produce the foreign exchange necessary to buy consumer goods and spare parts—not to mention paying off the country's international debt. As this situation worsens, how greater still will become the black man's cursed dependence upon the white, be he Rhodesian farmer or New York banker?

Further indication of the relaxed war here is the almost total absence of military activity. Absolutely no blackout or curfew is observed in Livingstone or across the river at Victoria Falls, where a dozen hotels and a casino run wide open all night. A Rhodesian sightseeing plane even makes hourly tourist overflights.

Coming out of the Barclay's Bank in Livingstone one morning, I met the tanned, lean, solid-chinned wife of an ex-colonial cattle farmer. She invited me to have dinner with her, her husband and two other couples at the Hotel Mosi-Oa-Tunya. Dinner was a superb T-bone steak—preceded by several rounds of gin and tonic. They talked in high-to-flat British accents in studiously low tones. Whenever the waiter came near there was a conspicuous falloff in conversation. They were beyond shock or disillusionment or even fear. It was evident that the three couples met like this about once a month after Saturday shopping to share the latest on the war, mismanagement, corruption and personal gossip. Today was a happier-than-usual day because one of the ladies had just returned from Cape Town with a freshly mounted diamond ring. She had found the stone (the size of a big bean and valued at $3,000) the year before on a sidewalk in midtown

Manhattan.

My hostess had been born here in the early '30s of South African parents. Her husband had come out with his family just before the war. The second couple had married in England and come out in 1949. The third couple were both born here in the '20s. Each family had elected to stay on after independence, when "more than three fourths of them [the whites] fled" to Rhodesia and South Africa.

Each of the ladies wore a long colorful cotton dress; the gents each had on the virtually obligatory colonial uniform—a freshly starched pair of khaki shorts, high white socks and a pressed khaki shirt.

Their land had not been confiscated outright—it would be more correct to say that they had been prospectively evicted. The land had been declared "inalienable and non-heritable" by the Kaunda regime. In other words, they could stay on and farm it as long as they lived, but when they died it would go to the state for redistribution—"although not necessarily to the Africans who have lived there and worked it with us all their lives," one said. "Those things have a way of working themselves out, if you know what I mean," he said in disgust.

"What irks me," said another, "is that both my children want to stay here and farm but I can't leave the land to them. And I know what will happen to it—the same thing the bloody *kaffirs** have done with all the other land . . . ."

He asked me if I knew that the country used to export more food and meat than any other British colony. "Hell, now you can't even find potatoes half the time. The bloody *kaffirs* have let every one of those farms go to seed." He told me that I could go out now to any of the farms—and he named one particular large estate left by whites who had immigrated to South Africa—and that "you can't tell from the forest that there was ever even a farm there. It's unbelievable, it is."

Although these ex-colonials still make "quite a decent go of it," they are unable to spend their money outside of Zambia. Since their produce must all be sold locally they are paid in *kwachas*—the nonconvertible local currency. When traveling abroad, a couple might take out 300 *kwacha* (about $500 officially) which then was to be changed at an unfavorable discount rate in Rhodesia or South Africa. Special application could be made to take out more—for, say, a long trip to New York or London—but this was tedious and time-consuming. In fact, one of the couples had just come from the bank in an attempt to hurry such an application, which had been filed some three months before. They were planning to leave for London in two weeks, the woman said, to visit their children. They were shocked to learn, she said, that the application had been "misplaced," and that a new one, consisting of several pages and requiring the attachments of various official documents (tax receipts, residence permit, etc.) would have to be filed: "You can't imagine how angry I was after waiting in that queue for an hour only to be told they'd lost it. . . ." she went on.

For all their complaining, though, they seemed content to have stayed

---

*Arabic for "heretic," this is a perjorative and racist term, considered as grave an insult as "nigger," with which it is frequently and interchangably used.

behind. "We're certainly not getting shot at here, that's for sure," said one, referring to the situation in Rhodesia.

"And for what we are able to buy we can certainly afford to pay for it—if it would ever just get here," said another. He was speaking of hard-to-get items, like household appliances and parts for their farm equipment. Two of the couples were driving smart new Range Rovers. Their farmhouses, though remote, were serviced by electric power and a party-line telephone. There were only nineteen families left now, of the 100 in the Livingstone area before independence. "But I think most of us are glad we stuck it out. It's been hard, but. . . ." His eyes became misty and he looked out the window toward the falls. The waiter was nowhere nearby, and there was a long, uncomfortable silence.

Many of the letters and notebooks of David Livingstone had somehow been collected and preserved in the museum named after him in the town's center. I spent two afternoons there browsing through displays of his 1855 and subsequent diaries, various documents pertaining to discovery of the falls and the exploration of the Zambezi. So few people visited the museum these days that its staff was happy to accommodate almost any request to see additional material.

A whole section of the museum was devoted to Kaunda's revolutionary activities and the present regime. Actually, there had been very little armed rebellion and the colony was given independence on schedule in 1962. Dr. Kaunda is considered a political moderate and, with Julius Nyerere and Felix Houphouët-Boigny, is one of the most respected African leaders.

There were some rare photographs from the early days of British settlement. One picture of a British-supervised Arab auction of a young slave was worth 10,000 words. Also on display were assorted handcuffs and shackles used in the grisly business, along with maps showing the routes of the caravans and raiders. In the same case with the photograph of the slave auction were samples of the beads, trinkets and guns for which slaves were traded to the African raiders who had captured them. The most impressive taxidermy anywhere was in the Livingstone museum. Among the many predators exhibited was a magnificent leopard bringing down a waterbuck.

Out at the falls there was another, smaller museum dealing primarily with the geology of the falls themselves and with a *Homo erectus* living site found there. There were various brochures and books for sale, but the paleontological material was dated and the geology oversimplified.

In a park shelter just up from the museum, some 40 almost-desperate young vendors plied their souvenir trade. Their wares appeared to be locally made and of a natural quality superior to the mass-produced paraphernalia usually found in such places. Particularly impressive were assorted wooden heads and totems.

If I were a school- or Scoutmaster and planned a trip to Africa I would start at Livingstone. There is so much natural and human history here. Livingstonians—black and white—are among the continent's friendliest people.

There is one point in Africa where one is, at one moment, in four countries: South West Africa (Namibia), Zambia, Rhodesia and Botswana. I went there not out of choice but out of necessity: the only way to reach Rhodesia from Black Africa is to cross the Zambezi River between the police post at Mamboba in Zambia and the tiny Botswana hamlet of Kasungulu. Here one must participate in one of the most tedious little diplomatic prevarications of the road. The device is known as the Caprivi Caper to travelers. It involves touching briefly on the ridiculous 600-mile-long strip of South West Africa (through which the Germans once schemed to build a railroad to beat Rhodes's own to Tanganyika), then cutting back a quarter mile into Rhodesia. In any event, the procedure of traveling between these two Front Line nations and their declared enemy is another example of the flexibility with which official Black Africa deals unofficially with the economic facts of life.

Beginning in Tanzania, I was asked at each border to declare my ultimate destination. The code words, adopted by many years of the traffic, are "Botswana, to the Kalahari Desert." As you get closer to Botswana, they ask more and more questions, like what you expect to see in the desert and where you are going after that. The answers are "Bushmen" and "Dar es Salaam." I winced each time at the petty duplicity of this procedure, for all know that an overland traveler is going eventually into Rhodesia and South Africa. And they know that you know that they know. Yet the alternative to playing the game is not only refusal of entry but possible arrest as a mercenary or embargo violator. One simply cannot mention Rhodesia or South Africa. To do so is to violate the game rules.

I crossed the ferry with an empty black-driven Zambian cattle truck, returning ostensibly to Gaborone, in Botswana, after delivering beef to a farm near Lusaka. He cleared Botswana customs ahead of me and I didn't see him again—until a week later at Bulawayo, in Rhodesia.

The Botswana officials were surly and rude. I was told I was disrespectful, for having misspelled "Gaborone" (their capital) and for having put "Zambia frontier" instead of "Kasungulu." I was then dressed down for leaving blank the space for "wife" instead of writing "unaccompanied" and for merely writing an "S" instead of spelling out my middle name.

I knew from talking with other travelers that the post was a difficult one. Four Australians had been detained a week because one of them had a South African stamp in her passport. I was their first American customer for quite a while, so I was berated with political questions such as why there were so many American companies in South Africa. These were wily, intelligent young officials—two of them—around 30. They questioned me intensely on my itinerary. I answered as best I could but was not in a mood to be diplomatic and almost blew my stack when, after half an hour, it became obvious that they planned a prolonged game with me.

They, of course, sensed my irritation and delighted in it. Condescendingly, they presented me with an unexpected bill for $50 for "fees" and "insurance." I had no cash, but I would have gladly, I think, paid this dash to get them behind me. But I had only traveler's checks and the closest bank was in the village itself some five miles away. "You must leave something valuable so I know you will come back," the more aggressive of the two insisted. I was holding my billfold, which he seized and from which he withdrew my passport. Looking me straight in the eye he asked: "Do you already have your Rhodesian visa?" When I repeated that I was going to the Kalahari he said, "I see, you're going to the Kalahari, *then* coming back down through South Africa and Rhodesia?" And so it went. Finally, I persuaded him I would need the passport (which he had already stamped with a visa) to get the money for his fees. He said, "Then I take this." And he fished out my expired Master Charge card. I saw immediately I was safe but, just to make sure, I pretended to protest, then grudgingly withdrew. He and the other one grinned slyly at each other. "If you do not come back you have big trouble."

A quarter-mile down the dirt road, in the middle of nowhere, was a shingle with a hand-drawn arrow and the words "Rhodesia Customs." Down this side road, a half-mile away, was an utterly matter-of-fact border post. As he was stamping my exit visa the lieutenant remarked knowingly, "I thought you were going to Kalahari? That would seem to be impossible, now wouldn't it?" Momentarily shocked, I hesitated, and he said, "I see, you're going down to visit the falls first, right?"

"Yes, that's right," I said.

"But haven't you already seen them in Zambia?"

"Well, I. . . ."

"You just want to see them from both sides."

"Yes."

"When will you come back?"

"I can't say exactly," I said.

"Yeah, I know," he said, signed my passport and pushed it across the counter.

CHAPTER XXI

Mediterranean Sea

Nile River

Red Sea

AFRICA

Atlantic Ocean

Victoria Falls
Fort Victoria
Wankie
Bulawayo

Salisbury

ZIMBABWE
(Rhodesia)

SOUTH AFRICA

Durban

Indian Ocean

Cape Town

Grahamstown
Port Elizabeth

Cape of Good Hope

A hundred yards around a tight curve, the narrow dirt road ended in front of a tidy brick and concrete building. Two men, a black corporal and a white sergeant, in starched khakis with slung rifles, stood at ease.

"Good morning, sir," the sergeant said.

"Welcome to Rhodesia. Customs this way, sir," said the corporal.

Behind the desk was a young lieutenant in khakis. His bearing was relaxed, courteous.

"Had a rather long jaunt, haven't you, sir?" he asked as he rapidly affixed the visa stamps on looseleaf for insertion into my passport. "Don't suppose you'd want our stamp in there? Might cause you some unpleasantness."

When he said the visa and insurance fees came to $26, I pulled out a traveler's check. On the back was the Kenyan stamp invalidating the check in South Africa and Rhodesia. The lieutenant smiled at that, then stamped the checks and gave me my change.

A minimum on one's person of $750 (or the equivalent in sterling or other convertible currency) was required for entry into Rhodesia. (To enter South Africa, the minimum is $1,500, so many young Brits and Australians come to Rhodesia to work a while before going down.) The lieutenant counted the remainder of my checks, which came to only $600. He estimated the value of my vehicle at $1,000, however, added that amount to the checks and granted me entry.

Outside again, I was waved perfunctorily through the inspection island. "Drive carefully, sir," said the sergeant, saluting smartly. "Fifty miles an hour is about right. You may see our people out there, we have patrols here and there and you can't tell where they're likely to be."

There was a straight, wide concrete highway with broad shoulders. I had not seen a highway like this since France. It ran through lightly forested bushland. For five miles, I drove at 50, when suddenly, not 30 yards ahead, was a cluster of black-and-white striped oil drums crossed with planks. I hardly had time to get my foot to the brake pedal, stopping barely ten inches from the first barrel.

"You know, sir, I would have had to open up on you if you'd crossed the barrier," said a firm but polite voice. It belonged to a burly red-faced military police sergeant in camouflaged utilities with a slung but at-the-ready Browning automatic rifle. A younger man was with him. He also carried an automatic rifle. He was covering me from across the road at a very astute military angle.

I sensed by the sergeant's nervousness how close indeed I had come to forcing the decision upon them. He explained that I could expect from time to time to encounter similar checkpoints: "We usually throw them up on a curve like this." I followed his hand with my eyes and saw that indeed they had been on a curve. I must have had my mind on other things than driving.

"You'll have to be more alert, sir. You didn't see our sign?"

"Sign? What sign?" I followed his hand again. About 40 yards back was a tiny shin-high sign.

"Says 'police check,' " he said. "Now I would like to instruct you in a few simple precautions. We wear uniforms like these. [He turned so that I could see him from the rear.] We will all usually be white who will stop you but we do have black officers. They will look like this: constable!"

He pointed to the forest across the way as he shouted. There was nothing at first, then something moved. It was a black noncommissioned officer, also in camouflaged utilities and a neatly blocked cap. He presented his profile.

"Very well, recover!" At the command, the constable ducked back out of sight.

"You should really have no trouble, but then you never know. The thing to remember is never, never stop for anyone that is not dressed as we are. The terrorists have different uniforms, not at all like ours, and they are, of course, black."

He explained that the guerillas (always "terrorists") carried rifles with "carved magazines, Communist made—not square like ours." He gestured to the straight ammo clips beneath the breaches of their rifles. "Do you have a weapon?"

I said that I did not.

"Well, that's up to you, sir, but I—" he hesitated, then said, "where you from? Yank, I'll bet?"

I told him.

"Saw two of your fellow countrymen in here hunting just last week. Very good chaps they were."

He was, I saw, every bit the senior staff NCO—combat-seasoned, experienced, self-confident. The kind who would teach young second lieutenants how to lead, then pick up the platoon again as each new lieutenant became a casualty.

The next 30 miles to Victoria Falls I passed not a single vehicle. I felt like a sitting duck on a few of those long, lonely stretches. When I checked in at the police station, a convoy of a dozen vehicles was forming with two machine-gun-mounted pickup trucks to make the crossing in the opposite direction.

"Better stick with the convoys from now on, sir," the desk captain said. I told him I figured I would.

Two convoys a day, sometimes three, went south from Victoria Falls (at 7:30 a.m., 10:30 a.m. and noon). They went the first leg to Wankie, some 50 miles away. From there another convoy continued from Wankie itself and from the surrounding game reservation lodges.

Vic Falls was a town of tidy paved streets that could have been Anywhere, USA. The shops were full of clothes and canned goods and appliances, although there were quite a few empty buildings and "for rent" or "for sale" signs.

The people on the sidewalk were well dressed, courteous, eager to speak to a stranger: "Yes, straight on to the falls. Where you come from, by the way . . . ?"

I drove slowly down the main street, past the corner Wimpy Bar (a British hamburger chain as prolific as McDonald's in America), and across the railroad tracks. A huffing steam locomotive, probably the one I had seen switching from across the river, was busily arranging the night's mystery train of tarpaulin-draped gondolas.

From the tracks I could hear the thundering of the falls, even over the noise of the locomotive. Because the town was on a hill, I could also see across the full mist, clear to the Zambian side. I parked at the small ranger station and made my way down the brick path to the observation point overlooking Devil's Cataract, the furthest south of the some 50 chutes and easily the most turbulent. The top of the falls is recessed just a few yards so that what you have at Devil's Cataract is a double chute. Because the water is channeled into a cut above the upper chute (and because the chute itself is quite narrow), the volume and force of the water gives the illusion of being double that of the rest of the falls. Above Devil's Cataract is a statue of Livingstone looking out over the falls. The bluff opposite it is almost three times as long as the one on the Zambian side so that you can walk out opposite that many more chutes. The Main Falls, a giant cataract almost at the center of the river, sends up so much spray that you can barely see it when standing face-on. The rain forest on the Rhodesian side was full of kudu and small deer, but I didn't see any vervet monkeys or baboons. The forest extends further back from the top of the falls here, since the bluff is flat and extends into the surrounding hardwoods.

I took one of the Town Council's cheap-but-tidy guest cabins in the town center. A small shopping center nearby cut between two old lines of stores. All but one were vacant with "for lease" signs in the windows.

Anna Marie, the lovely director of the cabins, queried me at length on conditions over in Livingstone, her hometown. She hadn't been back since the border was closed in '74. She was determined to stick it out, "even though they bomb us from time to time. They can't hit a thing. The only time you have to worry about getting hit by a terr [pronounced "tear," as in "rip"] is when he's not aiming at you," she said, echoing a local aphorism. In the cabin, I found on the table a mimeographed sheet of instructions in case of attack.

I walked around the town visiting with store clerks and merchants. A middle-aged lady at the tourist information shop had migrated to the falls from England's Lake District some five years previously, to get away from "the hustle and hypocrisy of British life." The foreign tourist trade was virtually dead, "but we still get droves of Swiss and Germans and holiday makers from Salisbury and the Republic," she said, meaning South Africa.

WHAT TO DO IN A MORTAR ATTACK

BE PREPARED!!

Here are some of the things YOU can do to help—KEEP THIS NOTICE HANDY

1. Don't go outside to watch the attack—you could be injured, and men urgently needed elsewhere may unnecessarily have to leave vital work to help you.

2. Move into the safest part of your house. A cellar is ideal, otherwise a central corridor. Keep away from outside walls, try to have two walls each side of you and the smallest area of roof space above you. Take blankets and other necessities.

3. Tell children and servants NOW what to do, and where to go in an attack.

4. Keep away from windows and keep them open—flying glass can cause serious injury. Draw the curtains.

5. Don't use the telephone except in cases of real need. Remember the Civil Defense and Security Forces will need the telephone urgently. DON'T BLOCK THE LINES.

6. DON'T BLOCK THE ROADS. Stay Put. The Civil Defence and Security Forces must be able to move quickly.

7. Don't touch unexploded bombs OR FRAGMENTS. Report their positions to Police or Security Forces after the attack.

8. Don't shoot—unless you personally, or your family are being attacked. In bad light you could be shooting at our own men.

9. Do keep a simple first aid kit handy—with a torch.

10. Don't be worried by noise—noise hurts no one, and much of it will be our own retaliation.

KEEP CALM   STAY PUT

HELP OUR FORCES BEAT THE ATTACK!!

Two heavily rouged and pantsuited resident matrons at the town's newsstand shared the views of the others but were more resigned. Unlike most of the others, they had no plans to leave. "We'll stay, whatever happens," the older woman said.

There was a narrow grocery store on the side street with a meager stock of cellophane packaged crisps (potato chips) and other junk food together with assorted tins of beef. A refrigerator contained cheese, milk, and bologna cut on a small automatic cleaver. There were several cases of Coke and Lion beer. Near the door was a cooler of pop which also held a tray of ice-cream bars. The grocer and his wife each had the stern, bony look of humorless perserverance. A pale white woman with a shopping basket was gossiping with the wife in front of the counter as I walked in. Three black children came in behind me, opened the cooler and stood staring at the ice-cream tray. The wife scolded them for leaving it open so long and asked them to make up their mind. They each chose a chocolate popsicle, paid, and walked out onto the sidewalk. The grocer winced as the door slammed.

An old black woman came in and stood waiting patiently for the end of the gossip. A young black man with a grey delivery cap hurried in past her and interrupted: his change had been short and his boss had sent him back for the correct amount.

"Why didn't you count it here the first time?" the grocer asked him.

"I thought I did, sir," he responded.

"How do I know you just didn't fiddle the two dollars between here and Mr. Black's?"

"Oh, sir you know I not do thing like that." The delivery man grinned and shuffled nervously. The grocer gave him the two dollars, and he trotted back to his bicycle, which he'd leaned against a parking meter across the street.

I bought two Cokes to take out, paid the deposit and walked next door to Shaw's Hardware. There was something in the smell of these stores and the people in them that stirred memories of Mississippi summers of long ago.

Mr. Shaw, aged about 60, was behind the counter, drumming it morosely with his fingers and surveying his shelves of cloth and display cases of belts, knives, ropes, pencils and notebook tablets.

Mr. Shaw was furious with the Americans and the British. He referred to Dr. Robert Owen, the British foreign secretary, as a "damned fool whippersnapper still wet behind the ears," and to Ambassador Andrew Young as "a rich American *kaffir* who knows nothing about Africa." He recited the names of local families who had left the Falls area, among them many of his friends who had gone to South Africa. "I'll tell you one thing, by God," he said, "They may break Rhodesia but they'll never force those crazy Dutchmen to leave their country to the *kaffirs*. Why, they'll kill every one of them before they'll do it."

He interrupted his diatribe to serve a black customer seeking garden tools. The tools had to be fetched from a storeroom and they proved to be the wrong ones. He was surprisingly courteous, almost obsequious, as he returned to the storeroom.

"A very good customer, always pays his bills," he said when the man had gone. The store was not crowded, but there was a steady stream of seed 'n'

300

feed trade, most of it black. He climbed the ladder to retrieve a bolt of calico for a heavy African woman with four children. He asked after her family as he cut the cloth, and when one of the kids spilled ice cream on the floor, he genially had a clerk wipe it up.

Back at the counter he resumed his philippic. "Now what's a man like me to do—been here since way back before the war: my family, roots are here. Why should we leave? We built this country. We don't want apartheid up here—really never had it. Rhodesia's not South Africa. It's an open, integrated country. Public parks, restaurants, bars . . . anybody can go in, black, white or green. Oh, I know [the Western press] says they can't vote. They can too vote if they show they're responsible. If a *kaffir* can show he's a responsible property owner and can pass his school exam, then he can vote.

"But I'll tell you, the whole thing is a Communist plot, a Communist plot, that's what it is. The bloody Russians are going to take over southern Africa and then what will your Jimmy Carter say? Oh, they will scream and holler then, but it will be too late. Serve 'em right too, the whole lot of them, the stupid bloody British, too, the *kaffir*-lovin' bastards."

At the Wimpy Bar the following morning at breakfast I met a most unforgettable character, John Galsworthy. Twenty-nine years old, tall, gaunt, bearded, he had just returned to the mainland after fifteen months as the British Royal Society's camp administrator on Aldabra Island in the Indian Ocean. Having spent some time on the Galápagos Islands off South America long ago, I knew Aldabra's importance as a refuge for turtles and tortoises. It is, in fact, the only place besides the Galápagos where giant tortoises are found. When the United States and Britain announced the construction of a naval base there in 1966, there was such a protest from the conservationists that it was built on Diego Garcia instead.

The island, a part of the Seychelles chain, lies about 600 miles southeast of Mahé Island, the capital. It is about that far from the mainland coast of Africa. Aldabra is uninhabited except by a slowly rotating international community of some twenty scientists and a half-dozen native helpers. Almost its entire surface is covered with a sinewy tough brush called *pemphis.* The growth is so thick and tall (up to ten feet high) that it is impossible to walk through in most places. Because of this nuisance, travel around the doughnut-shaped island is by motorboat through the central lagoon. Navigation has to be done at high tide, however, since the lagoon all but dries out at low tide.

John's job was to attend to the comfort and convenience of the scientists and to try occasionally to contact the outside world by wireless. His radio would receive, but audible transmittals were a problem. His usual contact was the Kenya navy dispatcher at Mombasa, who would relay any messages on to London or to Mahé Island. The admiralty in Mahé didn't like this, and there was a lot of friction until, finally, the only ship to call regularly at the island, the Kenya freighter *SS Nordvaer,* was ordered to call first at Mahe. "Since there is no airport, any emergency evacuation might prove difficult," John said.

301

There was a small aerodrome a mile south of town where, for fifteen Rhodesian dollars, you could fly over the falls in a twin-engine Cessna. The flights lasted about 30 minutes. In midstream the plane carefully kept just to the Rhodesian side. I asked the jocular pilot if he'd ever been shot at. "Not that I know of," he jested. His wife knitted in the hangar, fussing occasionally at a disobedient Spaniel and gossiping with the receptionist. I had gone up with a party of four German tourists from the Victoria Falls Hotel. We made four passes over the falls at various angles and altitudes. I was able to see all the chutes at once and, below them, the zigzagging gorge. On the way back, the pilot buzzed a lone bull elephant who was browsing intently on a small island. From the air it was clear why the guerillas had been able to move about so easily. The terrain was mostly semi-desert scrub brush but with long stretches of timber near the Kasungulu Highway.

Along the riverbank were high, thick weeds and marsh grass. The town had been attacked for the second time in six months the Sunday night before I arrived—about fifteen terrorists, according to the police chief. They had hit just at the south edge of town, at a motel about 300 yards from the airstrip. My first question was if they could hit the motel, why not the airstrip, which was certainly a more exposed and desirable military target? The guerillas, the chief said, avoid contact wherever possible. The airstrip has a half-dozen black guards and an army "ready squad" nearby. The guerillas prefer to hit "soft" targets such as farm houses, hotels, and lone vehicles.

Guerilla strategy, here as elsewhere, is not military conquest *per se*, but conquest through destruction of the population's morale and will to resist. In this they have been, to a degree, successful, particularly among the black population. Favorite targets are monasteries, where nuns and hospital patients are shot, as well as pro-government villages in which the chiefs, or "head men" as they are called, are executed. Because of the increasing number of whites leaving the country (some 9,000 in 1976; 16,000 in 1977), they have also been somewhat successful in weakening white resistance.

Although there were many complaints about the falloff in the foreign tourist business, there seemed to be a good deal more than was let on. In addition to the four Germans and their party of twenty, I also met and visited with three French families, a honeymooning Swiss couple (with matching red velvet pantsuits) and the American missionaries. Except for the Germans, however, these were independent travelers, not group tourists.

I bought stamps and mailed some letters and postcards. I noticed that the Rhodesian currency was the first that didn't have a picture of the current chief of state on it. It was also interesting to see so few official portraits of Prime Minister Ian Smith, who is immensely popular among whites. This contrasted sharply with the vast number of photographs of black and Arab chiefs of state (usually in military uniform or carrying the local scepterlike talisman of power) I saw in virtually every building and market stall north of the Zambezi.

> Not only [money] for their schools, but where is the money to
> come from for their food, clothing and medical attention? Up to
> now the white population has footed this bill, but with the advent
> of a predominately black government, which seems inevitable,
> will there be sufficient cash to finance these essential services?

Thus read the August 5, 1977 edition of the *Wankie and Falls News*, a mimeographed news sheet.

Calling for family planning among blacks beginning with sex and hygiene education at the primary level, it echoed a standard white preoccupation. Time and again I was to hear something like this: the reason there are 7,000,000 Africans is because of white medical care. Most black children used to die at childhood or soon afterward. In 1900 there were only 200,000 blacks in all of Rhodesia. But the white man's medicine and civilization eradicated disease and filth; thus the blacks, unable or unwilling to practice birth control, multiplied disproportionately.

What is overlooked by the whites is that in 1900 the white population of Rhodesia was barely 10,000. Recently, it was just under 300,000. There was, in other words, almost an exactly identical exponential rate of increase among whites, although granted, a large part of the latter was due not to births but to immigration. Still, it seems unfair to accuse the black Africans of negligently creating a disproportionate demand on the country's resources.

Late each afternoon while I was in Victoria Falls, all able-bodied men donned their camouflaged jungle utilities and reported to an assembly area. They were then assigned to various sentry and listening posts. Large troop carriers ferried them about with their motor and other support units. Strategic points, such as the railroad, post office building and each hotel were guarded by two or three black troopers. Several mobile units roved the asphalt and dirt roads with enough fire power to counter any conceivable assault. Then A. Zambezi River Lodge and Elephant Hills Casino (which ran all night) had special protection. There was a sundown curfew for all Africans, and whites were urged not to move about unnecessarily.

During the four and a half days I was there the town was not attacked, although within the previous month several local farms had been hit and their African laborers killed. So vulnerable were the farms along the river here that the white owners had all moved into town, making only occasional daylight inspection tours. Paydays varied since a favorite guerilla tactic seemed to be ambushing the farmer when he drove out to pay his workers.

At that time, reports of military activity were released by the Combined Forces Headquarters to the press. The foreign press was exempt from military censorship, and the local press used its best judgment. This meant usually following CFH guidelines and, frequently, just printing CFH handouts. Now, however, a system of direct censorship has been imposed, and all copy (foreign as well as local) must be reviewed in advance by censorship officers in Salisbury.

There is, with one exception, no censorship of political criticism of the government, be it local or foreign in origin. Indeed a great deal of coverage is given to British and American (as well as Soviet and front line) criticism of the Smith regime. The exception is that no statements by Joshua Nkomo or Robert Mgawe, the leaders of the United Front, are allowed.

The press was at the time giving prominent play to a government order evicting Africans from a previously all-white residential area in Salisbury. (Pronounced "Saul's bury," I was sternly told.) In view of the government's policy of gradually eliminating all segregation of public places, this was a surprise. The reason given for the eviction was that housing segregation was still legal and that private rather than public rights were involved.

Americans familiar with our own recent segregationist lexicon will have an approximate idea of the some-of-my-best-friends-eat-watermelon vignettes prevalent here from the Prime Minister's response to a question concerning covenants which restrict the rights of Jewish citizens to purchase land. The *Rhodesia Herald* reported, "He was forced to acknowledge their validity but said they applied to 'green eyed,' Irish or anybody else should the landlord so proscribe."

Several cars—Fords, VW's and Mercedes-Benzes, full of scrubbed and friendly white faces—stood in line. Flaxen-haired tots played in the back seats, and pale, hollow-cheeked young clerks in white shirts and thin black ties stood against the fenders. The line had begun to form around 10:00 in the parking lot at the police station and now numbered some twenty. In and out several times wheeled two small Ford pickup trucks, each with a middle-aged police reservist riding shotgun with a 12-gauge. In the back of each was an automatic rifleman who covered another reservist at the base of a .50-caliber machine gun mounted desert-rat style on a swivel. A large protective metal guard rose halfway down the barrel. Each reservist wore a helmet and flight jacket with heavily padded camouflaged utilities. The machine gunner faced forward and alternated the weapon from one side to another over the top of the cab. The rifleman leaned against the cab and faced to the rear.

The sergeant driving the first pickup called, "All drivers up here, please!" We were told to keep 50 feet between vehicles and to maintain a speed of 55 mph. It was a small convoy, so we would go a bit faster than usual. No trouble was expected, "but just the same our intelligence is that terrorists are in the area." If there were an ambush, we were to "keep moving unless your car is disabled. If you have to stop, pull off onto the left shoulder and the rear escort will cover you." They had already escorted one convoy, without incident, that morning.

The convoy drove into the gentle hilly countryside. There was no other traffic for the entire 70 kilometers to the police station at Wankie. Waiting for us there was a twenty-car convoy from that town. After fifteen minutes for the pickups to refuel, we were again briefed, and the lead pickup drove out. This truck was mounted with the strangest-looking contraption: a steel cylinder, some three feet in diameter, which completely enclosed a machine gunner and his weapon. I had thought that this convoy would go all the way to Bulawayo. However, about 30 kilometers south of Wankie was a police roadblock. The passengers of an African bus were on the shoulder being searched by African troopers. As we passed, our escorts, without any warning, pulled over and stopped. The patrolman directing traffic waved us on through alone. Evidently those in front assumed, as did I, that this was the end of the convoy. A Mercedes and a Range Rover spurted off around me and in no time I realized that I was driving alone through thick brush country.

When I reached the village of Lupane I decided that I would wait there for the convoy, which I thought must surely be following me. When after about fifteen minutes it didn't, I decided to inquire whether the road ahead were safe and, if so, continue. The only people there were blacks, and I asked several of them who were standing around the general store and gas station, but they didn't know. One of them said there was a mission not far away and I should inquire there. I drove in the direction he indicated for about three miles when I met a Volkswagen with two white Catholic sisters coming the other way. They told me that there was only a morning convoy (at 9:30) from Wankie but that most local drivers did not worry about taking it, since the most dangerous part of the highway was to the north, between the falls and Lupane. But after Lupane it was relatively safe. I therefore decided to drive to Bulawayo in company with the next car that passed. I returned to the main road and waited.

Very shortly thereafter there drove by three off-duty soldiers breaking in a new Ford at under 30 mph. When they saw me parked on the shoulder they slowed and asked if I needed any help, and I told them that I was waiting for someone to convoy with to Bulawayo. A tall, athletic fellow in the back yawned irritably and stretched his arms as the other two allowed that I shouldn't be so concerned: "We drive this once or twice a month and so far we've not seen a thing. Of course, we never drive after 3:30 p.m.—that's when they will hit you because our security forces only have a few hours to track them down before dark." That's when I learned that no one drives anywhere in Rhodesia except in the middle of the day.

They may have been nonchalant, but the two in front each had on flight jackets and the older one was literally riding shotgun. He patted his barrel and grinned: "Just in case."

I drove with them for about half an hour, then became impatient at the pace and decided to drive on in alone. The sisters had said the road was safe, and these gents would be quite a while getting there—at 30 mph. Except for two cars of whites that sped around me, I saw only one other vehicle, with an old African at the wheel. The trip was uneventful, and I arrived in Bulawayo about 4:30.

It was with some surprise that I opened Monday's paper to read that guerillas had attacked the Catholic Regina Mundi Mission at Lupane less than two hours after I had talked to the sisters. They had robbed the mission personnel, taken their weapons, and marched the church's building contractor, a Mr. Rudy Kogler, out into the woods. Just at the edge of the clearing, Mr. Kogler had pulled a concealed .32 midget pistol and killed the guerilla leader, whereupon he was killed by the others, who quickly fled. According to the sisters, Mr. Kogler sacrificed his life to protect them from execution. Five sisters had been executed by guerillas at another mission only a few miles away the previous October.

Two days later I read that at 6:00 p.m. on the highway twenty kilometers south of Lupane, a truck with a half-dozen Africans as passengers was ambushed. One of them, a Mr. William Mutandoro, had his left leg shot off. As he tried to crawl to cover in the middle of the highway, he was again wounded repeatedly. His right leg was later amputated in Wankie Hospital. One of the passengers, a girl working in Zambia who had come home to visit her ailing father, was also seriously wounded.

Bulawayo could have been Peoria, Joplin, Fort Smith, or Topeka: big wide clean streets, Protestant churches, smartly bricked shopping malls, Pizza Huts and neatly trimmed lawns bordered with irises, roses and tulips. Here and there stood a modern one-story concrete-and-glass professional building skirted with potted shrubs and skinny saplings. There were 1930s banks redone with gold and pseudo-marble facades, yet enough new mini-skyscrapers to give the town the look of an emerging commercial center. It was Sunday, and there was hardly any traffic. I drove past several garages and a used-car lot with streamers and pennants fluttering in the breeze ("Cut rate prices on all custom models"). A team of Africans was cleaning out debris from Saturday night's bash at The Southern Sun.

I parked in front of the Grand Hotel, which looked as if it had been a pioneers' hangout. The lobby was boarded up. Upstairs was an old folks' home. I walked on up the street: nothing. That's when I saw a well-dressed gent taking snapshots of the town center. His name was Louis Bolze, he said, and the photos were for a book he was publishing about Bulawayo. His business was called Books of Rhodesia, a reprinter of old African diaries and manuscripts in handsome hardback volumes. He suggested that I stay at the Selbourne, which was also an old hotel with character but well managed. We chatted for a while and he asked me over to his home for a visit. We arranged to meet at the King's Head pub in the Selbourne.

Once Louis had given me a chamber-of-commerce tour of Bulawayo, we returned to his home, where he lived with his wife and two sons, Adrian and Simon. I was sipping on a Lion lager and listening. "We don't want to keep the black man down," he continued, "we want to bring him along." What the white Rhodesians wanted, he said, was a gradual "sensible, responsible transition" that will "let the talent rise" regardless of race. Majority rule is "a noble concept" but "without safeguards there would be majority rule just once," then there would be civil war and an eventual dictatorship and destruction of "this civilization we have built up in the past eighty years."

The two cultures (white and black) are "poles apart," according to Louis. But they are getting closer. "He's adopted many of our ways and we've er. . . ." But African culture was still simply much too undeveloped to permit blacks to take over the management of the country. He reiterated how superior white medical care had resulted in a black population explosion: "So you can say, we've brought the problem on ourselves by our own generosity." Black medical care was only a fraction of the cost of the same care for whites, he said. White taxpayers, in other words, have subsidized it for them. He said that the black hospital in Bulawayo had better cancer treatment than the one for whites. "They have a cobalt machine. Whites go there for treatment. . . ." He continued: "No other African country has a clinic in every major village as we do in Rhodesia. There is no doubt about it, Africans are better off here than they are anywhere else."

He talked about domestic servants, who are exempt from the rigid housing segregation laws. These blacks, he said, live in servants' quarters, "not in the townships but here with us, for free. We take a boy or girl right out of the bush, never had any training, and we pay him or her thirty-five dollars a month. Now that doesn't sound like much, but all his meals are free, his lighting [not only electrical power but candles and a flashlight, since not all servants' quarters are wired for electricity]." He also said that a family would pay an African's bus fare to and from his family home in the townships once a week.

As I listened I felt within a certain cumulative disgust—not at my host, who was a kind, considerate fellow, but at the human condition. Here were echoes of the same pitiful rationalizations, presented with the same logic, I had heard so many countless thousands of times in my own country and around the world. Granted, his arguments sounded more convincing considering the relative cultural levels of the races in Rhodesia compared to those in Europe and America. I knew I would continue to hear the same line both eloquently and crudely expressed for the whole time I was in southern Africa, and I also knew that I would probably never hear the other side, since Africans distrust whites, even foreigners (not to mention the fact that the few articulate and outspoken blacks are banned, in exile or dead). Still I listened, and I knew that there was some unpleasant truth in what he was saying, namely that the Africans would make a hell of a mess of things if given immediate majority rule.

The simple fact is that Africa has not experienced the renaissance which is the necessary prelude to the informed public opinion essential for self-government. And it doubtless will take many generations for this to occur. In the meantime, each country will be ruled by a succession of more or less wastrel dictators, their tribal cronies and European "advisors." Yet when one considers that it took Europeans 500 years to do these things, perhaps the Africans should be allotted at least a few decades. The unfortunate thing for the Louis Bolzes is that there is no way to protect them in the interim. They will simply have to suffer. And while that is easy for an outsider to say, it is impossible for a white African to accept. To expect that he will watch his wealth and heritage confiscated, squandered and Swiss-banked by a self-proclaimed savior strutting about in a field marshal's uniform, without fighting, with the consolation that this is but the necessary adolescence of maturing African democracy, is to expect too much. There is little solace for Louis Bolze in the moral certainty of Dr. Julius Nyerere's dictum: "Men will never accept deliberate and organized humiliation as the basis of existence."

The only friend Rhodesia had had was South Africa, Louis said. "We're sort of like first cousins," he said, mentioning that Cecil Rhodes and the British South Africa Company had settled Rhodesia from South Africa. Indeed most of Rhodesia's whites claim to trace an ancestor back to the

South African English settlers of the 1830s or to the Voortrekkers, who settled the Transvaal and many of whom later moved on into Rhodesia. The Rhodesian National Police still calls itself the British South Africa Police, even though the company has long since been dissolved and the colony has been self-governing since 1920.

Regarding the South Africans, Louis noted that their support of Rhodesia since UDI (Unilateral Declaration of Independence) in 1966 had not been altogether out of first-cousin altruism. He referred to South African merchant's acting as middlemen in the transshipment of Rhodesian chrome and other products (thereby enabling third nations to legally circumvent the United Nations' embargo).

"Of course, they've made a pretty profit," he observed. "Charged us dearly for it. But that's only fair. I suppose we would have done the same thing if it were the other way around."

Because of the embargo, he said, Rhodesia had been forced to become self-sufficient in almost everything it needed: shoes, guns, suits, tobacco, hardware. "You name it, we make it." He described how a machine gun factory had been put together in a very few months and boasted that even the Israelis had bought some of their weapons.

Ironically, although the United States has forbidden the importation of Rhodesian chrome, the Soviet Union (self-proclaimed godfather of the "Zimbabwe People's Revolution") has had no qualms about it. The Russian State Trading Corporation, using dummy agents (usually in London and Hong Kong), purchases high-grade Rhodesian chrome through South African middlemen. When the ship (under a flag of convenience, most often Panamanian or Liberian) is at sea, the Russian "agent" then sells the chrome to American purchasers at a nice profit, delivering at the same time a third-country certificate of origin required to get the cargo past American customs. Hence, the net result of the American embargo on Rhodesian chrome has been the same chrome still coming in, but at a vastly increased cost which is, as usual, passed on to the consumer in higher retail prices and added inflation—with the Russians pocketing a considerable profit.

The Bolze house was a handsome split-level of brick and native stone. It was built on and into great granite *monotopa* boulders, for which the district is famous. They had built it twenty years earlier, "when this was all what we call 'bush.'" There is now a quilt work of other, similar homes in what obviously is the prestige neighborhood—with its own public pond-studded park that comprises several hundred acres with walkways and gardens.

The house was surrounded by a twelve-foot-high native-rock wall which is interwoven with the boulders. There is a rich interior garden of shrubs and flowers adjacent to an immaculate teardrop swimming pool. The street outside the wall was softly floodlit that night, but there was no watchman or dog or other sign of exceptional security, other than a stubborn padlock on the ornate French doors to the drawing room from the patio.

Louis's private den sat atop the two largest boulders, the largest of which extended through the ceiling and was specially floodlit from the garden below.

For style and luxury, this home would rival any in the most exclusive American suburb. Yet there was something heavy and alien about its presence here.

Louis's younger son, Simon, was partially deaf and had a speech defect. He had lagged several years behind in school until very recently, when he had suddenly made such progress that everyone—including his teachers—was surprised. Louis was very proud of him and talked in some detail about the various special local programs for handicapped children and how much he and his wife and their friends had learned from their experience with Simon.

When he drove me back to the hotel he invited me to drop by the publishing house the following day. I did so, and we had another long visit. Later, I ordered a number of his volumes for my library.

The next day was a Sunday, and I rose early and took a long walk. Passing Saint Mary's Catholic Church and hearing a choir inside, I decided to go in. The mass was served by eight black youths, and there were perhaps a dozen blacks seated in no particular order throughout the congregation. The sermon was on faith and was built around the verse "Where your treasure is, there will your heart be also." It was preached in that unwavering, matter-of-fact monotone, the British ecclesiastical accent—the voice of ultimate boredom. Still, the congregation was rapt and the offering generous.

That night I had a long talk with Mr. Douglas Shepherd, a retired octogenerian architect. He had served in the Royal Air Force during World War II. I thought how interesting it was that so many Rhodesians had served with the British armed forces. Louis Bolze had been with the South African engineers, attached to the British Eighth Army in North Africa and Italy. Their mission had been to rebuild railroads blown up by the retreating Germans. After the war, Mr. Shepherd had been involved somehow officially (he refused to say exactly) with the old Federation of Northern Rhodesia, Southern Rhodesia, and Nyasaland, which the British had formed in the '50s to pave the way for eventual independence of the three territories as a federal republic. However, it was dissolved in 1962, when Northern Rhodesia (having become Zambia) and Nyasaland (having become Malawi) opted out.

Overhearing Mr. Shepherd's explanation to me of the ill-fated union, a well-dressed gentleman slightly in his cups came over and angrily interrupted him, shouting that the real reason for the dissolution was that "the Rhodesian politicians stole all the federal money," an allusion to allegations heard at the time that the union had been unfairly dominated by the white Southern Rhodesians who had spent common tax money on roads and other projects in present-day Rhodesia to the neglect of the other two countries.

The following morning I reported as directed to the tourist information center where I had been assigned to an official tour of the Black Townships with some British tourists. The tourists didn't show, however, so I went alone with a Mrs. Nadabunda (phonetic), an official tourist office guide.

We toured a vocational school carpentry course first, where some twenty high-school-aged students were at work on tables and chairs under the supervision of a black journeyman. Next we went to an arts-and-crafts training center for "desperate" women. There were separate weaving and crocheting rooms. In the former were several looms; in the latter, 30 women sat on the floor sewing, stitching and crocheting. In one room, baskets were being woven with sisal fiber. There was a pottery shop with two electric kilns operated by remote control with pulleys and a crane/hoist system. The kilns were lifted and moved around the room to various stacks of freshly cast pottery. The young men and women were busily molding the pottery on electric potters' wheels.

In this center was a small Carnegie-sized municipal library, one of five in the township. There seemed to be no censorship of the content, since I found volumes of and by Marx and Marcuse, a biography of Lenin, the thoughts of Mao Tse-tung, and President Kaunda's "Letter to my Children." There were stacks of old *Time* and *Newsweek* magazines and current issues of *The Christian Science Monitor*. A small children's section was spacious and colorfully decorated but sparsely stocked.

The last item on this tour was a visit to the black residential areas. Mrs. Nadabunda explained to me that most of Rhodesia's blacks live not in the urban but in the rural townships in the bush, and that visits to them by Europeans are prohibited except in special circumstances. I was to later observe while traveling overland through some of them that they were little different from those north of the Zambezi.

Mrs. Nadabunda drove me over two hours through neighborhood after neighborhood of monotonous green and grey rows of neatly trimmed yards and fences. Although she drove at my direction (this having been one of the selling points of the tour) I searched in vain for the squalid bidonville shanty town I knew must surely lie beyond the very next neighborhood. Nor was there the usual gaggle of beggars and street urchins, even around the two large markets at which we stopped. The point was made repeatedly that no loafing about or soliciting of alms was permitted.

Throughout the residential areas, hydraulic-compress garbage trucks were at work. Each house had a neatly placed refuse or garbage can which, according to Mrs. Nadabunda, was picked up at least once a week.

At the last market we visited were long, covered stalls of assorted herbs and delicacies. These included many spices, caterpillars, ground (pea)nuts, and chilis (dried red peppers). There was also colorful Indian corn (called "maize").

There was a variety of snuff and chewing tobacco that would have rivaled that of any London tobacco shop. The sweet-smelling snuff is mixed with soda before being wrapped in cylindrical rolls of old newspaper for selling. It is arranged in rows on soap crates according to grade and amount.

Mrs. Nadabunda naturally refused to be drawn into a political discussion, although we were alone. She did, however, take strong exception to my observation that one of the internal leaders, Bishop Muzorewa, appeared to have a strong national following. She was of the Matebele tribe and said that Joshua Nkomo, the leader of one of the factions of the United Front, had a much stronger following in Matebellaland. She favored, she said, a peaceful solution but said that every faction (including the guerrillas) should be included.

That night I ate dinner at a place called Gray's Inn, where the waiters wore the ridiculous red fezzes that are the standard uniform of black servants in swank establishments south of the Zambezi. The wine steward, a very short fellow named Jimmy, brought out a bottle and asked if I had ever tasted that kind before. No, I said, was it Rhodesian? Yes, grapes grown right here. The label read "Rouge Sec (Red Dry) Table Wine 'B' " from Monis Wineries of Bulawayo. He poured a sampler. It had a bitter, acid taste; I smiled and said I was not drinking just then. He understood. Still holding out the bottle as if it were the reason for our continued conversation, he queried me on America and whether I had ever been to New Orleans. Why New Orleans? He had always listened to jazz, he said, knew all the top and not-so-top musicians. Said he saw Duke Ellington once. He'd worked at a hotel in Salisbury until five years ago. "Seen a lot of them there," he said. He preferred Bulawayo—not as much politics, he said.

Of course, civic Bulawayo had another side: the one with the raw hamburger doused with runny ketchup across the table from bigoted, stranger-hating snobs. And the scruff-dusty traveling man soon learns that Rhodesian bars cling desperately to that ubiquitous colonial talisman of civilization, the tie: no tie, no beer. So out I went and bought a nice narrow blue number: with a red and green flower to wear with my bush jacket.

After dinner the last night in "Big B" I had a small glass of brandy at Grandpa's Bar next door, courtesy of E. C. McLarnon, "an old Scotsman," he said, who had graduated from engineering school in Belfast, Northern Ireland, in 1936 and then fought with the British Eighth Army in north Africa. He had come back here and worked 25 years, mostly running switch engines out of the copper mines up in northern Rhodesia and the Congo. The railroad had presented him with a gold Bulova wristwatch when he retired in 1962. He lived alone in a pension, he said. He asked me to write him a letter and let him know how I was doing and what I was seeing; I said that I would.

When I went back by Books of Rhodesia to say goodbye to Louis Bolze I mentioned that I might drive out into the Monotopas to take a look at Cecil Rhodes's grave. Louis looked off and said, as much to himself as to me, "Out there you'll find that the country's fairly empty, desolate. You'll find yourself pretty much alone. Perhaps Sunday would be a better time."

He said that people picnicked out there on Sunday, going out in groups—not really *convoys,* but not unarmed, either.

I did not wait for Sunday, but drove on to Salisbury instead. Although I drove from mid-morning to late afternoon, there was almost no traffic. At one time I drove for 40 miles (before Gwella) and did not see a single other

311

vehicle. Almost everyone, I later learned, takes the plane or train. They rarely drive and never do so alone. There were no convoys operating between Bulawayo and Salisbury.

Salisbury was smart, clean, a kind of little Dallas or San Diego, stacked with a half-dozen 30-story banks and hotels—the people wary, tense, stoic but garrulous, solicitous of strangers, especially Americans. I took a small room at the Courtney Hotel.

Everyone was talking about the dynamiting Saturday of Woolworth's branch store. The explosion had killed eleven people and blinded and mangled many others. The front page of the paper one morning carried pictures of two men who had each lost his wife and two children in the blast. When the news of the Lupane killings was also discussed in a lobby downtown, I mentioned that I had been there only a couple of hours before the shooting. The people just looked at me and shrugged, as if to say, "So what else is new?" The same reaction greeted even the gratuitous mayhem of the Woolworth explosion. Human beings seem to become accustomed to outrage—their own as well as that of their enemies.

I was able to locate a friend, Ann Willis, from Hampshire, England, whom I had met in Formentera the year before. She was working as a receptionist at Wankie Park Lodge, which I had passed on the way south from Victoria Falls. I phoned her, and we had a good visit. Needless to say, there were few guests for her to receive. The park was teeming with guerillas infiltrated from Botswana; Ann's lodge was an armed camp.

Salisbury was much like Bulawayo, with its neat, manicured parks and squares; streets swept, washed, tidy to monotony; terse-lipped, thin-smiling shop ladies, correctly solicitous yet reserved; immaculately dressed, pale-faced professional men exuding that sweet, crafty, aftershaved essence of Gothic unction. Politics was a subject easily stimulated. I repeatedly listened to the repertoire of grievances against the villains Owen, Carter, and Young.

There was, oddly, no visible public segregation. All facilities such as bars, buses, parks, restrooms, cafés, lunchrooms, and tea rooms were legally open to everyone, without entry or seating restrictions. I saw, however, very few blacks venture into the more posh locations. This was a recent phenomenon and, of course, housing remained rigidly segregated. Both the vocational schools (colleges) here and in Bulawayo had a measure of token integration, as did the university. Admission requirements effectively barred most Americans. Over 80 percent of Rhodesia's army was black. Although there were no black officers at the time I was there, a publicly announced plan to train them was being prepared.

In the town mall's sidewalk cafe one morning, I met a young woman who, though South African (of English and Afrikaan parents), was now officially a resident of the new independent black homeland of Transkei. She was in Salisbury, she said, as a summer social worker helping to raise capital for the Rhodesian government's Tribal Investment Bureau and was to pay a visit that very day to the restricted (to whites) homeland village of Mrewa, some 50 miles northeast of the capital. After we'd talked for a while, she said she needed transportation since her car was on the blink. Would I mind driving her out there? She bought some sandwiches and potato salad, and we were on our way.

Mrewa was a half-dozen grocery and general stores and might have been any plantation town in the Mississippi delta. It had been raining lightly, and several score of passengers were waiting to board some rickety old school buses to take them to their homes many miles into the interior.

My friend was to interview the owner of the largest store and solicit his participation in an investment project. She explained that some black shop owners were quite wealthy. This one was probably a millionaire. The proposed project involved both the clearing of new land and the building of housing for its farmers. The project was to be funded from both public as well as private sources.

The wide dirt main street was pocked with puddles. Two black policemen stood under an overhang and surveyed the crowd of bus passengers, keeping a close eye on their sacks and shopping baskets. The policemen were relieved after a quarter-hour by a detail in a Land Rover. The Land Rover returned an hour later, and the policemen in it ordered all the passengers to line up against the wall of the store to be searched. After each one was searched, he or she was permitted to board one of the buses.

I walked over to the Zuvaguru Eating House, the local café, where I ordered hot milk-tea and chatted with a gent who appeared to be the owner. He was talking intermittently with an African truck driver from Salisbury about the village chief who, as well as his second-in-command, had been assassinated by the guerillas just the week before. It would be hard, he said, to find a replacement. I thought it interesting that he was so talkative in my presence, and in English.

The rain picked up while I was there, and each customer who dashed in gave me a stare—not exactly hostile, but rather surprised at my being there.

After a while I drove out to the Mrewa grain storage depot, one of several regional wheat and maize stockpiles where farmers, mostly black, who did not have silos would truck their grain to store it pending sale. Such facilities had recently become prime guerilla targets, and the compound had been fired upon during the attack of the previous week. The place was run by a white manager, the only white in Mrewa, who personally logged in and wrote receipts for each cargo of grain. He had for company a small white poodle. Neither of them seemed too friendly, so I drove back up to the village and made the rounds of the stores, finding them stocked fairly well with hardware, clothing and sundries, but not with a wide variety of food, other than canned meat, rice and spaghetti. Each store was crowded with people who had come by bus to do the week's shopping and locals come in out of the rain.

On the way back to Salisbury my friend explained that all business at Mrewa had to be conducted before dark—after dark, she said, the government could no longer guarantee the safety of the people. It was possible for the guerillas to strike anywhere and virtually at any time, although they rarely hit before 3:00 in the afternoon. She mentioned the killings of the previous Sunday. Even our visit had had to be arranged with the local police.

313

She had reconfirmed with them by phone from her office in Salisbury just before we had left, and they had told her that it was all right to come.

As we left the store where she had been conducting her interview, a young man tried to hitch a ride with us. He appeared to have been drinking. My friend was adamant that I refuse. Guerillas had lately been posing as hitchhikers, she said, then executing the passengers. Once again, there was a long stretch of empty highway, and we passed fewer than a dozen cars the full 50 miles. We were in Salisbury by 5:00. That night we visited the Coq D'or, a notorious but in fact subdued singles bar. The Arizona Steakhouse afterward served a good steak.

The next morning, August 11, 1977, the *Rhodesia Herald* carried the following stories on the front page:

1. The killing by guerillas of a nun and doctor at St. Paul's Mission near Lupane.
2. The funeral of the victims of the previous Saturday's Woolworth bombing.
3. The figures on the increased immigration of professional people and skilled workers from Rhodesia.
4. A mortar attack by guerillas on the Kasungulu border post. According to Rhodesian police, there were no injuries and most of the rounds fell in Botswana.
5. The following statement by Mr. Peter Normand, managing director of the Merchant Bank Rhodesian Acceptances:

   Life has become more difficult because of tightening of sanctions and the continuing recession. Finding buyers for exports is not easy as buyers are reluctant to involve themselves in a Rhodesian situation when a plentiful supply exists elsewhere. There is now a high degree of urgency for a settlement which will result in the lifting of sanctions.

The name of the new nation which is supposed to someday succeed colonial Rhodesia will be Zimbabwe. That is one of the few things that all of the black factions and, belatedly, most of the whites agree on.

Zimbabwe means "house of stones" in Shona and is the name given to the Stonehenge-like ruins of a people that probably lived between the thirteenth and fifteenth centuries east of the present-day town of Fort Victoria, about halfway to the South African border from Salisbury.

Although a lot of wild theories were advanced early on about the ruins being the handiwork of the Phoenecians or the "Lost Tribes of Israel" (someone even said they were King Solomon's Mines), most archaeologists now date their construction in the thirteenth century. This would mean that, indeed, they were built by pre-Muslim Arabs or Negroes—probably the latter and quite likely the remote ancestors of the Shona. Although the Shonas' direct Bantu ancestors arrived in the eighteenth and nineteenth centuries, they doubtless intermarried with earlier tribes who had them-

314

selves intermarried with the Zimbabweans. This theory is not universally accepted, least of all by the local white population. Until recently, local white opinion was inclined to exclude any connection with the Shona by saying either that the site was abandoned or that "the civilization was finally destroyed by invading Bantu Negroes."*

By the prevailing modern view, the place had been a small African village that grew into a mini-nation as a result of the Arab gold trade. By the end of the fifteenth century, its large population had ruined the land, cut the forest for miles around and could no longer live there.

During the last eighty years, the ruins have been both picked clean of artifacts and structurally restored (some would say over-restored) so that while the early explorers found lots of soapstone statues and crumpled walls, the present-day visitor finds half a castle and nothing else. Like any similar structure, the place was occupied by successive squatters, each one claiming primacy and kicking out his predecessor so that a little sample of every period's pots and beads is found there. These are interspersed with scatterings of trinkets traded from the coastal Arabs and Portuguese well up even to the twentieth century. Some of this debris is displayed nearby in a small museum.

What was happening to the artifacts, as well as to the folks who lived there when the white man came, is revealed in this item, reprinted by Huffman from the diary of one Willie Posselt, a hunter who visited Zimbabwe in 1899:

> ... I saw four soapstones, each carved in the image of a bird and facing east; [they] were planted in an old ruin wall within the enclosure. I examined the best specimens of the four "bird" stones, and decided to dig it out; but while doing so, Andizibi and his followers became very excited, and rushing around with their guns and assegais, I fully expected them to attack us. I went on with my work, but told Klass, who had loaded two rifles, to shoot the first man he saw aiming at either of us. By means of a native, who spoke a little Sesuto—as I did not know any Mashona—I was able to tell Andizibi that I had no intention of removing the stone but that I was quite prepared to buy it. This evidently pacified him, for I was not molested further. The next day I returned with some blankets and other articles, and in exchange for these received the one "bird" stone and the round perforated stone. The former was too heavy to be carried, and I was therefore obliged to cut off the pedestal. I stored the remaining stones in a secure place, it being my intention at a future date to return and secure them from the natives.**

The two principal ruins are the acropolis atop the dominant hill (about 300 feet high) and the Great Enclosure, a rock corral containing a 35-foot conical monolith, or tower, to one side and surrounded by a wall some 30

---

*T.N. Huffman, *A Guide to the Great Zimbabwe Ruins* (Salisbury: National Museum and Monuments of Rhodesia, 1976), p. 2.
**Ibid., p. 19.

feet high and from five to fifteen feet thick. The acropolis and the Great Enclosure were once connected by a quarter-mile of low wall and masonry—now scattered—which was the main village. The acropolis is accessible through a maze of connecting walls and narrow passageways.

An idea of how much labor was involved is gleaned from the fact that the "great outer wall" of the enclosure alone contains "an estimated 900,000 blocks of stone—the equivalent of two and one-half million bricks or 45 normal-sized houses."*

The scarcity of rocks in the vicinity suggests that those used in the construction of Zimbabwe came from the immediate area. The acropolis is ideal from a military standpoint—being inaccessible to an invader except one man at a time up through the warren of narrow passageways. The corral-like enclosure was probably a storeroom or harem or simply the dwelling place of royals of lesser rank. The tower has forever remained a mystery. Phallic symbol, fake or ceremonial grain silo—such have been ventured as explanations. The most simple explanation is that it was a watchtower and the base for a signal fire for communication with those on the acropolis, as well as sentinel stations further away. Whatever it was, the tower remains a fitting symbol of Zimbabwe as well as the enigma of black Africa: resilient, majestic, aloof—and unknowable by the white man.

One appreciates even more fully the military planning of its builders when it is realized that the acropolis was surrounded by a marsh until the 1950s, when it was drained to build a golf course. The only way across the moat was a narrow stone causeway which led to a formidable gatehouse, protected by spearmen stationed on the lower ramparts of the acropolis and in the maze of passageways.

A low, soupy fog settled over the ruins during the two days I was there. The fog accentuated the atmosphere of mystery and enabled me to take some unusual black and white photographs.

I had driven to Fort Victoria alone, there being no convoy for that stretch of the road to Beit Bridge on the South African border. At Enkeldoorn I picked up two hitchhikers: Ron Wright, an Australian, and his British friend, Peter Smith-Ainsley. They were draftsmen with an engineering firm in Salisbury and were on a weekend to the ruins. Ron had been there before and had spent time in some of the nearby townships. He said that the guerillas based in Mozambique had stepped up their raids into the Shona areas southeast of Zimbabwe. They had struck several days previously at a village called Zoka. Everyone expected them to try to attack the ruins sooner or later because of the symbol Zimbabwe held for their cause. That they had not yet done so was perhaps due to the large contingent of troops kept at Fort Victoria.

At Fort Victoria, we needed to purchase additional gasoline-ration tickets from the local police station. I had been given 225 of these at Kasungulu, but they had not gone far since I needed one for every liter

---

*Ibid., p. 29.

purchased.

The ruins were about fifteen kilometers from town. Just above them was a modern restaurant with some modest cabins called the Zimbabwe Ruins Hotel (ten dollars for bed and breakfast). The room was unheated, and it became quite cold at night in the drizzly weather. The lounge was not much warmer. I wore a wool sweater and jacket even while eating.

In the lounge watching television before dinner was a young Israeli mechanic who had been working for a garage in Salisbury for three years. Evidently because of his nationality, he had been exempted from the compulsory military service law which conscripts all aliens residing here longer than two years. This causes most British and Australians to leave just before their time is up. A few years ago they used to go out for a few weeks and then come back. The rules have been recently changed, however, to close this loophole.

Also in the lounge was a pleasant Italian couple, about 60 years old, who had just returned from a vacation in Argentina. They had come to Salisbury after the war and he had become a toolmaker with Rhodesia Airway. He had done well, he said, and planned to stay on, "whatever you [the U.S. and Britain] do to us."

Breakfast next morning was a platter of silver-dollar-sized pancakes, kidneys, bacon, red link sausage, ham-and-onion omelets, scones (big Scottish biscuits) and several kinds of fresh jam and preserves. It was a real spread.

There were three busloads of African tourists at a lodge just below the ruins. Although they drove up for a look at the ruins hotel, no blacks stayed there. I was told, however, that the facility is officially desegregated and that Africans do stay there from time to time.

Unlike the scene at Victoria Falls two weeks previously there was no lightheartedness among the 90 drivers of the gathering convoy at Fort Vic the next morning. A driver and his family had been ambushed and killed the previous afternoon, and the word was that the guerillas now intended to attack the route daily. Almost every car had its own rifle or shotgun. Some had pistols.

"The best deterrent," we were told by a sergeant, "is the *kaffir* factor." That meant the conspicuous display of any fire power would dissuade any guerillas sitting in ambush from firing. Not having a passenger or a firearm, I made both from an old navy seabag and a plastic bucket, the handle of which came down under the "chin" of the upright seabag like a soldier's helmet. Next I stuck the butt of an old ceremonial Kikuyu witch doctor's cane I had brought from Nairobi as a souvenir into the loop handle of the upright seabag and let the barrel of the cane protrude through the half-lowered window. Word of my scarecrow quickly spread, and people from cars parked a good distance away came up and inspected it approvingly and with a good deal of laughter.

Soon the convoy leader blew on his whistle and called for "all drivers and shooters" to assemble up at the lead truck. This was another pickup mounted with one of those cylinders from which protruded a .50-caliber machine gun. The helmeted head of the gunner was barely visible. As at

Victoria Falls, we were instructed that the convoy would travel at 90 kilometers per hour; if a driver could not keep up he would have to fall behind; if he had to stop because of mechanical trouble or for any other reason, he was to pull off onto the left shoulder and the rear guard would help him. There would be a tow truck, if necessary. Anyone with a firearm was reminded to keep the breech empty: "If anything happens, you'll have plenty of time to load." Finally, if there were an ambush, "Keep driving—no matter what you see or who's hurt; don't stop as long as you can keep moving."

There was a somewhat lighter mood as we returned to our cars and began to peel out behind the lead truck. I noticed that the jeep station wagon in front of me had Minnesota license tags: only the third car I had seen since Algiers with U.S. tags. There was an accordion effect at first, but gradually we reached 90 kilometers per hour and stayed there. The flat, low country was interrupted occasionally by a river or creek, and the guards on the bridge waved heartily at us. We made the 200 kilometers—without an ambush—to the Lion and Elephant Motel at Bubye Junction in just over two hours and fifteen minutes. Tea and coffee were ready, and African waiters lunged at us with trays of dry ham and cheese sandwiches. Convoys were good business for the L and E.

Just as I bit into a sandwich, I was joined by a stout, somewhat over-weight man, about 38 years old, wearing pressed Rhodesian army khakis. "Say, that's you in the Land Cruiser with the Arkansas tags, isn't it?" It was the Minnesotan I had seen in the station wagon—he was from Duluth. He had driven down here to pick up a gun collection he had shipped over from the states. It had just arrived from South Africa but had been impounded by Rhodesian customs. He would have to show them his special permit to bring it in.

His wife had told him he had too many guns and he'd have to choose between them and her. "I tried to turn it [the guns] into a business, but it didn't work," he said. "So, I chose the guns and came to Rhodesia. It's like the States was 25 years ago, free and open."

When I said he must have been in 'Nam, he said, "No, I missed it. I was too old. Missed Korea too. They said I had a bad back."

He was a bigger guy than I had first realized. Strapping was not exactly the right word, but he was really big—like he could have been a linebacker once but hadn't been in shape for quite a while. He talked in quick, short phrases in a deep voice. He'd been in Rhodesia 90 days—in the army for three weeks. The corporal stripes weren't his, he said, but they were on the only shirts big enough for him. "You going to stay in Rhodesia?" he asked. When I hesitated as if to say, "That's an idea," he said, "You have a skill, don't you? What's your skill?"

When I told him I was a lawyer he frowned and drew back a little and said, "Well, I don't know about that. . . ." I could tell he didn't particularly like lawyers.

The lead gunner blew three long blasts on his horn and we were away. The remaining 50 miles to the border were uneventful. I cleared customs and immigration, and at 4:00 p.m., August 14, 1977, crossed the Limpopo

River into the Republic of South Africa.

The bridge was being repaired, and traffic was forced into a single lane. The lane was covered at both ends by sandbagged bunkers bristling with machine guns. Two Rhodesian soldiers in jungle utilities and a blond South African trooper in dark bush khakis stood chatting and smoking at midspan beneath a faded bronze medallion of Cecil Rhodes.

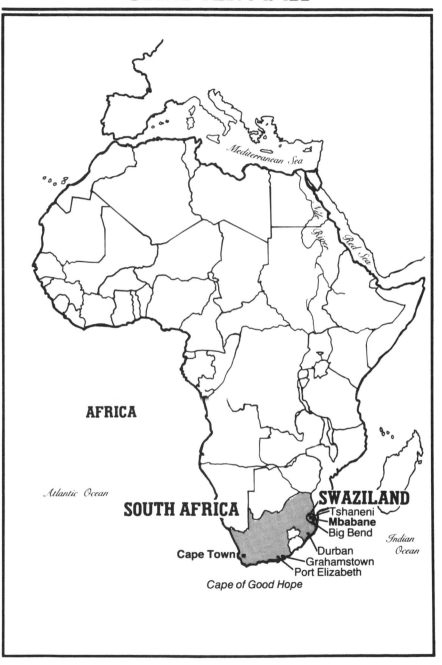

CHAPTER XXII

The first thing one notices when entering South Africa are the separate queues for blacks and whites at customs and immigration. These are marked by signs which read "Blanc-White" and "Non Blanc-Non White." The reason they don't just say "Black" is that Asians must also line up with the blacks unless special facilities are available to serve their particular "class," which is usually not the case.

I was made to purchase South African car insurance and to make proof of my solvency. I was asked whether I had enough to ship the car and still live for the month I'd said I was spending there. I was admitted only after I named the specific bank in Cape Town to which I had ordered another $1,000 wired from my Little Rock bank account. I also told the officers—who were stiff and formal, not relaxed like the Rhodesians—that I was shipping the Toyota C.O.D. to New Orleans.

I spent the night at the class "C" Hotel Louis Trichard in the center of the town by that name. A ten-member family of Rhodesian asbestos mine owners (each son managed one of the family's three mines) were gathered around the fireplace in the large, otherwise empty, dining room, and at their warm invitation, I joined them.

They spoke in Afrikaans except when speaking directly to me. They had immigrated to Rhodesia from the Transvaal in the 1940s. They had just returned from Brazil, where they had for three weeks been the guests of some local miners. The official purpose of their trip was to consult with a Brazilian firm, but the real reason was to investigate the prospects for emigration.

They had been very impressed with Brazil, the old man in particular. "One people, many races," he kept saying. The father and mother, now grandparents, and their three sons and their wives—all were considering moving to Brazil, according to the old patriarch. They did not believe that even a moderate Rhodesian government could resist black political pressure to expropriate most private capital. Although the conversation was dominated by The Problem, the assets of Brazil ran such a close second that I knew they had already decided to emigrate and that they would do so comfortably.

The head waiter's name was Joe Sadiki. He stood straight and reserved against a column a good distance from the table. He commanded the service with a soft voice and an easy gesture. Yet his expression, almost of contempt, never changed. The next morning before I left, I had him pose for a photograph before the hotel.

My route south was through the eastern Transvaal. In one little town after the other I had the same feeling that I could have been back in the southern or midwestern United States. There were scores of people bustling along paved streets full of shops and boutiques and supermarkets. It seemed as if I could have stopped at any one of them and seen someone I knew or who might know someone I knew. Then passing out into the open country, the veld, there was another world: vast semi-desert interrupted only occasionally by pineapple and banana plantations, all leading toward the mountains of the Transvaal.

I reached the Blyde River and climbed along its canyon for many miles, passing as I did some of the most dramatic mountain scenery anywhere. At one point I looked back through a maze of rocks rising out of the gorge to the plains below. The mountain was tilted just enough forward so that against the plains far below, I had the illusion of a double horizon.

The youngest asbestos miner had spoken of a mountain hamlet, an all-but-abandoned mining town called Pilgrim's Rest, where there was a cheap pension with good home cooking. The way he liked to eat, I figured it was worth a stop. So just after dark, after a twenty-minute climb from Graskop, I drove down into the village, and there I spent some of my happiest days since Paris.

Gold made Pilgrim's Rest a boom town in the late 1880s and '90s. At its peak, around 1920, it had a population of over 10,000. Today it is down to about 350. That includes maybe 75 old-timers, many of them retired, and maybe that many newcomers who work at the hotel, a few small craft shops, and the Transvaal Provincial Authority, which had purchased virtually the whole town and planned to restore it as a tourist attraction after the fashion of Central City, Colorado. So far, nothing much has happened because of a lack of further funds. The pleasant result is that the miners' houses still look like miners' houses. At the north edge of town is the African, or nonwhite, compound, a neatly arranged village of some two-score mud houses where the African workers live.

The village is 30 miles as the crow flies from Kruger National Park, southern Africa's richest game preserve. It lies in a central valley of the eastern Transvaal mountains, which sometimes get a foot or two of snow on the higher slopes—as they did my last day. Mount Anderson, at 12,285 feet, the highest point in southern Africa, rises just to the south between Pilgrim's Rest and Sabie, the region's sawmill town. The snow there was so deep that the pass on the road to Johannesburg was closed.

At the village center was the Royal Hotel. Its dining room was the one mentioned by the asbestos miner, and the food was, as he had said, superb. Out on a ridge northwest of town were three well-kept turn-of-the-century miners' houses, somewhat larger than the usual cabins, which were rented to tourists. Since it was winter, the off season, I was able to get one cheap, at eight dollars per day. It had two bedrooms, a large living room with a fireplace and a very large kitchen containing an old woodburning stove.

The hotel bar is famous, having been a mission chapel at LM (local jargon for the Mozambique port of Lourenco Marques). It was dismantled board by board and brought up here by the first owner back in the '20s. There is a handsome paneled backbar with a wide selection of African brew, imported whiskey, and Cape wine, which is reputed by many to be the best in the world, excluding those of France.

Although several dirt tracks carved a few hundred feet up the mountain to dead ends, there was only one street: the highway that ran over to Graskop, a seedy little railhead ten miles over the ridge. The blacktop ended just north of town and a dirt road carried on into the pine forest. Gold miners and timber companies had strip cut the woods early in the century. Present-day trees had been planted as a result of commercial and government restoration, which was apparent from their alignment in neat rows.

My first night at the "church" bar in Pilgrim's, I met a leather craftsman named Dennis. Being an outsider, he had forced himself to learn about the town. Through Dennis I met Georgy, another outsider, but of longer residence, who became my very dear friend and served as my unofficial hostess and source of invaluable local lore and color. It was she who introduced me to Christian Marcus, prospector, fisherman, storyteller, sage.

Christian Marcus sat on his front porch holding court and making fishing flies: he was reminiscing of his childhood, having been born here, in this very house, in 1910. He had been a prospector almost all his life. Still had two good claims, although "I have to slip away from my wife to work 'em."

He talked of The Problem, offering his opinion of the various politicians. What he really liked, though, was fishing. He told me the story about a big trout he'd caught—or almost caught—down in the Blyde River one day on one of his homemade flies. He had seen "the old rascal" for years down there but never able to get him to so much as nibble. He had taken to fashioning different flies just for him, but none of them ever worked. Once, the fish had swum over (he could see him in the deep pool) and nibbled at a white fly but after a few seconds he darted off: nothing satisfied him. "He was a big 'un, too—twenty-five inches long." Mr. Marcus reckoned he weighed 23 pounds. I told him I had heard of trout at ten, twelve pounds but rarely bigger. "Twenty-three pound," he repeated.

This one afternoon he'd gone down to the river and walked his way slowly up to the pool where the "big 'un" lived. "It was the white fly, I think," he said. The very first cast there was a strike. "I could tell when the line went deep and heavy it was him," he said. "The little ones just get up on the water and dance and splash around. The big ones go deep." Then he remembered that he had forgotten to follow his customary practice of putting the net into the water before casting.

He must have played the fish for half an hour—he wasn't sure—but "it sure was a heck of a fight." When he had finally brought it near the bank, he tried to slip the net in slowly, but it startled the fish. The trout broke away and dived again into the depths of the pool, where it wrapped itself around some snags.

"I could see him down there, as clear as day," he said. "I had my shirt and pants off and I was just about to dive in when the line snapped. I guess it just wasn't my day."

Still, he said, he wasn't discouraged. Someday he would hook him again. Mrs. Marcus, who had joined us, brought out a box of his flies and he showed me how he made them with hatpins, chicken and partridge feathers.

He had spent World War II at Beberia Island in Somalia. "Spent most of my time fishing," he said. He had fished off of the fantail of the yacht the army had requisitioned to take the troops up there. They had called at Mombasa but the men weren't allowed ashore, so he had missed Kenya.

Mrs. Marcus moved her chair closer to us. Still, she did not talk except to serve the tea. It was now ready, and she poured us each a cup. There were biscuits—the dry, light and crunchy crumpets that quickly become soggy when dunked in the tea—on the silver tray under the napkin, which I noticed was of finely embroidered soft linen, slightly yellowed. "I brought it with me from the Free State," she said of the service when I complimented it.

"He was one of my best friends," Mr. Marcus said of her first husband. "When we were together all those years I never thought I'd wind up marryin' his widow." (She smiled at this.)

The claims in the valley were the richest in the country, he said, getting up to 30 ounces of gold for one ton of ore. Freelance panning, however, is not legal—you have to have a registered claim, and the government tightly regulates those. It hadn't always been that way, though, he said. Time was when the valley was full of swindlers and claim jumpers. He began talking about old times and telling stories:

In about 1910 two Scotsmen got into it over a local lassie—a barmaid at the saloon where the church is now. The combatants challenged each other to a duel. The seconds secretly arranged to pare the lead off all the rounds so that both rifles were loaded with blanks. When they fired, one of the seconds broke a goat's bladder full of blood over his man's head. The blood-sodden victim passed out, and the "victor" was told, "You killed him, you better run!" He did, and hid out in the mountains for more than a month before somebody could find him and tell him it was all a joke.

Then there were the sluice robbers, who caused lots of trouble. They'd slip up at night and scrape off the gold sediment that a miner hadn't cleaned off his sluice. This one particular thief was caught red-handed one night. They shaved half his head and half his beard and railed him out of town, after telling him they'd kill him if he ever came back. Well, two days later somebody saw him slipping up over the hill. Christian pointed out back of the house. "One of them takes a rifle and shoots him clean through the head, and he falls down just there—by the church, lying crossways." They buried him as he fell, perpendicular to the other graves, and put up a marker: "Robber's Grave." (Later, I walked up behind the church and, sure enough, found the grave just as Mr. Marcus had said. There was a tombstone with no name, just

"Robber's Grave.")

Judging by the tombstones, most of the people buried up there had been born in Wales and Scotland. One had been born in Tasmania, of all places. The town history, written by a former postmaster, says there are also some Americans buried in the cemetery.

And Pilgrim's Rest had its share of ghosts. A Mr. Paine, it seems, cut his throat in a suicide attempt. Some neighbors found him barely alive and rushed him to the old hospital up over the mountain, where the Provincial Authority office is now. They covered him with a blanket to keep him warm and when they arrived with the stretcher and pulled off the blanket, they found he had opened the wound even further and finished the job.

A year later to the day, people began seeing a black dog come down the road and go to the house where this old man lived. Horses would balk and shy away from it. One youngster claimed he saw the dog turn into a man without a head but nobody believed him. Still, a lot of people had seen the dog. Just the year before, the fellow who lived across the street from the house asked Mr. Marcus if a man had died there with his throat cut. Mr. Marcus said yes. The gent said he thought so. He then described how he had seen a figure in a white robe, more like a nightgown, walk up the street late one night with a lantern shining—a really beautiful old-fashioned lantern, like they'd used back around 1900. He watched this robed specter walk right up to the old Paine house and start to go in. He woke up his roommate and they crossed the house toward the light in the back room, the bedroom where they had found old man Paine. When the two men saw the figure just standing there, with the candle held high over its head, one of them cleared his throat as one might, politely, to announce his presence. Whereupon the figure turned abruptly and with a sweep of its right hand made a slashing gesture under the chin as one does to signify cutting the throat. At that moment the lantern went out. When they finally groped their way back to the porch, the specter had disappeared, but on the porch was a frightening black dog that growled at them, baring its teeth. They ran out the back, and when they returned with a light there was no sign the house had been entered and the dog had gone.

Ginger Bates ran the town's bottle shop. He sold just about every brand of good—and not so good—potion from Chivas Regal to demon rum. Ginger's name came from his now-almost-vanished red hair and his gingerly complexion. Almost every morning when I'd walk up through the village, there Ginger would be chatting away with one of his early customers, perhaps a tourist from the Royal Hotel, but as often as not, a Pilgrim's African. He served his African patrons over a counter in a separate room that opened onto the street just next door. The counter was really a continuation of the one in the white store. A sign over the white entrance read, "Europeans only."

Ginger had the reputation as the friendliest man in town, and he would've got on right away with any "good ole boys" who might have shown up. He had been born in Johannesburg and come up to Pilgrim's in

1939. Then came the war. He enlisted and was sent, of all places, to Madagascar, "to keep the Japs from using it as a submarine base." He then followed most of his fellows to northern Africa and on into Italy with the British. He came home in 1945 and went to work up in the copper belt (southeast Zaire and western Zambia) as a surveyor.

What he liked most was riding the railroads. "No better rail system anywhere then," he said. "Why, we could ship copper all the way to Lobito [in Angola] or to Beira [Mozambique]. Now there's only the one line [the one across the bridge at Victoria Falls] and they can barely run that one with our help—or the help of the Rhodesians." He became very upset when he talked about the way the railroad had run down.

Irene had lived golden days in southern California and Fort Lauderdale, resulting in three beautiful daughters: Leila, seven; and Eve and Dawn, six-year-old twins. She'd left her last lover, a self-styled yacht bum in Florida, five years back and come home with the kids. Leila's father was black, and when she'd shown up last year at the elementary school in Graskop there had been quite a row. But Irene "just doubled up and barged on through," and an exception was made for Leila. She was, after all (according to one school board member), "an American citizen, and anyway, her little twin sisters are white."

They had lived in a series of prospector cabins and TPA housing and had just moved up to a happy blue house with a high porch only a short walk from the Pottery Shop where Irene worked. The twins spent most of the day there with her while she painted and managed the inventory of local crafts and art, including a number of cheerful paintings by Cheryl Bert, the shop's attractive owner and the wife of the town druggist.

Irene occasionally did caricatures, and when I saw her work, I asked her to do one for me.

In addition to leatherwork, Dennis did etchings and copper crafting at the village smithy. When I met him, he was carving the village logo (profiles of two brawling prospectors) on the big copper keys of the Royal Hotel.

He'd come up from Johannesburg ten months back to escape the "heavy scene" there. His parents and friends had criticized him relentlessly for his bohemian life. He had lived for a year in a farming commune prior to coming here and had not corresponded with his family in many months.

He was perhaps the closest to a member of the counterculture that I found in South Africa. His poetry, mostly unpublished, reflected the disenchantment and naïveté of his American counterparts. His immense sensitivity to the poverty and mistreatment of Africans naturally had not endeared him to the local establishment. Yet even his independence in attempting a personal solution to The Problem was complicated by his awareness of the enormous cultural differences involved. He was not optimistic: he foresaw as the only bloodless solution a republic of independent black and white states. I thought to myself that if this intelligent, sensitive person had such difficulty in finding his own solution to The Problem, how much more difficult it must be for other South Africans to do so.

Compared to the press in Black and Arab Africa, the South African press enjoyed relatively broad freedom. Criticism of the government and individual ministers was sometimes bitter and prolonged. Disputes between the ruling Nationalist Party members were printed as well as statements by the opposition.

Strictly prohibited was any mention of or quotation from persons or political parties who had been banned. At the time I was there, this included some 1,000 whites and blacks, among whom was the late poet and political activist, Steve Biko. He was later murdered by the police while I was in Port Elizabeth. However, the details of Biko's death, the result of beatings and lack of medical attention, were thoroughly reported by the *Rand Daily Mail*, which persistently criticized the police as well as the Minister of Justice who attempted to whitewash the incident.

World criticism of apartheid was printed regularly, as well as texts of United Nations speeches indicting the South African government and calling for rebellion to overthrow it. But similar statements by banned South Africans were censored.

The World—"our own, our only paper," as it was called—was, in August of 1977, the country's only African daily. Its running lead stories included the Soweto* riots and the government's closing of some 40 schools there. A typical issue, that of August 18, carried these items together with the report of the sentencing of Paul Lanya, 28, for terrorism. He was given 30 years at hard labor (on extenuating circumstances) instead of death. There was a photograph of his wife and friends, several of whom were giving the clenched-fist black-power salute. In another story, a teenager who had been kidnapped and carried into Angola by SWAPO** guerillas had lived to tell about it. His sister, also kidnapped, was still a hostage.

The so-called "popular" press is typified by the *Star News*, a Johannesburg paper which thrives on murders, rapes and other sensational unpleasantness. Court news and dockets that one normally finds discreetly reported in the back page of a Western metropolitan paper receive conspicuous *Star News* coverage in the manner of the *National Enquirer* in the United States or *Evening Standard* in Britain. As in its tabloid counterparts, few facts are given of any event beyond the immediate gory details.

---

*The all-black Johannesburg suburb, which is the base of operations of various guerillas and activist groups operating clandestinely in the country. Their covers are frequently blown, and they are arrested and their caches of arms and pamphlets seized. The frequency and accuracy of these raids is indicative of the power and efficiency of the Bureau of State Security (BOSS), the ubiquitous secret police that has the reputation of turning tough revolutionaries into babbling informants.

**South West African Peoples Organization. This standard guerilla practice of kidnapping youngsters from schools and missions for training in the host country as insurgents is used successfully by both Rhodesian guerilla movements.

Racism runs a close second to crime in the *Star News,* which puts heavy emphasis on terrorism and governmental incompetence. Stories of graft and corruption in Black Africa are a daily staple. The annual meeting of the chiefs of state of the Organization of African Unity in the Gabon several months before was receiving wide coverage.* However, another issue of the *Star* carried a *Los Angeles Times* copyrighted article on Kenya's relatively smooth and prosperous transition to majority rule.

Phyllis Patterson ran the Print Shop, a health-food store next to Irene's new house. I selected a jar of blackstrap molasses from her cornucopia. I had never seen so many jars and tins of herbal goodness. This business was also owned by the Berts, whose drugstore was doing well, also.

Phyllis had drifted around Europe in the late '60s and was a veteran of the 1968 Paris street "revolution." The following year, she had taken a near miss by a tear-gas canister in the LSE London riots. She then met an American named Preston who smuggled her into Morocco in a sailboat.

Plucky and feisty, she taught yoga once a week at Sabie. When not meditating, Phyllis supervised the village from her perch at the top of the town. She did not hesitate to offer advice when she deemed it necessary.

Phyllis and Mike, her husband, a ruddy, bearded lumberjack of a fellow, lived in a modern forester's house twenty miles into the woods. They invited me to spend the night, and Mike's superintendent and his wife came over to visit. Although they were the only neighbors for miles and the men worked together every day, it was the first time they had visited socially in some months.

The next morning Mike drove me in his Toyota pickup on his morning inspection, during which we visited several logging crews on site. The first of these was composed of a dozen Africans who were pulling previously felled logs up a hillside with a cable run by a John Deere tractor. Two men would follow the end of the cable guy down the hill until it came to a log. They would then chain the log to the device and signal the operator, who would retrieve it, moving the cable along a thicker, stationary one. Other men waited in shifts at the top to stack the logs. Another crew was loading logs onto a truck from such a stack with a forklift. When some of them would fall off the stack, three men on the ground would retrieve them.

We drove to the boundary of the company land and the national forest. It was easy to tell where the government's land began since its trees no longer grew in neatly planted rows. Just over the fence was a 300-foot cliff over which trickled the headwaters of the Blyde—the river whose canyon, just 40 miles below, forms the magnificent gorge up which I had driven.

---

*Among item's prominently reported: the flying in of 50 Rolls Royces which went unused because their chauffeurs disappeared with them; the spoilage of food which had to be replaced with supplies from Rhodesia and South Africa; the alleged $500 million cost of the meeting.

Georgy Schoeman's little house sat high on the hill about 200 yards down from the Tea Room restaurant she managed. Georgy had been in Pilgrim's a year and was about ready to move on. She'd done a lot of reading, she said, and a lot of thinking. She was one of those tall, golden women for whom South Africa is famous. I was to see them more frequently as I approached the Cape.

Her father, a geologist, was German in origin; her mother, colonial British. Her mother had been born in Burma, but her family returned to England during the war, where she became a map-room spotter of enemy aircraft for the RAF. After the war, she joined her brother and his family in Kenya. They left Kenya during the Mau Mau rebellion.

Georgy's house was a miniature museum of antique chairs, clocks, and bric-a-brac from the 1890s. It was one of the oldest houses in town and sat by itself. It had a wide front porch from which you could see beyond the strip-mined gulch that cut below the village, on to green fields and pine forest. At the top of the opposite ridge was a prospector's cabin, whose ribbon of grey smoke trailed constantly into the blue Transvaal sky. There wasn't much traffic down this way since the blacktop ended a quarter of a mile further on. Beyond that was only the logging road out toward the Pattersons'. Phyllis said that if you followed the road far enough and were able to pick your way through its maze of interconnecting trails, you'd eventually hit the Johannesburg highway.

Georgy and I would sit on her porch each evening and watch the day go down while we drank her special hot spiced tea. Georgy was a sister spirit and a great companion.

I went with Phyllis to a flower show in Sabie and there met Ian Marx. Ian lived with his daughter, Cindy, in an old house above the sawmill. He was a geologist with Placid Oil Company of South Africa, a subsidiary of Placid Oil of Dallas, and was then engaged in tying up as many gold mining claims and leases as possible. The company, owned by the family of the late H.L. Hunt, was seeking to reopen some dormant gold mines in the region. Although most of the larger mines had long been closed or abandoned, they had recently become profitable again because of modern extraction methods, bulk shipping, and skyrocketing prices for bullion. Whereas the gold had once been removed from the ore here (with 40 percent being lost in cooking off the sulfur), it was now economical to ship the unrefined ore to the buyer in the United States or Europe. The buyer would then refine it himself, using sophisticated techniques which saved most of the gold itself, together with a much greater quantity of by-product, such as copper. The Hunts, Ian said, felt certain that the price of gold would exceed $500 an ounce by 1980, which, of course it did.

Visiting Ian was his octogenarian mother-in-law from Salisbury, Mrs. Mabel Renaud. Her ceaseless tales of life in the Congo rain forests early in the century were classics of the age of the Empire. For a decade she and her husband had shipped and sold sundries to the workers in the copper mines. They'd run a series of small stores on both sides of the present Zaire-Zambia border near Lake Mweru. Plying the Luapula River, they bought fish from the natives who dried and smoked them on the shores of the lake. When the fish had dried two or three days in the sun, they would be stacked in a thatched smokehouse for a week's smoking, after which they were shipped by steam barge to Kilwa or Kasanga for distribution to the mine and railway workers.

Once their old paddlewheeler had sunk with boxes of gears and thousands of pounds' worth of heavy equipment. The natives located the wreck, however, and raised it. The entire cargo (and the Renaud's fledgling business) was saved. "I could tell they had found it when I heard them singing as they rowed towards us from across the lake," Mrs. Renaud said. "I'll never forget it."

The river was full of hippos, and many times Mrs. Renaud had had to be carried across a stream by the porters. "I was terrified one would eat me," she said. "I never got used to them."

Her daughter, Ian's wife and Cindy's mother, was in the Rhodesian police reserve in Salisbury. Cindy took out her photo album and showed us pictures of her mother's military training.

Ian prided himself on his unusual friends and the following morning took me to see John Carstairs and Gale Pulliam, who lived in the national forest about 20 miles south of Sabie. After meandering for an hour on back-country rut roads, we suddenly came to what looked like a barn—an 80-foot-long shed. A troop of yelping mongrels surged to greet us. Up the hill behind them, from a stovepipe shack, emerged a tanned and beautiful couple who waved and smiled down at us. The barking abated and we climbed up past all the wagging tails.

Carstairs was a jack-of-all trades: carpenter, welder, lumberjack and geologist. He held no degree, having dropped out of college his senior year, but it soon became apparent that, for him, school had been a waste of time.

In the shed below, we quickly learned, was the *Lisa*, a 50-foot steel-hulled yacht which would, they hoped, soon carry them around the world. John had begun building it seven years ago on a hull purchased from a fellow in Johannesburg who had given up sailing. He and Gale had been working on it together for over three years. Another year and it would be ready for the sea.

Lighting in the barn, as well as in the cabin, was provided by bulbs wired to an old automobile generator which was powered by a giant water wheel retrieved from an abandoned gold mine nearby. John straw-bossed five or six claims for a local company. "We're not getting rich," John said, "but we're making enough money to get us to the day when we finally sail."

Gale left us momentarily to fetch the day's washing from a 50-gallon drum which was turned by a machine belt attached to the water wheel. A spring trickled over the wheel's blades just fast enough to keep the entire apparatus in constant motion. "All she has to add is a half-dozen pine knots for agitators, and we've got the world's cheapest washing machine," John said. Returning with the wash, Gale produced some fresh-baked bread and a jar of elderberry jam, which we washed down with generous glasses of home-brewed ginger beer.

Ian had to get back to Sabie early, so John and Gale offered to put me up that night in a miniature house trailer recently purchased from a spiritualist prospector who had supposed his visions to be leading him to "a nugget as big as a pig's head." I soon fell asleep to the lulling whack/whack/whack of the water wheel.

Although Kruger is the game park outside East Africa most noted for its animals, I did not have any unusual encounters. There were assorted elephants, gazelle, eland and some rather scrawny wildebeest. I did run into a troop of rambunctious baboons, who were on a mesa which overlooked the park about halfway to Lower Sabie from the main gate. One of their number sat watch in the fork of a tall snag. When he saw me stop beneath it he attempted to descend, whereupon the snag collapsed, bringing him down with it. Overcoming his momentary loss of composure, he came over to panhandle. He reached up and when I didn't respond he jumped onto the hood as if to prevent my continuing until I had paid his toll. I tossed a crust of bread onto the ground, and that momentarily diverted him. But when I started the engine he remounted the hood and grabbed the windshield wipers. It was not until I had reached 20 mph that he jumped off, having in the meantime startled an oncoming car full of elderly ladies.

I soon arrived at Komatipoort without incident and drove out to look at the Mozambique border. From the border post, I could see the trains at Ressano-Garcia. The South African engineers ran several trains daily between there and Lourenco Marques (now Maputo). In addition to running the railroads, South Africans also managed the port there, under contract to the Mozambique government. Some 10,000 Mozambique citizens work in South Africa and cross back and forth regularly with special permits.

I drove on to Tshaneni, the northernmost town in Swaziland. The road turned to dirt at the border, and it was difficult to find the town in the dark without road signs. A maze of unmarked dirt roads led in all directions. Finally I found a road crew who gave me directions. I checked in at the Impala Arms, a hotel regionally famous (for its good, cheap dining room) and run by Don Wilkinson. I noticed there that I had picked up another flat tire, the second of the trip. I changed it the following morning after a hearty English breakfast.

Swaziland is a 17,000-square-mile kingdom of a half-million inhabitants. Inhabited exclusively by the Swazi (who fled there in the eighteenth century to escape the persecutions of the Zulu) it has a homogeneity rare in Black Africa. The British had prevented the Republic of South Africa from annexing it, and, in 1968, granted its independence. The king of Swaziland is Sobhuza II, and his official portrait, in the regalia of a Swazi warrior chieftain, is more impressive than that of any chief of state. He has proved a nimble diplomat—balancing his dependency upon South Africa with political overtures to Black Africa through Mozambique, with which the kingdom shares a 100-kilometer frontier. A railroad runs from Mbabane and Manzini to Maputo. Like their Mozambique cousins, many Swazis work in

332

An overly curious baboon becomes an unexpected hitchhiker. Kruger Park, South Africa.

South African mines. The number so employed in 1976-1977 was some 40,000.

The only paved road in the country is between Mbabane and Manzini. Its dangerous hills were choked with traffic and frequent white crosses commemorated the mayhem. One curve had had twenty people killed in separate crashes. Many of the vehicles carried South Africans on their way to weekends at the Holiday Inn-Swazi casino complex just east of Mbabane.

I had been told to check with the British consulate in Mbabane to see if I needed another visa to re-enter South Africa. (For some reason, the South African mission was closed.) The desk officer told me that my first visa was still good. On the way back I stopped at the Swazi Inn and Casino. I found it to be another of those great plastic domes of white opulence in the midst of African poverty. Of course, the argument is the usual one that foreign investment of any kind benefits the natives. Maybe it does, but it was hard to see how Swazi dirt farmers were profiting from the gambling.

Before 8:00 p.m., customers were allowed to enter the casino without a tie. Bush jackets and muddy jungle boots, however, were frowned upon, which was why I got the hard stares from the toughs at the door. An elegant Swazi cashier disdainfully sold me twenty one-rand chips for the last change I had, except for $500 in traveler's checks. I figured I needed 200 rand to make the Cape.

The roulette table was surrounded by four thin, milk-faced boy-men in dark suits. They reminded me of sharks. Their cold fish eyes drilled me, then glanced at one another in a kind of sinister, smirking mirth. They were watching a blonde lady, caked with rouge and bulging against a tight yellow evening gown, who was betting 200 rand a throw. She was on her fifth gin and tonic, she said. A chubby gent in khakis and beach togs was betting a fistful of five-rand chips on numbers 32 and 36 at every spin. He was losing, but not as much as the woman. There were two other people: a businessman, about 30, in a grey blazer and blue trousers, and what was probably his wife, a grim little brunette with a heart-shaped mouth. They were nervously betting four or five rand a throw and breaking about even. They tended to play the colors and the odd-even. A man in an ice-cream suit and goatee, a dead ringer for Colonel Sanders (with silver mirror sunglasses) was having some luck covering the last third of the board.

I checked the sharks during the spins and they didn't signal the croupier—or at least if they did, it wasn't very conspicuous. It looked like a straight table. Also, house sharks don't hang around if there is a hot table: they don't have to. The customers are hawked by the guy in the ceiling who runs the magnet that pulls the ball into a safe number. Also, the table had only one zero. Most wheels run with a double-zero green as well. That increases the house's odds considerably.

I watched a few more turns, then tossed a chip down on the green. The spin: zero it was, 35:1 odds. I pocketed 30 of my newly won chips and spread five around, one of them on "9." The spin: "9" it was, another 35 prize chips. Could I win three in a row? I spread my chips around again, one on "12" . . .

and "12" it was. To make it short, I ran it up to 260 rand in just under half an hour. I then bet five on individual numbers the next two spins and lost them all. I walked over to the cashier with all of those one-rand chips in my bush hat. When I passed the table on the way out, it was business as usual. Nobody had even noticed I was gone, except the sharks, and they weren't smiling.

By 4.00 p.m., I was raising clouds of dust on the road to Big Bend, my gas tanks full, courtesy of the Swazi Casino. They also bought me half a fried chicken at Mr. Rooster. The French fries weren't bad either.

We sat on the quilt next to the rusted chassis of an ancient tractor behind the house of the village prefect. He was a regular client.

She inhaled forcefully, emitting as she did a long gurgling, hissing sound. After a series of these gasps she began chanting, in Swazi—a long sing-song cadence.

The head waiter at the Big Bend Inn had brought me there at the direction of his boss man. The night before we had talked of sorcery and witchcraft, and he was convinced that the old woman was a witch.

"She's told people things about themselves nobody else could have possibly known," he said, allowing that she once told an Afrikaner his best friend would die in a wreck within the week, which he had. She could conjure the past, and some said she had summoned the voices of the departed. Additionally, she was a healer of no small reputation. The innkeeper, Mike Green, didn't believe the talk about the voices of the dead, but of her prescient powers he was certain.

She wasn't there when we first arrived at the concrete market pavilion. I sat inside on a table of watermelon, swatting flies and reading the remnants of the *Sunday Tribune,* with which someone had wrapped his fish.

Then I saw her, waddling toward the market at 200 yards—I knew it was she: at least 350 pounds of witchdoctor, laden with beads and skins, necklaces of all colors and wrist bands of red and white and green. Her hair was short and mud-caked, Masai-style it seemed: a kind of super-henna. She greeted the market people regally. They smiled respectfully and stood quickly aside, almost bowing. She passed a few words with some of them and glanced disinterestedly in my direction.

"She see you in short time, Mastah," my guide said. "She have first visit in house." She shuffled on toward the little house, her beads and trappings swaying in the wind. In a quarter of an hour I was called by the guide.

She bade me sit at the far end of the blanket and did not "mastah" me as the guide had done. I noticed that the children that had hung around me at the market had disappeared; not a soul was even peeping in the distance, although surely she was the village's chief event.

Suddenly, from within the folds of her dress they came: a half-dozen bones of various sizes, two of which were leg bones of fowl with beads inserted at each end. There were two sets of dice—green and red—and several worn dominoes, four old copper coins and assorted loose beads and sticks. The largest object was a conch shell. In all, there must have been two pounds of enchanted debris strewn across her blanket.

Waving her hands over the lot, she repeated the hissing spasm, rolled her eyes until only the whites were showing and scooped the items again into her garment. Shaking and stirring them she repeated the routine, her eyes still rolled into the whites. Just as she reached a frenzy, she flung the talismans so that they fell in the queerest arrangement, the larger of the beaded drumsticks resting well beyond the rest. The conch lay open, facing it.

My guide now interpreted her sing-song voice. I was prepared for the worst. Better I had not come, I thought. Ignorant bliss would at least permit hope, no matter how vain.

"Very good, very good . . ." she was saying.

But her trance was better than the fortune.

After telling me the obvious (that I had come a long way, that I had occasionally had difficulty with the vehicle but each time had been able to overcome it), she told me that if I would drive slowly and not drink too much and buy a five-rand set of her special magic beads, I would finish my journey, get rich and not fall off my horse. That sounded good enough, but she didn't have any beads for sale just then and told me to come back later. When I asked her if the clove necklace hanging from my rearview mirror would do, she said it was powerful medicine, but not as powerful as her own. The fee for all that was one rand, to which I added a 50-cent tip. My head-boy guide also got one rand.

Back at the hotel, I busied myself writing letters and sending them in envelopes decorated with beautiful Swaziland stamps. They are collector's items and I hope that the people to whom I sent the letters have saved the stamps.

I talked to Paddy O'Reilly, the manager of the irrigation division of the Big Bend River Corporation. The corporation had placed 18,000 acres of sugar under cultivation since 1956 and now employed some 30,000 Swazi workers. Scores of the company's giant double-bin cane wagons would roll their way to the mill every morning at sunup. O'Reilly and his wife had been here ten years and hoped to retire here.

Sugar is, after maize, the country's chief crop. In 1976, Swaziland produced 96 tons per hectare, the world's sixth most efficient rate. Swaziland is one of the few Black African nations that is self-sufficient in agriculture. It is the only one of the neighbors of Rhodesia and South Africa that does not depend upon one of them for food.

The company general store was well stocked with merchandise. Employees traded at special prices and guards stood at the gate to keep out strangers, but no one said anything to me.

The next day I drove to Lavumisa, the post on the southern Swazi border with South Africa. Thinking I had seen the last of the police checks, I was surprised at the bridge on the Pongola River by a military police barricade. An officer explained that they were searching for stolen automobiles and that the culprits were white.

I continued past Richard's Bay to Tongaat where I camped on the beach and jogged three and a half miles both that night and the next morning.

The next morning at Durban I read that the *Windsor Castle,* a mail-passenger liner, was leaving on her last voyage to London. I phoned the steamship office, but she was booked solid from Cape Town. I was now sensing the end of my voyage and decided to hug the coast and make the Cape straightaway.

It was midafternoon when I left Durban westward on the freeway to Pietermaritzburg. I thought it strange how quickly I had adjusted since Bulawayo to paved streets and freeway ribbons. For the preceding eight months, except for Abidjan and Nairobi, I had been either in the wilderness or bidonvilles of Black Africa. Yet this seemed not to affect in the least my reacclimation to freeway driving.

CHAPTER XXIII

At dark I came to the River Umzimkulu. A sign in front of a sleek complex of police and customs buildings proclaimed:

YOU ARE NOW LEAVING THE REPUBLIC OF SOUTH AFRICA.
YOU ARE NOW ENTERING THE REPUBLIC OF TRANSKEI.

Thus I entered a country that, until a month ago, I hadn't known existed.

In front of the South African border hut was a long line of Africans waiting for South African entry visas. A few were waiting to reenter Transkei. A solitary lieutenant in khaki and a blue overcoat filled out and meticulously stamped three copies of six separate forms dealing with everything from vehicle registration to currency control. It was a tedious process and required twenty minutes. I do not know why I was put at the head of the line, but I suspect that even in this "independent" African republic, it was because I was white.

In 1976, Transkei was the first of eight homelands to be declared independent by South Africa. No other country recognizes them. Most of these lands are sanctuaries for terrorists or patches of separated lands inhabited by one or two tribal groups. The main Transkei tribal group is the Xhosa.

Transkei does, however, comprise some of the best plateau farm land in the country and has some 200 miles of Indian Ocean coastline. Its estimated population in 1976 was 2.4 million. It is not self-sufficient, however, and depends upon South Africa for its food, energy and consumer goods. As in all the black enclaves of southern Africa, the currency is the South African rand.

As in Swaziland, there are many white residents who carry on pretty much as they did before independence, although in the role of managers, since all property in Transkei is state-owned.

Clearing customs, I found myself in the town of Umzimkulu and parked in front of the weathered old hotel of that name. In the lobby were a dozen Africans watching television. Just then there came a shrill whistle, and as I turned I saw that it emanated from a tough, wiry old Afrikaner at the desk. *What on earth could he be doing that for?* I wondered. Suddenly, three African porters shuffled in from the rear porch, one after the other, as if in some bad vaudeville routine. The manager ordered one of them to take my gear, but I politely refused. I asked him if he had a room and what the price would be. It was cheap—7.5 rands, including breakfast—and I followed one of the porters to my room.

After a hot bath, I finished a couple of letters I'd begun in Tangaat and went up to the dining room for dinner. Umzimkulu was a small village, and this was the only restaurant in town. The hostelry was conveniently situated for travelers and had been a stop on the old stage and rail lines. Now it was on the main in-coastal route connecting Cape Town and Port Elizabeth with Durban and other points north.

Sitting in the lobby talking to the manager and his wife was a heavy British woman of about 28 and her six-year-old half-black son. Her legs were thick and varicosed, and she could walk only with great difficulty. The boy, however, was as bright and healthy as you'd ever see. He didn't stare or gawk but bounced right up and asked me what I was doing, where I'd come from and—when he learned I was an American—if I was a cowboy.

The old Afrikaner acted like the boy's grandfather, sternly but kindly admonishing him not to irritate me. Whenever the boy said "ain't," the old gent posed stiffly and shook his finger, repeating, "isn't."

They had been in Transkei since February, when the woman had flown down to Johannesburg from London to try to join her husband, a Zulu businessman who ran a small African nightclub in Soweto. "They [South African immigration] took one look at me and the boy and refused us entry," she said. The only thing she could do was to catch a connecting flight to Umtala in Transkei. She tried to get a visa from there, but they had absolutely refused her reentry. She was at her wit's end. Her husband had done all he could, she said, but there was not much else he could do because the South Africans simply didn't want a white woman living in Soweto with a black man.

The child, meanwhile, had begun school in Umzimkulu and, understandably, was not doing very well. "Oh, he gets the work OK, that's no problem. He's the smartest boy in the class." But he rattled his teachers and intimidated his peers with his precocious conduct. I dined next to them and answered a hundred questions for him.

The next morning on the way to breakfast he tapped me from behind and smiled. I was happy to see him. The night before, when he had found out I was an American, he had wanted to know if we had jungles in the United States. I said maybe one in Florida and pointed on an old wall map to the Everglades. He asked if there were "beasts" and how many, and we spent an hour talking about snakes and alligators. Tigers? No, I said, but we did have wildcats. I drew him a fairly good picture of a bobcat.

Later, as I was checking out, the manager brusquely reprimanded me for offering to stake my new friend to 50 cents' worth of candy: "He gets too much candy now . . . everybody stuffs him. Spoiling him, it is." The boy was off to school with another child, and I bade him goodbye. The *grand pere* whistled, and the porters—all three of them—shuffled in. I again begged off and carried my own gear.

All that day I drove over rolling green hills and plateaus and occasional semi-desert. The rocky coastal road was lightly traveled, and I saw only two vehicles the whole afternoon. At dusk I reached Port St. Johns, a fishing village at the mouth of the Umzimkulu River in the remote, rugged country of the Wild Coast. The few people who lived here made a living as subsistence farmers or by working for one of the white or colored merchants that had stayed on as managers. The businesses consisted of two hotels, a few bars and eat shops and a park of roundavels next to the mountain on the south side of the beach. Down in the village was the Needles Hotel and Nelson's Pot Restaurant (after a giant copper kettle in the entryway said to have been used by Lord Nelson). Jimmy and Frankie, the English couple who ran the place, had come there eighteen months before, they said, because they liked Transkei's politics and weather.

(Transkei is officially integrated. Although stories of graft and incompetence abound, they rarely involve Europeans, who remain aloof from politics. White farms and businesses have been confiscated by the government, but for fairly good sums guaranteed by the South African government. White citizens of Transkei may renew their South African citizenship at any time.)

Back in the 1930s, Port St. Johns was the chief port for this region of the coast but when Port Elizabeth was given development priority, St. Johns dried up. With independence for Transkei, most of the white inhabitants sold out to the government and left.

The remains of the Port Authority house rested in front of a caved-in dock a quarter of a mile from the mouth of the river. Its rotted crossbeams swung limply in the wind. Although it looked abandoned, the house was in fact inhabited by the African port captain and his family. They lived in what had been the records room, which was packed with loose straw matting. The captain at first demanded petulantly to know what I was doing there, but when he learned that I was an American he relaxed and offered me a tour.

The dock works had been formidable in their day but had not been used, the captain said, since 1945. Living in the waterlogged timbers along the riverbank were a family of feisty tree hyraxes who dutifully scurried through their danger drills, looking up at us and emitting grunts and hisses until the captain tossed a small stick in their direction.

After the tour, I patronized the fish and chips store just off the town square, run by a colored family. They served delicious pickled onions and the helping of fish was generous and tasty. I ate off of a sports page of the *Rand Daily Mail* in the town park. The beach ran right up to the park, and I walked out to visit with two crayfishermen who were wading in the low tide. Between us the mud was quick, and I sank up to my knees. The fishermen grinned nervously but kept on netting.

A road around the mountain on the south beach led to a half-moon bay at the neck of which was a tea room in a stand of trees. A garden of tropical flowers was beginning to bloom. I was the only customer, ordering a Coke from one of the three willowy African girls shimmying to a radio's offering of Elvis Presley. The reception was bad, and the surf provided a rhythmic filter for the tinny crooning.

I paid the tab and climbed the cliff along an eroded goat trail until I could see a lighthouse. There was a view of the coast for miles to the south, but I could not see the beach at St. Johns. A woman wrapped in bead necklaces and a cloak of hide strips rushed suddenly down the hill past me. I started: she looked exactly like the Swazi witch doctor. She trotted on in a great hurry without returning my greeting. *An emergency housecall,* I thought.

I was only the third guest that week at the roundavels, and Mr. and Mrs. Pat Pinnock, the managers, were most kind. Their smart little cottage above the campsite had been remodeled, "for the rest of our days." The house was surrounded by trees and just enough in defilade from the beach to avoid the full gale. My cabin had two army cots, and Mrs. Pinnock put fresh sheets on one of them. I set up the camping stove, made coffee and wrote in my diary for an hour and a half.

The coast was blanketed at this time with a constant mist, and only for brief moments did it lift enough for the sun to break through. But the next day a long break came at noon, and I took advantage of it to climb the cliff above the camp. A narrow dirt track wound for a quarter of a mile up to the concrete lighthouse. There were signs stating that use of the trail was forbidden, but Mr. Pinnock advised me to ignore them. A no-trespassing sign on the open gate in the driveway proclaimed that the lighthouse was the property of South African Railways and that intruders would be prosecuted. Such facilities as lighthouses, telephones and other utilities, I learned, were still run by the South Africans.

In the small yard beyond the lighthouse, and skirting its edge, was a variety of shrubs and flowers on a thick blue-green lawn. A gardener knelt with his back to me, yet I had the distinct feeling that he knew I was there. I mumbled a pleasantry, then walked past the lighthouse to a narrow black-earth trail which led up the mountainside. As I gained the trail I felt the full gale of the warm wind as it danced on the blades of grass and scrub-brush leaves. The surf was rolling in on grand white swells to pound into the rocks just out of sight below the hill. Occasionally there was a glimpse of spray. Far down the beach I could see the waves spending themselves on the sand of the half-moon bay. When I reached the crest, the roar of the surf had become only intermittent gasps smothered by the wind.

On top was what appeared to be a two-room shack beside which rose an impressive radio antenna. As I drew closer, a dog inside began barking ferociously. There was a window covered with what looked like shelves reversed against the panes. I walked around to the other side and called in but received no answer. Through the window I saw what could have been a military communications center. Perhaps it was the lighthouse radio shack. But whatever it was, there were shelves of charts and pencils and protractors, and on a table lay a sophisticated radio transceiver and earphones.

Behind the house I discovered a half-acre garden planted with a dozen neat rows of fat, blue cabbages. Beyond the cabbages were some tomato stakes and a stand of corn. The garden was carefully tended and seemed to have been recently topsoiled, since the mountain was otherwise poorly sodded.

343

As I turned to leave, I noticed a wisp of smoke rising from the stovepipe chimney in the rear. Draped over the railing of the back porch was the cloak of hides worn by the woman who had passed me so hurriedly on the trail the day before. As I approached, the dog's voice dropped into a low, rolling growl. I paused. From overhead came the calls of shrikes and gulls. The sun had disappeared into the mist again.

I hiked back down to the village the way I had come. The gardener was no longer at the lighthouse, and the gate was closed and locked. A man at the Needles Bar said that no one lived there now. The beacon comes on automatically at dusk, he said, and clicks off at dawn.

The Needles Bar had an elegant wooden staircase descending into the area behind the bar. This was the style of the old English pubs in which the barman and his family live in the second story overhead. I have seen pub children in England dragging dolls and peeping from behind the banisters at the guests below. Here there were no children, but the landing was adorned with a handsome grandfather clock which chimed happily every quarter hour.

Mrs. Pinnock was a bustling and immaculate English grandmother whose attention to the last detail of a guest's comfort was simply a matter of course. The Pinnocks had lived in various places in the Republic as Mr. Pinnock's career in the British South African Police (BSAP) flourished. Suddenly, he was passed over for promotion and reassigned for no apparent reason. He soon learned it was because of his political views. He had been a member of the Progressive Party, a relatively liberal party opposed to apartheid. Its members were soon, for all practical purposes, purged from the police force: no raises, no promotions. Mr. Pinnock's job became so intolerable that he took an early retirement and came here. Things had been going well until just a few months back when he'd had a stroke. Now he would walk with his cane to the park bench on the road above the beach and look out to sea with his binoculars. Some ships passed close enough that he could read their names, and he kept a kind of log of them. The Pinnocks gave me the name of their son, who was a copy editor with the *Argus* newspaper in Cape Town.

Grahamstown could easily have been one of those steepled American college towns where Doric facades, McDonald's arches and used car lots somehow coalesce into civic propriety.

Grahamstown seats several colleges and finishing schools, of which the most prestigious is Cecil Rhodes University. Founded and funded by its namesake, its students have a reputation as the hard-drivingest, beer-drinkingest, fast-talkingest skindivers, hang gliders, and stunt parachutists south of the Zambezi. And since not much of that goes on north of the river they know they are "Africa's finest." Their swarthy, mischievous grins seemed a contrived counterpoint to the drawn, gothic faces of the local gentry.

But not all of them.

Some were quite serious: pale, earnest, can-do, gee-whiz faces, dimpled

344

boyish smiles, engaging locution: nascent machinated politicians of the first order. Attempting to crash their bar at the Rhodes Union (I told the bouncer, "Cecil sent me"), I was at first refused out-of-hand. But when they learned I was an American vagabond, I was admitted at the command of their president, who adopted me, escorted me to the bar and introduced me around. After a few moments' pleasantries, the conversation resumed the course it had taken before the interruption.

Talking as much to each other as to me, their conversation went like this (as I noted that evening in my journal):

> One must remember that the Black man has—without exception—rejected western culture and civilization every time he has been exposed to it. . . You [Europeans and Americans] educate them at Harvard and Oxford and the LSE and Berkeley and they are erudite and cultured with the best of you. But get them back to Kenya or Zambia or Nigeria and they revert to type. They set up one-party dictatorships and shoot or jail their opponents. We're not going to have that here. If we were to institute majority rule today, there would be one free election then there would be a blood bath because the losers would never accept the outcome. (Can you *imagine* the Zulu consenting to be ruled by the Xhosa?) And the winners would not sit still for their opponents attacking them in the daily press. They would exterminate their opponents and close the press. The concept of a Loyal Opposition is alien to the African's culture. . . .
>
> Yet how do we live up to the ideal of equality and still protect democracy? That is the failure of *apartheid*. It really says that the African is forever inferior, stupid and that he can never learn tolerance and decency. We don't believe that but we have to bring him along slowly, gradually, unmistakably. There have to be property and achievement standards of citizenship. Once someone has, say, graduated from high school or, say, even passed an exam that he can read and write then he should immediately be qualified to vote. But he would lose that right unless he attended classes in government and citizenship and passed these exams for, say, a period of two or three years. But not only Africans but whites as well—everyone—would be subject to the same rules, follow the same course of study and pass the same tests. . . .
>
> In the meantime, say, over a period of twenty years, or less if I had my way, anyone with full citizenship in the "new republic" [everyone who had passed the exams] would be permitted to move and live and work anywhere. When a sufficiently large number of adult Africans—say 50%—had successfully matriculated [become citizens] then the program could be said to be successful and the restrictions gradually lifted—even for those who had not attained the required levels, although that would be over a period of 5, 10 or 15 years: a kind of gradual universal phase-in, if you will, of universal suffrage.

The person doing most of the talking was a sauve, ingratiating young man—almost unctuous, in a way monotonous, but very serious and self-

345

controlled. He drank a heavily toniced gin, which he camouflaged with water when the tonic ran out and the others were not looking. He chose his words carefully. I felt like a reporter interviewing a Congressional candidate.

Another young man was a farmer's son, from the northern Transvaal—cotton, cattle. His wife and child were in Cape Town visiting her mother. The woman had been strong-armed by a black and her purse stolen, and that brought the subject around to crime in the veld.

All of these things were to be hashed out with "the Prime Minister of this country this very time tomorrow night," said the intense young man with the watered-down gin and tonic, who was to meet with him in Pretoria. The occasion was, I gathered, a youth leadership conference sponsored by the National Party. This lad was president of the local student chapter.

A third student was a stocky, athletic gent who remained grim-faced and solemn throughout the conversation, although occasionally nodding his head in agreement. His father was a famous lawyer in Durban, according to one of the others. He nursed a substantial vodka Collins which the bartender regularly refilled.

I was absolutely forbidden to touch my tab, and as soon as my bottle of Amstel lager was dry, another appeared alongside the empty. I was showered with names and addresses of friends and friends-of-friends and at midnight was given a hearty farewell.

I knew how quickly these self-styled young liberals would be hissed and hooted by their European and American peers. Yet I had seen the shock, bewilderment and resignation of those same peers—who had come as eager cultural missionaries to Peace Corps and diplomatic outposts from Niger to Kenya Coast. The one thing they all shared was the basic assumption that their culture (or at least its political organization and tool-using methods) was better for the African than the African's own traditional way of doing things. Whatever the merits of this assumption (and stratigraphically, remember, they are dubious), the Islamic, Christian and Marxist missionaries—each in his own way and in his own time—have come here with it. Yet the African has cleverly resisted them all by assimilating just enough of their perfunctory trappings so as not to incur their wrath or discourage their largesse, all the while retaining his indomitable animism.

The result of this *modus vivendi*, however, has been the African's ultimate dependence on the tools, weapons, and governing skill of foreigners, without respect to the official designation of his cartographical entity as tribal homeland, colony or republic.

It is this perpetual dependence that must be escaped if Africa—indeed, the entire third world—is to achieve self-sufficiency and political dignity. In the meantime, there is little cause for optimism. For in the whole of Black Africa, some 45 separate states, a government has never been voted out of office.

I stayed in Grahamstown at the once-commodious Hotel Goodwood, run by two wary, terse-lipped ladies who appeared to have surfeited long ago on the antics on Doris Lessing's children of violence. The walls and floors of my room sweated old-wood scents of a thousand graduations, homecomings and disappointments.

There was a bar where I was served stale draft beer and vetted scrupulously by the manly clientele—a fireman, two night watchmen, a steeplejack, and two truck drivers. Yes, I was most impressed with the country, I told them, and would tell my friends there were good people, too, in South Africa. Carter was probably OK, the steeplejack said, but had bad advisors, like Andrew Young. They all recommended the Union Club and the museum of the 1920 English settlers. I said I wouldn't miss either site. One of the truck drivers bought my beer.

The next morning I checked out after breakfast, but the man at the desk insisted that I leave the Toyota out front until I had seen the museum. The porters would watch it. "We've never had any trouble here, but you never know...."

The names in the museum were familiar ones: McKenzie, Shaw, Phillips, Madison, Jones, Patterson.... They'd packed up everything—or sold it—and taken their families and come down here to homestead and farm and seek a new life. But instead of a land of milk and honey, they'd found semi-desert wasteland and hostile natives—the Bantu. There were years of privation and skirmishes, not only with the Bantu but with the equally xenophobic Afrikaners. But most survived, and eventually a thriving community was built, farms prospered, and they and their sons and daughters became Britain's bulwark in Cape Province against the recalcitrant and ungovernable Boers.*

There were photographs or cameo portraits of most of them—several hundred in all—in a kind of gallery of honor in one hall on the ground floor. You could tell that they were as hearty and devout a group of immigrants that ever sailed for a new world. I couldn't help thinking that, in 1820, they could just as easily have gone west, to America, and today be celebrated as pioneers and frontiersmen.

I made Port Elizabeth about 1:30 and continued on around the bypass. Someone had said that Storm River mouth was a remote, secluded place and might be worth a few days. I decided to check it out.

Storm River is the most spectacular of the Wild Coast's twenty short, turgid rivers. It cuts a magnificent gorge, the bottom of which is barely visible in the shadows of the canyon walls. The walls branch into graceful buttresses that arch up from the streambed and almost join several hundred feet above the river.

---

*The British seized Cape Province from the Dutch in 1795. Although they receded it, they seized it again in 1814, when it became a British colony. The settlers of 1820 constituted Britain's first concerted effort to settle the new colony with loyal subjects. It was as the direct result of this British encroachment that many Dutch farmers pulled up stakes and pushed inland on their Great Trek. These *voortrekkers* migrated through what is now Natal and the Orange Free State, and eventually to Transvaal. Some of them even continued into Rhodesia at the end of the century.

Entrance to "Whites Only" mens' restroom. Storm River Park, South Africa.

Next to the bridge was a cliff with a longwise view of the gorge. There was a restaurant behind the observation area. Signs on the toilets and the restaurant itself restricted entry: "White Only."

A few miles beyond the bridge was a dirt road to the river's mouth. This area was a national park, and a black forest ranger was collecting a one-rand camping fee. At the bottom of the road leading to the beach was a lodge-style restaurant and twenty or so duplex cabins. To the north and west were gentle folds of a bay that led to the river mouth. You couldn't see up the river from the lodge, and it was too late to climb the steep trail that led over there, so I walked to my cabin. I set up my camping gas stove on the concrete porch and had made but a few notes in my journal when I was distracted by the soft harmony of a guitar and folk duet from the adjoining room.

Michael was twenty, a theater set-light man; Julie, three years older, was a guitarist from a family of musicians. They'd just returned from Cape Town, where they'd played with friends at a place called the Pizza Den, a hangout where the customers bring their fiddles and banjos and join the bluegrass regulars. They were a happy, gentle couple. They'd been reading Kipling's *Just-so Stories* and had me read aloud "How the Rhinoceros Got His Skin." We strummed and sang and told stories until very late, and I enjoyed their company.

The next morning I climbed the trail to the river, tarrying down a side path to a small pearl-shaped cove. Its white sand was that morning undisturbed.

The forest was rich with flowers freshly bloomed, among them lilies of incomparable beauty. I got up very close and photographed one with a bee inside. There were a dozen other varieties of wildflowers and plants and a vine that smelled like jasmine. After a half-hour's climb I came to a suspension footbridge from the center of which I looked upstream into the gorge and downstream out to sea.

I'd given up, coffee for eight days at that time (I later made it fifteen). I think you tend to drink more on the road and it's such a pleasant, looked-forward-to diversion. Without exercise, however, the caffeine poisons your system and races your heart and makes you nervous and quarrelsome. Tea with milk (morning tea) had become a habit since Olduvai and I would have an extra cup or two at mid-morning to replace the stronger coffee.

The road back of the cabins was a good jogging trail and I put in two 40-minute runs the next afternoon and the following morning. I was exhilarated by the friendly thrashing and churning of the sea on the rocks below the cabin and the windy, grey-blue sky.

I drove on, coming in mid-afternoon to a forest beach called Nature Valley, a quiet place with hillocks before the sea. I look a long walk and on returning, found a German and three attractive Afrikaner girls looking over the jeep. He was a senior engineering student at Stellenbosch University. The girls were X-ray technicians in Cape Town.

They invited me to the Why Not Tea Room at Plattsberg Bay. One of the girls, Luna Ludeke, was from South West Africa, or Namibia. She rode with me, and we talked about the Namib Desert. She'd spent quite a lot of time in it with her father, who was a farmer near Otjiwarongo.

It was late when we left the tea room, and I decided to stay in Plattsberg Bay for the night. After goodbyes to my friends, a high-school student and his girlfriend in a customized '56 Chevy directed me to the modest Lookout Hotel on the ridge overlooking the bay.

I had a good run while a nonplussed elderly couple watched me from their maroon Cadillac in the Dutch Reformed Church parking lot. I would jog up just even with the lot and run back a quarter of a mile to the edge of the hill. When I finished I walked over and said "Hi," and the lady invited me to join them for church and dinner. ("You can even stay in our home if you want.") I would have been too late for church but I accepted the invitation to dinner. They were to have picked me up at the hotel but they didn't show. I suppose I *had* looked awfully scruffy in my raggy running gear.

I took my time driving the next day, stopping here and there in lush forests beside long golden meadows to photograph flowers and open spaces. Not without reason do they call this "The Garden Route."

Then, from the plains, I climbed unexpectedly up the slopes of the Little Karoo range and from Dutoit's Pass I saw False Bay and the peninsula leading to the Cape. I pulled over and stopped briefly and thought of how long it had been and how far I had come. I thought of the ritual three circles I had made at the mosque at Moulay Hassan.

At 4:15 p.m., September 5, 1977—some fourteen months since leaving Paris—I drove into Cape Town. I drove downtown and parked on an empty street, got out, stretched and looked around. Seeing the worn tires, I thought of them plowing and churning through the Hoggar, Chad, Ngorongoro.

I needed a place to stay—cheap, with a good bed and a place in which I could safely park my vehicle and stow my gear. I asked around for a pension, preferably an old colonial-style boarding lodge or weekly rental hotel. After a half-dozen dead ends I found the Helmsley-Green Park on Hof Street Gardens. It had a family dining room and a pleasant, easygoing clientele of university students, secretaries and friendly old ladies. The color TV in the big lounge attracted half the house and quite a few nearby residents. The Pizza Den, a singing club and restaurant, was adjacent to the lobby. Its folk and bluegrass music filtered gently up through the walls until midnight. The only bar in the hotel (beer only) was the Den's. It served hotel guests through a special side door as well. The hotel porter would bring the beer (and a reasonable pizza) to the veranda out back. There were lots of trees, shrubs, flowers and, sometimes, sunshine. It was quiet there, a good place to write.

Hof Street Gardens ran uphill toward Table Mountain, the massive rock that rises over 3,000 feet above the town. The mountain attracts a constant parade of clouds that keep it and the town in fog and showers. In the summer (our winter), there is much less rain and lots more sunshine; but just then it was the end of their winter, when a day was rarely free of inclement weather. Additionally, it was quite cool and wearing a sweater or light jacket was necessary.

Table Mountain dominates Cape Town like the Matterhorn dominates Zermott or Cheyenne Mountain, Colorado Springs. It is visible from almost everywhere and its relief appears on billboards, phone books, business logos and in all manner of advertisements and brand labels. A cable car goes to the top, but because of foul weather, it was closed most of the time I was there. Rescue operations for lost or stranded climbers are routine. Just after I arrived a fifteen-year-old boy was found suffering from exposure and broken bones after an ordeal of six days.

The streets of the downtown area near the Helmsley were lined with trees and gardens. The houses were mostly mid-nineteenth century, although there were a few mansions dating from the late eighteenth century and, here and there, the usual modern apartment blocks. The business district, only a ten-minute walk from my hotel, was like that of any other major city. The flavor of Cape Town was rather like that of Charleston or New Orleans or perhaps San Francisco of 50 years ago. On the walls of a good many buildings some bereaved individual had stenciled images of Elvis Presley with blue and red aerosol paint. One radio station was still playing whole albums of the singer's songs, now several weeks after his death. The *Argus, Star* and *World* were carrying running exposés of old Presley girlfriends and hangers-on under teaser headlines.

Jogging, facilitated by the beauty of my surroundings, again became a regular morning habit. I would trot up Hof Street Garden, past the tennis courts, through De Waal Park, and up to the entrance to the town reservoir. There was a walkway around the reservoir into which the water-flow control house and Table Mountain were reflected in perfect symmetry.

The first few days in Cape Town, I slowly took care of shopping and shipping arrangements and walked around town meeting and talking to residents. It felt good to have new clothes, a bath every day and a regular place to come back to at night. Eventually, I left the jeep parked at the hotel parking lot and walked everywhere.

The South African Automobile Association (AA) office made all the necessary arrangements to ship my jeep to New Orleans on the next available vessel, which was scheduled to depart November 23. Even if I could have sold it for its replacement value (new ones had almost doubled in retail price since 1973), the import duty and sales tax would have eaten up 90 percent of the sale. Some travelers return to Kenya to sell their vehicles. The taxes there are much lower, and it is most profitable for overland tour operators, for example, to sell their Bedfords in Nairobi after each trip. Indeed, profit from such sales is usually enough to cover expenses.

But I had no desire to sell my Toyota, it having been my only constant companion for over a year.

I developed the habit of going to town along the central garden walk that bisected the national gallery grounds and the Dutch East India Company's old gardens. The gardens, begun in 1652 to grow vegetables for the fledgling colony, were now a floral masterpiece. Most area wildflowers were represented, along with many varieties of roses, tulips, and pansies. The light in the gardens was constantly shifting with Table Mountain's weather. The result was a kaleidoscope of color and contrast not unlike that of Paris.

Yet upon this botanical palette were implanted austere and ponderous sculptures, marbled specters that celebrated Afrikaner founders and school-men and, inevitably, Cecil Rhodes. Two statues were erected to the memory of the late General Jan Smuts, the wartime Prime Minister and opposition party leader who vehemently rejected apartheid until his death in 1953.

One morning, I heard on my way back to the hotel through the park the dull thud of an explosion toward downtown. It was a bucket bomb, according to the security police who quickly gathered. Strewn about were a number of leaflets of the African National Council, the banned black revolutionary group. The police hurriedly collected the leaflets while stiffly ordering the curious passersby to move on. According to a friend, one of these devices went off somewhere in town at least once a week. The leaflets were stacked on top of the actual explosive and separated from it by a thin

Statues of Afrikaner heroes in the Botanical Gardens, Cape Town, South Africa. Although General Smuts (left) is today revered, he strenuously opposed the introduction of apartheid after World War II.

metal plate. When the bomb, a timed device, goes off, the leaflets are dispersed.

The reason for the bucket-bomb method of dissemination is simple: The penalty for distributing such material is death. Merely possessing such a leaflet is a ten-year prison offense.

At the Pizza Den the following Monday, I met a Frenchman who said he'd been working on a top secret South African nuclear project. When I asked him if there was any truth to Russian and United States reports that South Africa was planning to test an atomic bomb in the Kalahari Desert, he said that they didn't need to test it; they had it and it worked and if threatened they would use it. He said they had "artillery tactical" nuclear devices as well. He was slightly in his cups. I saw him there once again but he didn't bring the subject up—nor did I.

An English woman I met there typified the quandary of so many people.

She enjoyed the good South African life, she said, but she knew it couldn't last. "They all want to make arrangements. I'm lucky, with my family back in England." In that way, most of the English residents *are* lucky. They can always go to Australia, Britain, Canada, or the U.S. But the Afrikaners have no place to go. This woman had gone back to England once but returned three years ago. Now, she said, she'd decided to go back for good.

One morning I dropped by the editorial office of the *Argus* and looked up Don Pinnock. Don made up the inside pages of the paper which had earlier been known as the *Press Argus*. With its diet of crime, race, broken hearts and gore, it was like having the *National Enquirer* as your family daily. "It's frankly hamstrung by the insipid sensationalism of the lower-class English press—which we've copied," a co-worker of Don's said.

I had to wait in the messenger room on the fourth floor before getting in to see him. The messengers were colored and Indian teenagers. They wore old-fashioned railroad-porter-styled uniforms and caps and jumped up one after another as they were summoned.

Don lived with his girlfriend, Patch, in Kloof Neck, a kind of artsy and young-professional section of town on the ridges separating downtown from the beaches. Don usually rode his motorcycle to work but walked on a clear day. Patch drove their car—a '66 Mercedes—to her classes at Cape Town University where she was majoring in Religious Studies. On the rear window was a small but prominent sticker: "Apartheid Must Go."

I found the lifestyle of Kloof Neck exquisitely bourgeois. Although the rate of inflation had recently been higher in South Africa than in most industrial countries, consumer prices here were still cheap, mostly due to the abundant supply of cheap labor. Vegetarianism was currently the vogue, but even if you ate meat daily, food prices were still a bargain. Gasoline was $1.60 per gallon (it was running to $1.80, as in Transkei), but apartment rental was half that of major American and European cities.

Don and Patch had met in Salisbury several years back when he was working as a reporter for the *Rhodesia Herald*. He'd covered sports and politics. Before that he'd spent a couple of years in Europe and Morocco. He recounted having had to escape the Spanish customs police at Algeciras who mistakenly thought he had entered the country illegally. He'd managed to slip unnoticed into the harbor, backpack and all, and swim out to a friend's yacht. Several days later, the yacht capsized and sank off Ibiza. Fortunately, they were able to float to the island in their life jackets.

Later he had lived in Morocco for several months—far in the country, he said, near the Algerian border: "A bus ran out there once a week then waited a week before it left."

They had me over for dinner one evening: celery and spinach soup, baked bananas, okra, asparagus, lots of herbs and spices, such as onions, parsley, peas and crumbs for the salad. I brought along a guest, Lisa, a photographer I'd met the day before on the beach at Sea Point. I had stopped there on the way down to the Cape, and she'd come along with her dog. We hit it off, and she volunteered to be my guide.

353

Inevitably, the after-dinner conversation gravitated toward The Problem and the problem of journalists, in particular. The sordid history of journalistic oppression was reviewed, including the story of a friend of Don's, a British wire service man, who had been jailed the previous fall for ten years for disseminating ANC propaganda. I recalled having read of it in London at the time and seeing pictures of his pregnant wife attending the trial. He had been sent to the political prison called Robben Island. According to Amnesty International, there were more than 400 such prisoners there as of May, 1977. The island, an Alcatrazlike facility, is located off-shore near Cape Town. There is neither early parole for good behavior nor any kind of furlough, and visits are permitted only at Christmas.

We talked about the options one opposed to apartheid might exercise: editorial criticism, public speeches, opposition-party candidacy at elections, stickers on cars. Yet, in print, to even mention a banned organization or person or to quote one of them was to risk conviction under the Terrorism Act of 1967 which defined "terrorism" as any activity likely "to endanger the maintenance of law and order."

Other reporters Don knew had received official warnings from the Bureau of State Security about their "suspicious activities." Private mail—particularly foreign mail—was routinely opened, read and microfilmed by BOSS agents. A South African journalist had to exercise the utmost caution in what he said. Indeed, the less he wrote the better, particularly if he was under suspicion. (Much of my correspondence from friends in South Africa contains perfunctory recitations of how good things are there and how wicked are the foreign opponents of apartheid. These weird polemics, strained and contrived, appear suddenly as non-sequitur paragraphs in personal letters from utterly nonpolitical people.)

Most journalists eventually surfeit and shrug their shoulders and give way to a kind of resigned despair: the final realization of personal helplessness. All the hours of talking, the clever metaphors, the well-reasoned arguments come to naught. The courageous refuse to resign and continue to work as best they can in their own private ways to influence events. Yet, they have to be careful: the penalties are draconian and inflicted with a vengeance.

Don spoke longingly of his travels in northern Africa, particularly Morocco, and of his plans to study full time at Cape Town University. He was majoring in African History and Social Studies there. Studying sociology in Cape Town was like being in a living laboratory, he said. One could see daily the most unique interactions among human beings anywhere on the planet.

Don repeated an allegory he said he had read somewhere comparing the races of man to mountain climbers climbing a bottomless cliff to an unseen summit. From time to time, each climber must rest. Some go to sleep resting and are seen as stupid and lazy by the others as they pass. Yet the others too soon must sleep themselves.

I visited them frequently and Don and I kept a chess game going for several days which, we finally agreed, ended in a draw. Patch would fix tea while we talked about meeting up some day on the road . . . at sea . . . I told them of John and Gale and their yacht on the mountain near Sabie, and we relived north Africa, Morocco, Ibiza.

One mid-morning I took the commuter train to Stellenbosch, seat of Stellenbosch University, the jewel of Afrikaner pedagogy. I walked along the streets of white-columned homes and dormitories and talked with neatly scrubbed students and their professors and loquacious lady administrators. There were two big house museums, one of which had an enormous eighteenth-century colonial kitchen with copper kettles, ladles, knives and all the rest.

At Stellenbosch I noted that every menial and many skilled tasks seemed to be performed by Africans. Here and there among the mansions black gardeners clipped and trimmed. A yellow electric-company bucket lifted two black linemen to a transformer. The bulldozer on Dorp Street was run by a black operator. Even the pallbearers in the white cemetery were black, as were, of course, the gravediggers.

As the commons cafeteria filled to overflowing, some thespians, resplendent in Elizabethan garb, trooped about the hall heralding a current festival. Two history students, one from Johannesburg and the other from Durban, lectured me on American intervention in other people's affairs. An engineering student from Salisbury asked many questions about Zambia, where he had been born before his father moved to Rhodesia. He hadn't been back in twenty years.

I needed to get my visa extended, and running from one bureau to another took the better part of a day. They demanded proof of solvency, and $900 in traveler's checks wasn't enough. The Standard Bank gave me a voucher letter (they'd corresponded and knew my stateside balance), and finally the visa was extended—for two weeks.

I packed all the spare parts and loose gear into steel boxes and delivered them to the shipping agency's warehouse. (The heavier items, such as the battery, I'd given to Don and Patch.) Before taking the jeep to the AA garage, I cleaned the spark plugs and carburetor and blew out the various filters at a Shell station not far from the hotel. The mechanic was a former Rhodesian farmer who received an annual check for 4,000 rand from the Zambian government for his confiscated farm. He wasn't sure how much longer they would honor the commitment, he said, but he was keeping his fingers crossed.

The next-to-last morning I visited the local Magistrate's Court. The court building was early '20s British-administrative style, with a cold, austere facade and equally austere within. The ground floor was divided into eight divisions, each containing an assize conducted in English or Afrikaans.

There were no hearings that morning in English, so I asked for the most interesting case and the bailiff directed me to a handsome wooden courtroom. A rose-colored bench dominated counsel and witness tables from a threatening height. Behind it sat a bewigged, hollow-faced judge who appeared disdainfully disinterested in the four scruffy Africans before him. Although I couldn't understand a word of Afrikaans I had a good idea what was going on.

One of the young blacks was testifying from the witness box. He was answering the questions of a black-robed prosecutor who stood in a box on the opposite side of the room. The prosecutor was looking off contemptuously into the distance with a slightly affected twitch in his neck. He occasionally twisted his mouth into a sly, knowing grin and rolled his eyes.

The witness stuttered and lost his voice and pointed toward the other three youngsters who stood in the prisoner's dock. They wore colorful but seedy street clothes. One sported a red-and-white striped T-shirt. Two had combs in their hair. They shifted their weight from one foot to the other.

The public gallery was separated into two sections by a heavy oak divider that spanned the length of the room waist-high. I was the only spectator in the white section. In the section marked "Nie Blanc" were some twenty tidy African men and women and a half-dozen small children who were also neatly attired, the little girls in brightly colored dresses. The men's faces carried cold, empty expressions; the women's, sad ones. Two of the women were sobbing. One of them was very old. The children's faces were eager, curious.

The judge seemed to be sleeping as the witness's testimony continued. Occasionally he would shake himself awake and leaf through some papers. Then he would close his eyes again.

When the young man stopped talking, the prosecutor gathered his wind and rattled off a brisk, incredulous, sneering query which sounded like "Do you mean to tell this court . . . ?"

The day I went with Lisa to the Cape we stopped at Simonstown on the way back. The town was a quarter-mile frontage of stores and a small harbor on the Indian Ocean side. There was a pub there called The Lord Nelson (First Pub to the Cape).

I was all the way inside when I noticed that Lisa had stopped cold at the door. A dozen or so men at the bar were staring at us silently. When I asked what gave, she said, "It's not a ladies' bar—I can't go in."

When one of the gents heard my American accent he got off his stool and showed us the way to the ladies' bar next door. I had an Amstel lager and Lisa ordered a glass of white Cape wine. We laughed at the ladies' bar rule—although ten years before in the States, men-only bars had not been unusual.

The conversation came around to baboons. We'd seen two troops of them in the nature reserve on the way to Cape Point and we talked about how destructive they were in farming country. I told her some of the stories I had heard in Zaire, of how baboons can tell whether or not a farmer is armed and do not flee if he isn't. She'd heard of baboons stealing African babies left unattended. I had read of chimpanzees doing that but had never heard it of baboons.

She made an effort at teaching me some Afrikaans:

Te-wees
to be
Gaan
to go
Find
to find
Neem
to take

It was a musical language and she spoke it with an easy, flowing rhythm:

Hoor
to hear
Slaap
to sleep

"The verbs you must always learn first," she admonished.

She asked what other languages I spoke and I said only a very little Spanish and some terrible French. She chose the Spanish:

Hacer
to do
Ir
to go
A tardecer
the coming of the late afternoon

But my mind was back at the Cape.

Just as we passed the last troop of baboons, the two oceans came into view—first the Indian, at the end of a side road posted, "NIE BLANC: BEACH FOR NON-EUROPEANS ONLY," and then the Atlantic, beyond a slight depression in the peninsula to the west. A moment later there was a beach in that direction with a road marked, "COLORED ONLY."

"They have the best beaches," Lisa said, "much better than ours."

It was raining when we came to the end of the road, but it soon let up and we climbed the ridge overlooking the rock at Cape Point. We each posed in turn for the Instamatic with the rock and the two oceans in the background.

The afternoon was still overcast, but far to the south there were generous patches of blue. Somehow the sea breeze was warmer here than on the beaches at Cape Town.

All in all, there was a mild wind and a mild-looking sky.

Place de la Contrascarpe
Paris
April 30, 1978

...and the air smells now, as if it blew from a far-away meadow; they have been making hay somewhere under the slopes of the Andes, Starbuck, and the mowers are sleeping among the new-mown hay.

—Herman Melville

Mary Leakey at Laetoli Base Camp, July 1977.

The author with Jean Guy Gaynard, his pilot over Lake Tchad, March 1977.

Dr. David Livingstone's Mission at Bagamoyo, Tanzania.

ABOUT THE AUTHOR

Born at Quantico Marine Base, Virginia in 1941, Sandy S. McMath grew up in Hot Springs, Arkansas, and the Grant County community of Cane Creek, where the family settled after his father, Sid, had completed two terms as one of the most innovative and progressive governors of the New South.

During high school and college, McMath worked as a laborer with the Arkansas State Electric Cooperative, as an Interior Department surveyor's assistant in the national forests of Oregon and northern California, and as a merchant seaman for American President Lines between San Francisco and Hong Kong.

He attended Arkansas public schools and was graduated with honors from Castle Heights Military Academy, Lebanon, Tennessee, in 1959. He received his B.A. degree in history from the University of Arkansas, Fayetteville, in 1963 and was graduated in 1966 from the university's School of Law, where he received the Robert A. Leflar Award for outstanding scholarship in Torts. He was admitted to practice in Arkansas in 1966 and, in 1970, in California.

Following law school, McMath, who had previously earned his commission as a second lieutenant, entered the Marine Corps and was posted to Vietnam, serving with the Ninth Marine Amphibious Brigade in 1967 out of Okinawa and the Third Marine Division out of Dong Ha and Quang Tri in northern I-Corps during 1968. He was awarded a number of service ribbons, together with the Navy Commendation Medal with Combat "V."

362

Discharged with the rank of Captain in January of 1970, McMath spent six months traveling through Central and South America, following which he attended the University of London on the GI Bill, receiving his Master of Laws Degree in International Law from the London School of Economics in 1971.

Returning to Little Rock, he served as Chief Deputy Prosecuting Attorney, then entered private practice with his father and two brothers, Phillip and Bruce. The McMath Law Firm is recognized nationally as one of the oldest and most successful personal injury firms in the United States.

Following his landmark victory in a recent case against an automobile manufacturer for the crippling of a young woman, the ATLA *Law Reporter* (official journal of the Association of Trial Lawyers of America) said of McMath:

> [The case] . . . represents an advocacy accomplishment of the highest order. With insight which is innovative in its acuity, daring and depth, [McMath] contended that product misuse is no defense when encouraged or invited by the product producer.
>
> The lawyering that went into the preparation of plaintiffs' case in [this] tragedy exemplifies creativity along with courage, constancy and concern.

With the same resourcefulness and tenacity with which he has represented his clients, McMath the trial lawyer became McMath the explorer – organizing and executing a fifteen-month passage alone through some of the most desolate terrain on earth.

The author is a Fellow of the International Academy of Trial Lawyers, the American Board of Trial Advocates and, since 1981, a member of the visiting faculty of the Center for Trial and Appellate Advocacy, Hastings College of the Law, University of California, San Francisco.

McMath is married to the former Allison Boyer Van Pelt of Blaine County, Idaho.

If a book's measure is its praise by readers who've "lived the country," *Africa Alone* is a traveler's landmark. The first edition, which sold out from word-of-mouth, has stirred hundreds of laudatory letters from, among others, Peace Corps volunteers, missionaries, businessmen, a safari pilot, two bush physicians and reknowned anthropologist Mary Leakey, who readily agreed to write the foreword to the COLUMBUS AND COMPANY edition.

McMath drove alone by jeep from Paris to the Cape of Good Hope, crossing the Sahara Desert, the Congo rain forests and the Sengetti where, following a close encounter with hunting lions, he met Dr. Leakey.

Leakey signed the author on as her foreman at Olduvai Gorge and charged him with building a 35-mile earth road out to the remote site of Laetoli, where she had recently discovered what are now recognized as the oldest fossil remains of early man (a precursor of *australopithecus*) and the footprints of three individuals of the species encrusted in sun-hardened ash from a nearby volcano.

McMath, with some twenty Mkumba tribesmen, built the road, established a base camp and re-located most of the Olduvai operation to the site.

Following his work at Olduvai-Laetoli, McMath traveled extensively through Zambia, Zimbabwe (then Rhodesia) and South Africa. Returning to Paris, he finished this narrative from his journals in April 1978.

Deciding the do the trip alone, and without institutional "sponsorship," permitted the author spontaneously to follow his intuition, keep a hard-scrabble perspective and, in the end, execute a writing free of obeisance to mass marketing and political convention. The result is a raw account of Africa as seen by a trained observer with no ax to grind or audience to please.

The view from this window onto the "Dark Continent" is as encompassing today as when it was first opened by the author. In the swift decade since this crossing, Africa has changed little. The sun is yet eclipsed by winds of locusts and goat-sythed soil, as the Sahara continues its march toward Zaire. Once-proud farmers, whose fathers repelled Mussolini, remain drought-scourged starvelings under Marxist tyranny in Ethiopia. Apartheid continues to deny suffrage and process to South Africa's majority, whose numbers have been swelled by thousands of Africans fleeing persecution and malaise in neighboring countries. Elsewhere on the continent, democracy has fared poorly: In the quarter-century since "independence," in not a single one of some 45 new nations has a government *ever* been voted out of office. Military and one-party dictatorships are everywhere entrenched. Only in South Africa is there a functioning multi-party system and an open press, but even these are subject to Apartheid's onerous "banning" laws. Poachers have decimated the elephant population (then over two million) to under 700,000 and have hunted the black rhinoceros and mountain gorilla virtually to extinction. West Africa's *franc bloc*, led by the Ivory Coast, still prospers relative to the rest of the continent; Kenya has substantially increased its manifold revenues from tourism; and Tanzania's Olduvai Gorge continues to disclose its fossil treasures to scientists following in the footsteps of Mary Leakey.

Written in the tradition of the *recit de voyage* of Boswell, de Toqueville, and Stanley, this record of one traveler's journey through that Africa is an insightful and prescient account that laymen and scholars alike have found not only a stimulating read, but a valuable primary source.

Index

Bol 112, 117-121. (overflown 120)

Bolze, Louis 306-309

Bongo 143

Bosse Be, La Malagache restaurant in Treichville 89, 93

Bossembele 130-131

bowling, Kisangani 158

Brazil, Rhodesian immigration to 332

bread, Algerian army confiscating 28

British Bilma Sands Expedition 38-39

British South Africa Company 307

British South Africa Police (Rhodesian National Police) 308, 344

Botswana 293

Bouzous, 32, 41

Bubye Junction 318

bucket bomb (ANC), Cape Town 351-352

Bukavu 179, 276

Bulawayo 304-312

Bureau of State Security (BOSS), South Africa 354

Burns, John 34, 40, 42

cable ferry at Rutshuru River 168

Cabo Beberias 15

Cameroon 109-111

camel, cheese of, 62; replacing horse in Sahara 83, caravans to Bilma 63-65; *photo*: 103

Canadian, surveyors, Kano 107; backpackers murdered by guerillas at Victoria Falls 289

Cape Buffalo, goring tourist 204; in Ngorongoro Crater 204-207; story by Hugo Van Lawick 214; at "Treetops" 226-229; at "The Ark" 229

Cape of Good Hope 350, 356-357

Cape Town 350-357, University 353, 354

capitaine 116, 154

Caprivi strip 293

Carstairs, John 331-332, 355

Casablanca 17-19

Ceuta 15

Chad 110-129; Lake 80, 87, 109, 112-121

cheetah 206, 212-213, 217-218, 244

Chewa 288

"Chi Chi," Greek restauranteur and trader at Tamanrasset 33-34, 36, 38

children, slave trading in across Sahara 32-33; stoning by in Morocco 21-22, 24; with glaucoma 102, 243; torturing animals 84, 158

chimpanzees 273, 356

Chinese, aid to Bangui (rice planting) 134; Dar to Lusaka Railroad 190, 276-279, 283-284

cholera 19

chrome, Rhodesian, profiteering in by Soviets in circumvention of U.N. embargo 308

CIA, author is suspected of being agent of by Peace Corps volunteers 112, 117

Claustre, Mme. Francoise, kidnapped anthropologist 114

Club Mediteranee at Grand Bassam, Ivory Coast 93-94

coal, in Niger 87

cobra 196; recounted by Hugo Van Lawick at Ndutu 215; black mamba mistaken for 248; at Laetoli 254

Combined Forces Headquarters (Rhodesian Military Command) 303

convoys, Free French 44-45; Rhodesian 304-306, 316-318

Cooner, Joel 22-25

Courtney Hotel, Salisbury 312

cruelty to animals in zoos 84 (Niger); 158 (Zaire)

Cyangugu 180

"Daniel," Olduvai worker 253

Dar es Salaam 190, 270-279

"dash" (bribery) 80, 99, 108

"David," Olduvai tracker 242, 248

Davis, Alan 70-73

Deacon, Doreen and Jack 91, 93

"Deebo," Olduvai carpenter 251, 253

Delamere, Lord, Bar (Nairobi) 220-221

"Dennis," leather worker, Pilgrim's Rest 324, 327-328

Depachtere, George, supervisor of "Gala" brewery at Mondou 123

Diego Garcia 301

Djerma 83-84

Dodoma 272, 279

Domino, Hotel (Niamey) 84

Driftwood Lodge, Milindi 264

"Dune-go," Mt. Kenya climbing guide 232-235

East African Airways, dispute over 189

East African Wildlife Society 223

East Asians, black market dealing 156, 191, 272; expropriation by Black governments 191; education of children 192

Eboue, Felix 114

ecarpi 162

Edmonston, Mary 147, 149-152, 163-164, 180

"Edward," Olduvai guide 213, 241, 245, 251

eland 245

elephants, poached for tusks 223; at "Treetops" 228-229; trampling crops 224; on Mt. Kenya 232; black-cotton tracks at Laetoli 253; in Selous Park 279; at Victoria Falls 302

Elizabeth I, at "Treetops" 226, 229

Encounter Overland 138, 154; 171-172

Endima, "Mama" (Kenyatta) 189, 223

Endolyn, Lake Eyasi, Masai Catholic Mission 245

English, difficulty in understanding as spoken in Nigeria 108; taught by Peace Corps volunteers 71, 76, 130; little used in East Africa 193

Enkeldoorn 316

Epulu game park 162

Etoile du Chad, restaurant 119

Eyasi, Lake 203, Masai Catholic Mission at 245

Fachi 64

Fathers of the Holy Spirit (Peres du St. Esprit) 275

Faya, overrun by Toubou rebels 115

"fetish" [Ghanan lagoon spirit] 98-99

fire, in French television crew van in Sahara 30-31

fishing with throwlines, Milindi 264-267 (photo: 267)

flash flood, in Aden desert, story of 121

"Flying Doctor" 245-246, 251

fording rivers in flood 184, 187, 196-197

Fort Foureau (Kousseri) 110

Fort Victoria, Rhodesia 314, 316-317

Foster, Mike 62-65

Formentera 14-15, 312

Foucould, Father, French missionary to Tuareg, Tomacheck linguist and martyr 37-38

fox 242

France, Bank of as guarantor of CFA currency 155

Free French, African veterans of 82 (status, pensions and extortion from); Chadian base of Eboue and Leclerc 114-115; convoy tracks still in sand 44-45; freight pilot for 119

French: colonial administrative policy 108; emphasis on language and culture 108, 262; television "RAID" through Africa 28-31; dominance of technicians and contract workers, Ivory Coast 88-89; uranium mine at Arlit 42; Volunteers for Progress 70; west to east crossing of Sahara 38-39; nuclear project in South Africa 352

"Front Line" states 290

fuel, buying on black market in Zaire 155-157; capacity carried by Land-cruiser 15; hoarding 51, 109, 155-157; riots 109, 157; tank bolts severed by welder 193 (collapse and escape of gasoline 196)

Fulani 112

funeral dance, Ghana 97

Herakunta volcano 172, 232

Hernandez, Miguel 15

hippopotamus, report of killing children, CAR, 138; in Selous Park 279; in Virunga Park 166; Luapula river 331

Hirafok 34

Hoggar mountains 34, 36-37; *photo* center-4

homo erectus 216, 222, 224

homo habilis 216, 217, 224

Hotel Training School, Dar es Salaam 272-273, 277, 279

Houphet-Boigny, President of Ivory Coast 92, 292

Hunterston, Nigel 143-144, 147, 151, 166

Hunterston, Robert 151

hyraxes 232, 342

Ibiza 14, 353, 355

Immalman 38-39

Indolyn 212

Infilise, Alice and Phil 119

In Gall 58

In Guezzim 48-52

International Academy of Trial Lawyers 65, 91-94

"Irene," artist at Pilgrim's Rest 327

Irunga 279

Isaka 282-283

Israel, aid-hospitals in hostile nations (Tanzania) 192;

"Ivan," French agriculturalist, Niger 72, 74, 76

Ivoire, Hotel 89-90, 92

Ivory, carvings by artisans at Kisangani 157; smuggling: to Central African Empire from Zaire for transport to Paris 136; to Hong Kong from Kenya 223

Ivory Coast 87-99

"Jack," the Texas fish-spotter pilot at Abidjan 90-91, 95

jackals 210, 241, 242

japati cakes 243, 253

Jeffers, Sidney 143-144; 166-173, *photo by*: 114

Jesus, Fort 263-264

"Jo Jo," Sahara merchant and inn-keeper 33-40, 44, 62 (*photo*: 35)

Jones, Wyn 177

"Jooma," Mike Mehlman's houseboy 207, 218

Joyce camping at Agadez 60-62, 65

Kabibo, Olduvai camp cook 211, 240, 243, 247, 250, 253, 256, (*photo*: 197)

Kadi, Jalou 192-193

373

374

as Laetoli foreman 216; breaking ankle in fall 245; restricted to cabin 247; on crutches 251; Dalmations kept by 211-213, chased 241; in Nairobi 239; Laetoli fossils, discovery of 215-216; library of at Olduvai base camp 210-211, 245; Mkumba tribesmen preferred as workers 217; Mkumba language spoken 193; Olorgesalie, discovery of site by 222; short wave radio contact with Nairobi 212; special permission needed to cross Tanzanian border 216; story of old Masai abandoned by hyenas 248; supervision of archeological digging 217; taciturn personality of 210; Havana cigars smoked by 258; treated by "Flying Doctor" 245-246; *zinjanthropus*, discovery of 9, 199; inspection trip with author to Laetoli site 259-260 (*photo with author:* 238)

Leakey, Phillip 212, 215, 224

Leakey, Richard 84, 224, 262

Leakey, Valerie 212

leopards, as danger 211, 245; at "Treetops" 229; on Mt. Kenya 232

lepers, *photo:* 114

Limpopo river 118, 318

Lindley, Rowan, 221, 262

lions: killing Masai shepherd boy 211; man-eaters of Tsavo 262; broken down next to, Rutshuru 169-170; at Lion Hill 198-199; in Olduvai Gorge 211-212, 240; stories by Hugo Van Lawick 214-215; roaring at top of Ngorongoro Crater 202; lioness with cubs in Ngorongoro Crater 207; hunting gazelle on Laetoli road 243-244; at Virunga Park 166

Lion and Elephant Motel, Bubye 318

lion flies 198, 213, 241

lips, of women stretched with bottle caps 122-123

"Lisa," the photographer at Cape Town 353, 356-357

"Lisa," the "pet" cheetah at Olduvai-Ngorongoro 206, 212-213; 217

Livingstone, Dr. David 275-276; 286-287

Livingstone, Zambia 286-289

locusts, eating as source of protein 60

Logone and Shari, Hotel ("Chez Magna") 110

Logone, river 110-111; flood-irrigation project 123

Lorca, Garcia 15

Losi 288

"Lucas," Olduvai truck driver 246

"Lucy," the Australian hitchhiker 196, 199, 215

Ludeke, Luna 349

Lupane 305, 306

McKinney, Robin 202-217, 239

McLarnon, E.C. 311

McMath, Anne and Sid, 91, 93, 94

Magistrate's Court, Cape Town 355

Mahe Island, Seychelles 301

Maiduguri 109

376

Monkey Bar (*Bar du Singe*), Bangassou 135

Monotopas 311

Morgan, Barbara and Lee 61-62

Morocco 15-25

Mosi—Oa—Tunya "The Mist that Thunders." Victoria Falls 288; Hotel 289-290

Moulay Hassan, oasis of 29, 350

Mrewa, Rhodesian homeland 312-314

Munro [err. sp. Monroe] Rex 39-54, 73

Museum, National, of Niger 83-84, 225; of Kenya 84, 224-225

Mushinda 268

muskrat (*zibethica*) 130

Mussolini, 1936 treaty with France as basis for Libyan claim to Tibesti 115

Mutandoro 306

Muzorewa, Bishop 311

Mwanza 191-199

Nadabunda, "Mrs.", Black Townships guide, Bulawayo 310-311

Nairobi 218-226, 239-240, 262, University 222; compared with Dar es Salaam 271-272

Namibia (Southwest Africa) 92, 349

Naro Maru River 234; Lodge 235

National Geographic 9, 199

natron (saltpeter) 118

Natron, Lake 222, 259

N'djamena 111-121, Grand Hotel 115

Ndutu 210, 213-215, 246, 251

"Nelson, The Lord," pub 356-357

New Avenue Hotel, Nairobi 222

New Florida Bar, Nairobi 221

New Mwanza Hotel 192-193

New Zealand girl raped by Algerian officials 50-51

Ngorongoro Crater 201-207, 232; Lodge 203-204, 240

Nguigmi 80

Niamey 83-86; 99

Niger 52-86; 99-107

Niger River 86, 99

Nigeria 107-109

Nkomo, Joshua 304, 311

Nordvaer, SS, Kenyan freighter to Seychelles 301

Norfolk Hotel, Nairobi 220-226

Nyahanga 196

Nyau excorcist cult, dances 288

Nyerere, Dr. Julius 189-190, 270, 307

Nyirangongo volcano 170-171

Oasis Bar, N'djamena 121

Olduvai Gorge and Base Camp: *australopithecus 216*; black mamba killed at 248-249; cheetah entering 212; daily work and dining schedule 256; described 199-200; Dogs (Dalmations) in 211-213, 241; first visit to by author 199-201; grid excavation technique used in 217; *homo erectus* 216, 259; *homo habilis* 216, 217; library at 210-211; lions in 211-212, 240-241; managed by Tanzanian Department of Antiquties 200, 216; Masai origin of name 201; Mkumbas as main work force in 200, 201, 217, 245; museum at 201-202; quartz inselbergs described 242; short wave radio contact with 212; sites: DK 200, 217; JK 259; toilet facilities 240; vegetables purchased for 250; windmill-generated power 240; *zinjanthropus* found in 9, 199; river 199, 201

Olorgesalie 222

Olympia Hotel, Kisangani 153-154, 157-159

O-Maroe, barge captain, N'djamena 119

Omolo, Francis 222

O'Reilly, Paddy 336

Organization of African Unity 329

Ouaddi 112, 115

Ouagadougou 86-87

Ouaka River 133

overgrazing, as contributing factor in desertification 42, 57, 61, 74

palm oil plantation, Ivory Coast 88

Pan-African Congress on Pre-history 262

"Pascal," Cameroon truck driver 118

Patterson, Phyllis and Mike 329-330

Pavica Plantation 134

Pavillion Vert Hotel, Ouagadougou 87

Peace Corps 34, 42, 61, 63, 70-73, 76, 82, 85-86, 93, 98, 112, 116-117, 119, 121-123, 130, 133, 135-137, 179, 263, 276, 346

pemphis 301

"Per," Norwegian manager at Gibbs' Plantation 250

Peulh 66

phosphates, mined in Western Sahara 17-18

pickpockets, thrown to death from top of stadium in Nigeria 108

Pilgrim's Rest 323-330

Pinnock, Don and "Patch" 353

Pinnock, Mr. and Mrs. Pat 343-344

pirates, raiding shipping at anchorage off Lagos 109

Pizza Den, Cape Town 349, 350, 352

poaching 223

poker, playing in sand storm 54

polders, on Lake Chad 115, 120 (described)

Polisario, guerillas in Western Sahara 17-18; Libyan recruitment of Tuareg for 85

Pongola River, police barricade at 336

Port St. Johns 342-344

poste restante, Nairobi 221

Presley, Elvis 342; post-death graffiti, Capetown 351

Preventive Detention Act (Kenya) 189

Progressive Party (South Africa) 344

puff adder 147, 162, 254, 255 (*photo*)

Pullam, Gale 331-332, 355

Pumwani, Nairobi slum 223

Pygmies 163

Qaddafi, Colonel Muhammar 114

Quest Four 62

Rabat 17

rabbits, attempt to raise in Sahel 74

railroads: Ivory Coast 87-88; Kenya 220, 268; Mozambique 289, 332, 327; Rhodesia 288-289; South Africa 327, 332, 355; Swaziland 332; Tanzania 190, 277-279, 283-284; Upper Volta 87-88; Zaire 153, 288-289, 311; Zambia 288-289, 311

Rainbow Inn, Victoria Falls 287-288

rainbow, lunar, at Victoria Falls 287-288

Rand Daily Mail 328

rape, of New Zealand girl by Algerian officials 50-51

rat, great white 151

Regina Mundi Catholic Mission, guerilla attack on 305

Renaud, Mabel 330-331

Ressano-Garcia 332

"Rex Hotel and Clock Tower," Dar es Salaam 273-275

Rey, Marie Josie 262

Rhinoceros 227-229

Rhode Island Reds (chickens) as breeding stock in Sahel 76

Rhodes, Cecil 288, 307, 311 (grave), 319, 351, University 344-347

Rhodesia 294-319

Rhodesia Herald 304, 314, 353

robber(s), execution of in Nigeria 108; furloughed robber a hitchhiker 125, 129-130; in Nairobi 225-226; gold sluice robber's grave, Pilgrim's Rest 325-326

Robbin Island 354

Rotary International, sponsor of "Flying Doctor" 246

roulette 334

Royal Hotel, Pilgrim's Rest 323-324

Royal Society, The [British] 301

Royer, Flossie and Ralph 61-62, 65

Rudolf (err. sp. "Rudolph") (Lake Turkana) 224, 262

Rusumu Falls 184

at Beit Bridge 322; insurance and proof of solvency required 322; relative press freedom compared to Black and Arab countries 328; operation of Mozambique rail and port systems 332; operation of "homeland" utilities 343; nuclear capability 352

Soviet math teachers 123, 130-131

Soweto, riots 328, white wife of resident 341

spy, author suspected of being: by Peace Corps volunteers in Chad 112, 117; by Tanzanians 277-279; by Zambians 284-286

squid, as fishbait 265-266

Standard Bank, Cape Town 355

"Star Club," Nairobi 221

Star News 328-329

steel, produced near Lake Victoria ca. 700 AD 249

Stellenbosh University 355

"Stephen," the Mkumba foreman at Olduvai 204-217; 244-259; (*photo* 205)

stick-wheel, child's game of, 16, 118

Storm River 347-349

Sutton, Peter 36-65

Swahili 193

SWAPO guerillas 328

Swazi 332

Swaziland 332-336

Swiss, girl swept over Koto River

Falls and drowned 134; abandoning land rover, Ngorongoro 204; jumping ferry queue, Virunga Park 168; at Victoria Falls 302

Table Mountain 350-351

Takeita 76

Takoukant 66, 70

Tamanrasset 28, 31-45

Tanganyika, Lake 273

Tanout 67-73

Tanzania 184-218; 239-260; 269-279

Tegguidda In Tessoum 55-56, 259

Telouess 64

Tenere desert 64, 83

termite mound, *photo* 128

Tetouan 15-16

Tierney, Jackie 72-76, 99-102

Tilley, Phil 39-54, 73

Timbuktu 34, 99

Tongaat, beach camp 337

Toubou 85, 112-115

Toy, Steve 122-123

Transkei, tribal homeland 312, 340-344

travellers checks, phony reports of theft 156; attempt by Kenyan bank to invalidate for use in Rhodesia and

South Africa 222; cashing of "invalidated" checks by Rhodesian immigration officer 296

"Treetops" 226-229

Treichville, 89-90, 93

Tribal Investment Bureau (Rhodesia) 312-313

Trichard, Hotel Louis 322

Tuareg, at Agadez 60-67; at Matameye (photo) 77; at Kano 107; at Tamanrasset 31-41; at Tanout 72-73; women equal 33; caravans through the Erg of Bilma 63-65, 83; as guards 60-62, 85, 107; recruited by Libyans as guerillas and oil workers 85; at oasis of Assamaka 52; tea 73

tyrannosaurus rex, skeleton of found in Tenere Desert 83

Ubangui 131, 133

ugamaa (Tanzanian socialism) 190-191, 248, 271, 276

Uganda 164-171, 225

Ugandan refugees in Rwanda 182-183

Umzimkulu 340

Unilateral Declaration of Independence (UDI) 308

United Front [Rhodesian guerillas] 290, 304

Upper Volta 86-87, 99

uranium, in Niger 42, 87; in Tibesti 115

Ushasha 196

Van Lawick, Hugo 210, 213-215

Van Stein, Franz 272, 279

Velle river 143

Victoria Falls 286-303; Livingstone's journal description 286-287; lunar rainbow 287-288; Rhodesian side, description 298; Zambian side, description 286-287; railroad bridge and traffic over 288-289; "Boiling Pot" 289; "Devil's Cataract" 298; Canadian backpackers murdered 289; author's overflight 302; (photo center-7)

Victoria Falls, Rhodesia 298-304; Hotel 302; curfew and anti-guerilla patrols 303; civilian attack order 299

Victoria, Lake 188, 190, 196

Victoria, Queen 190, 287

Virunga Game Park 165-170

volcanos, eastern Zaire (Nyirangongo and Herakunta 170-173)

Voortrekkers 308, 347

wait-a-bit thorns 242

Walls, Dick 116-117

Wankie 297, 304, 307, Park Lodge 312

Wanke and Falls News 303

wasps 138

Waza National Park (Cameroon) 109

wells, construction of for irrigation in Niger 61; in Chad 117

Western (formerly Spanish) Sahara 17-18, 20; Tuareg recruited for fighting in 85

Whould, David and Sara 288

Wilhelm II, Kaiser 190

Williamson, Terry 138, 143, 177, 218

Willis, Ann 312

Wilson, Tom 221-222; 226, 262

Wimpy Bar 298, 301

windmill electric generators at Olduvai Gorge 201

Windsor Castle 337

witch doctor 135, 335-336

Woolworth's, Salisbury, bombed 312

World Bank 123

World Church Service 61

World, The 328

Wright, Ron 316

Xhosa 340

Yacouba, Ibrahim Mainisara 70 71

"Yoca," Olduvai truck driver 246

Zagora 23

Zambesi River 279, 280, 286-303

Zambia 279-294; railroad and truck shipping duplicity with Rhodesia during "war" 288-289

Zanzibar 267, 274-275

"Zanzibar," Dar es Salaam 273-274

Zimbabwe (ruins) 314-316

Zinder 66, 70, 73

zinjanthropus bosei 9, 199

Zulu 332

Zuvaguru Eating House, Mrewa 313